Sustainable Innovations in Management in the Digital Transformation Era

Digital Management Sustainability

Sustainable Innovations in Management in the Digital Transformation Era

Digital Management Sustainability

Edited by

Rania Nafea
Shabana Faizal
Dorota Jelonek
Narendra Kumar
Jayendira P. Sankar
Ilona Paweloszek

Routledge
Taylor & Francis Group

LONDON AND NEW YORK

First published 2024
by Routledge
4 Park Square, Milton Park, Abingdon, Oxon OX14 4RN

and by Routledge
605 Third Avenue, New York, NY 10158

Routledge is an imprint of the Taylor & Francis Group, an informa business

British Library Cataloguing-in-Publication Data
A catalogue record for this book is available from the British Library

Library of Congress Cataloging-in-Publication Data
A catalog record has been requested for this book

ISBN: 9781032584775 (pbk)
ISBN: 9781003450238 (ebk)

DOI: 10.4324/9781003450238

Typeset in Sabon LT Std
by HBK Digital
Printed and bound in India

Contents

List of Figures

List of tables

Foreword

It is with great pleasure that we present to you the proceedings of our first international conference on Sustainable Innovations in Management in the Digital Transformation Era (SIMDTE) held on May 2–3, 2023, in Manama, Bahrain. This event marks the first collaboration between the College of Administrative and Financial Sciences (CAFS) at the University of Technology Bahrain (UTB) and FIRST India, represented by Dr. Narendra Kumar. This conference represents a milestone in our ongoing journey towards academic excellence where we aspire to become a renowned platform for the exchange of ideas, collaboration, networking, and learning.

I am pleased to present the proceedings of this conference, which serves as a testament to the intellectual curiosity, rigorous scholarship, and innovative spirit that defines our academic community. This compilation offers a snapshot of the significant strides we are making in sustainable innovations and digital transformation and provides a roadmap for future research and development.

The breadth and depth of contributions in these proceedings are truly impressive, spanning a wide range of topics from Artificial Intelligence trends to Innovations in DNA sequencing to the latest trends in business. They reflect the collaborative efforts of a diverse group of researchers, practitioners, and thought leaders from 4 continents around the world.

I would like to extend my deepest gratitude to all the authors for their high-quality contributions, the reviewers for their critical insights and constructive feedback, and the organizing team for their tireless efforts to ensure the success of this conference.

As you delve into these proceedings, I encourage you to approach each paper with an open mind. The ideas and findings articulated here have the potential to spark new thoughts, stimulate lively discussions, and inspire innovative solutions. Despite the challenges that we have faced over the past year, our community has shown resilience and adaptability in continuing to advance our collective knowledge. I do not doubt that the insights and ideas shared in these proceedings will play a critical role in shaping the future of management innovations and digitalization.

Thank you for being part of this journey. Your participation, inquisitiveness, and commitment to pushing the boundaries of our understanding are what make SIMDTE a vibrant and enriching experience.

Dr. Haitham Al Qahtani
Vice President Academic Affairs
University of Technology, Bahrain
December 2, 2023

Preface

Esteemed Participants,

It is with great pleasure that I welcome you to the recently concluded conference, held on May 2–3, 2023, in the beautiful Kingdom of Bahrain. This pivotal conference was focused on "Sustainable Innovations in Management in the Digital Transformation Era". In an age defined by rapid technological advancements and digital innovation, the way we understand and carry out management is continually evolving.

The conference brought together thought leaders, industry professionals, academics, and innovators from around the globe to share insights, exchange ideas, and catalyze change. The digital transformation era has not only revolutionized our personal lives but has significantly impacted the business landscape. It became a strategic priority, driving companies to reassess their business models, reinvent their strategies, and redefine their value propositions. Amidst this change, ensuring sustainability, building resilient, adaptable, and future-proof businesses became a central theme.

During the conference, we delved into how digital transformation was reshaping the management landscape and explored innovative approaches to ensure sustainability. We discussed strategies to foster a culture of continuous learning and adaptation, to harness digital technologies for sustainable growth, and to balance the drive for innovation with the need for ethical, responsible conduct.

The conference featured a blend of keynote addresses by Bahraini industrialists and businessmen, panel discussions, workshops, and networking sessions. A dynamic group of speakers shared real-world experiences and provided practical insights into the challenges and opportunities of managing in the digital era. Topics such as the role of artificial intelligence in sustainable management, the impact of blockchain technology on supply chain management, and the importance of data analytics in decision-making were explored.

I would like to extend my sincere gratitude to the conference committee members who worked tirelessly for the past six months to bring this conference and proceedings to life—*Dr. Shabana Faizal, Dr Nidhi Menon, Dr. Reem Abdalla and Ms. Mariam Al-Salman*. Your commitment to advancing the discourse on sustainable management in the digital era is deeply appreciated.

As we continue to navigate this exciting realm of digital transformation, I hope the insights from this conference will inspire you, challenge your thinking, and equip you with the knowledge and tools to drive sustainable innovation in your respective fields.

Thank you for your participation and contribution to the success of this conference. I look forward to our continued engagement in the pursuit of sustainable management innovations.

Dr. Rania Nafea, Conference Chair
Associate Professor, University of Technology Bahrain
December 2, 2023

Acknowledgment

Dear Attendees,
We would like to extend our deepest gratitude to each and every one of you for your participation in our annual conference. We understand the time and effort required to attend such events, especially amidst your busy schedules, and we are immensely grateful for your commitment and contribution.

A special tribute goes to FIRST India, represented by Dr. Narendra Kumar, in helping us organize this conference. A huge gratitude to all the authors who displayed exceptional patience and commitment to higher education. Your contributions have significantly enriched our knowledge base and sparked important discussions that will undoubtedly lead to progress in our field.

We would also like to specifically acknowledge our keynote speakers: Dr. Narendra Kumar from India, Prof. Dorota Jelonek and Dr. Ilona Paweloszek from Poland, Dr. Dalia Younis from Egypt, and Dr. Arifusalam Shaikh and Dr. Carlos Bazan from Canada. Your insightful presentations were a highlight of the conference, providing invaluable perspectives and stimulating thought-provoking dialogue.

Our generous sponsors - Gulf Financial House (GFH), Batelco, and Khaleeji Commercial Bank—deserve a very special acknowledgement. Your support helped transform our vision into reality, and for that, we are truly grateful.

We express our deep gratitude to our strategic partners – Bahrain Small & Medium Enterprises (SMEs) Society and Bahrain Association of Banks (BAB). Your attendance and continued support of sustainability and innovation practices have been instrumental in the success of this event and the further development of these important areas in our region.

Our heartfelt thanks go out to the organizing committee. Your tireless efforts, dedication, and meticulous planning have made this conference a resounding success. *Dr. Shabana Faizal, Dr Nidhi Menon, Dr. Reem Abdalla and Ms. Mariam Al-Salman—* without your efforts, this event would not have been possible.

Last, but certainly not least, we want to thank all attendees. Your active participation, insightful questions, and shared experiences truly enriched the event. We hope that you found the conference informative and worthwhile, and we look forward to seeing you at our next event.

Once again, thank you for your valuable contribution to this successful conference.

Dr. Rania Nafea, Conference Chair
Associate Professor, University of Technology Bahrain
December 2, 2023

About the Authors

Dr. Rania Nafea, currently an Associate Professor of Entrepreneurship and Management at University of Technology Bahrain, has obtained her Bachelor of Business Administration in Finance and MBA in Marketing and International Business from the American University in Cairo – Egypt. She holds a Doctorate of Business Administration (DBA) from Maastricht School of Management in the Netherlands in the field of knowledge management and innovation, with an interest in leadership and culture. Dr. Nafea believes in the importance of diverse experience to bridge the gap between industry and academia. Her industry experience spans several multinational and regional companies including HSBC, British American Tobacco (BAT), and Logic Consulting. She has held teaching posts in Egypt, Dubai, Saudi Arabia and Canada. She is a well-published author of several papers and multiple book chapters with IGI publications in the areas of organizational and national culture, company performance, entrepreneurship, and education and is the holder of several certifications including the Advanced Project Management Certificate and the Chartered Manager designation from the Canadian Institute of Management.

Dr. Shabana Faizal received her PhD from the Bharathiar University, India. She worked for six years in India and has been working in Bahrain for 4 years. Overall, she has 8 years of academic experience and 2 years of industry experience. Further, she has published articles in various high-impact journals and presented a good number of papers at conferences. Presently, she is an assistant professor in Business school and is the Research chair at the University of Technology Bahrain in the Kingdom of Bahrain. Her current research interests include marketing, management, and digital business.

Prof. Dorota Jelonek is a full professor of Economics at the Faculty of Management of the Czestochowa University of Technology in Poland. Her scientific and research interests focus on solving problems related to the implementation of management information systems in enterprises and improving management information processes. She is the author of 6 books and the editor of 10. Additionally, she has authored or co-authored 250 articles in Polish and foreign journals and book chapters. She previously held the positions of Associate Dean for Science and Dean of the Faculty. Since 2019, Prof. Dorota Jelonek has been the President of the Scientific Society for Economic Informatics and is a member of many societies, including the Polish Association for Innovation Management and the Informing Science Institute.

Dr. Narendra Kumar is a Professor in the School of Applied Science, NIMS Institute of Engineering and Technology in Jaipur. He has worked more than 28 years as faculty member, Dean, Joint Director and Director in various engineering institutes and universities. He is one of the founding members of Forum for interdisciplinary research in mathematical Science and Technology (FIRST), and a member of more than a dozen academic forums in India and abroad. He has published more than two dozen books in the domain of mathematics, statistics and computer science and engineering, and more than 70 research papers in national/international journals. His key areas of research work are Mathematical modeling, Theory of relativity, Data science, Image processing and network security.

Dr. Jayendira P. Sankar received his PhD from the University of Madras, India. He worked for ten years in India and working in Bahrain for six years. Overall, he has 16 years of academic experience with senior fellow HEA-UK and academic fellow CIPD-UK. Further, he published several articles in various high-impact journals and presented a good number of papers at conferences. Presently, he is the assistant professor of MBA and head of the digital business research center at the University of Technology Bahrain in the Kingdom of Bahrain. His current research interests include development economics, human resource management, and teaching-learning.

Dr. Ilona Paweloszek has a Doctor of Economics in the discipline of Management and Quality Sciences, a graduate of the Faculty of Management of the Czestochowa University of Technology, specializing in "development management and consulting." She also completed pedagogical studies in training teachers of technical subjects. She has been a researcher and didactic employee at the Faculty of Management of the CUT since 1999, currently as an assistant professor at the Department of Management Information Systems. From 2002–2006, she researched mobile technologies in knowledge management, the usability of mobile solutions, and their integration with enterprise information systems. Her scientific and research interests focus on using semantic web technology, big data, and data mining to support managerial decisions. She is the author of several dozen publications, including three original monographs. She is a member of the Scientific Association of Business Informatics and the Polish Association for Production Management.

1 Understanding the Factors that Influence the Intention of Kuwaiti Entrepreneurs to use Technology Using the UTAUT Model

Ali AlMas[1,a], Ahmad Alsaber[2,b], and Rania Nafea[3,c]

[1]American University of Kuwait (AUK), Kuwait
[2]Assistant Professor, College of Business and Economics, American University of Kuwait (AUK), Kuwait
[3]Associate Professor, College of Administrative and Financial Services, University of Technology Bahrain, Salmabad, Bahrain

Abstract

Financial literacy has risen dramatically across the board over recent times. After this shift, people began taking more control over their financial management by implementing budgetary planning, saving strategies, and investment tactics. It is essential to gauge the public's enthusiasm towards cutting-edge technology during its development. This investigation focuses on determining the contributing elements that shape the acceptance and utilization of a digital financial literacy app among workers from diverse social and economic backgrounds in Kuwait. This study constructed the proposed model's six primary constructs based on the existing frameworks of TAM, UTAUT, and Usability models. The factors to be considered in this study are as follows: firstly, performance expectations; secondly, expected effort; thirdly, social influence; fourthly, resources and cost; fifthly, subjective happiness; and finally, deliberate conduct. The statistical assessment of all hypotheses in this study was conducted using SmartPLS methods.

According to this study, it is recommended that workers with lower socioeconomic backgrounds should not receive financial literacy education using digital platforms due to their limited proficiency in technology. The UTAUT model has been commonly used in gauging the level of technology implementation. The UTAUT framework employs four key factors to assess the diffusion of emerging technologies. The UTAUT model has been widely utilized to assess novel technologies, utilizing four key elements to delineate public reception of emerging gadgets and systems: The outcomes are anticipated to enhance women's impact across various domains within society. The potential benefits derived from the utilization of extensively researched technology are predicated upon optimistic assumptions. A quantitative assessment of the effort necessary to utilize the technology effectively. One determinant that can impact the broad acceptance of technology is social influence, which pertains to the manner in which individuals are influenced to utilize it. Facilitating conditions pertain to evaluating the technological infrastructure's extent and effectiveness in facilitating and streamlining the utilization of the technology. This study's findings suggest that a digital platform may not be the most efficient means of conveying financial literacy to individuals from lower-middle socioeconomic backgrounds due to their limited familiarity and comfort with technology. This methodology is employed to ascertain the potential of digital applications in facilitating the enhancement of individuals' financial literacy comprehension, particularly with regard to gender. Using digital applications in financial literacy

[a]Fatmaalkhoder@gmail.com, [b]aalsaber@auk.edu.kw, [c]rania.nafea@utb.edu.bh

training has contributed to enhanced knowledge among Kuwaiti entrepreneurs regarding fund management.

Keywords

Financial knowledge, Kuwaiti entrepreneurs, technology adoption, UTAUT model.

Introduction

Background

The definition and interpretation of financial literacy can vary depending on the source and context. According to Bannon et al. (2014), financial literacy is defined as the capacity to make sound judgments and engage in suitable acts in the present and future utilization and administration of monetary resources by the U.S. Government Accountability Office (GAO). The comprehension of financial alternatives, the exercise of prudent financial decision-making, careful budgeting, and the adept management of challenges arising from life circumstances, including job loss, retirement savings, or funding a child's education, collectively constitute this domain.

The central objective of financial literacy pertains to effectively managing one's finances by applying knowledge and comprehension of monetary matters. According to McKenzie (2009), it is posited that financial literacy extends beyond mere skill and knowledge, encompassing a potential for universal attainment. Individuals can be considered financially literate if they can effectively identify appropriate resources that provide the knowledge needed to make informed decisions while being aware of their constraints in specific financial categories. At this point, an individual's financial literacy can be gauged by assessing the degree to which they have progressed in cultivating the necessary financial behaviors that facilitate sensible financial decision-making.

Global Research

The global landscape of public administration is transforming because of the rapid progress in flexible technology. In modern times, mobile technology serves various purposes, including facilitating interaction and entertainment and enhancing taxpayer-funded enterprises' accountability, awareness, and capacity. Mobile technology, characterized by its wireless and portability capabilities, plays a crucial and expanding part in the public sector's ability to provide dependable information and services to individuals, regardless of location or device. The online purchasing habits of individuals have been substantially transformed because of the mobile and networking sectors advancement. A significant proportion of the global population utilizes smartphones equipped with the Internet to engage in mobile shopping, wherein they seek, acquire knowledge about, and purchase various products or services. Simultaneously, a staggering number of approximately 4 billion individuals utilize mobile applications to leverage the functionalities offered by social media e-platforms.

Nevertheless, a significant majority of marketers, precisely 73%, believe that their respective organizations' social media marketing efforts have yielded a certain degree of effectiveness (Nikou and Economides, 2017). As a result, creators have shifted their focus to capturing and enticing clients through social networking sites such as YouTube, Pinterest Facebook, Instagram and Twitter. Performance expectancy is the degree to which a person expects that employing a system will result in improved job performance results.

Kuwait Experience

Approximately 90% of firms in Kuwait are SMEs—defined as small and medium-sized businesses, with a total count between 25,000 and 30,000. According to Zainal et al. (2022), the industrial and construction sector comprises 30% of the total market. On the other hand, the retail and hospitality segments constitute 40%. In Kuwait, Small and Medium Companies have been categorized based on size, asset valuation, and income. SMEs are characterized by fewer than 50 workers in Kuwait, possessing an asset base of KD 500,000 or less, and generating annual sales of KD 1,500,000 or less, as defined by the National Fund for SME Development (2013).

Despite their notable contributions, MSMEs continue to encounter numerous obstacles, including the persistent difficulty of securing finances from established banks. Due to MSMEs' negative or non-bankable characteristics, access to financing from banks is difficult, resulting in their profit potential being neglected. This often stems from MSMEs' challenges in effectively managing their financial operations. Nevertheless, banks require documentation that accurately reflects the current financial status of MSMEs to support their bank facilities applications (Sawaean and Ali, 2020).

The National Survey of Financial Literacy and Inclusion study determined that Kuwait demonstrates an impressive level of financial literacy, one that is more than 60% of the population (Saeedi and Hamedi, 2018). It is arguable that Kuwaitis have an understanding of financial institutions and posit a great degree of trust in the ways in which these organizations conduct their business. When engaging in technological innovation, it is of utmost importance to comprehend the level of acceptance exhibited by prospective clients. According to Blut et al. (2021), the prototype e-learning platform will be subject to testing using prominent models that assess various factors influencing acceptability, specifically, the technology acceptance model (TAM), the Usability model, and the Unified Theory of Acceptability and Use of Technology Model (UTAUT).

Search Productivity

The enhancement of financial literacy initiatives aimed at equipping young individuals, particularly aspiring entrepreneurs, with the necessary skills to become competent personal financial managers upon entering the market and establishing their households can be further optimized by comprehending the potential impact of financial literacy on economic behavior and decision-making.

Aim and Objective

The purpose of this research is to evaluate the model financial literacy smartphone application using the TAM, UTAUT, and the Usability of Technology Uptake by MSMEs in

Kuwait. The elements utilized in this study encompass the following: expected effort, expected behavior intentions, expected performance, expected resources and costs, expected efficiency, and an acceptance prototype.

Literature Review

Prior studies have identified various factors that affect technology adoption among entrepreneurs. These factors encompass perceived usefulness, ease of utilization, social impact, and facilitating aspects. Nevertheless, examining these factors in relation to Kuwaiti entrepreneurship has been limited to a few studies. This study addresses the gap above by applying the UTAUT model in the context of Kuwait. This research investigates the effects of effort expectancy, performance expectancy, social influence, and facilitating environments on Kuwaiti entrepreneurs' inclinations to use technology. The following six key constructs of the model have their respective details presented:

Performance and effort expectancy (PE): This defines how MSMEs owners perceive technology could enhance their firm's performance and assess the system's simplicity.

Facilitating conditions (FC): Defines an individual's faith that an administrative and technological structure could minimize technology utilization.

Satisfaction (SAT) defines how a consumer's general view could impact the acceptability of technology.

Social influence (SI): evaluates how users' technology acceptance is influenced by how friends and family utilize it.

Learning attitude (LA): Impacts consumers' desire to use technology to learn.

User perception (UP): the level of comprehension of technological concepts.
Continuance intentions could be described as the subjective capacity of an individual interacting with technology.

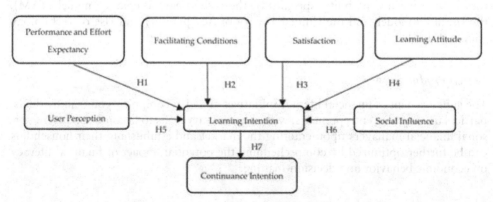

Figure 1.1 Presents the conceptual model of this research.

Seven key hypotheses that will be evaluated in this study include:

H1: *Performance and effort expectancy (PE) positively impacts learning intention (LI).*

H2: *Facilitating conditions (FC) positively impact learning intention (LI).*

H3: *Satisfaction (SAT) positively impacts learning intention (LI).*

H4: *Learning attitude (LA) positively impacts learning intention (LI).*

H5: *User perception (UP) positively impacts learning intention (LI).*

H6: *Social Influence (SI) positively influences learning intention (LI).*

H7: *Learning intention (LI) positively impacts continuance intentions (CI).*

Methodology

The pilot study of this research employed the UTAUT Model as its theoretical framework. This particular approach aims to assess the efficacy of digital tools in addressing the knowledge disparity pertaining to financial literacy among Kuwaiti entrepreneurs. The study employed a structural equation modeling approach to evaluate the various factors that influence the intentions of Kuwaiti entrepreneurs to adopt technology. The data-gathering tool employed in this study consisted of self-administered surveys that necessitated participants to respond to the provided questions. The target population involves female and male Kuwaiti entrepreneurs that aim to employ technology in their operations. A sample size of 383 is recommended.

Data Collection

Data and opinions from respondents were collected using a questionnaire. The research employed two questionnaires, one relating to the participants' demographic information and the other focusing on the primary hypotheses. A questionnaire aimed at participants to uncover demographic information about their basic characteristics, such as gender, marriage status, age, job title, educational qualifications, smartphone habits, and technological proficiency, was used. Respondents were obtained through web-based platforms like Facebook, Twitter, and LinkedIn. The survey was conducted through these platforms. The range scale of responses extended from 1 (strong agreement) to 5 (strong disagreement).

Statistical Method

The provided table displays various statistical measures, including the mean, item-rest correlation, standard deviation, Cronbach Alpha, and factor loading. These measures contribute to a clear and comprehensible solution, indicating that the study items effectively load onto a single factor influencing Kuwaiti entrepreneurs' intention to utilize technology. The factor loading for the elements exceeds the lower level of 0.6. Therefore, it is advisable to eliminate objects with factor loads below 0.60 from subsequent analysis (Awang, 2015).

Results

Data on the demographics of respondents are contained in Table 1.1. Around 43.3% of those surveyed were identified as women, while approximately 56.7% were men. The largest segment of participants comprised individuals aged between 20 and 35, 76.7%, and 36–45-year-olds constituted approximately 16% of the sample. Fifty percent of the participants had a bachelor's degree, highlighting this attainment as the predominant demographic. According to the findings, roughly 52.7% of participants were employed by private organizations, whereas 47.3% worked for public entities. The demographic information shows that 24.7% of individuals are married, while 74% are single. The responses indicated a wide range of technological know-how among the participants, with 16% having used technology for 2–3 years, 7.3% reporting minimal experience (less than one year), and most (76.7%) possessing extensive knowledge beyond five years.

Table 1.1: Demographical information.

	Total sample (n = 150)
Gender	
Female	65.00 (43.30%)
Male	85.00 (56.70%)
Age	
Less than 19	5.00 (3.30%)
20 to 35	115.00 (76.70%)
36 to 45	24.00 (16.00%)
over 46	6.00 (4.00%)
Marital Status	
Married	37.00 (24.70%)
Single	111.00 (74.00%)
Widowed	2.00 (1.30%)
Working	
Private Job	79.00 (52.70%)
Public Job	71.00 (47.30%)
Qualification	
High school	10.00 (6.70%)
Two years diploma	22.00 (14.70%)
Bachelor	75.00 (50.00%)
Master	31.00 (20.70%)
PhD	12.00 (8.00%)
Experience on Technology adoption	
One year or less	11.00 (7.30%)
2–3 years	24.00 (16.00%)
More than 5 years	115.00 (76.70%)

Statistical Results

A partial least squares path modelling (PLS) analysis was performed to examine whether the independent variables FC, SAT, SI, LA, UP, LI, and PE were sufficient to appropriately represent the data. We were able to compute the weights associated with the structural model using the path weighting scheme. PLS-PM's principal purpose is to adequately show the extensive variables network and their interrelationships; this is the method's fundamental objective. The assessment of the PLS-PM model involved an evaluation of the validity of both the structural and measurement models. Figure 1.2 depicts a representation of the PLS model.

The latent construct must exhibit a positive correlation with each indicator to establish reflective indicators. If there is a rise in the value of the latent variable, each indicator is also expected to exhibit a rise. Sanchez (2013) describes this concept as indicators of one-dimensionality. Cronbach's alpha (α) and Dillon-Goldstein's rho (ρC) were the statistical methods that the researchers utilized in order to evaluate the markers of one-dimensionality (Sarstedt et al., 2019). When the values of Cronbach's alpha, Dillon-Goldstein's rho, and ρA are sufficiently high (>0.7), it is possible to make the assumption that the indicators are unidimensional. The fact that all latent variables are unidimensional lends credence to the notion that the correlations existing within the latent variables and the indicators that correspond to them are acceptable for PLS-PM. The information of Dillon-Goldstein's rho and Cronbach's alpha are presented in Table 1.2.

In addition, an assessment was conducted to determine the average variance extracted (AVE) for every construct, thereby verifying the strength of the correlation with every latent variable and its corresponding indicators. The convergent validity analysis also considered the communality and loading of each construct.

The assessment of convergent validity involved the computation of the average variance explained (AVE) for every construct (Sarstedt et al., 2019). A latent variable with an AVE of 0.50 or higher suggests that it explains at least 50% of the variability in the observed indicators (Henseler et al., 2009; Chinn and Fairlie, 2010; Sarstedt et al.,

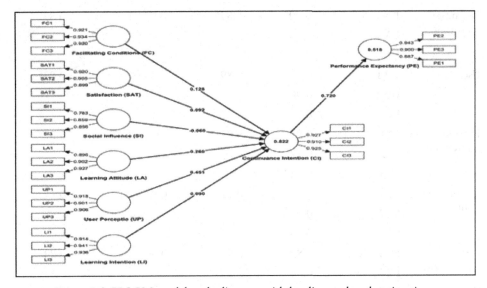

Figure 1.2 PLS-PM model node diagram with loading and path estimations.

2019; Sanchez, 2013). AVE is evaluated solely based on reflective factors. Every latent variable accounted for a significant portion of the variability in the indicator, as none of the latent variables had an AVE value less than 0.5. Table 1.2 presents the mean values for vehicle expenditure data.

To ascertain the reflective indicators that exhibited inadequate loadings on the latent variables, an analysis was conducted on their commonalities and factor loadings. According to Chinn and Fairlie (2010), Henseler et al. (2009), and Sanchez (2013), it is recommended that every latent variable construct of an indicator should have an explanation for at least 50% of its variance, as indicated by a loading of at least 0.707 and a communality of 0.50. If the loading is not adequate, it can be concluded that it is insufficient. The loadings of all reflective indicators were high, indicating that they accounted for a significant proportion of the variability in their respective latent constructs. Table 1.2 displays the communalities and loadings of the measuring model.

Table 1.2: One-dimensionality indicators for each and every latent construct, in addition to an outer model for the PLS-PM model.

Dimension	Item	Loading	Cronbach's alpha (α)	Dillon-Goldstein's rho (ρC)	AVE
Facilitating conditions	FC 1	0.92	0.92	0.93	0.86
	FC 2	0.93			
	FC 3	0.92			
Satisfaction	SAT 1	0.92	0.89	0.90	0.82
	SAT 2	0.91			
	SAT 3	0.90			
Social influence	SI 1	0.78	0.79	0.82	0.70
	SI 2	0.86			
	SI 3	0.86			
Learning attitude	LA 1	0.90	0.89	0.90	0.83
	LA 2	0.90			
	LA 3	0.93			
User perception	UP 1	0.92	0.89	0.90	0.83
	UP 2	0.90			
	UP 3	0.91			
Learning intention	LI 1	0.91	0.92	0.92	0.87
	LI 2	0.94			
	LI 3	0.94			
Continuance intention	CI 1	0.93	0.91	0.91	0.85
	CI 2	0.91			
	CI 3	0.93			
Performance expectancy	PE 1	0.89	0.90	0.90	0.83
	PE 2	0.94			
	PE 3	0.90			

The Fornell-Larcker criterion was employed to assess the discriminant validity of the reflective indicators (Hair et al., 2014). The correlations between the scores of the constructs were contrasted to the square roots of the AVE for every construct. The Fornell-Larcker criterion is considered to be violated when the relationship within a given construct among other constructs surpasses the square root of its AVE. None of the constructs violated the Fornell-Larcker criterion, indicating the absence of multi-collinearity. Table 1.3 shows the Fornell-Larcker criterion, wherein the diagonal entries represent the AVE values of the constructs, while the lower triangle displays the correlations between the constructs' scores.

Table 1.3: Fornell-Larcker criterion results.

	FC	SAT	SI	LA	UP	LI	CI	PE
FC	.94							
SAT	.81	.92						
SI	.64	.79	.84					
LA	.79	.82	.76	.92				
UP	.77	.83	.76	.85	.92			
LI	.76	.81	.77	.88	.89	.94		
CI	.79	.81	.71	.86	.88	.85	.93	
PE	.67	.76	.67	.71	.74	.72	.73	.92

Note. The average variance extracted from the constructs is represented by the diagonal, and the correlations between the construct scores are shown in the lower triangle.

Evaluating the internal or structural model involved utilizing the R^2-values and Goodness of Fit for every endogenous variable. The internal regression pathways were analyzed using the latent scores computed by the model. The diagram presented in Figure 1.1 shows the internal model as a node diagram.

The R^2-values were computed for every endogenous variable to evaluate the suitability of the correlations between the latent variables. Sanchez (2013) argues that it is recommended that each endogenous variable possess an R^2-value greater or equal to .20. All R^2-values exhibited significant magnitudes, suggesting that every relationship is suitable for inclusion in the model. Table 1.4 displays the R^2-values.

Table 1.4: AVE values as well as R^2-values for every construct.

Construct	R^2	Adj. R^2
CI	.83	.82
PE	.53	.52

The GoF index can be computed as a metric to evaluate the predictive capability of the PLS-PM technique in forecasting future outcomes. The GoF index is derived by considering the geometric mean value of R^2 and the average communality of every latent variable. The concept of good model fit is described as having a GoF index that exceeds .90. Conversely, a GoF index within the range of .70 to .89 shows an acceptable level of quality (Sanchez, 2013; Chinn and Fairlie, 2010). If the GoF index is below or equal to .70, it indicates that the model has a low level of predictive capacity. Based on the goodness-of-fit metric, it can be said that the model's fit was satisfactory, and its predictive ability was average (GoF = .74).

The threshold for significance in the regressions was fixed at α = .05. To elaborate, the particular value of B (.78), when paired with the impressively high t-scores (15.01) and the p-value (>.001), highlights the potent ability of FC to forecast CI. As the level of FC rises, the projected value of CI increases by approximately .78 units. B, with a value of .80, and a t-value of 16.24, with a p-value of .001, suggests that a one-unit rise in the SAT score is associated with a predicted rise of .80 units in the CI. Logically, one can deduce that a high SAT score forecasts exceptional cognitive abilities. When these values are considered together (B = .70, t-value = 11.86, and p-value .001), they create a powerful argument for the notion that SI rises by one unit, corresponding to an identical growth in the predicted value of CI.

B, with a value of .85, a t-value of 19.43, and a p-value of .001, suggests that a one-unit increase in LA is associated with a predicted rise of .85 units in the value of CI, which shows LA strongly predicts CI. B at .88, with a t-value of 22.19 and a p-value of less than .001, shows that UP significantly predicted the CI. Specifically, a unit rise in UP is linked with a perceived rise of .88 units in the predicted value of CI. B was found at .84, with a corresponding t-value of 18.56 and a p-value of .001, which suggests that a unit rise in LI is associated with an expected rise of .84 units in the dependent variable CI. These data establish a robust link between LI and CI, indicating their interconnected nature. A statistically significant positive link exists between PE and cognitive intelligence, as witnessed by the observed value of B = .72, which suggests that for each upward shift in CI, there is an expected augmentation of around .72 units in PE expectations at t-value = 12.61 and p-value = .001. The regression outcomes are presented in Table 1.5.

Table 1.5: Regression results for every path.

Bath	Beta-Value	T statistics	P value	Remark
H1.1: FC → CI	.13	1.73	.08	N.S.
H1.2: FC → CI → PE	.09	1.69	.09	N.S.
H2.1: SAT → CI	.09	1.04	.30	N.S.
H2.2: SAT → CI → PE	.07	1.03	.31	N.S.
H3.1: SI → CI	−.06	.78	.43	N.S.
H3.2: SI → CI → PE	−.04	.79	.43	N.S.
H4.1: LA → CI	.26	2.16	.03	Supported
H4.2: LA → CI → PE	.19	2.13	.03	Supported
H5.1: UP → CI	.45	4.32	<.001	Supported
H5.2: UP → CI → PE	.33	4.11	<.001	Supported
H6.1: LI → CI	.09	.63	.53	N.S.
H6.2: LI → CI → PE	.07	.62	.53	N.S.
H7: CI → PE	.720	15.81	<.001	Supported

With a score that is .055 points lower than the threshold, the current model is considered to be within the allowed range for the "standard root means square residual" (SRMR) metric. SRMR Saturated model equals .06, SRMR Estimated model equals .076, Chi-square equals 820.12, and NFI equals .80.

Discussion

The research investigates the factors influencing technology acceptance among individuals with varying socioeconomic backgrounds, specifically focusing on financial literacy education. The study builds upon the theoretical frameworks of UTAUT, TAM, and usability theory to comprehensively understand this phenomenon. Specifically, efforts and performance expectations, possibilities, and social influence do not significantly influence continuation intentions. The findings indicate that Kuwaiti entrepreneurs decided to adopt the technology after recognizing its benefits. This gives rise to notable statistical correlations among individuals' performance expectancy, user perception, and learning attitude, thereby facilitating their enhancement of financial literacy knowledge through digital platform use. This can be attributed to the significant number of socioeconomic users who possess knowledge and comprehension of the technological aspects required for proficient utilization of the applications.

Integrating digital sites into a financial literacy training initiative is expected to enhance the comprehension of financial literacy among Kuwaiti entrepreneurs. The utilization of digital platforms facilitates the acquisition of financial literacy, motivating an increasing number of businesses to pursue this objective actively. This finding illustrates that employing a digital platform is the most effective approach for imparting financial literacy knowledge to Kuwaiti entrepreneurs.

The researchers validated the TAM and determined that a favorable disposition towards acquiring knowledge has a substantial impact on the socioeconomic standing of individuals utilizing the system and their inclination to continue using the system within a professional setting. This finding aligns with hypothesis H4.1, which has been confirmed (T = 2.159, p = 0.031). The statistical evaluation at a T-value of 2.132 and a p-value of 0.033 presents a considerable impact of performance expectancy on learning intentions among low-income users. Similarly, a T-value of 4.317 and a p-value of 0.000 were achieved, indicating a substantial impact of user perception on learning intentions among high-income users. Both hypotheses, H4.2 and H5.1, were accepted based on these findings. One of the three identified criteria, which indicates learning attitude, is the statement "Learning financial literacy through the mobile app is enjoyable," exhibiting the highest loading. Individuals who download this software do so to augment their understanding and proficiency in the field of personal finance. The conclusion aligns with the findings reported by (Peng et al., 2022). This observation suggests that individuals utilizing mobile applications positively intend to enhance their financial literacy. Given that the observed factors exhibited the highest loading factor, it can be inferred that they would significantly influence users' learning intentions if the online learning setting offered all the necessary resources to enhance their financial literacy (SAT2). The study by Zhou et al. (2019) illustrates the correlation between user satisfaction and app stickiness and the user's motivation to learn.

For instance, if the application incorporates all the desired features that users require to achieve their objectives or enhance their knowledge, its impact on their learning intentions will be substantial. A relevant positive correlation exists between higher continuation intentions and higher performance expectations (T = 15.808, p = 0.000). The elements that significantly influence individuals' intentions to continue a particular course of action will also impact their expectations regarding performance outcomes. This is because the intentions to continue substantially affect individuals' expectations regarding their performance outcomes, as approved in Hypothesis 7. The results indicate that the facilitating conditions (T = 1.689, p = 0.091) did not significantly affect continuance intention (H2 was rejected). This is due to people's proclivity to oppose the application due to their need for greater resources and support (Cho et al., 2020). According to Venkatesh et al. (2003), facilitating aspects do not impact continuation intention. The subsequent variable, social influence (T = 0.783, p = 0.434), did not yield a statistically significant impact on the intention to continue (H3.1 rejected).

Integrating a digital platform within a financial literacy training initiative can potentially enhance the financial literacy knowledge of Kuwaiti entrepreneurs. This demonstrates their proficiency in utilizing digital media as an instructional tool for imparting financial literacy skills to entrepreneurs in Kuwait. The utilization of digital platforms has the potential to enhance the accessibility and convenience of acquiring financial literacy skills, thereby fostering a greater inclination among Kuwaiti entrepreneurs to engage in financial education. The outcome would be extremely beneficial.

Future Research and Limitations

The major goal of this study was to identify the elements that influence entrepreneurs' technological adoption intentions. The findings of this study carry significant implications and are anticipated to contribute to the advancement of mobile applications designed for entrepreneurs. The need to carefully evaluate the study's limitations arises due to its restricted demographic sample scope. The study was successfully conducted within the defined parameters of its objectives. Further research is warranted to explore additional factors from various theories, models, and societal barriers.

Moreover, increasing the sample size to investigate a more representative portion of the Kuwaiti population is recommended. Further investigation can be conducted on a macro-level enterprise. Furthermore, it is recommended to undertake further investigation into non-technological strategies; this includes practical, hand-on education, to enable Kuwaiti entrepreneurs to improve and develop their financial literacy.

References

Awang, P. (2015). SEM Made Simple: A Gentle Approach to Learning Structural Equation Modeling. Bangi: MPWS Rich Publication.

Bannon, S., Ford, K., and Meltzer, L. (2014). Financial literacy programs in the workplace. *The CPA Journal*, 84(9), 67.

Blut, M., Chong, A. Y. L., Tsigna, Z., and Venkatesh, V. (2022). Meta-Analysis of the Unified Theory of Acceptance and Use of Technology (UTAUT): Challenging its Validity and Charting a Research Agenda in the Red Ocean. *Journal of the Association for Information Systems*, 23(1), 13–95. doi:10.17705/1jais.00719

Chinn, M. D., and Fairlie, R. W. (2010). ICT use in the developing world: an analysis of differences in computer and internet penetration. *Review of International Economics*, 18(1), 153–167.

Cho, H., Chi, C., and Chiu, W. (2020). Understanding sustained usage of health and fitness apps: incorporating the technology acceptance model with the investment model. *Technology in Society*, 63, 101429.

Hair, Jr F. J., Sarstedt, M., Hopkins, L., and Kuppelwieser, V. G. (2014). Partial least squares structural equation modeling (PLS-SEM) An emerging tool in business research. *European Business Review*, 26(2), 106–121.

Henseler, J., Ringle, C. M., and Sinkovics, R. R. (2009). The use of partial least squares path modeling in international marketing. In Sinkovics, R. R., and Ghauri, P. N. (Ed.), New Challenges to International Marketing (Advances in International Marketing, Vol. 20), Emerald Group Publishing Limited, Bingley, pp. 277–319. https://doi.org/10.1108/S1474-7979(2009)0000020014

McKenzie, V. M. (2009). The Financial Literacy of University Students: A Comparison of Graduating Seniors' Financial Literacy and Debt Level. University of South Florida.

Nikou, S. A., and Economides, A. A. (2017). Mobile-based assessment: integrating acceptance and motivational factors into a combined model of self-determination theory and technology acceptance. *Computers in Human Behavior*, 68, 83–95.

Peng, P., Ao, Y., Li, M., Wang, Y., Wang, T., and Bahmani, H. (2022). Building information modeling learning behavior of AEC undergraduate students in China. *Behavioral Sciences*, 12(8), 269.

Saeedi, A., and Hamedi, M. (2018). Financial Literacy: Empowerment in the Stock Market. Springer.

Sanchez, G. (2013). PLS Path Modeling with R. Trowchez Editions, Berkeley, (vol. 383), pp. 551.

Sarstedt, M., Hair Jr, J. F., Cheah, J.-H., Becker, J.-M., and Ringle, C. M. (2019). How to specify, estimate, and validate higher-order constructs in PLS-SEM. *Australasian Marketing Journal*, 27(3), 197–211.

Sawaean, F., and Ali, K. (2020). The impact of entrepreneurial leadership and learning orientation on organizational performance of SMEs: The mediating role of innovation capacity. *Management Science Letters*, 10(2), 369–380.

Venkatesh, V., Morris, M. G., Davis, G. B., and Davis, F. D. (2003). User acceptance of information technology: Toward a unified view. *MIS Quarterly*, 425–478.

Zainal, M., Bani-Mustafa, A., Alameen, M., Toglaw, S., and Al Mazari, A. (2022). Economic anxiety and the performance of SMEs during COVID-19: a cross-national study in Kuwait. *Sustainability*, 14, 1112.

Zhou, L., Bao, J., Setiawan, I. M. A., Saptono, A., and Parmanto, B. (2019). The mHealth app usability questionnaire (MAUQ): development and validation study. *JMIR MHealth and UHealth*, 7(4), e11500.

2 Artificial Intelligence Trends in Business Services and Industry in Terms of Sustainable Innovations in Management

Dorota Walentek

Czestochowa University of Technology, Poland

Abstract

Artificial intelligence (AI) technology is increasingly used in various aspects of human life. The aim of the article is to identify trends in the use of AI in business services and industry in terms of sustainable innovations in management. An additional goal was to determine whether and how the size of the population, the level of development of citizens and GDP per capita affect the interest of residents in information about the use of AI in business services and industry. The study was conducted using the virtual ethnography method. It was checked what kind of aspects of artificial intelligence the users of the www.google.com search engine are most often interested in. The research area was narrowed down to the category of business services and industry. The results were presented on a global scale and, additionally, 30 countries were selected where AI enjoys the greatest interest among www.google.com users. The most frequently searched areas including the term artificial intelligence were identified: business intelligence, technology, companies, analytics, system, machine learning, business, data analytics, course, marketing, data science, big data and automation.

Keywords

Artificial intelligence, AI, virtual ethnography

Introduction

Artificial intelligence (AI) is a technology that is gaining more and more interest among users around the world. In 2021, 141.24 thousand patents were filed worldwide for solutions based on artificial intelligence. This is more than 30 times the number of patents filed in 2015 (HAI, 2022). The rapid development of the AI market is primarily a huge opportunity for organizations. They can visibly improve supply chain efficiency and increase competitive advantage by offering products and services that are more attractive to customers.

The aim of the article is to identify trends in the use of AI in business services and industry in terms of sustainable innovations in management. An additional goal was to determine whether and how the size of the population, the level of development of citizens and GDP per capita affect the interest of residents in information about the use of AI in business services and industry. The study was conducted on a global scale.

dorota.walentek@pcz.pl

In addition, countries with the highest level of interest in AI were selected. Statistical data available on the website www.trends.google.com were used for the calculations.

AI has been the subject of scientific research many times, especially in recent years. In 2000, the number of articles searched in the Scopus database under the term artificial intelligence was 3,270, in 2010, 12,285, and in 2022, as many as 33,128. In the Business, Management and Accounting category, the number of publications was: 73 in 2000, 193 in 2010 and 1457 in 2022. A significant part of them concerned the area of machine learning (Alon et al. 2022), AI-based applications used in management (Mishra et al. 2023) and the use of artificial intelligence in individual industry sectors (Smallman 2022). But current research on the level of user interest in AI is lacking. This study is an extension of existing scientific research devoted to artificial intelligence by identifying global trends in searching for information on particular issues related to AI. In addition, the article presents the level of interest in the use of AI in 30 selected countries. The study is up-to-date as it focuses on the last 12 months (April 2022–March 2023) and is based on the google.pl search engine database used worldwide.

Literature Review

The term AI can be understood in two ways. In a general sense, it refers to the non-existent computer software that thinks and works independently. In a narrower sense, AI refers to software that uses special algorithms to identify patterns in the database and predict future events related to the analyzed data (Raj and Seamans 2019). Bordot (2022) draws attention to the basic difference between existing algorithms and artificial intelligence: the existing technology enables the task to be performed, and the artificial intelligence algorithm is designed to learn how to perform specific tasks.

In the Web of Science (WoS) database, the first publications on artificial intelligence were published in 1989. The total number of articles in all WoS categories by March 1, 2023 was 46,827, and in the Management and Business categories 2,076. Until 2016, inclusive, the number of publications on AI remained at a similar level: from 3 in 2003 to 25 in 2016. A moderate increase in the interest of scientists from the given categories in this area of research took place in 2017 and 2018 (38 and 69 publications, respectively). A significant increase in interest is noticeable starting from 2019: 156 publications. In the last year presented in Figure 1, the number of articles was 434.

Researchers described, among others, machine learning (Olugbade et al. 2022; Kuntz and Wilson 2022; Krajcer 2022), data mining (Cai et al. 2022; Huang et al. 2022; Bajdor, Pawełoszek 2020), pattern recognition (Song and Fan 2022; Amiri et al. 2022), human-computer interaction (Balmcombe and De Leo 2022; Shao 2022), big data analytics (Jelonek 2017; Jelonek et al. 2019), and virtualization of resources acquisition processes (Jelonek et al. 2013). A large part of the publications was also devoted to computer vision (Corke et al. 2022; Kitaguchi 2022; Gumbs et al. 2022), natural language processing (Shaik et al. 2022) and algorithm (Ma et al. 2022; Zhu and Jing 2022). Researchers have also addressed the potential impact of AI on unemployment with mixed results. Bortod (2022) and Bailey (2022) argued that AI will increase unemployment. Naude (2021) believed that AI does not increase unemployment in the short term, but it may increase it in the long term. Nguyen (2022) made the impact of AI on unemployment dependent on the inflation rate. Anakpo and Kollamparambil did not find any negative impact of AI on unemployment. In turn, Kohli (2020) and Lu and Lu (2022) believed that artificial intelligence technology can reduce unemployment, as long as employees constantly educate themselves in the use of new technologies.

We are currently seeing an increasing share of AI technology in human life (Thomas 2022). The main sectors that use artificial intelligence are: healthcare, manufacturing, customer service, transportation, media and education. In the USA in 2021, over 3% of job advertisements in the IT industry were related to AI (HAi 2022). The value of the AI industry amounted to USD 55–60 billion. According to estimates for the years 2021–2026, the AI market will grow by approx. 38–40% on average annually, and in 2026 it will reach the value of USD 300–310 billion. The largest increases concern the BFSI sectors: USD 550–560 million, telecom & IT: USD 490–500 million, retail and e-commerce: USD 470–480 million, healthcare and life sciences: USD 460–470 million, automotive and transportation: USD 270–282 million USD, government: USD 280–300 million and manufacturing: USD 240–254 million (Markets and Markets 2022).

Thanks to the increasing use of AI technology, it supports the implementation of sustainable innovations in organizations. These are innovations in which companies take into account the three pillars of sustainable development: environment, society and economy. Sustainable innovations are therefore characterized by a much greater level of complexity than traditional innovations (Lv et al. 2018).

The implementation of sustainable innovations in business is based not only on the conventional abilities of employees. It also requires the development of environmental management capabilities, collaboration across supply and value chains, risk and brand equity, and the management of intangible assets (Berghout 2014). AI technology can be extremely helpful in a coherent combination of the abilities just mentioned (Jelonek et al. 2020).

Research Methodology

The aim of presented study is identification of trends related to the use of AI in business services and industry in terms of sustainable innovations in management. An additional goal was to determine whether and how the size of the population, the level of development of citizens and GDP per capita affect the interest of residents in information about the use of AI in business services and industry. The presented study was conducted on March 1, 2023 and covered the period from March 1, 2022 to February 28, 2023. Four research hypotheses were defined: *Country's population size determines the level of interest in using AI in business and industry* (H1), *The level of development of citizens significantly affects the degree of their interest in using AI in business services and industry* (H2), *The amount of GDP significantly affects the interest of residents in using AI in business services and industry* (H3) and *Business intelligence is one of the most searched areas related to AI* (H4).

Virtual ethnography was chosen as the research method. Trends related to the use of AI were determined on the basis of the percentage of user queries entered in the www.google.com search engine. There was no focus on the absolute number of queries. Trends were selected using data from www.trends.google.com. The main search term for all the calculations below was artificial intelligence. The results were narrowed down to the category of business services and industry and the period of 12 months preceding the survey, and more specifically to the period from 01/03/2022 to 28/02/2022.

The study was conducted on a global scale. In addition, the 30 countries whose inhabitants most often search for information on individual aspects of artificial intelligence in the google.com browser were presented. In order to verify H1, data from the World Bank (Worldbank 2023) was additionally used. In order to verify H2 and H3, Human Development Report 2021/2022 (HDR 2022) was used. A report containing information on both the Human Development Index and Gross national income (GNI) per capita from 2017. Human Development Index (HDI) is the geometric mean of standardized indicators for three key dimensions of human development: long and healthy life, knowledge and standard of living.

The correlation between the number of inhabitants, HDI and GNI of a given country and the level of their interest in the subject of AI was determined using Spearman's R. All calculations presented in this article were made in the following programs: Statistica and Excel.

Empirical Results

To verify the H1 hypothesis (Country's population size determines the level of interest in using AI in business and industry), 30 countries with the highest level of artificial intelligence popularity in the www.google.com search engine were selected (Table 2.1).

Table 2.1: Countries with the highest artificialintelligencesearchpopularity .

No.	Country	Search popularity	Population (2021)	HDI (2021)	GNI per capita in USD (2017)
1	Papua New Guinea	100	9 949 437	0,558	4009
2	Eswatini	82	1 192 271	0,597	7679
3	Fiji	80	924 610	0,73	9980
4	Botswana	44	2 588 423	0,693	16198
5	Ethiopia	43	120 283 026	0,498	2361
6	Zimbabwe	43	15 993 524	0,593	3810
7	Suriname	38	612 985	0,73	12672
8	Malawi	37	19 889 742	0,512	1466
9	Rwanda	37	13 461 888	0,534	2210
10	Namibia	29	2 530 151	0,615	8634
11	Malta	25	518 536	0,918	38884
12	Iceland	23	372 520	0,959	55782
13	Guyana	20	804 567	0,714	22465
14	Singapore	17	5 453 566	0,939	90919
15	Kenya	17	53 005 614	0,575	4474
16	Benin	17	12 996 895	0,525	3409
17	Madagascar	17	28 915 653	0,501	1484

(continued)

Table 2.1: Continued

No.	Country	Search popularity	Population (2021)	HDI (2021)	GNI per capita in USD (2017)
18	Arab Emirates	16	9 365 145	0,911	62574
19	Qatar	16	2 688 235	0,855	87134
20	Pakistan	15	231 402 117	0,544	4624
21	Ghana	14	32 833 031	0,632	5745
22	Uganda	14	45 853 778	0,525	2181
23	India	14	1 407 563 842	0,633	6590
24	Luxembourg	13	640 064	0,93	84649
25	Bahrain	13	1 463 265	0,875	39497
26	Nigeria	13	213 401 323	0,535	4790
27	Zambia	12	19 473 125	565	3218
28	Mozambique	11	32 077 072	0,446	1198
29	China	11	1 412 360 000	0,768	17504
30	Sudan	10	45 657 202	0,508	3575

Source: Own study based on www.trends.google.com (01.03.2023), Worldbank 2023 and HDR 2022

Artificial intelligence search popularity is measured on a scale of 0 to 100. A value of 100 indicates the country in which the term was most searched for out of all www.google.com queries in that country. A value of 50 indicates a country with half the search level. A value of 0 would indicate a location where a given entry was either not searched at all or there is not enough data for that entry. Importantly, the higher value refers to the percentage of all queries in a given country, not the absolute number of queries. Therefore, a small country with 70% of all searches for artificial intelligence on www.google.com would score twice as much as a huge country with 35% of artificial intelligence searches.

Papua New Guinea had the highest percentage of inquiries in the above list. However, this does not mean that 100% of the search terms in this country were related to artificial intelligence. Based on the data presented by www.trends.google.com, it is not possible to determine the absolute number of queries. Starting with country number 2 in the list (Eswatini), all countries refer to Papua New Guinea. For example, the percentage of searches for artificial intelligence in small Fiji was 80%, and in huge China only 11% of the percentage of searches found in Papua New Guinea. The ranking shows the 30 countries with the highest percentage of searches. The Population (2021) column shows the population of a given country according to data collected by the World Bank from 2021 (World Bank 2023). The data in the columns: HDI (2021) and GNI per capita in USD (2017) was obtained from the Human Development Report 2022 (HDR 2022).

The next step was to check whether the size of a country's population affects the percentage of searches for artificial intelligence by the inhabitants of a given country. Spearman's rank correlation was used, assuming $p > 0.05$. Spearman's R was (−0.44469).

This means a moderate infl uence of the country's population on the popularity of the search query. Hypothesis H1 was positively verifi ed. Interestingly, the study found an inverse effect. That is, in the above group of countries, the larger the population, the lower the percentage of artifi cial intelligence searches. However, it should be emphasized once again that this does not mean a lower absolute number of searches for a given term. The data are statistically signifi cant (p=0.01381).

When verifying the H2, the focus was on the size of the Human Development Index. Spearman's R was (−0.06346) for p = 0,739012. Thus, no statistically signifi cant relationship was found between the level of development of citizens and the degree of their interest in using AI in business services and industry.

In the next step, the hypothesis H3 was verifi ed. Used GDP per capitol data collected in HDR (2022). No statistically signifi cant relationship was found between the size of GDP and citizens' interest in using AI in business services and industry (Spearman's R = 0,00089 and p = 0,9962).

Finally, H4 (Business intelligence is one of the most searched areas related to AI) was verifi ed. Based on data from www.trends.google.com, a list of the 20 most popular passwords entered by users was prepared, including the term artifi cial intelligence (Table 2.2). When preparing the list, duplicate items or items that did not contribute anything to the study (e.g., artifi cial intelligence pdf) were manually removed.

Table 2.2: Terms searched by www.google.com users with artificialintelligence.

No.	Search queries	Search popularity
1	Artificial intelligence	100
2	What is artificial intelligence	77
3	Artificial intelligence business intelligence	58
4	Artificial intelligence technology	46
5	Artificial intelligence companies	43
6	Artificial intelligence analytics	42
7	Artificial intelligence system	36
8	Artificial intelligence machine learning	32
9	Artificial intelligence in business	31
10	Artificial intelligence data analytics	30
11	Artificial intelligence in business intelligence	30
12	Artificial intelligence company	27
13	Artificial intelligence course	25
14	Artificial intelligence marketing	23
15	Artificial intelligence data science	22
16	Artificial intelligence systems	22
17	Machine learning and artificial intelligence	21
18	Artificial intelligence big data	19
19	Artificial intelligence and data analytics	19
20	Artificial intelligence automation	18

Source: Own study based on www.trends.google.com (01.03.2023)

The popularity of searching for individual items listed in Table 2.2 was determined by www.trends.google.com on a relative scale, where 100 indicates the most frequently searched term, 50 for a search term twice as low, and e.g., 10 is a search term ten times less than the first password. The keyword most often searched with the term artificial intelligence on www.google.com was ai artificial intelligence (value 100). Other thematic areas related to the main keyword are: business intelligence, technology, companies, analytics, system, machine learning, business, data analytics, course, marketing, data science, big data and automation.

The business intelligence area was listed twice: in third place (58 value) and in the context of artificial intelligence in business intelligence in eleventh place (30 value). Thus, hypothesis H4 was confirmed: business intelligence is in the group of areas most often searched for with the term artificial intelligence. What's more, this term is at the forefront of the most searched terms.

Conclusion

Sustainable innovations are becoming more and more popular among managers in various market sectors. Many organizations not only pay attention to their profits, but also take into account the environment, society and economy on a larger scale. Artificial intelligence (AI) technology can contribute to supporting decision-making processes within the organization through a thorough analysis of the needs of stakeholders, society and environmental protection.

This article presents a list of the most frequently discussed topics related to artificial intelligence by researchers. It has been shown that AI technology is an important topic from the point of view of science and from the point of view of managerial practices. It was also checked in which countries on a global scale user of the www.google.com search engine are most interested in the subject of AI. It turned out that the percentage of people searching for information about artificial intelligence is higher in countries with smaller populations. Calculations were made for the category: business services and industry.

The results of the study are important for managerial practice, as they show that AI technology supporting sustainable innovations in management is of great interest not only in countries with a large population or high economic growth. Managers in small countries can also use AI technology to develop the level of implemented innovations. What's more: artificial technology can be an opportunity for small countries for proportionally faster economic growth than in countries where AI is already used. By knowing in which countries, the subject of AI is proportionally the most popular, organizations can more efficiently choose the locations of their foreign branches. For this purpose, it is worth checking the level of knowledge of the inhabitants of a given country in the field of implementing sustainable innovations based on AI, branch maintenance costs, tax regulations and social and environmental conditions.

The study did not show any statistically significant correlation between the level of development of citizens and the degree of their interest in using AI in business services and industry. The level of interest in AI is also not affected by GNI per capita. It is worth noting, however, that the study was conducted only for a group of 30 countries with proportionally the greatest interest in using AI in business services and industry. It seems advisable to conduct a study on a larger group of countries.

The result of the study was also the identification of the most frequently searched areas on www.google.com with the term artificial intelligence. These areas are: business intelligence, technology, companies, analytics, system, machine learning, business, data analytics, course, marketing, data science, big data and automation. As the literature review in the theoretical part of this article has shown, most of the above topics have already been described many times by researchers. In the course of further research, it is worth paying attention to the course area. It is particularly appropriate to deepen the knowledge on the use of AI technology in business services and industry.

Sustainable development requires that organizations take into account social, economic and environmental impacts during implementing innovations based on AI technology. In the near future, the ethics of AI will spread. It is worth noting that AI ethics should be implemented in all countries of the world, not only by those with the largest population, territorial range and GNI per capita. Omitting the ethical area in AI-based solutions may prevent the effective implementation of sustainable innovations.

References

Alon, I., Bretas, V. P., Sclip, A., and Paltrinieri, A. (2022). Greenfield FDI attractiveness index: a machine learning approach. *Competitiveness Review: An International Business Journal*, 32(1).

Amiri, M., Jafari, A. H., Makkiabadi, B., and Nazari, S. (2022). Recognizing intertwined patterns using a network of spiking pattern recognition platforms. *Scientific Reports*, 12(1), 1–17, DOI: 10.1038/s41598-022-23320-8.

Anakpo, G. and Kollamparambil, U. (2022). Effect of automation on unemployment: The case of Southern Africa. *Development Southern Africa*, 39(4), 516–527. DOI: 10.1080/0376835X.2021.1978931.

Bailey, D. E. (2022). Emerging technologies at work: policy ideas to address negative consequences for work, workers, and society. *ILR Review*, 75(3), 527–551. DOI: 10.1177/00197939221076747.

Bajdor, P., Paweloszek, I. (2020). Data mining approach in evaluation of sustainable entrepreneurship. *Procedia Computer Science*, 176, 2725–2735.

Berkhout, F. (2014). Sustainable Innovation Management. In: Mark Dodgson, David Gann and Nelson Phillips (Eds), The Oxford Handbook of Innovation Management, Oxford: Oxford University Press, pp. 290–315.

Bordot, F. (2022). Artificial intelligence, robots and unemployment: Evidence from OECD countries. *Journal of Innovation Economics Management*, 37(1), 117–138, DOI: 10.3917/jie.037.0117.

Cai, Z., Li, H., and Cui, W. (2022). Design of multiobjective dynamic software development based on data mining algorithm. *Security and Communication Networks*, DOI: 10.1155/2022/4444061.

Corke, P., Dayoub, F., Hall, D., Skinner, J., and Sünderhauf, N. (2019). What can robotics research learn from computer vision research?. In The International Symposium of Robotics Research (pp. 987–1003). Springer, Cham.

Gumbs, A. A., Grasso, V., Bourdel, N., Croner, R., Spolverato, G., Frigerio, I., ... and Elyan, E. (2022). The advances in computer vision that are enabling more autonomous actions in surgery: a systematic review of the literature. *Sensors*, 22(13), 4918. DOI: 10.3390/s22134918.

HAI (2022), Artificial Intelligence Index Report 2022, Stanford University. https://hai.stanford.edu/research/ai-index-2022 [28.12.2022].

HDR (2022), Human Development Report 2021/2022. https://hdr.undp.org/data-center/documentation-and-downloads [01.07.2023].

Huang, Z., Feng, C., and Feng, Z. (2022). Analysis of ideological and political classroom based on artificial intelligence and data mining technology. *Wireless Communications and Mobile Computing.* DOI: 10.1155/2022/7081165.

Jelonek, D., Stepniak, C., Turek, T., and Ziora, L. (2013). The influence of virtualization of resources acquisition processes on the enterprises competitiveness. ICETE 2013—10th International Joint Conference on E-Business and Telecommunications; 4th International Conference DCNET 2013,—10th International Conference on ICE-B 2013 and OPTICS 2013—4th International Conference on Optical Communication Systems, 2013, pp. 320–327.

Jelonek, D. (2017). Big Data Analytics in the Management of Business, MATEC Web of Conferences, 125, 04021.

Jelonek, D., Stępniak, C., and Ziora, L. (2019). The meaning of big data in the support of managerial decisions in contemporary organizations: Review of selected research. *Advances in Intelligent Systems and Computing*, 886, 361–368.

Jelonek, D., Mesjasz-Lech, A., Stępniak, C., Turek, T., and Ziora, L. (2020). The artificial intelligence application in the management of contemporary organization: theoretical assumptions, current practices and research review. *Lecture Notes in Networks and Systems*, 69, 319–327.

Kitaguchi, D., Watanabe, Y., Madani, A., Hashimoto, D. A., Meireles, O. R., Takeshita, N., ... and Ito, M. (2022). Artificial intelligence for computer vision in surgery: A call for developing reporting guidelines. *Annals of Surgery*, 275(4), e609–e611. DOI: 10.1097/SLA.0000000000005319.

Kohli, G. (2020). Pitfalls of digitization with respect to traditional businesses and employment. JIMS8M: *The Journal of Indian Management & Strategy*, 25(1), 28–33. DOI: 10.5958/0973-9343.2020.00004.6.

Krajcer, Z. (2022). Artificial Intelligence in Cardiovascular Medicine: Historical Overview, Current Status, and Future Directions. *Texas Heart Institute Journal*, 49(2), e207527. DOI: 10.14503/THIJ-20-7527.

Kuntz, D. and Wilson, A. K. (2022). Machine learning, artificial intelligence, and chemistry: How smart algorithms are reshaping simulation and the laboratory. *Pure and Applied Chemistry*, 8, 1019–1054. DOI: 10.1515/pac-2022-0202.

Lu, C. H. (2022). Artificial intelligence and human jobs. Macroeconomic Dynamics, 26(5), 1162–1201. DOI: 10.1017/S1365100520000528.

Lv, W. D., Tian, D., Wei, Y., and Xi, R. X. (2018). Innovation resilience: A new approach for managing uncertainties concerned with sustainable innovation. *Sustainability*, 10(10), 3641.

Market and Markets (2022). https://www.marketsandmarkets.com/Market-Reports/artificial-intelligence-market-74851580.html [28.12.2022].

Mishra, A., Tripathi, A., and Khazanchi, D. (2023). A proposal for research on the application of AI/ML in ITPM: intelligent project management. *International Journal of Information Technology Project Management*, 14(1), 1–9.

Naudé, W. (2021). Artificial intelligence: neither Utopian nor apocalyptic impacts soon. *Economics of Innovation and New Technology*, 30(1), 1–23, DOI: 10.1080/10438599.2020.1839173.

Nguyen, Q. P. and Vo, D. H. (2022). Artificial intelligence and unemployment: An international evidence. *Structural Change and Economic Dynamics*, 63, 40–55. DOI: 10.1016/j.strueco.2022.09.003.

Olugbade, S., Ojo, S., Imoize, A. L., Isabona, J., & Alaba, M. O. (2022). A Review of Artificial Intelligence and Machine Learning for Incident Detectors in Road Transport Systems. *Mathematical and Computational Applications*, 27(5), 77. DOI: 10.3390/mca27050077.

Smallman, M. (2022). Multi scale ethics—why we need to consider the ethics of AI in healthcare at different scales. *Science and Engineering Ethics*, 28(6), 63.

Shaik, T., Tao, X., Li, Y., Dann, C., McDonald, J., Redmond, P., and Galligan, L. (2022). A review of the trends and challenges in adopting natural language processing methods for education feedback analysis. *IEEE Access,* 10(1), 1. DOI: 10.1109/ACCESS.2022.3177752.

Shao, Y. (2022). Human-Computer Interaction Environment Monitoring and Collaborative Translation Mode Exploration Using Artificial Intelligence Technology. *Journal of Environmental and Public Health*, 2022. DOI: 10.1155/2022/4702003.

Song, X. and Fan, L. (2022). Pattern Recognition Characteristics and Neural Mechanism of Basketball Players' Dribbling Tactics Based on Artificial Intelligence and Deep Learning. *Mathematical Problems in Engineering*, 2022. DOI: 10.1155/2022/1673969.

Thomas M. (2022). The future of AI: how artificial intelligence will change the world. https://builtin.com/artificial-intelligence/artificial-intelligence-future [03.03.2022].

World Bank (2023), Population, total, https://data.worldbank.org/indicator/SP.POP.TOTL [03.03.2023]

Zhu, Z. and Jiang, M. The role of artificial intelligence algorithms in marine scientific research. *Frontiers in Marine Science*, 9, 781. DOI: 10.3389/fmars.2022.920994.

3 Project Management Maturity: A Descriptive Study in Software Engineering Field

Niveen Mohamed Mahmoud Ahmed[1,a] and Hisham Abdelsalam[2,b]

[1]Head of The Foundation Department, Kuwait Technical College, Kuwait
[2]Professor, The Egyptian E-Learning University, Egypt

Abstract

The purpose of the study aimed to explore the relationship between organizational culture as an independent variable and the maturity of project management as a dependent variable by building confirmatory factor analysis model, The sample of the study consisted of 223 individuals form two regions (North America, Middle East).

As for the methodology, the analytical descriptive statistics method was used to describe the background properties of the study sample, as well as the use of the principal component analysis, confirmatory factor analysis, as well as the artificial neural networks model to show the relative importance of the variables included in the confirmatory factor analysis model.

The findings indicated the safety of the factorial structure of the study variables using the method of factorial analysis (principles component analysis–PCA) to load the study variables on the main dimensions, and the degree of belonging of the sub-variables to their chosen dimensions was emphasized based on literature review and the conceptual framework of the study using the emphasizing factorial analysis, which confirms the overall integrity of the model and the degree of suitability of the data in the selected sample. The value of the $\chi2$ significant at p-value = 0.05, confidence interval = 0.95.

In conclusion, confirmatory component analysis technique examined the link between dependent and independent variables as well as created composite indicators, allocated variable weights, and figured out how closely related variables are to one another across important dimensions. It also verified the data's applicability and quality, as well as the model's overall functioning structure's integrity.

Keywords

Confirmatory factor analysis (CFA), organizational culture, principles component analysis, project management maturity, software engineering.

Introduction

To effectively deliver a project's productivity in terms of time, expense, and conditions is the primary goal of effective project management techniques and technologies (Zwikael et al., 2018). Project management aids in maintaining control over challenging activities that must be accomplished while considering time, cost, and

[a]N.ahmed@Ktech.edu.kw, [b]habdelsalam@eelu.edu.eg

risk constraints, the need to include experts from various fields, and the coordination between many departments and businesses. Low project execution costs are a result of high project management maturity. Companies with higher levels of project management maturity perform better and have a greater chance of success (Silva et al., 2019). Maturity models are particularly important for project-oriented businesses to achieve greater effectiveness and efficiency (Backlund et al., 2014).

Literature Review

Project Management Maturity Model

Several project management maturity (PMM) models have been constructed by the scholars. According to Mittermaier and Steyn (2009), in 2003 a standard model, that is, organizational PMM model (OPM3) was developed under the stewardship of the Project Management Institute (PMI). Yazici (2009-a, 2009-b) states that integration, critical assessment, and improvement is incorporated in the PM practices in the OMP3 model. The model is efficient in supporting organizational development and provides to strengthen the overall process and construct a relationship between the project and corporate goals. Multiple capabilities are identified at each level of hierarchy. The capabilities result in the outcomes which can be measured by metrics and indicators.

Another model which was constructed in line with the PMM model is project management process maturity model. It allows measurement of different levels of PM by performing integration among the nine areas of PM knowledge along with project processes which can be quantified. The model is a one way forward in measuring the project performance and practices. The knowledge areas are measured against the actual performance of the project which provides data in quantitative form. Other maturity had been developed, for example, Baldrige National quality award (BNQA) and quality management by European Form. The maturity model aims at identifying the development made within a project, that is, next level achieved over time (Backlund et al., 2014).

Kerzner (2019) stated that the PMMM (Project Management Maturity Model) is efficient in analysing the execution phase of delivery systems, identifying areas which need improvement, baseline where improvement is required is identified, and periodic assessment helps in determining whether improvement is executed or not. The changes required in the project and company's infrastructure are indicated. No single PMMM can satisfy all the needs of a project, as every company has different objectives, resources, and maturity periods. The PMM can be defined as an ongoing process which reassesses the delivery system and organizational infrastructure. The aim of introducing PMMM is to meet organizational objectives, with minimum error.

Criticism of Applying Project Management Maturity Model

PMMM can be misapplied because of error in the organizational assessment, and because of the difficulty involved in determining the correct maturity level at present time. Choice of wrong assessment tool has proved to be a factor which adds inconsistency and achieves desired outcomes. Furthermore, organization ignores intangibles assets such as creativity, trust, customer involvement to name a few. The PMM model is not efficient in adapting rapidly with the changing technology within the system. Measurement of progress is difficult and crucial at the same time. Literature summarized that PMMM does not have any theoretical base and is the major limitation (Backlund et al., 2014).

Research Problem

Any new concept that is defined and philosophy is developed and used for a certain period of time serves as a test period that illustrates methodological problems for this concept, the most important of which are measurement problems, despite the literature dealing with the maturity of project management as well as organizational culture, most of these literature omitted the factorial composition of each dimension that includes several variables and tested them statistically in terms of building safety and quality standards of the working model, so this study was to highlight an important approach to address that problem.

Methodology and Model Specifications

Based on the problem of the study, the descriptive analytical approach was used using the applied method to collect and analyze data and test hypotheses, the study adopted the case study methodology, and the questionnaire was used to collect data from the respondents, analyze the data collected from the recovered questionnaires, and use appropriate statistical methods. The desk survey was conducted, searching the databases available to view theoretical and field studies and research and reviewing the literature of the subject with a view to crystallizing the foundations and premises on which the theoretical basis of the study is based.

Statistical Methods Used

Descriptive statistics (arithmetic Mean, standard deviation, trend strength, coefficient of difference, rank) to illustrate the values of the mean and the divergence of opinions on the elements of the questionnaire.

Statistical analysis of the statistical methods has been carried out using the Ver statistical package. (Version 26.0)—Statistical Package for Social Sciences (SPSS).

Sampling and Data Source

The study was based on a well-rounded questionnaire, including 3D of independent variables (organizational culture); Accuracy and Competency of Management Improving Customer Satisfaction 'Employees Qualifications to Achieve Goals, (5) dimensions of project management maturity (dependent variable); Embryonic 'Executive' Line-Management 'Growth' Maturity. The study sample consisted of 223 individuals who were selected as a simple random sample and the questionnaire was distributed to them and the questions included in it were completed and then the data was entered on the computer system in preparation for analysis.

Conceptual Framework

The philosophy of constructing the conceptual framework Figure 3.1 of research is based on the existence of a direct relationship of the influence of the independent variable (organizational culture) on the dependent variable (with its five elements: Embryonic, Executive, Line Management, Growth, Maturity), and another indirect relationship via an intermediate (region).

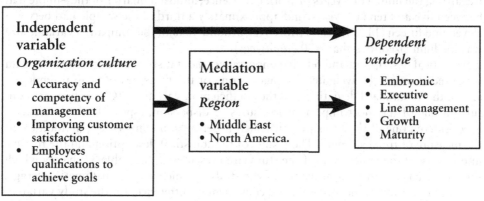

Figure 3.1 Conceptual framework.

Empirical Results

Descriptive Statistics

Table 3.1: Background characteristics of the study sample.

		Overall (N=223)			Overall (N=223)
Gender	Male	120 (53.8%)		11–15 years	68 (30.5%)
	Female	103 (46.2%)	Experience	5–10 years	54 (24.2%)
Region	Middle East	104 (46.6%)		Less than 5 years	39 (17.5%)
	North America	119 (53.4%)		More than 15	62 (27.8%)
Role	Sales/ Management	59 (26.5%)		Large (more than 500 employees)	12 (5.4%)
	Software Analysis	34 (15.2%)		Medium (less than 500 employees)	98 (43.9%)
	Software Deployment/ Maintenance (DevOps)	9 (4.0%)	co. Size	Micro (less than 50)	26 (11.7%)
	Software Development	86 (38.6%)			
	Software Planning/Design	17 (7.6%)		Small (less than 200 employees)	87 (39.0%)
	Software Testing	18 (8.1%)			

Table 3.1 highlights some of the background characteristics of the research sample of 223 respondents. The sample included around 54% more men than women, and 47% of the respondents were from the Middle East and 53% were from North America. The respondents worked in the following occupations: Almost 25% of the sample's workers are in sales or management. Software development accounts for almost 40% of the sample's labor. Additionally, there were few and a variety of other professions. Regarding the number of years of work experience, almost a quarter of the sample had between five and ten (10) years, and approximately a third of the sample had between eleven and fifteen (11–15) years. Moreover, around 40% of the company's variable size was medium-sized (less than 500 employees).

Statistical description and relative importance: the statistical description of the data was used through the weighted average as one of the measures of central tendency, and both the standard deviation and the coefficient of variations (CV), which are considered one of the most important measures of dispersion, especially the latter as it is considered one of the measures on which it depends in comparison, in addition to the measure of trend strength. The results of the statistical description and the relative importance of the dimensions of the study are presented in the Table 3.2 below which shows the basic statistical measures of the study sample such as (arithmetic average, standard deviation, trend strength, and coefficient of difference) for the study variables included in the basic axes, the descriptive results of the study sample showed that the embryonic axis ranked first in terms of trend strength with a value of 68.5%, then came in second place the axis of line management with a value of 68%, and finally the axis of accuracy and efficiency of management worth 65%. All axes came with a very close trend force which indicates the consistency of the study sample data and the high degree of homogeneity.

Table 3.2: Descriptive statistics.

Factor	Indicator	N	Mean	Std. deviation	Direction	C.V	Importance rank
Accuracy and competency of management (Sashkin 1996, 2002, 2013)	Q10	223	3.39	1.117	0.68	32.95	
	Q25	223	3.3	1.125	0.66	34.09	
	Q21	223	3.34	1.044	0.67	31.26	
	Q26	223	3.19	1.08	0.64	33.86	
	Q28	223	3.22	1.154	0.64	35.84	
			3.288	1.104	.658	33.6	8
Improving customer satisfaction (Sashkin 1996, 2002, 2013)	Q19	223	3.31	1.081	0.66	32.66	
	Q4	223	3.25	1.127	0.65	34.68	
	Q5	223	3.34	1.107	0.67	33.14	
	Q22	223	3.39	1.033	0.68	30.47	
			3.322	1.087	.665	32.73	4

(continued)

Table 3.2: Continued

Factor	Indicator	N	Mean	Std. deviation	Direction	C.V	Importance rank
Employees qualifications to achieve goals (Sashkin 1996, 2002, 2013)	Q29	223	3.48	1.134	0.7	32.59	
	Q2	223	3.29	1.027	0.66	31.22	
	Q18	223	3.31	1.26	0.66	38.07	
	Q11	223	3.46	0.928	0.692	26.82	
			3.385	1.087	.676	32.175	3
Embryonic (Kerzner 2019)	Q1	223	5.11	1.504	0.73	29.43	
	Q14	223	4.74	1.634	0.68	34.47	
	Q17	223	4.66	1.608	0.67	34.51	
	Q3	223	4.62	1.65	0.66	35.71	
			4.7825	1.599	0.685	33.53	1
Executive (Kerzner 2019)	Q10	223	4.74	1.717	0.68	36.22	
	Q13	223	4.84	1.65	0.69	34.09	
	Q20	223	4.74	1.733	0.68	36.56	
	Q5	223	4.15	1.674	0.59	40.34	
			4.6175	1.6935	.66	36.8025	6
Line management (Kerzner 2019)	Q12	223	4.74	1.606	0.68	33.88	
	Q19	223	4.73	1.546	0.68	32.68	
	Q7	223	4.82	1.645	0.69	34.13	
	Q9	223	4.66	1.724	0.67	37	
			4.7375	1.63025	.678	34.4225	2
Growth (Kerzner 2019)	Q11	223	4.65	1.68	0.66	36.13	
	Q4	223	4.68	1.691	0.67	36.13	
	Q6	223	4.61	1.57	0.66	34.06	
	Q15	223	4.55	1.708	0.65	37.54	
			4.6225	1.66225	.66	35.965	7
Maturity (Kerzner 2019)	Q8	223	4.46	1.668	0.64	37.4	
	Q16	223	4.71	1.724	0.67	36.6	
	Q18	223	4.6	1.78	0.66	38.7	
	Q2	223	4.77	1.644	0.68	34.47	
			4.635	1.704	0.6625	36.7925	5

Discussions

In a nutshell, descriptive statistics provide brief summaries of the sample and data measurements to aid in describing and understanding the characteristics of a particular data set. The mean, median, and mode, which are utilized at practically all math and statistics levels, are the most well-known types of descriptive statistics. By summing up all the data set's figures and then dividing by the total number of figures, the mean or average can be derived. In the current paper, basic statistical measures were used to describe the study sample such as the average and standard deviation and showed that the study sample tends towards the normal distribution, and also the measure of trend strength was used for the study axes and the variables they include to show any dimension more weighty and impactful, and finally the coefficient of difference, which is an absolute measure of the dispersion of data within the sample, was calculated.

Conclusion

Descriptive statistics are of high importance in all scientific research, especially those based on an opinion survey using the method of simple random samples, as they represent the first step in the statistical construction as a whole by identifying the variables and main dimensions under which those variables fall and then describing each variable separately and applying the basic statistical measures at the level of the main dimension to determine the degree of its importance among its counterparts from the different dimensions included in the study.

References

Backlund, F., Chronéer, D., and Sundqvist, E. (2014). Project management maturity models– a critical review: a case study within Swedish engineering and construction organizations. *Procedia-Social and Behavioral Sciences*, 119(0), 837–846.

Kerzner, H. (2019). Using the Project Management Maturity Model: Strategic Planning for Project Management. John Wiley & Sons.

Mittermaier, H. K., and Steyn, H. (2009). Project management maturity: an assessment of maturity for developing pilot plants. *South African Journal of Industrial Engineering*, 20(1), 95–108.

Sashkin , M., and Rosenbach, W. E. (1996, 2002, 2013). Organizational beliefs questionnaire: pillars of excellence. Organization Design and Development, distributed by M.L.R. Ltd.

Silva, R., Duarte, N., Barros, T., and Fernandes, G. (2019). Project management maturity: case study analysis using OPM3® model in manufacturing industry. In 2019 IEEE International Conference on Engineering, Technology and Innovation (ICE/ITMC) (pp. 1–8). IEEE.

Yazici, H. J. (2009-a). Does project maturity matter for organizational success. In Proceedings of the 2009 Industrial Engineering Research Conference, (pp. 356–361).

Yazici, H. J. (2009-b). The role of project management maturity and organizational culture in perceived performance. *Project Management Journal*, 40(3), 14–33.

Zwikael, O., Chih, Y. Y., and Meredith, J. R. (2018). Project benefit management: setting effective target benefits. *International Journal of Project Management*, 36(4), 650–658.

4   Why Do SME's Businesses Internationalize?—Factors Influencing the Decisions to Internationalize

Vishwas Chakranarayan[1,a], Tahera Sayed Abdulredha Jaafar[2,b], and Zahra Ali AlAali[2,c]

[1]Assistant Professor, Collège of Administrative and Financial Sciences, UTB Bahrain
[2]Graduate student, Collège of Administrative and Financial Sciences, UTB Bahrain

Abstract

Due to growth and sustainability, SMEs must consider internationalization in a changing environment. This abstract addresses two main research questions: 1) How do market factors affect internationalization strategy? 2) How do hindering factors affect SMEs' internationalization strategy?

The study examines how market variables affect SMEs' internationalization efforts to answer the first issue. It examines how market size, cultural variations, legal frameworks, and consumer behaviours affect market entry tactics, product adaption, and marketing strategies through empirical research and case studies. The investigation tries to understand how SMEs modify their internationalization strategies to capitalize on market opportunities and mitigate market risks.

In the second research topic, the study examines SMEs' internationalization barriers. These include financial, cultural, legal, and operational obstacles. The abstract synthesizes academic literature and real-world experiences to explain how these barriers hinder SMEs' strategic choices. It also examines how adaptable capabilities, strategic alliances, and new solutions might overcome these challenges and boost internationalization efforts.

This study sheds light on market characteristics, constraining factors, and strategic decision-making in SME internationalization. The findings have practical relevance for SMEs, policymakers, and scholars looking to understand international market difficulties. Understanding SMEs' strategic internationalization decisions is crucial for global company resilience and competitiveness as they continue to drive economic growth.

Keywords

Barriers to internationalization, internationalization, SME's.

Introduction

Few individuals understand the significance of business from the perspective of its participants. Businesses run modern economies. To be associated with a business, one must understand the daily challenges humans face. People start businesses to survive and pay their bills so that they can work and earn a living.

---

[a]v.chakranarayan@utb.edu.bh, [b]6ahooor84@gmail.com, [c]bh15501036@utb.edu.bh

Before beginning operations, organizations require business concepts. A business strategy is the plan for establishing and running a business. It is common in contemporary corporate strategies. Business owners may be required to obtain permits, certifications, and registration prior to moving forward. Therefore, it is essential to establish the company's standard structure. In many countries, corporations are considered legal persons with the capacity to own property, incur debt, and face prosecution. International marketing promotes companies on a global scale. The current business trend is international expansion because it is advantageous to the organization or product. Local is similar to a comfort zone in that it is cozy but unadvanced.

Details complicate globalization. Global trading takes place outside the borders of a single nation, with a focus on communicating with the global community and endeavouring to comprehend its culture, language, and customs.

International market segmentation aids in the formulation of a marketing strategy. Regional, economic, and cultural factors can have an effect on brand positioning, marketing management, and communication strategies. Consider how well your product or service meets the needs of your target market when devising a strategy. "Selling trash to a sawmill" The sawmill has adequate waste. What do they want and how do they want it presented?

Target marketing identifies categories of communication and messaging. Idioms, allusions, and even straightforward approximations (such as sawdust) can lose their meaning or offend those who do not share your culture.

Due to the global liberalization of industrial and commercial activity, both large and minor businesses are concerned about internationalization. It is no longer limited to foreign or daring enterprises.

The international community has evolved. Internationalization is no longer synonymous with traditional business practices. Because trade and export were difficult in the past, they conducted international business differently. International business incorporates company commerce, cross-border investments directed by financial institutions, governments, supranational organizations, etc. A corporation can internationalize by establishing an overseas production unit or by acquiring a well-known company. Such businesses are "born global" (Gibb and Szałucka, 2012).

Ahsan and Wyk (2018) identified three significant shifts that have had an effect on internationalization strategy. Small and medium-sized enterprises that have expanded internationally have achieved tremendous success. The second trend is novel models for entering international markets. In the 1960s, parent-subsidiary relationships were prevalent for obtaining competitive advantages. No longer is internationalization singular. Current implementation of the agreement is as a network.

Global corporations face difficulties. Local and multinational businesses encounter comparable challenges. The challenges are dynamic and vary by country, commodity, and service. It is difficult for participating nations to formulate trade policies. Global corporations face difficulties. Local and multinational businesses encounter comparable challenges. The challenges are dynamic and vary by country, commodity, and service. It is difficult for participating nations to formulate trade policies.

The conception and execution of global trade strategies influence global commerce. The international trade authorities and politicians impair the global economy (Taylor, 2007).

Diverse policies impact multinational corporations, and stringent laws typically impede their expansion. Numerous organizations have the capability to operate on a global scale, but few prosper because there are insufficient international paradigms that favor only a handful of multinational corporations.

The above discussion leads to the following research questions:

RQ1: How do the characteristics of a market fit into a strategic method to doing business abroad?

RQ2: How do things that make it hard to do business play into a strategic approach to doing business abroad?

People who are interested in business and want to start a business in a developing country like Bahrain could use this study. Participants would be able to understand in depth the things they need to think about before making a choice like this, as well as the things they need to deal with and control when moving to and working in a developing country. Since the research isn't limited to one field, it can be used as a guide by many big companies that want to do business in a growing country.

Literature Review

Market Characteristics

Rui and Yip (2008), along with Guillén and García-Canal (2009), investigate the expansion into international markets. Businesses, driven by intense competition, stringent regulations, and limited consumer understanding, pursue global expansion to tap into new markets, as highlighted by Lambe et al. (2002). When industry-specific partners either succeed or face challenges, organizations are compelled to reassess their strategies.

According to Magnani et al. (2018), internal issues within a company play a pivotal role in shaping internationalization strategy. The focus is on organizational dynamics, change management, and the role of transnational managers. Organizational dynamics encompass fundamental capabilities, market access (proximity to customers), firm integrity (speed, flexibility, or reliability), product performance, learning new procedures, legacy considerations, and crisis management (Pellegrino and McNaughton, 2015). The transformation of an organization requires essential elements such as communication, education, participation, negotiation, contracts, manipulation, and coercion.

Katsikeas and Pierce (1993) assert that the dominant firm plays a pivotal role in making decisions related to globalization and comparative advantage, encompassing factors like capacity, acquired stock volumes, and retail sales. Dunning's (1992) motivational variables, including resource searching, market discovery, efficiency seeking, and business strategy seeking, also contribute to these decisions. Research suggests that smaller firms in industrialized nations may have distinct motives for international expansion.

Globalization, deemed advantageous for most organizations, has positive impacts on societies as well (Cuervo-Cazurra and Genc, 2008; Lockyer, 2013). It enables corporations to leverage cheaper foreign manufacturing inputs, thereby enhancing efficiency and scope, aligning with Dunning's (1992) motivation model. Variable sectional rewards, local rivalry (Peng, 2009), and logistics preparation become crucial aspects of internationalization.

Baum et al. (2000) recommend evaluating the sector's ICT systems when formulating an internationalization strategy, as this process involves increased costs, including coordinating costs referred to by Johanson and Vahlne (1977) as inauthenticity costs. Progressive internationalization, when property and economic objectives are met, impacts foreign personnel management (Johanson and Vahlne, 2009; Autio, 2017), presenting multinationals with challenges related to capital, talent, data, economic factors, managerial issues, and external risks.

Global enterprises often engage in cooperation, where partnerships offer reciprocity, access to assets, relationships, resources, and cooperation expertise (Gulati, 1998; Pellegrino and McNaughton, 2015). The importance of partners in coalitions is emphasized by Baum et al. (2000), with considerations such as trust, interests, and culture potentially affecting coalition stability.

Peng (2009) employs the tactical triangle to direct corporations and organizations towards external markets. Bonardi and Durand (2003) advocate expanding business communities on a sectoral basis. The internationalization of a company is influenced by its size, particularly in the context of supply-constrained frontier markets (Yamin and Sinkovics, 2006), where border states collaborate by sharing scarce resources and culture to facilitate enterprise internationalization.

Numerous investigations, such as those conducted by Parkhe (2003) and Kotabe and Mudambi, underscore the influence of laws, culture, values, and relationships on the internationalization strategy of a company. Furthermore, there is an acknowledgment that the mitigation of transaction costs and operational risks significantly shapes decisions related to internationalization (Elbana and Child, 2007).

Certain proponents advocate the internationalization of a company based solely on external environmental factors and public opinion, often commencing with a thorough market analysis. However, this perspective is constrained by governmental administration limitations. A contrasting viewpoint emphasizes the importance of leaders' research and development, financial resources, technical skills, and distribution and marketing capabilities. In the context of modern commerce, rivals are not always a necessity, and smaller enterprises tend to be more adversely affected (Blomstermo et al., 2004).

According to Korsakien and Tvaronaviien (2012), small and medium-sized enterprises (SMEs) exhibit qualities of dynamism, adaptability, and innovation. Globalization demands human, technological, and strategic capital, but some companies overlook essential data. Smaller and younger businesses particularly require resources for identifying global commercial opportunities, partners, trade procedures, regulations, product specifications, and standards.

Korsakien and Tvaronaviien (2012) argue that interconnected businesses and organizations, sharing common goals and attitudes, can achieve synergies leading to reduced expenses. Examples of such cooperation benefits include co-payments, accelerated technology adoption, and improved interactions with business partners. Cooperation offers substantial benefits such as size economies, knowledge economies, and negotiating leverage, as well as moderate advantages like market adaptability and client proximity in the current economic landscape.

Struggling companies often adjust their strategies. Torkkeli et al. (2012) raise the question of whether a business, facing decline, should concentrate on a specific sector of the value chain while actively engaging in partnerships, network integration, and collaborations with both upstream and downstream organizations.

In line with the insights of Johanson and Vahlne (1977), it is highlighted that psychological distance poses constraints on the transfer of information between the firm and consumers. Successful internationalization mandates the acquisition of market-specific knowledge. Enterprises venturing into markets characterized by significant psychological distance are indicative of a globalizing trend.

These authors assert that possessing expertise in a country enhances market loyalty, emphasizing that knowledge and experience are instructive. Research suggests that the stages of foreign market participation are not necessarily sequential, as illustrated by examples like Magnani et al. (2018). This phenomenon is global, and a company's strategy may be well-suited for addressing geographical remoteness.

Location and social isolation are not critical factors for businesses. High-tech and R&D companies operating in multiple markets have the potential to reduce fixed costs, as highlighted in 2012. Creators demonstrate a commitment to international ventures, focusing on exports facilitated by local business networks in the process of internationalization. Small and medium-sized enterprises, despite limited resources, are capable of presenting innovative concepts (Gibb and Szaucka, 2012; Zhou and Wu, 2014). According to McDougall et al. (1994, 2000) and McDougall and Oviatt (1996), even small enterprises can engage in export activities, and many early internationalizers experienced success.

Experiments indicate that the scale of a company significantly influences internationalization opportunities, particularly the choice of entry points. Companies lacking access to global market resources often implement standard solutions (Fletcher and Harris, 2012), exposing themselves to risks and expenses associated with global expansion. However, small enterprises, constrained by financial limitations, are compelled to judiciously manage investment and risk (Acs et al., 1997).

In the early 1990s, Rennie (1993) presented empirical data on businesses that derived the majority of their revenue from exports within their initial two years of operation. McKinsey conducted an evaluation on the Australian Manufacturing Council (AMC), dividing 310 Australian corporations into two categories (McKinsey & Company and AMC , 1993). The research highlighted those robust regional businesses prioritized exporting, demonstrating a sustained 27-year commitment. Notably, 20% of all new businesses and 76% of small enterprises, generating around $16 million in revenue, engaged in exporting, successfully competing with global giants. These entities were labeled "global immigrants" by Rennie (1993).

Rennie's 1993 article significantly contributed to the formation of studies in this field (Servais, 1997). It emphasized the diversity of global identities. Oviatt and McDougall (1994) explored concepts such as "global start-ups," "early internationalization enterprises," and "global new ventures." Born global companies, according to Knight and Cavusgil (2004), possess a "significant strategic advantage through the financing and marketing of their products in multiple countries." Academic discussions have favored International New Ventures (INVs) and their role in global markets. While not explicitly named, respondents with a birth majority were compared to the following INVs.

H_{01}: The characteristics of a market do not affect the strategic approach to internationalization.

Inhibiting Factors

Buckley et al. (2016) highlight that internationalization efforts can face obstacles from external constraints. In strategic management, the evaluation of various factors is commonly conducted through the SWOT and PESTEL matrices. Interestingly, the utilization of these two matrices has proven effective throughout much of this century. However, certain limitations hinder their comprehensive examination, especially when viewed from a global perspective.

The impact of country-of-origin regulations and data related to target locations constitutes another dimension of this process, as discussed by Katsikeas and Pierce (1993). Additionally, the assessment of labor costs plays a crucial role in decision-making. Legislation characterized by an open-minded approach, particularly favoring the export of raw materials, seems to underpin this conclusion. Moreover, in conjunction with the European Union Society's initiatives aimed at fostering small and medium-sized enterprises, international corporations are required to equip individuals for employment, as emphasized by Pellegrino and McNaughton (2015).

The Uppsala Method, as proposed by Johanson and Vahlne (1977), significantly influenced the internationalization process. Swedish enterprises in Uppsala established a pattern for internationalization, with the market competence hypothesis deemed plausible. Market knowledge, encompassing both the firm's accumulated experience in each market and the conceptual gap between the home country and the host country, is integral. However, Lam and White (1999) argue that the Uppsala model falls short in adequately identifying internal obstacles and challenges faced by managers during internationalization-driven organizational change. Their examination focuses on leadership challenges encountered by organizations undergoing internationalization.

According to adaptive modeling, internationalization occurs when a business adjusts to economic, organizational, and personnel management challenges (Pellegrino and McNaughton, 2015; Ahsan and Van Wyk, 2018). This brings us back to the second hypothesis.

H_{02}: The inhibiting factors do not affect the strategic approach to internationalization.

Methodology

This research employed various methodologies to investigate the factors influencing businesses in their decision to expand globally. The study adopted a mixed-method design. To identify Small and Medium-sized Enterprises (SMEs) that have either already internationalized or are considering doing so, a list of around 50 SMEs was compiled for data collection. For this research, individuals at the management and supervisory levels within these SMEs were selected to participate. However, out of the 50 scheduled respondents, only 42 responded to the inquiry.

Regression Analysis

For modelling the relationship between two sets of variables regression is the most frequent used application of statistics. The research led to the development of a predictive regression model. Regression analysis helped us examine the relationships or effects of independent variables on dependent variable. Several factors may influence these interactions. We used it to investigate and measure the strength of a relationship between the variables, it provided an estimate of the future relationship between those variables. Regression enabled us to determine which variables are most significant, which ones you can disregard, and how they interact with other factors.

Empirical Results

Regression analysis results follow:

Table 4.1: Regression analysis.

Model summary				
Model	R	R square	Adjusted R square	Std. error of the estimate
1	.959[a]	.920	.917	.18477

[a]Predictors: (Constant), Inhibiting factors, Market characteristics

Coefficients					
Model		Unstandardized coefficients		Standardized coefficients	t	Sig.
		B	Std. Error	Beta		
1	(Constant)	.16	.138		1.197	.234
	Inhibiting factors	.088	.057	.084	1.542	.002
	Market characteristics	.828	.078	.821	10.602	.000

[a]Dependent variable: Strategic approach to internationalization

Source: Author's compilation

Table 4.1, you can find the outcomes of the regression analysis involving Inhibiting factors, Market characteristics, and the dependent variable (Strategic Approach to Internationalization). The regression coefficient of 0.088 for Inhibiting factors and Strategic Approach to Internationalization suggests a positive and statistically significant relationship between these two variables, indicating a robust and positive connection. The associated p-value of 0.0026 signifies significance, suggesting that Inhibiting factors indeed have a noticeable impact on Strategic Approach to Internationalization.

Contrary to our primary research hypothesis, the findings indicate that Inhibiting factors do have a discernible effect on Strategic Approach to Internationalization. Moving on to Market characteristics and Strategic Approach to Internationalization, both variables exhibit positive regression coefficients, signifying a favorable relationship between them. The p-value of 0.000 indicates a strong and significant association. Consequently, the second research hypothesis is also refuted in this scenario.

The effectiveness of the study is evident as the majority of respondents expressed a strong agreement with the findings. Traditional economic research on globalization primarily concentrates on large enterprises (Rowden, 2001; Buckley and Ghauri, 1999). Large businesses possess advantages over Small and Medium-sized Enterprises (SMEs) in overcoming barriers related to markets, economics, politics, and risks when venturing into the global arena. SMEs, on the other hand, encounter distinctive challenges, including constraints in personnel, capital, technology, and other resources. Hollenstein (2005) identifies country-specific laws, national regulations, market demands, and resource limitations as obstacles to SME internationalization.

Conclusion

This study delved into the internationalization of Small and Medium-sized Enterprises (SMEs). Our findings indicate that market characteristics and constraints significantly impact the globalization strategies related to internal resources and economies of scale. It is observed that entering new markets is crucial for SMEs as they seek new customers.

Various factors, including networks, venture capital, transaction costs, assets, and talent, play pivotal roles in enabling organizations to globalize. Given that SMEs contribute significantly to GDP and employment, they are integral to every economy. Evaluating contacts, venture capital, intrinsic traits, transaction costs, resources, and capabilities is crucial for SME internationalization, a well-explored field.

Foreign influences act as catalysts for SME internationalization, with institutional constraints driving growth and triggering initial overseas activities. Externally sensitive SMEs actively engage in internationalization to overcome local institutional limitations. Factors such as size, ownership, operating style, external investment, business groups, and clients may impact SME internationalization. The tertiarization of services and internationalization contribute to growth, with the flourishing of international service commerce, especially due to advancements in Information and Communication Technology (ICT).

Despite globalization and increased competition prompting many enterprises to expand abroad, numerous SMEs continue to rely solely on domestic markets, facing constraints due to national limitations. In Europe, a substantial percentage of enterprises engage in international trade, while a smaller fraction has overseas affiliates, branches, or partnerships, indicating a limited consideration of globalization among European SMEs despite intense global competition in their markets (European Commission, 2008).

Several studies have established a link between SMEs' profitability and globalization. Proactive internationalization is associated with increased growth, enhanced competitiveness, and corporate sustainability. However, small firms worldwide encounter challenges in expanding, struggling to identify commercial prospects, partners, and foreign opportunities.

While our study significantly enhanced our understanding of SME internationalization, it has certain limitations. Future research should extend its focus to other countries to develop more comprehensive theories and practices related to SME globalization. Despite the findings, there remains a need for additional research to explore how strategic attention indirectly influences SME performance. Given our study's focus on SME internationalization, it would be intriguing to delve into the analysis of cultural norms and institutional theory.

References

ACS, Z. J., Morck, R., Yeung, B. (1997). Small medium enterprise in internationalization.

Ahsan, M., & van Wyk, J. (2018). Going Past Entry Mode: Examining Foreign Operation Mode Changes at the Strategic Business Unit Level. *Journal of Managerial Issues*, 28–46.

Autio, E. (2017). Strategic entrepreneurial internationalization: A normative framework. *Strategic Entrepreneurship Journal*, 11(3), 211–227.

Baum, J., Calabres, T. & Silverman, B. (2000) The makeup of alliance networks and the performance of Canadian biotechnology companies

Baum, J. A., Calabrese, T., & Silverman, B. S. (2000). Don't go it alone: Alliance network composition and startups' performance in Canadian biotechnology. Strategic management journal, 21(3), 267–294.

Benito, G., Petersen, B. & Welch, L. Towards more realistic conceptualisations of foreign operation modes. J Int Bus Stud 40, 1455–1470 (2009). https://doi.org/10.1057/jibs.2009.54

Blomstermo, A., Eriksson, K., Lindstrand, A., & Sharma, D. D. (2004). The perceived usefulness of network experiential knowledge in the internationalizing firm. Journal of international Management, 10(3), 355–373.

Bonardi, J. P., & Durand, R. (2003). Managing network effects in high-tech markets. *Academy of Management Perspectives*, 17(4), 40–52.

Buckley, P. J., & Ghauri, P. N. (2004). Globalisation, economic geography and the strategy of multinational enterprises. *Journal of International Business Studies*, 35, 81–98.

Buckley, P. J., Munjal, S., Enderwick, P., & Forsans, N. (2016). Do foreign resources assist or impede internationalisation? Evidence from internationalisation of Indian multinational enterprises. *International Business Review*, 25(1), 130–140.

Cuervo-Cazurra, A., & Genc, M. (2008). Transforming disadvantages into advantages: Developing-country MNEs in the least developed countries. *Journal of international business studies*, 39, 957–979.

Czinkota, M. R., Ronkainen, I. A., & Moffett, M. H. (1999). International Business, edition.

Dunning, J. H., & Lundan, S. M. (2008). Multinational enterprises and the global economy. Edward Elgar Publishing.

Elbanna, S. & Child, J. (2007). Influences on strategic decision effectiveness: Development and test of an integrative model. Strategic Management Journal 28, 431–453.

European Commission (2008) – Entrepreneurship in Higher Education, Especially Within Non-Business Studies—European Commission, Brussels

Ferreira, J. J., Fernandes, C. I., & Peris-Ortiz, M. (2018). How agents, resources and capabilities mediate the effect of corporate entrepreneurship on multinational firms' performance. *European Journal of International Management*, 12(3), 255–277.

Fletcher, M., & Harris, S. (2012). Knowledge acquisition for the internationalization of the smaller firm: Content and sources. *International Business Review*, 21(4), 631–647.

Knight, G. A., & Kim, D. (2009). International business competence and the contemporary firm. *Journal of international business studies*, 40, 255–273.

Gibb, Y., & Szalucka, M. (2012). The FDI behaviour of polish companies: equity based entry modes and their impact on performance.

Guillén, M. F., & García-Canal, E. (2009). The American model of the multinational firm and the "new" multinationals from emerging economies. *Academy of Management Perspectives*, 23(2), 23–35.

Gulati, R. (1998). Alliances and networks. *Strategic management journal*, 19(4), 293–317.

Hair J., Black B., Babin B. (2010) Harper Edition, 7th edition, Multimodal Market Research, London, United Kingdom.

Johanson, J., & Wiedersheim-Paul, F. (1975). The internationalization of the firm: Four Swedish cases. *Journal of management studies*, 12(3), 305–322.

Johanson, J., & Vahlne, J. E. (1977). The internationalization process of the firm—a model of knowledge development and increasing foreign market commitments. *Journal of international business studies*, 8, 23–32.

Johanson, J. (2009). The Uppsala internationalization process model revisited: From liability of foreignness to liability of outsidership. https://econpapers.repec.org/article/paljintbs/v_3a40_3ay_3a2009_3ai_3a9_3ap_3a1411-1431.htm

Puck, Jonas F., Holtbrügge, Dirk, and Mohr, Alexander T. 2009. Beyond Entry Mode Choice: Explaining the Conversion of Joint Ventures into Wholly Owned

Katsikea C. and N Pierce (1993), International Marketing Journal Marketing, 'Lengthy export stimulants and company characteristics in a European LDC.'

Kogut, B. (1989). The stability of joint ventures: Reciprocity and competitive rivalry. *The journal of industrial economics*, 183–198.

Korsakien, R., & Tvaronaviien, M. (2012). The internationalization of SMEs: An integrative approach. *Journal of Business Economics and Management*, 12(2).

Kraus, Niemandt Besler, M., (2018) 'Global impact of leadership styles on the internationalization of 'born-global' enterprises'

Lam, L. W., & White, L. P. (1999). An adaptive choice model of the internationalization process. *The international journal of organizational analysis*, 7(2), 105–134.

Lambe, C. J., Spekman, R. E., & Hunt, S. D. (2002). Alliance competence, resources, and alliance success: conceptualization, measurement, and initial test. *Journal of the academy of Marketing Science*, 30(2), 141–158.

Lockyer, K. (2013), Strategy Dialogue, Oxford, UK, A Strategic Plan to change the estate of prisoners. A study on the organizational structures with the use of methods towards Beijing's changing market. Together with the structure of exams in the business journal studies.

Madsen, T. K., & Servais, P. (1997). The internationalization of born globals: an evolutionary process?. *International business review*, 6(6), 561–583.

Magnani, G., Zucchella, A., & Floriani, D. E. (2018). The logic behind foreign market selection: Objective distance dimensions vs. strategic objectives and psychic distance. *International Business Review*, 27(1), 1–20.

McDougall, G. H., & Levesque, T. (2000). Customer satisfaction with services: putting perceived value into the equation. *Journal of services marketing*, 14(5), 392–410.

McDougall, P. P., & Oviatt, B. M. (1996). New venture internationalization, strategic change, and performance: A follow-up study. *Journal of business venturing*, 11(1), 23–40.

McDougall, P. P., Shane, S., & Oviatt, B. M. (1994). Explaining the formation of international new ventures: The limits of theories from international business research. *Journal of business venturing*, 9(6), 469–487.

McKinsey & Company and Australian Manufacturing Council, (1993), Emerging Exporters: Australia's High Value-Added Manufacturing Exporters.

Kotabe, M., & Mudambi, R. (2003). Institutions and international business. *Journal of International Management*, 9(3), 215–217.

Parkhe, A. (2003). Institutional environments, institutional change and international alliances. *Journal of International Management*, 9(3), 305–316.

Pellegrino, J. M., & McNaughton, R. B. (2015). The co-evolution of learning and internationalization strategy in international new ventures. *Management International Review*, 55, 457–483.

Peng M. (2009) Global movement for strategic managegment South-Western Cengageter Learning.

Rennie, M. W. (1993). Born global. The McKinsey Quarterly, (4), 45–53.

Rowden, R. W. (2001). The learning organization and strategic change. *SAM Advanced Management Journal*, 66(3), 11.

Rui, H., & Yip, G. S. (2008). Foreign acquisitions by Chinese firms: A strategic intent perspective. *Journal of world business*, 43(2), 213–226.

Sapienza H. Aut E., George G., and Zahra, S. (2006) "An Capabilities Perspective on the Effects of Early 1on Company Sustenance and Development."

Torkkeli, L., Puumalainen, K., Saarenketo, S., & Kuivalainen, O. (2012). The effect of network competence and environmental hostility on the internationalization of SMEs. *Journal of International Entrepreneurship*, 10, 25–49.

Yamin, M., & Sinkovics, R. R. (2006). Online internationalisation, psychic distance reduction and the virtuality trap. *International Business Review*, 15(4), 339–360.

Zhou L., and A Wu (2014), 'Assignment of internationalization and performance outcomes: Investigating the mediating impacts of enterprise age and foreign orientation.'

5 Effects of Global Rebalancing—A Macro Economic Theoretical Perspective

Yoganandham G[1,a] and Jayendira P Sankar[2,b]

[1]Professor & Head, Department of Economics, Thiruvalluvar University, Tamil Nadu, India
[2]Assistant Professor, CAFS, University of Technology Bahrain, Kingdom of Bahrain

Abstract

This study examines the effect of the COVID-19 pandemic, supply-chain issues, and inflationary pressures that make economic recovery fragile. Emerging countries also face economic instability and asset price inflation due to excessive external borrowing. From a macroeconomic perspective, the study aims to evaluate the effects of declining global output, multilateralism, trade, investment, labor market recovery, and fiscal imbalances. The research employs a comprehensive literature review to summarize the current literature to highlight the effects of declining global output, multilateralism, trade, investment, labor market recovery, and fiscal imbalances from a macroeconomic perspective. The study highlights the importance of declining global output, multilateralism, trade, investment, labor market recovery, and fiscal imbalances in global rebalancing. Furthermore, it provides recommendations for international collaboration and government policy actions to promote sustainable and inclusive growth and to handle the challenges faced by the global economy.

Keywords

Global rebalancing, global output, multilateralism, trade, investment, labor market recovery, fiscal imbalance.

Introduction

The global economy encompasses all economic activities within and between countries, including industrial production, labor and financial markets, and natural resources and technology that affect economic development and growth. Developed countries' governments focus on these issues (Sankar et al., 2021). The World Economic Outlook Update in January 2023 predicts that global growth will decline to 2.9% in 2023 but rise to 3.1% in 2024 (IMF, 2021). Cross-border economic activity growth depends on five pillars: international trade, foreign direct investment, capital market flows, migration and labor mobility, and technology diffusion.

Globalization can offer potential economic benefits such as increased choice, higher-quality goods, increased competitiveness, economies of scale, increased capital

---

[a]drgyoga@tvu.edu.in, [b]jpsankar@utb.edu.bh.

flows, increased labor mobility, and improved international relations. However, the global growth rate is anticipated to reach its lowest point over three decades. While the 2023 global growth rate is predicted to be 0.2% higher than the October 2022 World Economic Outlook prediction, it still falls short of the long-term average of 3.8% (European Commission, 2020). Investment growth in emerging and developing nations is expected to remain below its two-decade average (Yoganandham, 2022). Smaller states rely heavily on foreign trade and financing and are more vulnerable to economic shocks.

Global growth is expected to slow to 1.7% in 2023, and per-capita income growth is also weaker than before the COVID-19 pandemic, exacerbating the development problem. Median income levels are eroded by inflation, currency depreciation, and underinvestment, particularly in the poorest economies, where efforts to reduce poverty have already stalled (Peterson, 2017). Income convergence has halted, as per-capita income growth in emerging markets and developing economies (EMDEs) is projected to average only 2.8% between 2020 and 2024 (Weaver et al., 2021). Immediate legislative action, such as fuel and agricultural subsidies, is necessary to promote growth and investment.

Continuing progress in Sub-Saharan Africa, where poverty rates are high, will be challenging, as per capita income growth is predicted to average only 1.2% over the next two years. EMDEs are projected to experience only a 3.5% increase in gross investment, which is less than half the average growth rate over the previous two decades and insufficient to sustain capital inventories (Latino et al., 2020). This study analyses macroeconomic theoretical perspectives on declining global output, multilateralism, trade, investment, labor market recovery, and fiscal imbalances to improve human growth in a globalized world.

Review of Literature

Investment in EMDEs is essential for achieving development and climate goals, as delayed capital accumulation can impede development and slow economic growth. EMDEs must create policies that generate and reward new investment to stimulate effect, increase median income, and eradicate poverty (Booth, 2020). This requires developing a robust regulatory environment, lowering startup costs, and improving property rights (Yoganandham and Sankar, 2016). Investment in public-private partnerships, international cooperation, and cross-border trade should also be increased to enhance energy access and switch to lower-carbon energy sources (Kabbani and Mimoune, 2021). Additionally, policymakers should divert inefficient subsidies to more beneficial purposes, such as private sector investment, time-bound, targeted grants, and climate investments (Olagunju et al., 2019).

The global economy comprises economic activities across countries, including products, services, people, expertise, and ideas (Shams, 2022). Due to synchronized policy tightening, deteriorating financial circumstances, and ongoing interruptions from the Russian Federation's invasion of Ukraine, global growth is predicted to slow to 1.7% in 2023, 1.3 percentage points below the previous projection (Leon et al., 2022). National policymakers must ensure that budgetary support is concentrated on vulnerable people, that inflation expectations are firmly anchored, and that financial systems are resilient to reduce the dangers of a global recession and debt distress in EMDE (Gai and Tong, 2022). Policies are also required to encourage a significant increase in EMDE investment to reverse the slowdown in long-term growth brought on by the converging shocks of the epidemic, the invasion of Ukraine, and the sharp tightening of global monetary policy (Vaquero-García et al., 2022).

The US, the eurozone, and China, the world's three main growth engines, are experiencing a downturn that negatively impacts EMDEs (Bechtel, 2022). Demand and supply shocks, currency declines, and tight labor markets contributed to global inflation. Due to extremely high inflation and restrictive monetary policy, the global growth rate has slowed to the point of a recession looming. The global financial environment has reduced fiscal headroom, but governments have taken steps to shield citizens and businesses from price increases. Global GDP is anticipated to fall to 1.7% in 2023, the third-weakest level in over three decades, with EMDEs expected to make up the majority of the gap in global trade (Halling et al., 2020).

The cost of living is anticipated to rise by 5.1% in low-income countries (LIC) in 2023 due to a worsening external environment. In Sub-Saharan Africa, where poverty is at its worst, per capita income growth is predicted to be the slowest, with a 3% poverty rate by 2030 (Białowąs and Budzyńska, 2022). Due to supply and demand considerations, especially in less developed nations, global inflation is anticipated to continue to be high for longer. To reduce the likelihood of debt crises in EMDEs, the international community must assist displaced people and others impacted by conflict or food hardship (Leon et al., 2022). National policy initiatives, such as bolstering macroprudential regulation and addressing financial vulnerabilities, must be added to global efforts to mitigate the risks to financial stability and crises. Exchange rate pressures can be reduced with the aid of foreign exchange interventions. EMDEs must invest significantly in their human, physical, social, and natural capital to compensate for losses and promote inclusive, green, and resilient growth (Lakner et al., 2022).

Methodology

A comprehensive literature review was conducted to identify the research theme, and based on the findings, a research agenda was proposed. According to Onwuegbuzie and Frels (2016), a comprehensive literature review is the best method to highlight the importance of the study topic using the existing body of knowledge. Further, the reason for using the comprehensive literature review is to summarize the current literature to highlight the effects of declining global output, multilateralism, trade, investment, labor market recovery, and fiscal imbalances from a macroeconomic perspective. Moreover, the information presented in the paper is based on selected scholarly articles (Google Scholar, Scopus, and Web of Science), conference proceedings, reliable databases, websites, and government publications. Also, the literature chosen was properly screened to ensure the data are reliable and the information is relevant to the effect of the global rebalancing context.

Discussion

Declining Global Output

The global economic recovery faces challenges due to COVID-19, supply chain disruptions, and inflationary pressures. Despite the prediction of a 4% increase in global GDP in 2022 and 3.5% in 2023, the GDP in 2021 was 3.3% lower than before the pandemic (WorldBank, 2023). Consumer spending and investment drove the global output recovery, but growth slowed due to supply-chain disruptions (Olasehinde-Williams, 2021). Emerging nations have experienced significant output losses due to the pandemic, and not all countries will fully recover, leading to increased poverty and inequality (Palomino et al., 2022). Access to vaccines is limited in underdeveloped nations, hampering economic recovery. Inflationary pressures are rising in wealthy and emerging countries, with the headline inflation rate increasing to 5.2% in 2021 (Islam, 2021). The solid economic growth projection of 5.5% in the US for 2021 is expected to slow to 3.5% in 2022 due to global supply chain disruptions, logistics backlogs, and the scarcity of industrial inputs (Attinasi et al. 2021).

Trade

Services trade has been weak due to limited foreign travel and tourism, but merchandise trade recovered in 2021 (Du and Shepotylo, 2022). However, ongoing inflationary pressures and labor shortages will persist into 2022, affecting economic prospects (Dafermos et al., 2023). The COVID-19 pandemic has led to an unprecedented monetary policy response from central banks worldwide, using unconventional tools such as large-scale asset purchase programs (APP) (Prabheesh and Kumar, 2023). Developed countries have utilized APPs to regulate financial markets, increase liquidity, and boost economic activity. APP has become the primary stimulus tool used by central banks in developed countries since March 2020, with a total of $10.2 trillion added to central banks' balance sheets. APPs aim to boost economic growth, employment, and aggregate demand while helping central banks achieve inflation targets (Ogunniyi et al., 2023). Central banks in developing countries have also implemented APPs to increase market confidence and reduce dysfunction. Empirical evidence shows that APPs have effectively stabilized financial markets, reduced borrowing costs, and promoted economic recovery during the global financial crisis and the COVID-19 pandemic (Adrian et al., 2022).

Investment

A faster-than-anticipated tightening of global monetary conditions could significantly impact investor expectations and capital flows to emerging nations, affecting portfolio allocations and investor expectations (López and Stracca, 2021). Investment has increased after the pandemic-induced depression, with China and the US leading. Still, investment growth in developing and transitioning countries that depend on fossil fuels will probably resume at the slow rate it had before the pandemic (Tian et al., 2022). The long-term effects of central bank APP on economic growth are uncertain, and evidence suggests that they may not significantly impact economic recovery once normal market functioning is restored (Jackson et al., 2021). Accommodative monetary policies have not encouraged banks to lend to the real economy, leading to the growth of unproductive "zombie" companies. Companies have used cheap liquidity for stock buybacks rather than new investments, negatively impacting capital accumulation and investment (English et al., 2021). Extended periods of ultra-loose monetary policies have led to significant macroeconomic and financial vulnerabilities, including excessive external borrowing and debt sustainability concerns in developing countries (Qureshi et al., 2022). Large-scale APP has led to asset price inflation, raising concerns about ever-growing asset price bubbles and financial stability (UN, 2022). The wealthy have benefited more than others from rising asset values, leading to adverse effects on income inequality, particularly affecting women. Central banks should consider the impact of APPs on allocation to address these issues (Carstens, 2021a).

Labor Market Recovery

Economic inequalities significantly impact the chances of robust, inclusive, and stable economic growth and healing. The employment levels are expected to remain below pre-pandemic levels with uneven job creation across regions, and poverty is expected to remain high worldwide, with some fragile economies projected to experience an increase in poverty (ILO, 2022). Inequality is growing within nations, with different populations experiencing uneven income and job recovery (Narayan et al., 2022). The pandemic has worsened the gender gap, with women's participation in the labor force and employment falling more steeply than men's, particularly in developing nations (Dubois et al., 2022). To address this, policies must put gender issues at the center of social security and labor market policies and support unpaid domestic labor for an inclusive and sustainable recovery (Johnson, 2021). Many countries face a debt crisis, and coordinated foreign assistance is necessary for debt relief (CEPAL, 2020). International solid collaboration is essential to defeating the pandemic, achieving sustainable development, and pursuing climate action (Filho et al., 2023). However, unequal access to vaccines and insufficient commitments to tackling debt issues highlight the need for more robust multilateralism to achieve a broad-based and inclusive recovery.

Fiscal Imbalance

Central banks face difficult decisions as they consider scaling back their APPs in response to rising inflation pressures (Carstens, 2021b). The challenge is to reduce bond purchases without disrupting financial markets and international financial flows. Removing support too quickly or delaying tightening for too long could lead to bad policy decisions (CBSL, 2022). However, the more significant concern is how central banks will stop making new purchases and shrink their balance sheets, which could significantly strain government finances, particularly in countries with large debt loads (IMF and World Bank, 2022). Developing nations with high levels of external debt denominated in hard currencies could experience substantial capital outflows and worsened debt sustainability due to higher interest rates following the termination of APPs (Heading and Zahidi, 2023). Central banks can use this opportunity to encourage climate action through complementary policies such as macro-prudential regulations and fiscal and taxation reforms (Khandelwal et al., 2022). Additionally, they can prioritize low-carbon investments and finance climate action by holding assets from firms with a lower carbon footprint (Ameli et al., 2020). In Europe, the economy returned to growth in 2021 but faced worker shortages and supply chain disruptions, especially in the second half of the year (Mukunoki, 2022). The Chinese economy slowed down due to restrictive measures, including temporary electricity rationing and the failure of a significant real estate company (Zanoletti et al., 2021). The Commonwealth of independent states (CIS) region's economy rebounded in 2021 but is expected to slow down in 2022 due to rising inflation, tightening monetary policy, and reduced financial assistance (UN, 2021).

Implications

The study highlighted the key implications, both theoretical and practical. Firstly, declining global output is the biggest challenge due to inflationary pressures, the COVID-19 pandemic, and supply chain disruptions. This leads to slower economic growth, and the decline in global output has implications for inequality, poverty rates, and employment levels. Secondly, international trade got affected due to COVID-19 due to affected tourism services and limited foreign tourism and travel. It has implications for economic prospects, labor shortage, and inflationary pressure. Thirdly, investments in EMDEs is vital in climate goals and achieving development with private-public partnerships, improved property rights, lower startup costs, and favorable startup cost. Therefore, the implications on long-term economic growth and neutralize financial vulnerability.

Fourthly, labor market recovery through reducing inequalities and uneven job creation for economic growth. Therefore, governments should focus on policies supporting unpaid domestic labor and addressing inequalities for sustainable recovery. Finally, the fiscal imbalance that will cause inflation pressure can be solved by avoiding the disruption of government finances and financial markets. Therefore, implications of the high level of hard currency denomination and external debt in termination of asset purchase programs and debt sustainability. Overall, implications need international collaboration and government policy actions to promote sustainable and inclusive growth and to handle the challenges faced by the global economy.

Limitations and Future Research

The existing literature provides valuable insights into the effects of global rebalancing from a macroeconomic theoretical perspective. But still, there are some limitations like data only from the world bank, IMF, and other organizations, specific details were not discussed, not based on specific country or region, and non-economic factors were not considered. In addressing the gaps, future studies could focus on an economic forecasting model with data, specific details of trade policy, and investment patterns; specific developed or developing countries or regions may be considered and reflect non-economic factors for a holistic understanding of the challenges and opportunities in the global economy.

Conclusion

In conclusion, international trade, foreign direct investment, capital market flows, migration, labor mobility, and technology diffusion will drive this growth. To mitigate the risk of debt crises and promote sustainable growth, EMDEs must prioritize human, physical, social, and natural capital investments. While global economic recovery is underway, it remains fragile due to ongoing COVID-19 infections, labor market issues, supply-chain bottlenecks, and inflationary pressures. Poverty rates have increased, with over 876 million people living in extreme poverty and rising inequality. Therefore, governments must adopt accommodating budgetary policies to support pandemic-related costs and alleviate suffering. However, international collaboration is crucial to ensure equitable resource access and promote inclusive growth.

Central banks have responded to COVID-19 with unconventional monetary policy tools, such as APPs, to stabilize financial markets and promote recovery. However, companies have used cheap liquidity for stock buybacks, reducing capital accumulation and investment. Excessive external borrowing has caused macroeconomic and financial vulnerabilities in developing nations, leading to asset price inflation and economic instability. To mitigate these risks, central banks should reduce APPs to lower inflation without disrupting financial markets. Finally, multilateralism is critical to ensuring equal and universal vaccine access, addressing debt problems, and accelerating the shift to low-carbon economies. This will provide a robust, inclusive, and sustainable recovery for all. Policymakers and stakeholders must prioritize these recommendations to promote a more resilient and equitable global economy.

References

Adrian, T., Erceg, C., Gray, S., and Sahay, R. (2022). Emerging-market central bank asset purchases can be effective but carry risks. IMF. 2022. https://www.imf.org/en/Blogs/Articles/2022/01/05/blog010522-emerging-market-central-bank-asset-purchases-can-be-effective-but-carry-risks.

Ameli, N., Drummond, P., Bisaro, A., Grubb, M., and Chenet, H. (2020). Climate finance and disclosure for institutional investors: why transparency is not enough. *Climatic Change*, 160(4), 565–89. https://doi.org/10.1007/s10584-019-02542-2.

Attinasi, M. G., Balatti, M., Mancini, M., and Metelli, L. (2021). Supply chain disruptions and the effects on the global economy. *European Central Bank*, https://www.ecb.europa.eu/pub/economic-bulletin/focus/2022/html/ecb.ebbox202108_01~e8ceebe51f.en.html.

Bechtel, G. (2022). Global assets mitigate global inflation. *Advances in Social Sciences Research Journal*, 9(3). https://doi.org/10.14738/assrj.93.11994.

Białowąs, T., and Budzyńska, A. (2022). The importance of global value chains in developing countries' agricultural trade development. *Sustainability (Switzerland)*, 14(3). https://doi.org/10.3390/su14031389.

Booth, A. (2020). The indonesian economy in transition: policy challenges in the jokowi era and beyond. *South East Asia Research*, 28(2). https://doi.org/10.1080/0967828x.2020.1739387.

Carstens, A. (2021a). Central banks and inequality. banks for international settlement. https://www.bis.org/speeches/sp210506.pdf.

Carstens, A. (2021b). Central banks facing pandexit challenges. banks for international settlement. https://www.bis.org/speeches/sp210629.pdf.

CBSL (2022). Financial system stability review—(2022). *Financial System Stability Review*.

CEPAL (2020). COVID-19: towards an inclusive, resilient and green recovery—building back better through regional cooperation. Cepal. United Nations. https://repositorio.cepal.org/bitstream/handle/11362/45551/4/COVID19TowardsAnInclusive_en.pdf.

Dafermos, Y., Gabor, D., and Michell, J. (2023). Institutional supercycles: an evolutionary macrofinance approach. New Political Economy Print-a-he (Print-a-head): Print-a-head. https://doi.org/10.1080/13563467.2022.2161497.

Du, J., and Shepotylo, O. (2022). UK trade in the time of COVID-19: a review. *World Economy*, 45(5), 1409–46. https://doi.org/10.1111/twec.13220.

Dubois, C., Lambertini, L., and Wu, Y. (2022). Gender effects of the COVID-19 pandemic in the swiss labor market. *Swiss Journal of Economics and Statistics*, 158(1), 1–29. https://doi.org/10.1186/s41937-022-00099-z.

English, B., Forbes, K., and Ubide, A. (2021). Monetary Policy and Central Banking in the Covid Era. London: Centre for Economic Policy Research. https://cepr.org/system/files/publication-files/60024-monetary_policy_and_central_banking_in_the_covid_era.pdf.

European Commission (2020). EU agricultural outlook for markets, income and environment 2020–2030. Report.

Filho, W. L., Minhas, A., Schmook, B., Mardero, S., Sharifi, A., Paz, S., Kovaleva, M., Albertini, M. C., and Skouloudis, A. (2023). Sustainable development goal 13 and switching priorities: addressing climate change in the context of pandemic recovery efforts. *Environmental Sciences Europe*, 35(1), 1–14. https://doi.org/10.1186/s12302-022-00701-4.

Gai, P., and Tong, E. (2022). Information spillovers of us monetary policy. *Journal of Macroeconomics*, 72. https://doi.org/10.1016/j.jmacro.2022.103401.

Halling, M., Yu, J., and Zechner, J. (2020). Bond and equity issuance activity during COVID-19. *SSRN Electronic Journal*. https://doi.org/10.2139/ssrn.3596114.

Heading, S., and Zahidi, S. (2023). The Global Risks Report 2023. Geneva. https://www3.weforum.org/docs/WEF_Global_Risks_Report_2023.pdf.

ILO (2022). World Employment and Social Outlook: Trends 2022. Geneva. https://doi.org/10.54394/dspl5113.

IMF (2021). World Economic Outlook, January 2021.

IMF and World Bank (2022). Making Debt Work for Development and Macroeconomic Stability. https://doi.org/https://doi.org/10.5089/9798400208591.007.

Islam, A. M. (2021). Impact of Covid-19 pandemic on global output, employment and prices: an assessment. *Transnational Corporations Review*, 13(2), 189–201. https://doi.org/10.1080/19186444.2021.1936852.

Jackson, J. K., Weiss, M. A., Schwarzenberg, A. B., Nelson, R. M., Sutter, K. M., and Sutherland, M. D. (2021). Global economic effects of COVID-19. The effects of COVID-19 on the global and domestic economy. *Congressional Research Service*. Accessed January 25, 2023. https://sgp.fas.org/crs/row/R46270.pdf.

Johnson, S. S. (2021). Addressing the caregiving crisis: The roles for employers and policy makers. *American Journal of Health Promotion*, 35(7), 1028–1029. https://doi.org/10.1177/08901171211030142a

Kabbani, N., and Mimoune, N. B. (2021). Economic diversification in the gulf: Time to redouble efforts. Brookings. 2021. Accessed January 18, 2023. https://www.brookings.edu/articles/economic-diversification-in-the-gulf-time-to-redouble-efforts/.

Khandelwal, P., Cabezon, E., Al-Farah, R., and Mirzayev, S. (2022). Macroprudential policies to enhance financial stability in the caucasus and central asia. DP/2022/006. Departmental Papers. (Vol. 2022). Washington, DC. https://doi.org/10.5089/9798400201240.087.

Lakner, C., Mahler, D. G., Negre, M., and Prydz, E. B. (2022). How much does reducing inequality matter for global poverty. *Journal of Economic Inequality*, 20(3), 559–585. https://doi.org/10.1007/s10888-021-09510-w.

Latino, L. R., Pica-Ciamarra, U., and Wisser, D. (2020). Africa: the livestock revolution urbanizes. *Global Food Security*, 26, 1–18. https://doi.org/10.1016/j.gfs.2020.100399.

Leon, D. A., Jdanov, D., Gerry, C. J., Grigoriev, P., Jasilionis, D., McKee, M., Meslé, F., et al. (2022). The russian invasion of ukraine and its public health consequences. *The Lancet Regional Health—Europe*, 15, 1–2. https://doi.org/10.1016/j.lanepe.2022.100358.

López, G. G., and Stracca, L. (2021). Changing patterns of capital flows. Bank for International Settlements (BIS). Accessed February 02, 2023. https://www.bis.org/publ/cgfs66.pdf.

Mukunoki, H. (2022). Comment on how COVID-19 medical supply shortages led to extraordinary trade and industrial policy. *Asian Economic Policy Review*, 17(1), 136–137. https://doi.org/10.1111/aepr.12367.

Narayan, A., Cojocaru, A., Agrawal, S., Bundervoet, T., Davalos, M., Garcia, N., Lakner, C., et al. (2022). COVID-19 and economic inequality short-term impacts with long-term consequences. Policy Research Working Paper 9902. World Bank Group. Accessed January 22, 2023. https://documents1.worldbank.org/curated/en/219141642091810115/pdf/COVID-19-and-Economic-Inequality-Short-Term-Impacts-with-Long-Term-Consequences.pdf.

Ogunniyi, O. R., Okunlola, A. F., Alatise, M. A., and Aregbeshola, R. A. (2023). Socio-economic inclusion and sustainable economic growth: Empirical analysis of nigeria and South Africa. *Cogent Economics and Finance*, 11(1), 2163077. https://doi.org/10.1080/23322039.2022.2163077.

Olagunju, K. O., Ogunniyi, A. I., Oguntegbe, K. F., Raji, I. O., and Ogundari, K. (2019). Welfare impact of globalization in developing countries: examining the mediating role of human capital. *Economies*, 7(3), 1–19. https://doi.org/10.3390/economies7030084.

Olasehinde-Williams, G. (2021). Is US trade policy uncertainty powerful enough to predict global output volatility. *Journal of International Trade and Economic Development*, 30(1), 138–54. https://doi.org/10.1080/09638199.2020.1806912.

Onwuegbuzie, A. J., and Frels, R. (2016). Seven Steps to a Comprehensive Literature Review. (1st ed.) Los Angeles, CA: Sage Publication Limited.

Palomino, J. C., Rodríguez, J. G., and Sebastian, R. (2022). The COVID-19 shock on the labour market: poverty and inequality effects across Spanish regions. *Regional Studies*, 57, 814–828. https://doi.org/10.1080/00343404.2022.2110227.

Peterson, E. W. F. (2017). The role of population in economic growth. *SAGE Open*, 7(4), 1–13. https://doi.org/10.1177/2158244017736094.

Prabheesh, K. P., and Kumar, S. (2023). How do the financial markets respond to India's asset purchase program. Evidence from the COVID-19 Crisis. Emerging Markets Finance and Trade Print-a-he (Print-a-head). https://doi.org/https://doi.org/10.1080/1540496X.2022.2148463.

Qureshi, M., Adrian, T., and Natalucci, F. (2022). Macro-financial stability in the COVID-19 crisis: some reflections. WP/22/251. IMF Working Papers. (Vol. 2022). https://doi.org/10.5089/9798400223532.001.

Sankar, J., P., Yoganandham, G., Kalaichelvi, R., John, J. A., and Kumar, B. U. (2021). Human resource digital transformation of IT sector in India. *Webology*, 18(1), 219–232. https://doi.org/10.14704/WEB/V18I1/WEB18085.

Shams, T. (2022). Review of mapping the transnational world: How we move and communicate across borders and why it matters. *Social Forces*, 101(1), 5–14. https://doi.org/10.1093/sf/soac025.

Tian, J., Yu, L., Xue, R., Zhuang, S., and Shan, Y. (2022). Global low-carbon energy transition in the post-COVID-19 Era. *Applied Energy*, 307, 118205. https://doi.org/10.1016/j.apenergy.2021.118205.

UN (2021). World Economic Situation & Prospects 2021. New York: United Nations Department of Economic and Social Affairs (UNDESA).

UN (2022). The Monetary Policy Response to COVID-19: The Role of Asset Purchase Programmes. Department of Economics and social Affairs. https://www.un.org/development/desa/dpad/wp-content/uploads/sites/45/publication/PB_129_FINAL.pdf.

Vaquero-García, A., Cadaval-Sampedro, M., and Lago-Peñas, S. (2022). Do political factors affect fiscal consolidation. evidence from Spanish regional governments. *SAGE Open*, 12(1), 1–9. https://doi.org/10.1177/21582440221085002.

Weaver, S., Shi, P. Y., and Rajsbaum, R. (2021). Building interdisciplinary research careers in women's health. National Institute of Health 30.

World Bank (2023). Global Growth to Slow through 2023, Adding to Risk of 'Hard Landing' in Developing Economies.

Yoganandham, G. (2022). A Theory-based evaluation of the causes and consequences of women headed households in Vellore town. *International Journal of Economics, Business and Management Research*, 6(2), 44–54. https://doi.org/10.51505/ijebmr.2022.6203.

Yoganandham, G., and Sankar, J. P. (2016). Financing renewable energy projects for the sustainable economic growth of India—Barriers and investment elucidations. *Research Dimensions*, 3(2), 66–68.

Zanoletti, A., Cornelio, A., and Bontempi, E. (2021). A Post-pandemic sustainable scenario: what actions can be pursued to increase the raw materials availability? *Environmental Research*, 202, 111681. https://doi.org/10.1016/j.envres.2021.111681.

6 Assessing the Productivity of Professionals Working Remotely Considering Cyber Security: A Case Study on INSOMEA Computer Solutions

Zainab Alhayki[1], Nandita Sengupta[2], and Muhammed Rizqy[2]

[1]MBA Student, University College of Bahrain, Bahrain
[2]Assistant Professor, University College of Bahrain, Bahrain
[3]Head of Business Administration Department, University College of Bahrain, Bahrain

Abstract

Remote work has been one of the most common way of work in most of the jobs and organizations. However, the security and privacy are not fulfilled, and many challenges could be faced while applying remote work. While many studies claimed that remote work would achieve better performance and productivity of the employees due to satisfaction and work life balance. Therefore, it is vital to assess the security principles and understand if this could affect the organization's privacy, productivity in terms of accessibility of the specific application and employee satisfaction. There are some studies related to accessing the productivity and effectiveness of employees working remotely. There are some advantages which motivate the employees to improve their performance by increasing their satisfaction level. But there are disadvantages while working from home. The study focuses on the way of overcoming these disadvantages with effective solutions along with the new services and intelligent technology that can be used for. These effective solutions can be applied while working remotely. These solutions include the technology implemented for working as well as monitoring the work. Furthermore, it is required to come up with rules and understand how working remotely could increase the productivity and effectiveness of employees while maintaining security.

Keywords

Cyber security, effectiveness, productivity, remote work.

Introduction

Working remotely increasingly becomes popular and new types of professional work. Many organizations are applying this technique for several reasons. One of the main is COVID-19 as people are not able to leave home or go anywhere, while work is supposed to continue. The second reason could be cost saving, as in the case of remote work, organizations will not need to offer office space and personal allowances such as car and accommodation for each employee. Also, it is a plan in case of any disaster or any situation that could avert employees from going to work. All the above reasons should not stop work and the organization must ensure business continuity, and sustainability and keep surviving the business in all situations.

With this change of moving to work remotely, a significant risk has been utilized. For instance, employees and organizations should be aware of the essential security principles to be able to adapt to work remotely successfully with the minimum-security risk that could be faced. According to ITERPOL (The International Criminal Police Organization), during their assessment of COVID-19's effects on security, it has been founded that there is a huge increase in the number of robust company infrastructures, governments, and huge companies that targeted by hackers. It is said that between January and April 2020 after doing the assessment, it has been detected around 50,000 malicious and 900,000 spam messages and emails with 700 malware incidents (Fortinet, 2022).

Ultimately, remote work is not a temporary solution that survives the business in a specific situation, remote work will continue to be used in most of the businesses within an organization that could use single office based and huge number of locations for work whether at home or any place. Therefore, it is critical to apply the security tips from the organization and management perspective to educate employees on how to manage sensitive data from home, keep monitoring and have control over the devices that are being used as part of the work to be able to identify and solve any error as soon as possible, validate the security effectively from the service provider and ensure no weaknesses in the security from both staff and organization. This could decrease the number of attacks that could impact and affect the organizations.

It is noticed that no studies are focusing on both security and productivity to be able to work from home and give solutions that cover both. Therefore, this research intended to fill the gap between employees' productivity and security challenges to ease the way of doing work from home while maintaining security. Also, this research will define the challenges faced by organizations and workers. After that, to come up with proper solutions and suggestions that fulfill the requirements of employees and organization management. Furthermore, assessing the productivity and satisfaction of employees based on work from home and on-site will be part of this study.

The structure of this paper will be as follows. Section 2 literature reviews. Sections 3 description of the sample and variables. Section 4 showing the methodology of the research. Section 5 discussion upon the empirical findings. Last section will be summary of the paper.

Literature Review

Previous Study on the Difference Between Working from Home and Working from an Office

Relevant theories have been reviewed to clarify more points regarding remote work. One of them is the boundary theory which justifies the difference between working remotely and working from an office from a different perspective. The main thing is the working hours where it will be fixed working hours in working from the office and flexible working hours for working from home. Furthermore, some organizations identify dress codes when it will be at the office. Also, there is a high cost for transport and accommodation in some cases while there is nothing like this when it comes to working remotely. However, the support and assistance will be high during working from the office while working online is required to deal with the issue individually. Furthermore, there is no freedom and time to spend with the family when it comes to working from the office and the opposite will be in the case of remote working as the worker can manage his time and have his responsibility to be accomplished within the due date. The theory also has discussed the boundaries that could block users from working from home and their ability to balance their personal life and work (Aczel, 2021). Within the theory, it has been stated that the position and the rules of each employee need to be separated to have clear boundaries which will be easy to finalize the task independently. However, the issues of this are the task itself and how they are related to each other which makes separating the rules much hared. Therefore, working from home required to have main communication between all employees as well as giving each employee full responsibility to accomplish his job. This could help in minimizing the time required to give a task to more than an employee as communication while working from home could be a block in some cases. Nevertheless, many online tools such as Microsoft Teams offer all the features related to teamwork and remove the boundaries that affect working from home. As the flexibility and mobilization have to decrease the blocking points.

Working from home is different than office work with advantages and disadvantages for both options. As stated by Frederick Herzberg satisfaction and productivity are the main factors that could affect the workplace (Le, 2019).

Work from Home: Cybersecurity Risks

One of the first researchers to examine this issue is Borkovich (2020). Government entities and private are the most targeted organizations for cybersecurity breaches because of their inability to recognize, plan, and educate the teleworker with the required test and keep updated with the new technology and security services (Borkovich, 2020). As remote works come with some dangerous security since the employees rely on the home connection which in most cases it is using the basic and default security. Furthermore, workers use their devices to accomplish some tasks with the hope of at least having technical skills to avoid any issues. According to the researcher, 70% of the workers confirmed that they faced IT issues while working from home, especially with the COVID-19 pandemic and it is stated that 54% of the employees wait for a minimum of 4 hours to solve the issue. There are many vulnerabilities with the network and device since there is no firewall or any blocklist of IP addresses. Furthermore, the most of employees' tasks could include any confidential information related to the organization and personal data related to employees and if it's on the internet, then the probability of cybercriminal compromising is always there. Cloud documents, email links, and attachments, dealing with third-party tools and services are all considered to be a vulnerability if security is not applied here. According to a CISCO report (Cicso, 2020), most financial enterprise is struggling to manage to work from home with the use of personal devices phone, and laptop, as many employees use their device and receive emails, open link, download attachments and upload through the device. These blurred lines between office devices and personal phones increase the risk and could fail the sensitive data to an unsecured environment. This required to apply of different security principles to protect both personnel and professionals with the use of multi-factor authentication, sensitive data labeling, controlling devices, and application with different tools available such as Intune, a Microsoft servicing tool that allows the organization to manage users' devices and help in protecting their data with the policies applied over all application used or required to be used with the organization (Leicham, 2022). As stated by the Microsoft report 52% of users confirm that Microsoft security and Intune tool helps in protecting their data from phishing and spam email with the evidence or security report generated monthly shows all details and risk level for each device and its compliance which shows the action required to be done to have a more secure device (Brenduns, 2022).

Barriers and Obstacles to Professionals Working from Home

It was evident that remote work has positive impacts on the productivity of the workers (Barrero, 2021), however, this does not mean that there are no setbacks. As stated, the most challenging thing are the absence of communication and face-to-face discussion, as this highly affects the quality of the work, (Ramos, 2020). In addition, employees pointed out that there is stress while working from home causes some difficulties with the feature of managing family life and work assignments. Different studies show that most workers keep receiving calls and tasks after working hours which makes it too hard to isolate themselves from their families and focus on the task given (Bloom, 2021). This result inability of the employee to focus while receiving and understanding the task as well as working on it. Furthermore, specific access related to work data and materials will be highly required especially when it is integrated with an application that can be accessed only via a work network and this is negatively impacting worker performance and productivity. In some studies, workers submitted several issues that they are facing while working from home such as the application installed on a personal pc has a different version that the one at the office which led to some issues. also, when it comes to signatures and formal requirements related to the government and bank requirements sometime could not be accepted as a digital signature or online soft paper (Akif, 2021). Thus, it is important to understand all employees' requirements to avoid any issues and decrease productivity.

Overall, identifying all challenges that could impact employees' performance will help in building a well-advanced environment with different methods that ease employees' work and organization management. This is considered is the main objective of this research.

The above literature review gives a conclusion regarding working online. employees do face challenges because of the mismanagement and security issues with the change in the workplace. Furthermore, recognizing all challenges will drive enterprises and administrators in applying processes and methods to minimize these struggles and sustain a healthy and secure workplace.

Data and Variables

Study Period and Sample

The study period spans over many years as this is considered not a new method of work. However, recently within the last 5 years and due to covid-19 situation, it is increased and become a popular way of working from home.

To construct the sample for this study, data will be taken from the different primary resources, as is the survey questionnaires that will be given to INSOMEA customers that are based in Bahrain and who are outside Bahrain with the limitation of organizations that have the possibility of remote work as well as work from the office. with an estimation of time to be taken to finish the survey is 5 to 7 minutes. The survey was shared with customers by email along with their employees if interested to do it. The survey was conducted in one language which is English, and it is used to collect the data as it gives the researchers the ability to answer this study's questions and to achieve the objectives.

Two types of data collection will be used in this study a questionnaire with the help of the online tool. It will consist of different types of questions such as checkboxes and open questions as well as multiple choice that are associated with the research goals and main questions. The first section of the questionnaires will be related to the respondents' personal information such as their age, gender, and current position in the work as this will be used to have a clear analysis of all responses and who the impacted people are. The second section of questions will be related to the working strategy and his experience, the security blocking points if and how can we tackle these issues from his opinion, and how the organization manages to work with these issues. The third section will be questions related to the satisfaction, productivity, and effectiveness of the employees and how they feel. A mention regarding the difference between working from home and remotely will be conducted with a rating question type which will be liked or dislike and each has a question and participant must answer with (0 = strongly dislike; 1 = dislike; 2 = somewhat dislike; 0 = not good; 1 = somewhat like; 2 = like; 3 = strongly like). The last section of the questionnaires will give the participant a space to provide his comment and any suggestions related to the improvements required to be able to increase the productivity of the employees.

Once this is done the analysis part will be taken care of with the use of the same tool as it will show different diagrams and charters based on the preferred and required.

Dependent Variable

Remote Work: It defines as the use of employees not having a physical fixed place in the organization within a specific time.

Mediating Variable

Cyber Security: It refers to the best practices and technological processes that used to control the system and network from cyber-attacks and breaches.

Independent Variable

Performance: Refer to the level of quality of the work along with a value of behavior over a specific period that benefits the organization.

Employee productivity: Employee productivity is defined as the amount of work produced over a specific period.

Productivity: the amount of work produced over a specific period.

Work-life Balance: It is defined as an individual that needs to succeed in both work and life and can manage both sides at the same level to fulfill his responsibilities in both.

Methodology and Model Specifications

The framework of this study is based on INSOMEA Computer Solutions customers that are available in Bahrain and outside Bahrain. Their response will make a huge effect on the result of this study. Based on the responses getting from them, it can reach the research aim which is to provide insight into employees working from home with high security and productivity. This study will include the main requirement that needs to be applied to secure the users' data and ease the way of working from anywhere and anytime without limitations.

The questions placed for this study are as below; (RQ1) what are the main security issues that affect the organization from allowing employees to work from home? and (RQ2) how to tackle the security challenges that organizations faced with the best user experience and efficiency. The third one is (RQ3) does working from home improve the efficiency and satisfaction of employees? And finally, (RO4) what are the security recommendations that need to be applied to secure the work environment with the ability to work remotely?

Along with the question, the main objectives of this study are to; (RO1) illustrates the correlation between the productivity rate and the security of professionals while working from home. and (RO2) identify the security challenges that could impact and block the organization from allowing their employees to work remotely in an effective way. And (RO3) to increase the productivity and effectiveness of employees while working remotely. Finally, (RO4) improves the security of the organization to meet the needs of employees working remotely.

Model Specifications

Hypothesis of this study is as follows:

H1: organizations face several security challenges with accepting employees working remotely and employees face many blocking points of the applied securities which affect productivity.

H2: the availability of both options remote work and work at the office has a positive and significant impact on the productivity and efficiency of employees.

H3: employees' productivity and effectiveness increase when working from home due to the balance between life and work.

H4: applying the required security affect organizations and employees positively to work remotely.

Empirical Results

Findings are represented below based on the research questions:

Giving the employees the ability to work from home could give many features, such as flexibility and productivity could be increased. However, some security challenges could appear here and organizations must consider.

Below are some of the security issues that could impact the organization in case of giving the employees the ability to work remotely.

1. Security of remote access: All employees need to get access to different resources including files, email, and other confidential data, when they are remote work. In this case a risk in access will appear in case the remote access in not controlled and not well protected.
2. Security of the devices: All users endpoints must be secured enough as a managed device. Also, it is crucial to have the latest update of anti-virus and other security software.
3. Attacks, social engineering and phishing: many attackers can take the advantages of knowing that the employees are working remotely and do the attack using different technique with social engineering to make the suitable trick to get confidential and private data and export the needed details.
4. Breaching sensitive data: Employees working in financial sector, they are dealing with sensitive information such as IBAN and CPR, therefore, it is high risk of any simple attack, as it could impact huge people in case of any comprised to their data.
5. Compliance requirements: Some organization could find some challenges to allow employees to work remotely because they need to follow the industry regulations and the laws related to information protection. This makes it more difficult to the organization.

How to tackle the security challenges that organizations faced with the best user experience and efficiency.

1. Access resources securely: Many security protocols need to be configured in each organization to make sure that every user access resources from any source with high security. This could involve MFA which is multi factor authentication and restrict the access for specific resources with Private network to get the data encrypted in the transit.
2. Securing endpoints: Organizations should secure each device that used by the employees by establishing different security policies and manages the device using MDM (Manage Device Management) to enforce security policies and wipe the devices in case of any emergency or attack.
3. Avoid new phishing attacks: Organization can tackle this challenge by providing security awareness regularly for all their employees and keep updated with new technology that can protect their data and keep all resources secured with latest technology that can handle the new attacks.

Limitations of the Research

One limitation of this study on assessing the productivity of professionals working from home with respect to cybersecurity is that it primarily focuses on quantitative data from survey responses. While this provides valuable insights into employee perceptions and attitudes towards cybersecurity and productivity, it may not capture the full complexity of the issue or provide in-depth analysis of specific cases or incidents.

Another limitation is that the study may not fully account for the diverse range of remote work environments and security practices across different organizations and industries. The findings and recommendations may be more applicable to certain types of organizations or work arrangements and may not be generalizable to other contexts.

Finally, the study may be limited by the potential for response bias, as survey respondents may not be representative of the wider population of professionals working from home. This could affect the generalizability of the findings and limit the ability to draw broader conclusions about the relationship between productivity and cybersecurity in remote work environments.

Conclusion

The survey results show that many employees prefer to work from home, provided that all rules are followed, and work is monitored to ensure smooth operations. However, there are several security challenges and restrictions on access that can hinder workflow and reduce productivity. Also, it is discussing the benefits and security challenges of allowing employees to work from home. It identifies several security issues that organizations need to be aware of, such as remote access security, device security, phishing and social engineering, data breaches, and compliance issues. To tackle these challenges, organizations can implement secure remote access, establish device management policies, provide security awareness training, use secure collaboration tools, and implement data protection policies and compliance measures. The research also discusses how working from home can improve the efficiency and satisfaction of employees, such as increased flexibility, reduced commuting time, improved work-life balance, reduced distractions, and a comfortable working environment. Finally, the article suggests that organizations can use Azure Virtual Desktop and Microsoft Teams together to provide a comprehensive solution for employees working from home, enabling secure and flexible remote work, enhancing collaboration and communication, promoting inclusivity and diversity, and increasing productivity.

Recommendations

Based on the findings of this paper, the following recommendation has been determined for future implementation of remote work in organizations: applying full security appliances and controls to achieve both objectives of improving employee productivity and satisfaction.

Recommendation for Addressing the Study's Problem

1. Configure full security principles: all organizations must configure the default and advanced security principles to mitigate the risk and attacks. This can be done by strict the employees of using virtual private network to access to the organization resources, Multi factor authentication with different security method of login to

be implemented. Also, all data needs to be encrypted, read and written. This will guarantee the organization confidentiality and integrity.

2. Setting up clear policies and rules: each organization based on their own environment has to set their own rules and policies. This involves old employees and new joining. For all employees it needs to have a regular session and explain each added policy or changed. For new joining, organization need to ensure that new employee join understand the policies and able to follow it with no exception. This will make the environment more controlled and secure in terms of employees.

3. Monitoring productivity: organizations need to monitor the productivity of their employees and determine the expected issue with the way of improving them and encourage their satisfaction. This can be included in the analysis of user activity insight that can be done through Microsoft Viva or any other tool, as it shows the spent time by the employee on each application and each task how long to takes to be finalized. The same will include the security breaches that happen to each user which also can be monitored and applying the required security based on group of users or individuals.

4. Applying the appropriate security policies: each environment need to set up their own security standard and each organization needs to train their employees based on the security applied. This will improve the productivity of employees since they will be aware of each tool, how it can be used properly and eliminate of mistake that could happen.

5. Security assessment: the organization will be more protected and improved if regular assessment has been done of their data and infrastructure. This assessment will show the vulnerabilities and missing security in their environment, furthermore, the assessment could perform penetration testing to have full picture upon the security of the organization. After that, a consultation and auditing on their security policy can be enhanced.

6. Foster communication: communication between the SOC team and other employees should be fostered along with the management. This will ensure that everyone is aware and has a good understanding of the reason behind each policy applied along with the regular feedback that can be got from all team members. Furthermore, in case of any potential risk, employees will have the visibility to address each security issue. This can be done by creating a team channel on Microsoft Teams or any other communication tool for reporting and incidents and feedback on any related security procedure.

Recommendation for Further Research

1. Effect of cybersecurity attacks on efficiency: further studies to constraint on the efficiency employees working from home and the importance of cybersecurity measures on remote work environments along with users. This also can include analysis of how the attacks could impact productivity and limit efficiency. Investigation with some research and study could be added and this will increase the level of the study.

2. Value of cybersecurity guidance and training: this is another vital area for research which will be highly efficient and beneficial in future research. Training on

cybersecurity and how it could improve the level of awareness for users. Also, the research could include assessment of different security programs that suites the organization environment in terms of financial, educational or commerce. Assessing the effect of different types of programs based on users' behavior with determining the best way of program to be delivered for training.

3. Automate responses: as extend to the topic that can be used in future research is to explore how organizations can work on automating the response of any attacks using runbook or predefined job. In case of any unexpected attack an automatic action can be applied instead of a manual response by the employee. Future research on this can avoid many issues that require to take a decision by managers and apply it manually.

4. The impact of online work on security: remote work and cybersecurity is another area of research that can be go deeply about with the focus on the examination of how the security can be changed based on the new tools that used by hacker for comprising the data. Also, it could include the investigation of different techniques that can be used to mitigate these attacks.

5. Generally, future studies in the above area can support the organization to implement better techniques and methods for managing the challenges faced by employees and cybersecurity to accept working from home. Also, to have a better understanding of how productivity and efficiency can be increased while working from home by accepting and following the security applied and rules.

References

Agarwal, V. K., Chanda, A. C., & Gupta, V. K. (2020). Review on Employee Productivity. Journal of critical reviews , 1156

Albert. (2020). Critical Review of Labor Productivity Research in Construction Journals . Critical Review of Labor Productivity Research in Construction Journals , 8.

Aziri, B. (2011). Job satisfaction: A literature review . Management research and practice.

Bhandari, P. (2022, December 5). Population vs. Sample | Definitions, Differences & Examples. Retrieved from Scribbr: https://www.scribbr.com/methodology/population-vs-sample/#:~:text=A%20population%20is%20the%20entire,total%20size%20of%20the%20population.

Bouchrika, I. (2022). Types of Research Design: Perspective and Methodological Approaches. Overview of Research Design, 1.

Cisco. (2023). What Is Cybersecurity? Retrieved from Cisco: https://www.cisco.com/c/en/us/products/security/what-is-cybersecurity.html

Clark, S. C. (2000). Work/Family Border Theory: A New Theory of Work/Family Balance. Human Relations, 349.

Diakun, N. (2018). Defining Cybersecurity. Defining Cybersecurity.

Freedman, M. (2022). Productivity Rising Among Employees Who Work From Home. In 2021, work-from-home productivity was often higher than in-office rates. Here's how to ensure this holds true for your team.

Gartner. (2022, April). Gartner Glossary. Retrieved from Gartner: https://www.gartner.com/en/information-technology/glossary/remote-work

Hanin, L. (2021). Cavalier Use of Inferential Statistics Is a Major Source of False and Irreproducible Scientifi

Insomea. (2023). Retrieved from https://insomea.com/

J.Motowidlo, S. (2003). Job Performance. In W. C. Borman, D. R. Ilgen, & R. J. Klimoski, Handbook of Psychology, Industrial and Organizational Psychology (p. 39). John Wiley and Sons, Inc.

Labour Market Regulatory Authority (2021)

O.Laccourreye. (2021). Mastering the descriptive statistics used in otorhinolaryngology. Mastering the descriptive statistics used in otorhinolaryngology, 8.

Lawal, A. K. (2019). Lean management in health care: definition, concepts, methodology and effects reported (systematic review protocol). 3.

Olson, M. H. (1983). Remote office work: changing work patterns in space and time. Communications of the ACM, 182–187.

Statistics. (2022). Slovin's Formula: What is it and When do I use it? Retrieved from Statistics: https://www.statisticshowto.com/probability-and-statistics/how-to-use-slovins-formula/

Veenhoven, R. (1996). The study of life satisfaction . Eötvös University Press, 11–48

Viviani, E. (2021). Energy Markets Forecasting. From Inferential Statistics to Machine Learning: The German Case. Energy Markets Forecasting. From Inferential Statistics to Machine Learning: The German Case.

7 Impact of ICT Tools on Knowledge Management in Enterprises: Remote Working Model

Anna Nowacka

PhD Student, Faculty of Management, Czestochowa University of Technology, Poland

Abstract

The impact of ICT tools is significant in an increasing number of industries and business sizes. It manifests itself in the implementation of small improvements to existing processes within companies, or large digital transformations. ICT tools can be described as a determinant influencing innovation, as well as an organization's competitive position in the market. Closely related to this is the strategic process of knowledge management in companies, which, through ICT tools, translates into the development of employees' intellectual capital. A research problem was identified in the application of ICT tools in knowledge management in the remote working model in IT and administrative companies. Qualitative research in the form of in-depth interviews was conducted to address the research problem. The paper shows that knowledge and its management is a very important process in companies, which, with the use of appropriate ICT tools, reaches all employees and creates added value. Furthermore, all the hypotheses posed in the article were positively verified.

Keywords

ICT tools, knowledge, knowledge management, remote working.

Introduction

Due to globalization and the increasing popularization and implementation of digital solutions, a great deal of attention is paid to the flow of knowledge within companies, and thus how to manage it so that it is accessible to all employees. It turns out that it is crucial to integrate knowledge into the strategy of companies and to develop it through tailored tools. Knowledge management is becoming a strategic process that affects the building of a competitive advantage and thus the organization's position in the market. The whole systemisation was developed before the coronavirus pandemic where most companies worked in a stationary working model. Using the remote working model, the problem arose of how to get knowledge to employees, how to keep it flowing and what tools to use to make it easier for employees to access knowledge. Organisations, boards of directors and managers were faced with the challenge of considering the best solutions to ensure smooth knowledge management. Employees have their own unique

anna.nowacka@pcz.pl

competences, skills, experience, which have a direct impact on building added value within the company. This added value is knowledge. Tools that enable the creation of repositories and the dissemination of knowledge play a key role. The aim of the article is to analyse how knowledge transfer takes place in companies, how ICT tools are used and whether remote working affects knowledge management in organisations. The article conducts a synthetic literature review, describes the research methodology, and presents the results and conclusions.

Literature Review

Remote working was defined when it was proven that all employee outputs through communication methods and technological tools could be transferred between employees regardless of the distances separating them. This experiment showed that through the use of technology, work can be done in a flexible and pro-employee way. It proved that employees do not need to do stationary work—to come to their employers' premises—and that they can perform all tasks directly on their computers and transmit the results of their work (Nilles, 1976, 2003). The popularisation of remote working has led to many definitions of it over the years. The first approach to defining remote working dates back to 1974. It was presented in a law in the Labour Code. Remote working was presented as work that: "May be performed regularly outside the workplace, using electronic means of communication within the meaning of the provisions on the provision of services by electronic means (telework). A teleworker is an employee who performs work (. . .) and communicates the results of the work to the employer, in particular by means of electronic communication" (Labour Code, 1974). In 2016, A. Jerhan presented remote working in a very concrete way: "Work carried out away from the employer's premises, depending on the form: at the employee's residence or elsewhere, sometimes on the move" (Jerhan, 2016). The ever-increasing implementation of remote working as a flexible form of employment has determined companies to implement a hybrid working model, which involves both the possibility to work from the employer's premises and the possibility to work remotely. This allows work-life balance to be maintained, which is of interest from the employees' point of view (Carnoy, 2000; Nowacka and Jelonek, 2022).

Figure 7.1 shows search trends for the words remote working (blue), hybrid working (red) and stationary working (yellow). The graph shows word searches over the last year by users in Poland in the Google Chrome browser.

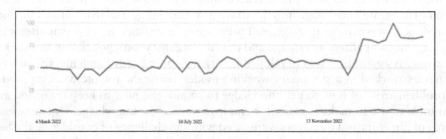

Figure 7.1 Trends for the words: remote working, hybrid working, stationary working.
Source: Google trends

It is noticeable that there is little amplitude of change in the search for information on remote working. In 2022, there was an area of interest for poles and it remained at a similar level in contrast to the topics related to hybrid and stationary work.

Knowledge management is one of the elements of a company's human resource management strategy. In knowledge management, the most important element is the knowledge of the employees, and in particular their intellectual capital (Drucker, 1999) and the ability to think abstractly and creatively (Jelonek and Stępniak, 2014). This is very much influenced by the widely understood information technologies and the digitalisation of functioning processes in companies (Mikuła et al., 2002). Based on many definitions in the literature, knowledge is a unique resource that includes: ideas, concepts, or know-how for effective use in decision-making (Drucker, 1999; Turban, 1992; Galata, 2004). Knowledge can be attributed with characteristics such as: inexhaustibility, which means that it will never run out, on the contrary it will be constantly increasing through new human experiences. An equally important characteristic is also its dominance in the context of the company's available resources. It stands out because it determines the company's position in the market. As already mentioned, it determines its competitiveness. It is also important from the perspective of the innovation solutions to be implemented. If an organisation does not have sufficient knowledge, it will not be possible to implement solutions that are based on this resource (Toffler, 1984).

It is important to look at knowledge management from two levels: the strategic dimension and the operational dimension. The approaches differ according to their functions within the enterprise. The strategic approach is directly related to the organisation's strategy and the factors influencing it, while the operational approach is related to internal processes within the enterprise. The strategic dimension relates to knowledge management as a component of the overall corporate strategy. It is as important as creating an organisational culture or developing technology. The operational dimension, on the other hand, presents knowledge management as a process that has a direct impact on the transfer of knowledge in a subjective approach (Skrzypek, 2002).

Figure 7.2 shows the trend of searches for the phrase: knowledge management in the last year by users in the Google Chrome browser. The graph shows how Poles' interest in this topic has changed. Periodic changes are evident, when there was hardly any interest and when there was an increased search for information on this topic.

A feature of the graph is the 3 spikes in interest in the subject. The first occurred in August/September 2022, another in November 2022 and early February 2023. This may indicate an interest in knowledge and its possibilities from the perspective of digital solutions being implemented.

Figure 7.2 Trend for knowledge management.

Source: Google trends

ICT technologies are having an increasing impact on companies and the business they run. They are therefore an integral part of the organisation that has a direct impact on efficient and effective working. The versatility of ICT makes it applicable to any enterprise regardless of its industry or size. The benefits can include: cost reduction, improved products or services, innovative solutions, optimisation of existing processes (Lewandowski and Tomczak, 2017). Modern ICT tools positively influence access to all information resources, which are placed in virtual environments. They have revolutionised the approach to data and information management in companies (Perechuda, 2013). Technological trends, as well as innovative approaches that use ICT tools, can include:

- mobility, which defines the growth in the use of mobile solutions in the industrial and business fields;
- cloud computing results in an intensive provision of ICT services and software. Systems are being adapted to current business models, ensuring their flexibility and rapid adaptation to user expectations; (Jelonek et al., 2014)
- dataset analytics focuses on the acquisition of highly specialised and valuable knowledge at the lowest cost;
- the industrial internet of things includes many process activities and, in the main, the remote management of objects that are interconnected in the form of chains. This can include: inventory management, supply chain management, energy consumption, etc.;
- IT security, which is playing an increasingly important role in business and industry. It is based on the implementation of software whose overriding objective is to secure and protect the enterprise at all possible levels; (Kwaśnik and Hetmańczyk, 2020)
- e-learning. (Jelonek et al., 2017)

A very big role in terms of technology is played by advances in communication technology, which is closely related to the transfer of information collections, which is changing the image of modern companies. It is also important to be able to acquire knowledge resources from the environment, e.g. using Big Data technology (Jelonek, 2017; Pawełoszek and Wieczorkowski, 2015). Many organisations are using ICT tools to improve communication processes inside and outside the enterprise, such as intranets and extranets (Chromiak-Orsa, 2016).

Methodology of Research

In-depth interviews were conducted between 27.02 and 04.03.2023. The respondents are economically active, working in large companies with more than 250 employees. Twenty-seven respondents took part in the survey. The study had a pilot character and the sample selection was purposive. It had to meet the following conditions: the survey was open to those working in IT and administration in specialist and managerial positions.

The article sets out the following research hypotheses:

H1: The implementation of solutions using ICT tools depends on the industry of the company.

H2: Knowledge management positively influences employees in companies in the IT and administration sectors.

H3: The remote working model determines the implementation of solutions based on ICT tools.

The interviews focused on the implementation of solutions based on ICT tools and their use in knowledge management transfer, also taking into account the remote working model. The qualitative study conducted was anonymous and participation was completely voluntary. The interviews took place according to a pre-prepared scenario. Each person was asked the same set of questions. The interview with the interviewee lasted on average 20 minutes.

The questions were phrased in a clear and simple manner.

Respondents were asked the following questions:

1) In your opinion, is knowledge management one of the key processes operating in a company?
2) What tools are used in your company to disseminate knowledge?
3) How can knowledge be acquired in your company?
4) Do you think it is important to use ICT tools nowadays?
5) Do you work in a remote working model? In which other model do you work?
6) Do you consider knowledge management in the remote working model to be a very important process?

Empirical Results

Twenty-seven respondents took part in the interviews: 12 women (44%) and 15 men (56%). The interviews were conducted with economically active people who are employed under employment contracts. All respondents (100%) are employed in companies with large company status. The survey covered people who work in the IT sector (60%) and in broadly defined administration (40%). They were divided into 2 groups of positions: specialist/expert (71%) and managerial (29%). All individuals have a university degree.

The questions asked in the scenario were answered by the respondents as follows:

1) In your opinion, is knowledge management the only one of the key processes operating in a company?

Out of a survey sample of 27 respondents—more than 80% answered that knowledge management is a very important process in a company. It provides key information, gives space for the exchange of experience between employees and continuously builds and expands know-how. Respondents from the IT industry confirmed that they have specifically implemented tools that support processes related to knowledge distribution, storage and absorption. Sometimes face-to-face meetings are not required. A big role is played by managers and their taking action in line with the company's strategy. In the case of administration, it is not always a sufficient budget to be able to implement digital-based solutions. There are cases where knowledge is not a very good medium to reach all employees.

2) What tools are used in your company to disseminate knowledge?

There are a lot of innovative solutions in the IT industry. Some of them are bought on the market and others are designed by IT specialists. Responses from those employed in the IT sector confirm that companies can afford to purchase modern technological solutions. They note that the transfer of knowledge between employees and the creation of a knowledge repository as a very important factor that determines a company's competitiveness and maintaining an advantage in the market. Respondents point out that the company's modern approach to technological development also means that they do not have problems with recruitment. Respondents mentioned such tools as an internal intranet, e-learning platforms, systems based on Learning Management Systems, Enterprise Resource Planning systems integrating all processes in the company. For administration, respondents mentioned tools such as an intranet, e-learning platforms, saving files on internal company resources. The overriding problem why there are no other more innovative systems is the lack of financial flexibility for such tools. Knowledge management is important, but this is not proportional to financial resources.

3) How can knowledge be acquired in your company?

Both respondents working in IT and administration answered that the main carrier of knowledge transfer is the exchange of knowledge between employees. The biggest carrier of knowledge is the employee himself. As far as external methods are concerned: participation in internal and external trainings, conferences, studies.

4) Do you think it is important to use ICT tools today?

Respondents representing the IT industry know what ICT tools are and what role they play in companies. They believe that without them, further development as well as the implementation of modern solutions would not be possible. In the case of respondents from the administration sector, it was necessary to explain at the beginning of the interview what ICT tools are and what role they play in companies. After explaining the basics, they unanimously agreed on the need to use them.

5) Do you work in a remote working model? In which other model do you work?

For the IT industry, all respondents (60%) answered that they work in a remote working model. Once a month, they have to be at the company or at company-wide events that assume attendance. As for this sector, it does not require coming to work. Respondents believe that this positively influences their attitude to work and the performance of their duties. In the case of administration, a hybrid working model is mainly used for 28% and a stationary working model for 14%, due to the fact that not all tasks can be done at a computer. There is a proportion of documentation tasks that are not referenced in the systems.

6) Do you think that knowledge management in a remote working model is a very important process?

All interviewees, even those who work in hybrid or onsite working models, agree that knowledge and its management is a fundamental process for the entire company regardless of its industry. Knowledge should be freely available to all employees. It is a resource that is inexhaustible and, on the contrary, an added value for any company. Respondents employed in administration point out that they would work even better if they had properly implemented systems for this.

Conclusion

The intensification of the use and usability of ICT tools has revolutionised the approach of companies to implementing innovative system solutions. Through the method of observation, companies have been paying attention to how and what benefits the implemented systems bring. It seems reasonable that without the global integration of processes and systems, the individual programmes existing in companies will not be maintained and developed in the future. There is also increasing speculation as to whether artificial intelligence and implemented robots will replace the work of employees. The consequence will be a reduction in employment in companies. In this view, knowledge and its proper management is very important. Knowledge is an element that all employees use and will continue to use even with large system integrations. ICT tools are a supporting factor and also provide opportunities for knowledge transfer. They provide opportunities for knowledge exchange, repositories, and contact between employees.

The first hypothesis (H1) was positively verified: The implementation of solutions using ICT tools depends on the industry of the company. Based on the respondents' answers, it is noted that the use of ICT tools depends on the industry of the enterprise. In the IT industry, the use of such solutions is common and popular. Companies invest in such tools because they want to facilitate the work of their employees and they know that the invested capital will pay off. The perception is different among employees who are employed in companies dealing with administration. Despite the implementation of ICT-based solutions, this is not so applied. Solutions are implemented when the situation demands it. This does not indicate that such tools are worth developing.

Hypothesis two (H2) was positively verified: Knowledge management has a positive impact on those employed in companies in IT and administration. The perception of the respondents is very similar. Regardless of the industry, employees are of the opinion that knowledge management is a key process in the entire functioning of the company. Sharing experience and skills creates a foundation on which the company can build and implement new innovative solutions. Employees' intellectual capital contributes to maintaining the company's competitive position in the market.

The third hypothesis (H3) was positively verified: The remote working model determines the implementation of solutions based on ICT tools. The use of ICT tools supports the performance of work in the remote working model. They contribute to the proper transfer of knowledge, as well as communication between employees and the company and employees. The implementation of new technologies also influences the internal development of the company, which is confirmed by the respondents' answers, despite the model in which they perform their duties. In the case of the research conducted, it is confirmed that everything depends on the industry and the financial resources that can be transferred to implement innovative solutions. Working in a remote working model should encourage companies to implement such solutions, which will support and build a strong position in the market.

The research conducted indicates that there is a correlation between the performance of the remote working model and the ICT tools used. An ICT-based solution supports companies in making employees perform remote work. The scheme would not be possible without the knowledge and remoteness of employees. It is acknowledged that knowledge management is a process that is gaining more and more importance and is becoming an increasingly significant process in the overall functioning of companies in the market.

References

Carnoy, M. (2000). Sustaining Flexibility: Work, Family and Community in the Information Age. Cambridge: Harvard University Press.

Chromiak-Orsa, I. (2016). The importance of modern ICT in improving intra-organisational communication. *Business Informatics*, 1(39), 48.

Drucker, P. (1999). Pro-Capitalist Society. Warsaw: Scientific Publishers PWN, (p. 43).

Galata, S. (2004). Strategic Information Management. Knowledge, Intuition, Strategy, Ethics. Difin, Warsaw (p. 50).

Jelonek, D. (2017). Big data analytics in the management of business MATEC web of conferences. *MATEC Web of Conferences*, 125, 04021. doi:10.1051/matecconf/20171250.

Jelonek, D., and Stepniak, C. (2014). Evaluation of the usefulness of abstract thinking as a manager's competence. *Polish Journal of Management Studies*, 9, 62–71.

Jelonek, D., Dunay, A., and Illes, B. C. (2017), Academic e-learning management with e-learning scorecard. *Polish Journal of Management Studies*, 16(2), 122–132.

Jelonek, D., Stepniak, C., Turek, T., and Ziora, L. (2014). Identification of mental barriers in the implementation of cloud computing in the SMEs in Poland. In Federated Conference on Computer Science and Information Systems, FedCSIS 2014, (pp. 1251–1258).

Jerhan, A. (2016). Remote working as a source of work function problems. *Opuscula Sociologica*, 2, 50.

Kwaśnik, Ł., and Hetmańczyk, M. (2020). On how ICT is transforming industry into Industry 4.0. https://przemyslprzyszlosci.gov.pl/o-tym-jak-technologie-ict-zmieniaja-przemysl-w-przemysl-4-0/

The Polish Labour Code (1974). Act of 26 June 1974, art. 67, § 1 and 2.

Lewandowski, J., and Tomczak, J. (2017). Modern ICT technologies as an opportunity for the development of micro-enterprises. *Scientific Journals Organisation and Management*, 68, 1217.

Mikuła, B., Pietruszka-Oryl, A., and Potocki, A. (2002). Business Management for the 21st Century. Difin, Warsaw (p. 69).

Nilles, J. M. (1976). The Telecommunications—Transportation Trade off: Options for Tomorrow. Wiley, (p. 87).

Nilles, J. M. (2003). Teleworking—A Strategy for Managing a Virtual Workforce. Warsaw: Scientific and Technical Publishing, (p. 25).

Nowacka, A., and Jelonek, D. (2022). The impact of the multi-variant remote work model on knowledge management in enterprises. applied tools. In Proceedings of the 17th Conference on Computer Science and Intelligence Systems, FedCSIS 2022, (pp. 827–835).

Pawełoszek, I., and Wieczorkowski, J. (2015). Big data as a business opportunity: an educational perspective In Proceedings of the 2015 Federated Conference on Computer Science and Information Systems, FedCSIS 2015, (pp. 1563–1568).

Perechuda, K. (2013). Knowledge Diffusion in a Networked Enterprise. Visualisation and Composition. Wroclaw: Publishing UE.

Skrzypek, A. (2002). Success Factors for the Company of the Future in a Globalised Environment. Lublin: Maria Curie-Sklodowska University Publishing House.

Toffler, A. (1984). The Third Wave: The Classic Study of Tomorrow. Bantam Books: United States of America.

Turban, E. (1992). Expert Systems and Applied Artifical Intelligence. Prentice Hall Collage: Macmillan.

8 Does Robotic Process Automation Will Shift Examination Process of the Universities in the Future?

Ms Sofia Khan[1,a] and R. K. Tailor[2,b]

[1]Research Scholar, Department of Business Administration, School of Business and Commerce (SBC), Manipal University Jaipur, Rajasthan, India

[2]Associate Professor, Department of Business Administration, School of Business and Commerce, Faculty of Management, and commerce (FOMC), Manipal University, Jaipur, Rajasthan, India

Abstract

The project of managing student's result was carried out in order to automate the previously manual procedures that were required in order to compile students' examination results. Obtaining information and rapidly transforming it into a product that customers want is a vital component to sustain in any business. This can be accomplished in today's world using computers and various applications or information technologies, and there is no denying that the educational system is society's backbone, it is geared toward developing young people's potential for the years to come. The term robotic process automation (RPA) refers to a type of technology that is finding more and more application as a tool that gives users the ability to automate, control, and update existing databases in an effective manner. This paper emphasizes how RPA is being used to integrate repetitive tasks within different departments of the universities and automate many of the processes that exist when managing Students' Examination Results. The solution provides the teachers and administration with the ability to convert the marksheets which are in pdf format into excel format automatically, leading to the requirement of fewer laborious and stressful duties, then the raw scores could be taken directly from excel files and automatically save in the database management system. The primary objective here is to develop an effective computerised system or software robot using UiPath that can substitute the manual processing and recording of results of students, which typically involves a lot of paperwork and is prone to errors. This article is explaining does RPA will shift examination process of the universities in the future?

Keywords

Artificial intelligence, machine learning, RPA, UI path studio.

Introduction

Robotic process automation (RPA) is the most recent automated business processing technology, and it's altering businesses in incredible ways attributed to software bots or artificial workers (Tailor, R. K., & Khan, S. 2022). RPA is changing the way business is done by automating and transforming key and manual activities within a company

[a]sofiakhanlagos@gmail.com, [b]rajeshkumar.tailor@jaipur.manipal.edu

(Mosteanu, 2022). RPA techniques and tools are made to carry out manual and repetitive work that would otherwise be done by human workers (Ahuja, Shefali & Tailor, R. 2022). The machines interact with various information systems through the front end, this software differs from other traditional ones. RPA not only helps businesses save money by reducing the workload and also errors made by workers (Osman, 2019).

To create tomorrow's worldwide citizens, education is crucial. The adoption of automated technology in universities has led to advancements like smart boards, online learning environments, smartphone applications for schools, and much more (Barman A, 2020). On average, staff in universities spend an entire day at work per week on tedious and routine duties and activities, which takes up more than half of their time. In today's new educational system, technology plays a significant part in automating activities based on rules, tasks that are repetitive, and tasks that are tedious that consume time (Gupta et al., 2022). Using RPA in education systems, paperwork, and labor-intensive procedures will be reduced. The RPA software is useful for various departments like administration, admission, Human resource, finance, placements, etc. (Khan et al., 2022). The use of RPA in universities enhances effectiveness and productivity, saves a lot of time, and allows highly qualified staff to work on various additional important duties (Thorave et al., 2022). RPA, a software robot is a virtual employee who mimics the actions of human and performs all the tasks more efficiently than human and results in better output in less time with less errors and reduction in stress.

Student administration system (SAS) is typically an enterprise resource planning (ERP) based solution that manages all of the information that is associated with the students, this is organized into sections and gives users access to an immense amount of information. The method maintains accurate records of the grades earned by all of the department's students at all times (Almgren J. E., 2021). The implementation of the ERP system, however, comes at a high expense. ERP specialists have very high costs and paying them consumes roughly sixty percent of the budget. The workforce, their schooling, and their understanding of how to make the system function correctly all play a role in determining how successful the project will be. As a result, RPA has also been widely used to perform manual processes in order to support procedures such as registration and data upload. Not only has this resulted in the automation of routine tasks requiring little to no involvement from a human workforce, but it has also led to an increase in the effectiveness of managing and storing students' examination results. One type of business process automation technology is robotic process automation which is built on artificial intelligence/digital workers or on software robots, RPA is also known as software robotics (Tailor, R. K., 2020). It is the gathering of several different automation technologies into a single toolset for use in a variety of situations. The reason to employ RPA in this project is to make it easy to automate it, thereby reducing the amount of work required by the instructors, thereby allowing to save time and ensuring that the final product was free of mistakes that are caused by human intervention (Kumar, S., & Tailor, R.K., 2023). Historically, ERP-based database solutions have been utilised in order to handle the student information management system. It is necessary to have a consistent operator who updates the student records in order to ensure that student records are continually updated. Even though manual data entry is an identified risk, it is one that can be reduced through the use of RPA. The application will handle the result information for students who have registered and appeared in the exams in different years, the marks that were obtained, etc will be recorded in the excel sheet for further use (Johnson, F., & Eide, S. S., 2018). The application will make the process of managing and downloading the results pdfs from email and recording them in excel format, it is significantly less complicated and much more efficient. RPA is a type of technology that not only optimizes processes but also increases the speed at which universities can operate (Tailor, R. K., & Khan, S., 2022). The goal of this project is to construct a system that will be able to handle information about students' examination results from all different semesters as well as from different branches and the grades students receive throughout the semesters as well as the production of reports. Due to the fact that the project is entirely constructed at the administrative end, access is only guaranteed to the administrator (Turcu, C., & Turcu, C., 2020, June). The creation of a software program to lessen the need for physical labour is the aim of the project. Despite the fact that there is a program that produces the results, it is not highly productive because there is a lot of time consumption and human resource consumption in the system, in completing a variety of activities, it is expensive, and also there is a lack of both data security and efficiency. At this point, the establishment requires an environment that is technologically sophisticated and computerized. And once it is implemented, it will reduce the severity of all the problems that were enumerated (Nadar et al., 2021).

Suggested Application of RPA

RPA is a software robot that uses software machines to simulate human business process execution. This means that the task is completed on the system using the same interface as a human (Lasso-Rodríguez, G., & Gil-Herrera, R., 2019). It types, selects, opens files, folders, applications, and shortcuts on keyboard are also used by it. It decreases human error and expenses. RPA eliminates the blunders to which human workers are prone, especially during lengthy repetitive tasks caused by fatigue and boredom. This results in more accurate, timely, and consistent work, preventing time and money from being wasted, and rectifying the work done previously (Lasso-Rodríguez, G., & Gil-Herrera, R., 2020). Utilizing RPA technology, the pdf file of student results can be converted to excel documents. It has also been discovered to be essential for automating ERP system processes. Using RPA, student result management in an ERP system can be managed efficiently and error-free. However, the installation and setup of the ERP is expensive. The consultants of ERP are extremely costly, consuming a large amount of the budget. Whether the system is functioning successfully is contingent on the talents and experience, capability of the workforce, including education and knowledge regarding the proper system functioning. Consequently, we favour RPA, it is a software robot that facilitates the construction, implementation, and management of the software robots that simulate human interaction with systems and software digitally. Same as humans, by mimicking them software robots understands displayed things on a screen, complete the accurate inputs, identify, and extract the data, navigate systems and variety of pre-defined actions, it can perform. However, software robots perform activities quickly, efficiently, consistently and accurately than humans can perform, without the need to take any kind of halt (Joshi, N., 2019).

Figure 8.1 explains how RPA software robot is developed using UiPath where the robot will receive the mails of attached marksheets from the examination department for conversion into excel. Then the robot will read the mails and download the

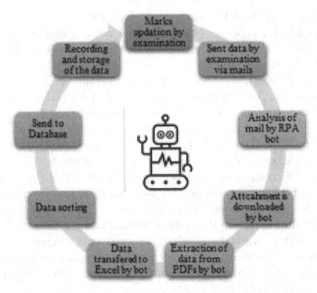

Figure 8.1 Result management system, using RPA software robots.

attachment in the file folder. Next step of robot will be to read the pdfs and extract the concerned data from pdf files and transfer them in excel format. The forms which are recorded in the excel file will then be transferred to different folder like completed folder and the robot will continue to perform the task for remaining pdf files. The data recorded by software robot in excel will be for all the student of all the departments. Now the assigned person will sort the data and send it to database for storing the data for further reference. Sorting the data and storing in the database can also be done by the robot. The database can be designed using computer application like firebase which can be used in student result management system. All the student result management system data and information can further be stored in system database.

Why is RPA Required in Examinations Department in the Universities?

Examination plays an important and major role in the university to function properly and helps to grow the university at a faster pace. There is process automation (PA) applied in the universities, multiple stakeholders have always been engaged in the PA educational ecosystem, which is also overloaded with tiresome tasks, it is costly to implement and requires a lot of skill, knowledge and expertise to handle, and with time there is need to upgrade the technology to the fullest to boost productivity (Khan, S., Tailor, R. K., Uygun, H., & Gujrati, R., 2022). Thus, there is a need to establish RPA in the universities. To implement software robot, it is developed through UiPath, Automation Anywhere, Blue Prism etc., RPA in the universities can eliminate a significant amount of manual labor and paperwork from school management processes. This enables the staff to concentrate on other important factors, improving efficiency and cutting down on mistakes (Nallasivam, 2022). Recording each data one by one takes time and effort, especially for courses with a large enrollment. For recording and storing the data, the RPA robot can be designed using a rule-based framework like UiPath.

The workload burden faced by examinations like recording each and every entry into excel and storing it into database by human, takes a lot of time and there are chances of high errors, and it becomes stressful, all this can be reduced with the use of RPA. RPA allows to set up software robots, define parameters, and check the requirements, receives and download emails, transfer the data from one format to another, and send the data to the database and finally mail it to the concerned departments. The software robots based on demand enables elastic stability, which means if there are large volume of data to deal with, it can easily and efficiently do it. There is no need to increase the workload of your current resources or recruit more. Compared to PA, RPA process produces quick turnaround times and contributes to cost savings while assuring process accuracy (Hurix, 2020).

Using RPA automation in the universities can maximise outcomes by allowing the staff to make better use of their precious time and indulge in more productive work. Numerous educational institutions are moving in the direction of robotic process automation, which greatly aids teachers and students in their various academic pursuits and is also beneficial in non-academic activities (Ippolito, P. P., 2019). RPA can increase output with less effort and decrease reliance on humans for all routine tasks. In the universities, RPA helps to eliminate data inconsistencies between various sources and keeps a log of every action the software robots take while conducting automation (Neethu V Joy, Sreelakshmi P G, 2020). Employees are able to conduct routine internal reviews and proactively identify and handle problems with compliance as a result.

Why UiPath Should be Used in RPA?

The UiPath platform is simple to use, and it is user friendly, has a vision of intelligent automation, extensive governance capabilities, and total product package. Other platforms like Automation Anywhere, Blue Prism, for example, demand significantly

Figure 8.2 Magic quadrant for robotic process automation.
Source: Gartner, 2022

The table below provides a quick snapshot of the leading RPA tools.

	Year Founded	HQ Location	Annual Revenue	Employees	Customers	Investment & Funding to date	Valuation
UiPath	2005	New York, NY	$968.7M	4,013	10,650+	$3.3B	$6.4B
Automation Anywhere	2003	San Jose, CA	$336.3M	1,600	5,000+	$1B	$7.3B
Blue Prism	2001	Warrington, UK	$218.4M	1,000	2,000+	$208.4M	$1.6B

Figure 8.3 Leading RPA tools.

Source: Corredor, 2021

higher coding skills, which lengthens the implementation process. With its ability to support the entire automation lifecycle, from discovery to measurement, UiPath has developed into the market's top RPA tool as shown in the Figures 8.2 and 8.3.

Automation Anywhere allows only restricted real-time collaboration between various developers. The platform from UiPath is designed with a wide variety of user groups in mind, including business technologists, fusion teams, and software engineers, throughout the process automation lifecycle. The near-term product plan for UiPath also includes Studio Web, a brand-new web-based design platform that can be used to build cloud automation. There is UiPath's pre-packaged, sector-specific solutions that shorten customers' time-to-value as well as the company's strong commitment to client success, training, and support. UiPath offers free, instructor-led, self-paced training in several languages that are specialized for various individuals, such as expert developers and business analysts. It also encourages the growth of a sizable online user group for cooperation and knowledge exchange. Attended robots of Automation Anywhere still only offer surveillance and deployment capabilities, and in the case of Blue Prism, essentially none at all. For many clients, UiPath offers the ideal blend of attended and unattended automation.

UiPath is frequently 3–4 times faster compared to other RPA products, making it one of the fastest and best RPA options in the market. Additionally, UiPath's attended robots have unmatched abilities. Attended robots assist human employees at their workstations and are started by the actions, instructions, or specific events that an employee performs as part of a particular workflow.

Workflow of RPA Software Robot Developed Using UiPath

Using UiPath, the workflow is developed, that facilitates the conversion of PDF file format into Excel format as shown in the Figure 8.4. The instructors will have easy access to this workflow on the learning management system. In this workflow, the pdf files will first be received or saved in the folder. This pdf file will then be transformed using the operation write text file into a text document. The pdf's contents will then be read using the action read text file and further transformed into the desired Excel file format.

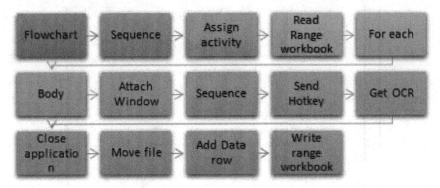

Figure 8.4 Workflow of RPA software robot developed using UiPath.

The sample of the input workflow and the results and output retrieved with the use of the workflow are presented in the Figures 8.5–8.11 presented below.

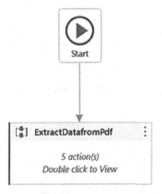

Figure 8.5 Workflow of Pdfs conversion to excel using UiPath.

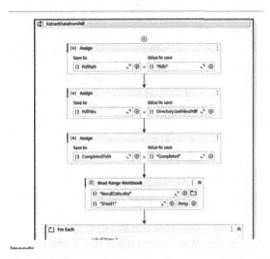

Figure 8.6 Workflow of Pdfs conversion to excel using UiPath.

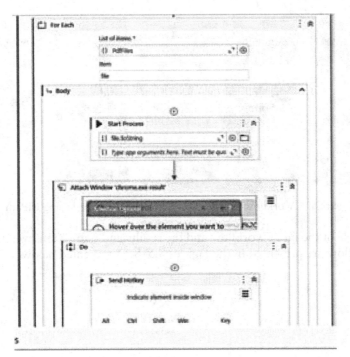

Figure 8.7 Workflow of Pdfs conversion to excel using UiPath.

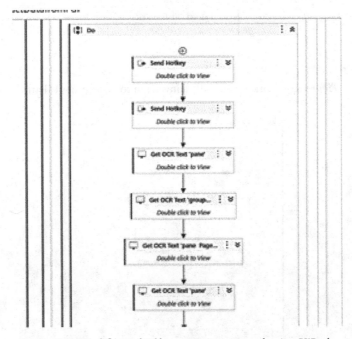

Figure 8.8 Workflow of Pdfs conversion to excel using UiPath.

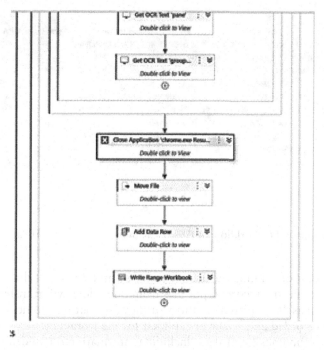

Figure 8.9 Workflow of Pdfs conversion to excel using UiPath.

Figure 8.10 Workflow of Pdfs conversion to excel using UiPath.

The developed workflow requires the result pdf file that is received from the concerned department through the mail, needs to be converted to excel format. The required excel sheet will be obtained after running the file is shown in Figure 8.9. For the demonstration, the Result pdf file is used as a sample that will be transformed into an excel sheet (ResultData) shown in Figure 8.9 using the workflow process developed.

	A	B	C	D	E	F
1	**Reg No**	**Name**	**Branch/Specialization**	**Semester**	**GPA**	
	190903014	MEGHNA DHURIYA	B COM (HONOURS) IN ACCOUNTING	II	7.46	
	191014006	RUCHIKA KUMARI	MASTER OF SCIENCE	I	8.00	
	190903014	MEGHNA DHURIYA	B COM (HONOURS) IN ACCOUNTING	III	8.2	
	191014006	RUCHIKA KUMARI	MASTER OF SCIENCE	II	8.47	
	190903014	MEGHNA DHURIYA	B COM (HONOURS) IN ACCOUNTING	VI	8.3	
	190903014	MEGHNA DHURIYA	B COM (HONOURS) IN ACCOUNTING	I	7.35	
	191014006	RUCHIKA KUMARI	MASTER OF SCIENCE	III	8.08	
	190903014	MEGHNA DHURIYA	B COM (HONOURS) IN ACCOUNTING	V	8.32	
	191014006	RUCHIKA KUMARI	MASTER OF SCIENCE	IV	10.00	
	190903014	MEGHNA DHURIYA	B COM (HONOURS) IN ACCOUNTING	IV	8.83	

Figure 8.11 Workflow of Pdfs conversion to excel using UiPath.

This is the outcome of running the demonstrated sample result pdf through the UiPath workflow. At the end the recorded pdf files from one folder will transfer to the different folder known as "Completed" in this workflow, so that it becomes easy to analyse which files are recorded and which are still left for the storage.

The entire system consists of data, including information on students' results. Faculty can interact with students in person and can keep track of and be updated on their progress. Users can have full access to the system, but with certain restrictions. Human interventions can be reduced with the implementation of RPA which will result in less burden and stress, accurate and efficient work and in enhanced productivity in the universities.

Conclusion

It is concluded in this study that the system will function properly, which means it will satisfy the end user's needs. The system will be user-friendly, enabling everyone to use the program with little to no errors. The goals were also accomplished by adhering to a process structure that included system assessment, design, and execution. The two actions that made up the system assessment were determining the requirements and structuring them. The first task was to gather information or requirements through communication with random people, workplace observations, and the collection of data from random individuals along with additional documents. Thus, using robotic process automation (RPA) technology can lessen the tedious job and relieve the faculty's stress or the burden to the staff related to the concerned work associated with result data entry. There has been an effort to use RPA as the backend technology, but there are still a few areas that need more research, particularly those that deal with the integration of unstructured data and offering crucial research ideas like a large amount of data that cannot be displayed in the rows and columns, which requires a lot of space for storage in the database, integration, and analysis of such data requires further research. This requires effective computations, queries, and records as well as transaction-keeping. The system interface could be enhanced in the near future with attractive, collaborative, and insightful representations. If a comprehensive solution has not been developed, improve the existing system by automating nearly all of the services offered by the institutions, converting it into a complete Learning Management System (LMS), and growing and expanding the system by developing multiple versions through user feedback. Therefore, it is concluded that application of RPA using UiPath in the university will result in enhanced productivity, timely completion of tasks or say before time completion, reduction in stress of students and staff. It reduces the chance of errors or blunders done by humans and also it reduces their burden, so that they could focus on other activities and task which actually need their attention, to boost the productivity.

References

Ahuja, Shefali and Tailor, R. (2022). Critical evaluation of application of robotic process automation on toll plaza. *Journal of Information and Optimization Sciences*. 43. 1801–1813. 10.1080/02522667.2022.2134368.

Almgren, J. E. (2021). Opportunities and Challenges of Robotic Process Automation (RPA) in the Administration of Education (Dissertation). Retrieved from https://urn.kb.se/resolve?urn=urn:nbn:se:kth:diva-296540

Barman, A. (2020). Transforming the education landscape with RPA. Retrieved from nalashaa: https://www.nalashaa.com/transforming-education-industry-with-rpa/

Turcu, C., and Turcu, C. (2020, June). On robotic process automation and its integration in higher education. In Conference Proceedings. The Future of Education 10th Edition 2020.

Corredor, F. (2021). Guide: Best RPA Tools and Why UiPath is# 1. https://www.auxis.com/blog/top-rpa-tools

Johnson, F., and Eide, S. S. (2018). An inquiry into robotic process automation implementation in institutions for higher education: a case study of RPA implementation at the section for admissions at the Norwegian School of Economics (Master's thesis).

Ray, S., Villa, A., Tornbohm, C., Rashid, N., and Alexander, M. (2021). Magic quadrant for robotic process automation. Von Gartner: https://www. gartner. com/doc/reprints.

Gupta, A., Prabhat, P., Sawhney, S., Gupta, R., Tanwar, S., Kumar, N., and Shabaz, M. (2023). Retracted: Robotic Process Automation use cases in academia and early implementation experiences. *IET Software*, 17(4), 600–609.

Hurix (2020). 6 ways to improve efficiency with RPA in higher education. https://www.hurix.com/rpa-higher-education/

Ippolito, P. P. (2019). Robotic process automation (RPA) Using UiPath. https://towardsdata-science.com/robotic-process-automation-rpa-using-uipath-7b4645aeea5a

Joshi, N. (2019). Here's what RPA means to the education sector. https://www.allerin.com/blog/heres-what-rpa-means-to-the-education-sector

Khan, S., Tailor, R. K., Uygun, H., and Gujrati, R. (2022). Application of robotic process automation (RPA) for supply chain management, smart transportation and logistics. *International Journal of Health Sciences*, 11051–11063.

Khan, S., Tailor, R. K., Pareek, R., Gujrati, R., and Uygun, H. (2022). Application of Robotic Process Automation in education sector. *Journal of Information and Optimization Sciences*, 43(7), 1815–1834.

G. Lasso-Rodríguez, R. Gil-Herrera (2019) Robotic process automation applied to education: A new kind of robot teacher? *ICERI 2019 Proceedings*, pp. 2531–2540.

G. Lasso-Rodríguez, and R. Gil-Herrera (2020) Training the teachers with assistance of robotic process automation, *INTED 2020 Proceedings*, pp. 8714–8720.

Mosteanu, N. R. (2022). Machine learning and robotic process automation take higher education one step further. *Science and Technology*, 25(1), 92–99.

Nadar, M., Naidu, V., Ragava, I., Rana, S., and Ravale, U. (2021). Student result administration system using RPA. *International Journal for Research in Engineering Application & Management (IJREAM)*. DOI : 10.35291/2454-9150.2021.0613

Neethu V Joy, Sreelakshmi P. G., 2020, Robotic Process Automation role in Education Field, *International Journal of Engineering Research & Technology (IJERT) NSDARM*–2020 (Volume 8–Issue 04).

Cristina-Claudia OSMAN, 2019. Robotic Process Automation: Lessons Learned from Case Studies, Informatica Economica, Academy of Economic Studies—Bucharest, Romania, vol. 23(4), pp. 66–71.

Palanivel, K., and Joseph, K. S. (2020). Robotic Process Automation to Smart Education. *International Journal of Creative Research Thoughts*, 8(6), 3775–3784.

Tailor, R. K., and Khan, S. (2022). Fintech in Investment Management for Modern Entrepreneurs. *Academy of Entrepreneurship Journal*, 28(2).

Kumar, S., and Tailor, R.K. (2023). Application of Robotic Process Automation (Rpa) in supermarket. *Academy of Marketing Studies Journal*, 27(S6), 1–5.

Tailor, R. K. (2020). Application of robotic process automation in queue system of shopping malls in India. International Journal of Advanced Research in Commerce, Management & Social Science (IJARCMSS), Volume 03, 234–238.

Tailor, R. K., and Khan, S. (2022). Robotic Process Automation (RPA) in the Aviation Sector. In Global Air Transport Management and Reshaping Business Models for the New Era (pp. 289–300). IGI Global.

Thorave, C., Dinesh A., Pratik B., Abhinandan G., and Mayur. (2022). Robotic Process Automation (RPA) in Education Industry. *International Journal of Advanced Research in Science, Communication and Technology*. Volume 2, 14–19. 10.48175/IJARSCT-4004.

9 Motivating Engineering Students to Participate in Highly Skilled Competitions

Husham M. Ahmed

Professor, College of Engineering, University of Technology Bahrain, Kingdom of Bahrain

Abstract

Encouraging and motivating engineering students to engage in highly skilled competitions can be a daunting endeavor, yet it plays a fundamental role in fostering their professional growth. These competitions offer an opportunity for students to showcase their skills, knowledge, and creativity to a wider audience. Unfortunately, most universities and schools face the problem of how to engage their students in high-level competitions that require specific skills, dedication, desire, patience, time, and hard work. In addition, the competitions require a substantial investment in resources and time commitment, which adds to the challenges of participation.

This study aims to share an experience and to discuss successful approaches for inspiring students who lack knowledge, skills and confidence in robotics and automation to passionately involve and enthusiastically participate in highly skilled scientific competitions and advanced technological challenges. in the field of robotics and automations. The key issue in encouraging student engagement in competitions are suitable motivation and effective training. Two approaches have been put into practice—tactical, aimed at addressing short-term issues, and strategic, focused on resolving long-term challenges. The results proved that incentives are a powerful motivator for students. They encourage students to work harder and push themselves to reach their full potential. It also proves that effective training is also crucial for encouraging student engagement in competitions. Training helps students to develop their skills and knowledge and gives them the confidence they need to participate in competitions. When students have a solid understanding of the subject matter and know what to expect in the competition, they perform well and enjoy the experience.

Keywords

Collaborative projects, engineering student motivations, student competitions, student incentives, students engagements.

Introduction

Enhancing and Improving the quality of student experience, with a particular focus in their engagement, has become a central objective and a a key priority of higher education and is gaining significant global attention (Patfield et al., 2022; Bryson, 2014).

---

hmahmed@utb.edu,bh

It provides students with a platform to showcase their enhanced thinking skills and expand their knowledge by offering them the chance to apply what they have learned through practical exercises. It offers an opportunity for students to demonstrate how their cognitive abilities can be improved and how they can effectively apply their acquired knowledge in real-life scenarios. By engaging in active practice and application, students can further develop and expand their thinking skills, ultimately enhancing their overall learning experience (Najdanovic-Visak, 2017).

The motivation for learning is a main problem in a modern university, where motivation is the source of activity that performs an urgent function and brings sense to the learning process. Activity without a motive or with weak motivation may not implement or may implement with weak results and would be highly unstable. The amount of effort a student takes to study depends on what she/he feels in a particular situation. Therefore, it is important during the learning process that students develop a strong desire to gain scientific experience and practical skills (Bazylev et al., 2014; Verner and Ahlgren, 2007).

Motivation refers to an inner psychological characteristic of personality, shows a person's attitude toward different activities. It is one of the key factors for successful preparation of highly qualified professionals with extensive knowledge, both in classical and in the most advanced fields of science and technology. Most schools and universities are facing problems involving young people in practical science. It is hard to motivate students employing abundant, but single theory. Often, they lose interest in the middle of the way (Bobtsov, et al., 2012; Zainuddin et al., 2020). Employing inter-group competitions engage students in learning subject content and finding creative solutions in ways that stimulate creativity through hands-on learning and team collaboration (Chen and Chiu, 2016). As a result, the competitions will increase interest and motivation not only in the subjects necessary for the development and control of robots, but also to other disciplines within the studying course (Bobtsov et al., 2012). In addition, participation in training program significantly improved student confidence and skilfulness (Fortune at al., 2018). Intrinsic motivation and student engagement have a significant effect on creativity. In fact, the key to a successful contest lies in whether the enterprise can understand students' motivation to engage in the contests and the factors affecting their creativity. When individuals are intrinsically motivated and actively engaged in their learning, it positively influences their ability to think creatively. This suggests that personal drive and active involvement play vital roles in fostering creative thinking among students (Tseng et al., 2022).

Xerri et al. (2018) reported that student engagement in academic activities in higher education plays a crucial role in determining overall student success. They found that factors such as peer relationships, teacher-student relationships, and students' sense of purpose for pursuing a higher education degree are key contributors to student engagement. Additionally, strong teacher-student relationships and a clear sense of purpose influence perceptions of student workloads. Moreover, the sense of purpose acts as a moderator in the relationship between teacher-student and student-student relationships, as well as perceptions of workload and student engagement.

In their study, Schuster et al. (2006) explored the key benefits that engineering undergraduate students gain by participating in team design competitions. The researchers found that these intercollegiate design competitions offer an effective way to involve students in design activities that go beyond their regular curriculum. When students come together outside of their regular class hours to collaboratively design, construct, and test a product for these competitions, an incredible transformation occurs. They cultivate a genuine passion for engineering. The researchers also emphasized the significant impact of advisor guidance on the success of the projects and the overall learning experience for the students.

This work showcased a triumphant experience of how both students and faculty can be encouraged to engage in highly skilled competitions and advanced technological challenges energetically and enthusiastically within the field of robotics and automation.

Problem Statement

The College of Engineering offers two programs: Mechatronics Engineering and Informatics Engineering. These programs are closely connected to the fields of control and robotics. Robotics serves as the core discipline, and the curriculum includes a substantial emphasis on both theoretical knowledge and practical laboratory experiments. Proficiency in mechanical, electronic, electrical, and computer engineering is crucial for success in the field of robotics.

There are two types of highly specialized competitions available in which students at the College of Engineering can engage and apply their knowledge, thinking skills, and most importantly robotic specific skills. The first competition is the GCC Robotics Challenge, which is a regional competition for the Arab Gulf Cooperation Council countries and is organized and supervised by the Institutes of Engineering Technology (IET). The second competition is the World Robotic Olympiad (WRO). It is organized and supervised by the World Robot Olympiad Association. The main goal of the competitions is to develop and enhance student's creativity, design, and problem solving through challenging and educational robotic tasks and activities. The competitions include a task whose main objective is to develop and enhance students' creativity, critical thinking, design and problem-solving skills through challenging educational robotics competitions and activities.

The primary challenge revolved around recruiting students who were willing to participate in those and other competitions. They were reluctant as it needs lots of preparation, testing and practicing in addition to the level of knowledge and specific skills in the field of Robotics, Programming, Control, and mechanical design. Moreover, the problem was further compounded by the fact that only fourth-year students were eligible to participate, thereby limiting the number of students who could engage in such activities. Additionally, close supervision from faculty members was necessary due to the advanced level of knowledge required. This is in line with the findings of Schuster et al. (2006) that advisor involvement plays a key role in both project success and student learning throughout the process.

In 2016, the College of Engineering received an invitation to take part in the inaugural GCC Robotics Competition. Unfortunately, the college had to decline the invitation due to a lack of student interest and participation. In January 2017, the College of Engineering received an invitation to join the 2nd GCC Robotics Challenge. The local round of this competition is scheduled for March 25, 2017, and the final round will take place in Qatar on April 29, 2017. Each university is allowed to have two teams participating in the local round, but only one team can qualify for the final round. Unfortunately, no students were willing to participate this year, citing similar reasons as the previous year. Furthermore, the timing of the local round coincides closely with the midterm exams, adding to the students' reluctance. It should be noted that the competition involves six rounds, each requiring the design of robots to perform six different functions.

A similar situation arises in the WRO (World Robot Olympiad) competition. This international competition allows two teams from each institute to participate in the local round, and the winning teams from the local round advance to the final round. In the previous two years, our college only entered one team, which managed to qualify for the international round as runner-up. However, this year posed a challenge as the students who had expertise and participated in the WRO competition in the previous two years had already graduated. The program heads faced difficulty in finding students who were willing to invest their time and effort in participating in this year's competition. Due to this predicament, they were even considering recommending against participating in the WRO competition this year.

The situation became more challenging due to the overlap of the local rounds of the WRO competition and the final round of the GCC competition in the same month. This necessitated the formation of separate teams of students and coaches for each competition, adding complexity to the logistics. Additionally, sourcing components, spare parts, materials, equipment, and other resources added pressure, as these items are not easily accessible in the local market and require both time and money for importation. This is in line with the concern expressed by Patfield et al. (2021) that academics are facing increasing pressure to demonstrate effective teaching, as higher education is now acknowledged as a crucial catalyst for competitiveness in the global knowledge economy.

Tactical Approach Solution

In order to effectively motivate faculty members and students, a tactical approach was proposed and put into action. Consequently, the dean of the college of engineering approached faculty members who have expertise in robotics. The dean sought their opinion on reducing their workload and dedicating more time to supervising students. The faculty members agreed to this arrangement, expressing their commitment to finding dedicated students and allocating sufficient time to fulfill their responsibilities. The proposal aligns with the findings of Cents-Boonstra et al. (2021), which revealed evident correlations between teacher motivation, their instructional practices, and student engagement.

On the other hand, in accordance with the teaching policy, every student is required to submit an in-course project for each subject they are enrolled in, at the end of every trimester. A proposal was presented to the academic council suggesting the substitution of student in-course projects with competition requirements in the GCC Robotics Challenge. This plan aims to enhance student motivation, particularly if it aligns with their work and studies. The academic council supported the idea because, basically, students in the preparation for such a high-level participation will acquire knowledge far more than ordinary simple in-course projects.

A meeting was called for the final year students and suggested the idea. Amazingly, more than twenty students agreed to participate in the competition. The specialized academic staffs chose the best ten students and were able to form two teams. The two teams worked hard and willingly spent all days long, including the weekends designing and testing their work. A meeting was organized for the senior students to present the proposal idea. More than twenty students showed interest in participating in the competition. The specialized faculty members selected the top ten students and successfully formed two teams. Both teams dedicated themselves to the project, investing long hours to design and test their work. In the local competition, the two teams confidently won first and second place out of five teams. The first team then advanced to the regional round in Qatar. They participated in the final round held in Qatar on April 29, 2017, and achieved the impressive fourth position out of a total of 13 teams.

To address the issue of student and staff availability for the WRO competition, a similar approach was taken. Two teams were created, consisting of six selected students. The local round of the competition happened just one week after the final exams and during the term break. In order to ensure continuous supervision during the preparation period, the faculty members overseeing the teams agreed to take turns sacrificing their vacation time, ensuring that at least one instructor was present at all times.

Once a team completed the design of their robot, they implemented another supportive tactic by inviting specialized faculty members to attend the testing phase. The faculty members provided valuable feedback, comments, and recommendations for further improvements. As a result, both teams that took part in the local round of the WRO competition secured the first and second places respectively. The winning team successfully qualified for the international round of the competition. Unfortunately, despite qualifying, the winning team was unable to participate in the final round in Costa Rica in November 2017 due to visa-related technicalities faced by some of the students.

Despite achieving satisfactory results, there was a need for a long-term solution to effectively encourage faculty and students to consistently participate in such competitions as well as other similar events. That is an interesting concept, and it aligns with current research in education, particularly the focus on achieving effective education for sustainable development. Howell (2021) highlights the importance of using appropriate teaching methods that actively engage learners in transformative learning experiences to promote sustainable development. This approach recognizes that simply imparting knowledge is not enough; instead, educators should provide opportunities for learners to critically analyze and apply the knowledge in real-life contexts, fostering a deeper understanding and ownership of sustainable development principles.

Strategic Approach Solution

A comprehensive and long-term strategy is crucial to enhance the participation of students in high-level specialized competitions. Practically, only fourth-year students possess the necessary knowledge and skills to participate in such events. The strategy should not solely rely on fourth-year students but instead, focus on attracting outstanding students from second and third-year levels by offering them the opportunity to attend specialized workshops that provide fundamental and specialized skills for designing and operating different types of robots. By doing so, the college will benefit from having permanent teams with exceptional accumulated experience for at least two or three years. In subsequent years, fresh outstanding students from second and third-year levels can join participating teams, thereby transferring knowledge and experience among participating students.

To implement this strategy, specialized faculty members initiated an intensive training course as part of the strategy implementation. A general meeting was subsequently organized for all second- and third-year students, during which the benefits and learning experiences that could be gained from competition participation were explained. In addition, videos and presentations from previous year's tournaments were shown to the students. Surprisingly, the workshop drew registrations from 84 students, which exceeded expectations.

The training program has been designed to be delivered in two stages: the basic stage and the advanced stage. During each stage, which lasts for two months, participating students acquire the necessary knowledge, general and special skills required for design and development of robots. The training program covers a variety of topics, including computer programming, engineering, physics, and mathematics. Students are also introduced to different programming languages, which are used for creating robot programs and advanced software development. Additionally, students gain knowledge in fundamental robotics concepts, such as kinematics, mechanical design, and sensors. Each stage involves four hours of classes on a weekly basis.

The 84 students who participated in the workshop were divided into four groups so that the students would choose the most appropriate timing for attendance that do not interfere with their lectures. When the first stage got completed after two months, 22 of the most creative and committed students that showed excellent performance were selected. They were enrolled in the advanced stage of the workshop. After completing the second stage, 10 students were selected to form the college's two teams to participate in the GCC Robotics Challenge. Another six students were selected to form the college's two teams in the WRO contest. The selected students represent a remarkable diversity in nationalities of both genders. At the same time, required resources of components, parts, instrumentation that the students may need in their preparations and work have been secured. To ensure that the 84 students attending the workshop were able to select a schedule that did not clash with their lectures, they were split into four groups. Following the completion of the initial phase after two months, the most dedicated and innovative

Results and Outcomes

In January 2018, the college of engineering received the invitation to participate in the 3rd GCC Robotics Challenge. The local round fixture to be on March 19, 2018, and the final round of all six GCC countries to be on April 21, 2018, and both rounds to be held in Bahrain at the University of Bahrain. The two selected teams carefully studied the competition instruction, regulations, and procedures. They started developing different design and ideas for the six different functions that the robots perform. In the local round, the students beat all other teams and won first and second place. The team that won the first place scored 100 points out of 120; the team winning the second place scored 91 points out of 120, while the third scored only 60 points out of

120. This clearly reflects the quality of work and competency of the two teams. The two-winning team received the invitation to participate in the final round on April 21, 2018. The final round commenced the week after the final exam directly, which gave the students very little time for final tuning and adjustment of the robots. Nevertheless, the two college teams won third and fourth place and only one point was the difference between the second and third place. Ten teams participated in the final round of the challenge.

In Jan 2019, the college of engineering has received the invitation to participate in the 4th GCC Robotics Challenge; a team has been formed from the same student cluster and won the first place for local round in March 2019 held at the University of Bahrain. The winning team represented Bahrain in the regional round took place on 6th April 2019 in the Canadian University of Dubai and won the excellent design trophy.

For the WRO competition, another team won the local round took place on April 2019 and represented Bahrain in the international round that took place in Gyor-Hungary on 8–10 Nov 2019.

In summary, since the motivation program started, all college of engineering teams have won all local rounds for GCC Robotic Challenges and the WRO Competitions and actively participated in the regional or international rounds.

The most important achievement was not only engaging and wining competitions, but the activities and the challenging environment have inspired many other students to request joining the teams during competitions preparations in such way that the preparation periods have become a training field for new participant. Unfortunately, these competitions have been suspended due to the spread of covid-19. This in This aligns with the findings of Xerri et al. (2018) study, which supports the importance of developing effective teacher-student relationships, facilitating positive student-student relationships, and communicating a clear sense of purpose to students. These actions can improve student engagement in academic activities and optimize perceptions of workloads. It is also in aligns with the research findings of Tseng et al. (2022), which suggest that intrinsic motivation and student engagement play a vital role in fostering creativity.

In school year 2022, The GCC Robotic challenge resumed online, and a team from the College of Engineering participated in the regional competition winning third place among the six teams representing the six GCC countries. The results align with the findings of a study conducted by (Jääskä and Aaltonen 2022). They discovered that the implementation of game-based learning (GBL) positively impacted students' motivation to study and comprehend project management concepts. The study also revealed that GBL can effectively prepare learners to handle uncertain situations that they might encounter in real-life projects.

The innovative and technologically advanced students of the new generation, who were mentored by their peers and guided by faculty members, showcased their talents at the international virtual expo of innovation product and system design in 2023. This event, known as "embracing the spirit of innovation and technology," took place on June 23, 2023. The students successfully designed, built, and tested two remarkable robotic creations. One of their creations, the tele-presence robot, impressed the judges and earned them the prestigious gold award. This robot allowed users to remotely interact with their environment and navigate through any space, providing a remarkable telepresence experience. Additionally, their smart self-leveling walker, another impressive invention, received the silver award. This walker demonstrated an innovative feature that automatically adjusted its balance to ensure stability and safety for users. The success of these students at the expo once again highlights the positive impact of effective training and close supervision. By nurturing and encouraging students' potential for innovation and creativity, they were able to push the boundaries of what was possible in robotics design. This agrees with the findings of Charosky et al. (2022), They observed that innovation competences can be developed based on the pedagogy chosen. However, the level of development may vary. Their research indicates that when utilizing a combination of a challenge-based approach and design thinking, skills like creativity, leadership, and entrepreneurship are more prominently fostered. The study also highlights that the development of competences is influenced by the planning and management of projects.

At present, the College of Engineering is encountering a common obstacle, which is to consistently uphold and improve their ability to foster a resilient team. This requires them to focus on motivating and training their members to think creatively and embrace innovation.

Conclusions

The implementation of a motivational approach proved to be highly successful, particularly with second and third-year students who often lack confidence and expertise in robotics. These students received excellent training and incentives, allowing them to compete with great skill, creativity, and resourcefulness. It is noteworthy that this program provided a unique opportunity for students to learn and thrive in their respective fields, acquiring a wealth of knowledge, skills, and practical experience. The incorporation of various motivational techniques, innovations, and creativity in this practice is expected to have a positive and long-lasting impact on the careers of the participating students. Additionally, it enhanced their soft skills and increased the effectiveness of working in teams and collaborating with others.

This endeavour has evolved to be more than just a motivator for students to engage in lengthy and challenging contests; it has evolved into a training ground that attracts fresh participants as they prepare for upcoming rounds of competitions. Exhibiting various robots and showcasing the exceptional work accomplished by the teams by means of demonstrations and video presentations during university-wide meetings has made a noteworthy impression on fellow students, leading to the inspiration of numerous new students to enroll in the mechatronics program. Several students and their parents have approached the university to inquire about the mechatronic program and the career prospects of their children after graduation. Upon witnessing footage of student achievements in competitions, they have been thoroughly convinced to enroll in the program.

In summary, encouraging students to engage in highly skilled competitions has advantages for both their personal and professional development. Training provides a chance to cultivate the essential skills needed to excel in such competitions and thrive in future careers. The benefits of training extend beyond merely winning competitions. This practical experience is crucial for students to grasp fundamental concepts in robotics and engineering, enabling them to make substantial contributions to the field.

Limitation and Future Research

Motivating engineering students to participate in highly skilled competitions can be challenging due to several limitations. Firstly, limited awareness and exposure among students regarding the benefits and opportunities these competitions offer may hinder their interest. Additionally, the demanding workload and academic pressures may overshadow students' willingness to invest time and effort into participating in such events. Furthermore, a lack of adequate mentorship and guidance within educational institutions can limit students' understanding of competition requirements and their ability to develop the necessary skills.

To address these limitations, future research should focus on exploring effective strategies to increase awareness and interest in competitions among engineering students. This can involve conducting targeted outreach programs, workshops, and seminars to educate students about the benefits of participating in these events. Moreover, studying the impact of competitions on students' academic and professional development can further strengthen the case for their participation, encouraging more students to engage in these highly skilled competitions in the future.

Acknowledgements

The author wishes to express gratitude towards all the faculty members who took part in the training program and oversaw the students' involvement in the competitions.

References

Bazylev, D., Margun, A., Zimenko, K., Kremlev, A., and Rukujzha, E. (2014). Participation in robotics competition as motivation for learning. *Procedia—Social and Behavioral Sciences*, 152, 835–840.

Bobtsov, A. A., Kolyubin, S. A., Pyrkin, A. A., Borgul, A. S., Zimenko K. A., and Evgeniy, R. Y. (2012). Mechatronic and robotic setups for modern control theory workshops. *The International Federation of Automatic Control*, 45(11), 348–353.

Bobtsov, A. A., Pyrkin, A. A., Kolyubin, S. A., Kapitonov, A. A., Feskov, S. D., Vlasov, S. M., Krasnov, A. Y., Khovanskiy, A. V., and Shavetov, S. V. (2012). Lego mindstorms NXT for students' research projects in control field. In 9th IFAC Symposium on Advances in Control Education, ACE, (pp. 102–106).

Bryson, C. (2014). Understanding and Developing Student Engagement. London: Routledge, Taylor & Francis Group Ltd.

Cents-Boonstra, M., Lichtwarck-Aschoff, A., Denessen, E., Aelterman, N., and Haerens, L. (2021). Fostering student engagement with motivating teaching: an observation study of teacher and student behaviours. *Research Papers in Education*, 36(6), 754–779.

Charosky, G., Hassi, L., Kyriaki Papageorgiou, K., and Bragós, R. (2022). Developing innovation competences in engineering students: a comparison of two approaches. *European Journal of Engineering Education*, 47(3), 1–20. doi:10.1080/03043797.2021.1968347

Chen, C. H., and Chiu, C. H. (2016). Employing intergroup competition in multitouch design-based learning to foster student engagement, learning achievement, and creativity. *Computers & Education*, 103, 99–113.

Fortune, J., Breckon, J., Norris, M., Eva, G., and Frater, T. (2019). Motivational interviewing training for physiotherapy and occupational therapy students: effect on confidence, knowledge and skills. *Patient Education and Counseling*, 102(4), 694–700. doi:10.1016/j.pec.2018.11.014

Howell, R. A. (2021). Engaging students in education for sustainable development: the benefits of active learning, reflective practices and flipped classroom pedagogies. *Journal of Cleaner Production*, 325, 129318.

Jääskä, E., and Aaltonen, K. (2022). Teachers' experiences of using game-based learning methods in project management higher education. *Project Leadership and Society*, 3, 100041.

Najdanovic-Visak, V. (2017). Team-based learning for first year engineering students. *Education for Chemical Engineers*, 18, 26–34.

Patfield, S., Gore, J., Prieto, E., Fray, L., and Sincock, K. (2022). Towards quality teaching in higher education: pedagogy-focused academic development for enhancing practice. *International Journal for Academic Development* (July 2022), 1–16. doi:https://doi.org/10.1080/136 0144X.2022.2103561.

Schuster, P., Davol, A., and Mello, J. (2006). Student competitions: The benefits and challenges. In Paper Presented at 2006 Annual Conference and Exposition, Chicago, IL. https://peer.asee.org/1055

Tseng, F. M., Weng, J. Y., Liu, F. W., and Hsie, M. H. (2022). How to design contests and motivate participants to engage in crowd innovation contests. *The International Journal of Management Education*, 20(3), 100722.

Verner, I. M., and Ahlgren, D. J. (2007). Robot projects and competitions as education design experiments. *Intelligent Automation and Soft Computing*, 13(1), 57–68.

Xerri, M. J., Radford, K., and Shacklock, K. (2018). Student engagement in academic activities: a social support perspective. *Higher Education*, 75, 589–605. doi:10.1007/s10734-017-0162-9

Zainuddin, Z., Shujahat, M., Haruna, H., and Chu, S. K. W. (2020). The role of gamified e-quizzes on student learning and engagement: An interactive gamification solution for a formative assessment system. *Computers & Education*, 145, 103729.

10 Structural Equation Model on the Sustainable Online Shopping Behavior

Shabana Faizal[1,a], Nidhi S. Menon[1,b], and Anand, J.[2,c]

[1]Assistant Professor, University of Technology Bahrain, Bahrain
[2]Assistant Professor, SRM Valliammai Engineering College, Chennai

Abstract

This research aims to understand which factors can have direct and indirect effect towards the online shopping behaviour of customers. The latent variables considered for the study are purchase intention, product information, privacy, price, convenience, advertising and shopping behaviour. Total of 558 responses has participated in the online survey. The data has been analysed and processed using the Smartpls 3.0. Descriptive statistics, correlation, factor analysis, regression, reliability test, discriminant validity and Path analysis were done to test the hypothesis. Five Hypothesis were considered for the study. The result shows that product information and advertising have a direct, indirect and total effect towards the shopping behaviour of customers. As per the path analysis purchase intention has a direct effect on the shopping behaviour. It is even observed that the intention to purchase the product can increase only if customers are confident.

Keywords

Advertising, convenience, privacy, product information, purchase intention, shopping behavior.

Introduction

Technological advancements and emergence of internet allowed the customer to access information of various product types (Urbinati et al., 2019). It is expected that by 2027, there will likely be 1.2 million users involved in the eCommerce market with various expectations. Since the pandemic, 86% of the customers in Bahrain have started to use online platform such as Shein, Amazon etc to purchase the products. In this study we would like to understand on the uncertainties influencing on the purchase intention of the consumers. Consumers would consider variety of factors before making a purchase in order to get benefit of the price spend for the product.

During pandemic university students at Jabodetabek support the fact that lifestyles and promotion has a significant impact on their online purchase intentions. There is no relation between the advertising and purchase or re purchasing intention (Samuel and Anita, 2023).

---

[a]s.faizal@utb.edu.bh, [b]nsmenon@utb.edu.bh, [c]anand1087jaya@gmail.com

Bahrain has done a significant upgradation of internet facilities towards 5G connections. As per Arabic coupon 2022, some of the barriers to e-commerce or online shopping are bad experiences and weak information related to products and prices. Online retail shops can utilize use friendly websites to help the clients improve the purchasing experience. Additionally the features, application, description of items can assist the customers in selecting the right products and services (Daroch et al., 2021).

According to Theory of Planned Behavior (TPB) attitude, perceived behavior and subjective standards have a significant impact on purchasing intention. These three factors predict intention, which in turn predicts behavior. According to (Liu et al., 2020). TPB framework is more applicable in predicting consumers purchase intentions Self-determination theory is the ability of the person to manage or make choices of their own life. Online consumers have the ability and the freedom to choose the products available on the shopping platforms

The structure of the paper has six sections. Section 1 on the introduction. Section 2 literature review. Section 3 sample of the study. Section 4 methodology. Section 5 discussion Section 6 conclusion.

Literature Review

Product Information and Shopping Behavior

Product information can considerably influence on the buyers shopping behavior (Zhao et al., 2021). Their study was emphasized on the production information and pricing. It has been recommended that the organizations to focus on the pricing strategies because it can inversely effected on cutting the operation cost. However product information was observed but the result of the study shows the significance that it has less effect in comparison to pricing. As per Kripesh et al. (2020), there is always a positive correlation between product information and the intention of the customers to buy the product. The study indicated that product information and website efficiency are the key factors for the customers to make online purchase.

H1: **Product Information has an effect on the Shopping behavior of the customers**

Privacy and Shopping Behavior

The indirect effect of privacy towards the attitude of the customers are mediated by trust, risk and usefulness. These can even effect on the behavior. Privacy is a perception depending on the dominance of the society. According the Yuniar and Fibrianto (2021) consumer perception can be on the several factors such as regulatory policy, acceptance of e-commerce, privacy protection and online information. Good privacy policy should be implemented by the organization and make it known to the users. Consumer tendency towards the privacy, security and information on the website has a stronger significant effect on the internet consumers. According to Bano et al. (2022) privacy concerns have a significant effect towards the attitude of the customers in using applications.

H2: **Privacy has an effect on the Shopping behavior of the customers**

Convenience and Shopping Behavior

Sholikhah et al. (2023) showed that convenience has the most significant direct impact on behavioral intention of the customers. The customers always prioritize online shopping to physical shopping as it requires less time. Kansra and Oberoi (2022) mentioned in the descriptive statistics that age, quality comparison, convenience has affected the youngsters in online shopping. The tangibility of the product acts as hurdles in online purchase intention. In an exploration study done by Alkaabi (2022), the UAE indicated that the customer considers convenience as a crucial factor which can be defined as rapid processes, efficient delivery, and easy access.

H3: **Convenience has an effect on the Shopping behavior of the customers**

Advertising and Shopping Behavior

The Strategy of the marketing is not only to target customers but also to go above the competitors. Consumers can be attracted by the advertisements but transparency in terms of pricing has more impact on the behavior. Online advertisement is another form of marketing or advertising that could deliver the message to the consumers. It can be an effective mode to influence on the perception of the customers. More importantly attitude can stimulate the buyer's behavior. Therefore, the organizers should understand the attitude before developing an advertisement (Jogi and Vashisth, 2021)

H4: **Advertising has an effect on the Shopping behavior of the customers**

Purchase Intention and Shopping Behavior

As per Herzallah et al. (2022) there is no relation between the trust, ease of use and purchase intention. The perceived risk by the customers does not have any impact on the intention towards purchasing the products (Zhang et al., 2023). When the purchase intention and purchase behavior resulted with 0.8181, it indicated that there is a significant affect between the variables.

H5: **Purchase intention effect on the Shopping behavior of the customers**
Based on the above literature review, we propose a conceptual model for this study

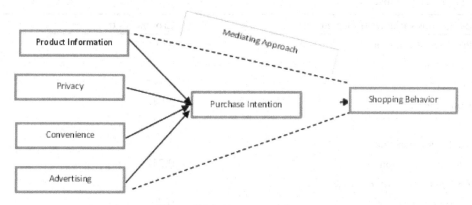

Figure 10.1 Conceptual frame.

Figure 10.1 a mediator approach method is used in this study to understand on the factors that influence on the customers hopping behaviour. In many research studies pricing has been considered an independent variables and majority of the results prove to be significant. Zhao et al. (2021) carried out the research path analysis, factor analysis and discriminant validity by using Structural equation model. The study's findings showed that university students in China believe that the association between product pricing and the purchasing decision-making process is statistically significant. In this study we are considering only product information, privacy, convenience and advertisements as exogenous variables (independent). Purchase intention will be the mediator because there are only few studies that has supports theses selected exogenous variables towards the online shopping behaviour of the customers. Secondly there are limited studies in understanding the perspective of the Bahrain customers.

Data and Variables

Study Period and Sample

A total of 588 customers participated in the survey. Based on the result in Crobech alpha, it can be indicated that all the variables are reliable from the pilot testing. It is widely used to estimate the reliability (Amirrudin et al., 2020). Alpha coefficient ranges from value from 0 to 1. Alpha value 0.7 is considered as an acceptable reliability. In Table 10.4 the alpha values of the variables are more than 0.7. This could be considered that the indicators and the items are reliable. The online survey questionnaire was distributed as a google form to the residents and the citizens of Bahrain. 61% of the respondents were employees and 25% were students. 35% of respondents' income level was between BD 500–BD1000. Dress, Household items, books, electronics, bags and accessories are the top prior online purchases done by the respondents.

Table 10.1: Cronbach's alpha.

Exogenous variables (Independent)	Cronbach's α
Product information	0.766
Advertising	0.804
Privacy	0.757
Convenience	0.746
Price	0.786
Mediating variable	
Purchase intention	0.752
Endogenous variables (Dependent)	
Shopping behavior	0.797

Methodology

A 5-scale Likert scale questions that ranges from strongly agreed towards disagreed is used to quickly assess the respondent's opinion. An online survey was used to gather data to validate the conceptual model and explore the study hypotheses. The sample population comprise of Bahrain residents who have an active experience in purchasing online products. A multivariate statistical method called partial least squares analysis (PLS) was used to test the hypothesis. PLS is a variant-based SEM statistical method developed to address direct, indirect and total effect of the exogenous and endogenous variable.

Empirical Results

Descriptive Statistics

The mean of the items are obtained from the respondents preferences on the basis of the Likert type scale indicated in the questionnaire. The overall mean stays between the range of 3.6 to 4.6 which means the respondents agree to the items or the statements mentioned in each latent variable. In convenience mean value is 2.6 which means the items are not agreed or rather disagreed. Product information (0.87) Privacy (0.404), Convenience (1.048) advertising (0.538) purchase intention (0.050) and shopping behavior (0.375) has positive skewness which indicate long right tail or more higher values. However, a value between –2 and +2 is typically seen as good. Skewness values between –1 and +1 are considered great (Hair et al., 2022).

Factor loading

A factor loading greater than 0.30 indicates a moderate association between the factor and the item (Tavakol and Wetzel, 2020). Factor loadings show how much a factor contributes to the explanation of a variable. Loadings might be between –1 and 1. Factor loading is to show the variance of a particular variable. The thumb rule in SEM approach is to have 0.7 or higher factor represent sufficient variance for the variable. The highest factor loading is 0.917 on the statement "I search for various online sites to find and compare the latest styles". The least factor loading is on "the description shown about products in the website is accurate" value at 0.425.

Pair wise correlation

The values of the correlation range from –1 to +1 which indicate that values nearing to +1 has strongest correlation. Increase of one latent variable product information will have an increase of convenience at 0.570 by meeting with the customers expectation. Expectation can add value towards the business because revenue is generated from the existing customers. Convenience has the medium relation towards the shopping (0.160) and this reason has to be investigated further in the future researches. 83% of the customers feels that convenience is very crucial to consider when doing the purchased. It could be because of the role of technology in e-commerce. Purchase intention (0.477) and Privacy (0.477) has an essential correlation with the shopping behavior.

Good fitness model

The Standardized Root Mean Square Residual (SRMR) is an exact measure of fitness for small samples size. A value of zero denotes perfect fit because the SRMR is an absolute measure of fit. In general, a value of less than.08 is regarded as a good fit (Hu and Bentler, 1999). In this study the estimate model result is 0.039 which is lesser than 0.08.

Discriminant validity

From the HTMT results generated from the PLS indicates that all the values are below the threshold of 0.85. There does not exist a collinearity problems between the variables. Advertising-shopping behavior (0.161), convenience-shopping behavior (0.445), privacy-shopping behavior (0.423), product information-shopping behavior (0.255), Purchase Intention-shopping behavior (0.478).

From the Figure 10.2 and Table 10.2, The product information and Advertising does have a total effect towards the shopping behaviors of the customers. The total effect is the combination of direct and indirect effect. According to (Chang and Chen, 2022) intention for purchasing the products can be improved with the customers involvement and the product knowledge. Privacy concern arises when the customers feels that their data are been shared to the third person or to the organization without consent. The factor loading results indicate that 67% variability explained "Online retailers provide marketing firms with customer information". There is a strong agreement from the online respondents that data's are been shared to the marketing firms. 80.4% variability explained in the latent variable advertising that "Online stores make promises they can't actually keep".

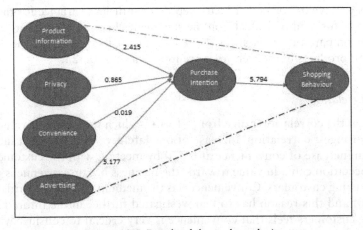

Figure 10.2 Result of the path analysis.

Table 10.2: Path coefficient.

Hypothesis		Direct	Indirect	P-Value	Decision
H1	Product information → Purchase intention → Shopping behavior	2.415	2.210	0.028	Accepted
H2	Privacy → Purchase Intention → Shopping Behavior	0.865	0.813	0.417	Rejected
H3	Convenience → Purchase intention → Shopping behavior	0.019	0.018	0.986	Rejected
H4	Advertising → Purchase intention → Shopping behavior	5.177	4.138	0.000	Accepted
H5	Purchase intention → Shopping behavior	5.794	-	0.000	Accepted

Conclusion

In many studies it has been proven that advertising has a direct effect on the shopping behaviour and it is still proved in this study with total effect. 45% of the responds agree that they are motivated to buy the products due to huge discount or offers seen in the advertisement. Online business can use various methods to motivate the customers. It is to make them aware subconsciously that their wants has to be satisfied and not the needs. This can be even related to the theory of reasoned actions. Stimulating an individual's intention to engage in a particular behaviour. Organizations are trying to be customer centric by offering the products based on the emotions, values and personalization (Pittman, 2023). After viewing advertisements each of the participants will rate on the advertisement and they will decide to buy the products. If the customer are taking too much of mental efforts to buy the products there are higher chance for a switch towards the pre covid shopping behaviour. Though convenience is a crucial point for the customers, they prefer to have a quick delivery. Augmented reality and Virtual reality concepts are giving chances for the customers to having a digitalized shopping which could satisfy their psychological needs. To an extend an urge to have quick delivery thinking can be controlled. Augmented reality is a huge success for Nikes among young demographics In the coming future the researchers need to have an investigation on the latent variable convenience and privacy.

References

Alkaabi, K. A. (2022). Customers' purchasing behaviour toward home-based SME products: evidence from UAE community. *Journal of Enterprising Communities: People and Places in the Global Economy*, 16(3), 472–493. https://doi.org/10.1108/JEC-11-2020-0187

Amirrudin, M., Nasution, K., and Supahar, S. (2020). Effect of variability on cronbach alpha reliability in research practice. *Jurnal Matematika, Statistika Dan Komputasi*, 17(2), 223–230.

Bano, S., Sarfraz, U., Salameh, A. A., and Jan, A. (2022). COVID-19 paradox: the role of privacy concerns and ad intrusiveness on consumer's attitude toward app usage behavior. *Frontiers in Psychology*, 13, 1–10. https://doi.org/10.3389/fpsyg.2022.836060.

Chang, M. Y., and Chen, H. S. (2022). Understanding consumers' intentions to purchase clean label products: evidence from Taiwan. *Nutrients*, 14(18). https://doi.org/10.3390/nu14183684NG.

Daroch, B., Nagrath, G., and Gupta, A. (2021). A study on factors limiting online shopping behaviour of consumers. *Rajagiri Management Journal*, 15(1), 39–52. https://doi.org/10.1108/RAMJ-07-2020-0038.

Hair, J. F., Hult, G. T. M., Ringle, C. M., and Sarstedt, M. (2022). A Primer on Partial Least Squares Structural Equation Modeling (PLS-SEM). (3rd ed.). Thousand Oaks, CA: Sage.

Herzallah, D., Muñoz-Leiva, F., and Liebana-Cabanillas, F. (2022). Drivers of purchase intention in instagram commerce. *Spanish Journal of Marketing—ESIC*, 26(2), 168–188. https://doi.org/10.1108/SJME-03-2022-0043.

Hu, L. T., and Bentler, P. M. (1999). Cutoff criteria for fit indexes in covariance structure analysis: conventional criteria versus new alternatives. *Structural Equation Modeling*, 6, 1–55. http://dx.doi.org/10.1080/10705519909540118

Jogi, S., and Kant Vashisth, K. (2021). Effect of Online Advertisement on Consumer Buying Behaviour-A Review. https://www.researchgate.net/publication/354161925

Kansra, P., and Oberoi, S. (2022). Determinants of online purchase intention among young consumers in Punjab. *International Journal of Social Ecology and Sustainable Development*, 13(6), 1–14. https://doi.org/10.4018/ijsesd.292041

Khan, Y., Hameed, I. M., and Akram, U. (2023). What drives attitude, purchase intention and consumer buying behavior toward organic food? a self-determination theory and theory of planned behavior perspective. *British Food Journal*, 125(7), 2572–2587. https://doi.org/10.1108/BFJ-07-2022-0564s in the current document.

Kripesh, A. S., Prabhu, H. M., and Sriram, K. V. (2020). An empirical study on the effect of product information and perceived usefulness on purchase intention during online shopping in India. *International Journal of Business Innovation and Research*, 21(4), 509–522. doi: 10.1504/IJBIR.2020.105982.

Liu, M. T., Liu, Y., and Mo, Z. (2020). Moral norm is the key. *Asia Pacific Journal of Marketing and Logistics*, 32(8), 1823–1841. https://doi.org/10.1108/apjml-05-2019-0285

Pittman, M. (2023). Social media scatters your brain, and then you buy stuff you don't need. *The Conversation*. http://theconversation.com/social-media-scatters-your-brain-and-then-you-buy-stuff-you-dont-need-201537

Samuel, S., and Anita, T. (2023). The relationship between trends in technology use and repurchase intention. *International Journal of Data and Network Science*, 7(1), 449–456.

Sholikhah, Pratama Sari, D. A., & Musyaffi, M. A. (2023). Exploring convenience motivation in the using delivery service intention. *Quality—Access to Success*, 24(192), 322–328. https://doi.org/10.47750/QAS/24.192.38

Tavakol, M., and Wetzel, A. (2020). Factor analysis: a means for theory and instrument development in support of construct validity. *International Journal of Medical Education*, 11, 245–247. https://doi.org/10.5116/ijme.5f96.0f4a

Urbinati, A., Bogers, M., Chiesa, V., and Frattini, F. (2019). Creating and capturing value from big data: a multiple-case study analysis of provider companies. *Technovation*, 84–85, 21–36. https://doi.org/10.1016/j.technovation.2018.07.004.

Urbinati, A., Chiaroni, D., Chiesa, V., and Frattini, F. (2020). The role of digital technologies in open innovation processes: an exploratory multiple case study analysis. *R&D Management*, 50(1), 136–160. https://doi.org/10.1111/radm.12313.

Yuniar, A., and Fibrianto, A. (2021). Consumer's privacy perception in online shopping behavior using e-commerce platform. https://doi.org/10.4108/eai.16-10-2019.2304352

Zhang, M., Hassan, H., and Migin, M. W. (2023). Exploring the consumers' purchase intention on online community group buying platform during pandemic. *Sustainability (Switzerland)*, 15(3), 1–13. https://doi.org/10.3390/su15032433

Zhao, H., Yao, X., Liu, Z., and Yang, Q. (2021). Impact of pricing and product information on consumer buying behavior with customer satisfaction in a mediating role. *Frontiers in Psychology*, 12, 1–11. https://doi.org/10.3389/fpsyg.2021.720151.

11 Examining the Relationships Among Service Quality Dimensions, Customer Loyalty, and Customer Satisfaction Towards Third-Party Online Food Delivery Apps in Kuwait

Dhuha AlSalman[1,a] and Rania Nafea[2,b]

[1]Master of Business Administration, Maastricht School of Management, MSM, Kuwait
[2]Associate Professor, University of Technology Bahrain, Bahrain

Abstract

Third-party online food delivery (OFD) applications (apps) have increased enormously in Kuwait. The objective of this research is to evaluate the impact of service quality dimensions of third-party OFD apps on customer loyalty, both directly and indirectly through satisfaction. The purpose is to identify the most significant associations among service quality dimensions, customer loyalty, and satisfaction. In addition, this paper intends to examine how self-efficacy and novelty-seeking factors moderate these relationships. In this study, service quality dimensions of third-party OFD apps include Efficiency, Fulfilment/Reliability, Privacy/Security, Personalization, Tangibility, Responsiveness, and Contact. By customer loyalty, the author refers to the two-dimensional approach of loyalty, both behavioral and attitudinal loyalty, presented as one dependent variable. Behavioral Loyalty in this research indicates customers' repeated purchase from third-party OFD apps in Kuwait, while attitudinal loyalty refers to the commitment and preference to use and order from those apps. The quantitative tool used was a survey questionnaire, and the total sample size was 432 users of third-party OFD apps. It was found that fulfilment/reliability, personalization, and tangibility, are significantly related to customer loyalty. Five dimensions, fulfilment/reliability, personalization, tangibility, efficiency and responsiveness play a crucial role in determining the level of satisfaction experienced by customers. Upon examining the mediating effect of satisfaction, it was found that fulfilment/reliability, personalization, tangibility, efficiency and responsiveness are indirectly related to customer loyalty through satisfaction. The results showed that fulfilment/reliability, personalization, and tangibility are the most significant factors to directly and indirectly impact customer loyalty. Self-efficacy and novelty-seeking were not found as significant moderators.

Keywords

Attitudinal and behavioral loyalty, customer satisfaction, service quality of mobile apps, third-party online food delivery apps.

Introduction

Amidst the rapid growth of online food delivery (OFD) apps in Kuwait, enhancing app services has become vital for sustaining customer loyalty. The research at hand

---

[a]duha_alsalman@hotmail.com, [b]rania.nafea@utb.edu.bh

examines the relationships among service quality dimensions, customer loyalty, and satisfaction with the aim of identifying the significant relationships affecting the two-dimensional customer loyalty, attitudinal and behavioral, towards third-party OFD mobile apps in Kuwait.

In the Middle East, the growth of OFD necessitates seeking competitive advantage to enhance customer loyalty (Sharma and Abdul-Waheed, 2018). In Kuwait, the number of third-party OFD firms increased from two in 2016 to seven in 2019 (Abdul-Ghafour, 2019) making it a competitive market. This study examined the users of OFD apps in Kuwait, including Talabat, Carriage, Zitaat, Jeebley, Cravez, Makan, and Deliveroo users. There is a knowledge gap, especially in Kuwait, with limited studies focusing on the impact of service quality dimensions of mobile sites, or mobile shopping apps, rather than of OFD apps (to be discussed in the next section).

Literature Review

This section discusses the concepts of the variables used, and the research hypotheses:

Online-Based Customer Loyalty

Online customer loyalty is characterized by a customer's positive "attitude" towards an online business, leading to recurrent purchases (Anderson and Srinivasan, 2003). Prior studies used different terms to describe online loyalty, such as customers' intentions to use the service (Ilham, 2018) and their online buying behavior (Shafiee and Bazargan, 2018). Other researchers took a two-dimensional approach, considering both attitudes and behaviors in assessing loyalty (Yusra and Agus, 2019).

Mobile Service Quality (M-Service Quality)

The SERVQUAL scale was introduced by Parasuraman et al. (1988), which consists of five factors of service quality: reliability, tangibles, assurance, responsiveness, and empathy. Yusra and Agus (2019) utilized the M-S-QUAL tool created by Huang et al. (2015) to evaluate the influence of service quality offered by food delivery mobile sites on customer satisfaction and loyalty. They used five variables: efficiency, privacy, fulfillment, responsiveness, and contact. Kuo et al. (2016) formulated a service quality model for mobile shopping apps, encompassing the following factors: fulfillment, efficiency, responsiveness, personalization, tangibility, privacy/security, and reliability. This study derived the independent variables from Yusra and Agus (2019), and Kuo et al. (2016) frameworks, and these variables are: Efficiency (EFF), Fulfillment/Reliability (F/R), Privacy/Security (P/S), Personalization (PER), Tangibility (TAN), Responsiveness (RES), and Contact (CON).

Efficiency refers to the ease of use and quick accessibility of a website (Parasuraman et al., 2005). Yusra and Agus (2019) emphasize that efficiency is highly associated with both customer satisfaction and loyalty. So, the following were hypothesized:

H1a: Efficiency positively influences Customer Loyalty.

H2a: A positive association exists between Efficiency and Customer Satisfaction.

Previous studies have established a strong relation between fulfillment/reliability, defined as the accurate and timely delivery of orders as promised (Wolfinbarger and Gilly, 2003), and both customer satisfaction and loyalty (Wolfinbarger and Gilly, 2003; Yusra and Agus, 2019). Similarly, reliability has shown significance in influencing satisfaction and loyalty in Kuo et al.'s (2016) study. Based on these findings, the following hypotheses were proposed:

H1b: Fulfillment/Reliability positively influences Customer Loyalty.

H2b: A positive association exists between Fulfilment/Reliability and Satisfaction.

Privacy/Security of mobile shopping apps was found to be robustly associated with customers' satisfaction level, besides significantly affecting their loyalty both directly and indirectly through satisfaction (Kuo et al., 2016). Thus, it was hypothesized that:

H1c: Privacy/Security positively influences Customer Loyalty.

H2c: A positive association exists between Privacy/Security and Satisfaction.

Personalization refers to tailoring the website to individual customer preferences and shopping behaviors (Zeithaml et al., 2000). Personalization was reported to have direct and indirect effects on the loyalty and satisfaction of customers towards mobile apps (Kuo et al., 2016). Accordingly, this research proposed the following:

H1d: Personalization positively influences Customer Loyalty.

H2d: A positive association exists between Personalization and Satisfaction

As stated by Kuo, et al. (2016), Tangibility is represented by the interface design of mobile apps, how often information are updated, and product variety. They highlight the significance of Tangibility for mobile service quality. Thus, it was proposed that:

H1e: Tangibility positively influences Customer Loyalty.

H2e: A positive association exists between Tangibility and Customer Satisfaction.

As per Parasuraman et al. (2005), responsiveness is assessed by the promptness of response and the effectiveness of problem resolution on a website. Yusra and Agus (2019) verified strong correlations among responsiveness of an OFD mobile site, customer satisfaction and loyalty, with satisfaction being the mediator. So, we hypothesized that:

H1f: Responsiveness positively influences Customer Loyalty.

H2f: A positive association exists between Responsiveness and Satisfaction.

Contact is the available assistance online or by telephone (Zeithaml et al., 2013). Yusra and Agus (2019) identified Contact as highly correlated with customer loyalty towards online food delivery services. Therefore, we proposed that:

H1g: Contact positively influences Customer Loyalty.

H2g: A positive association exists between Contact and Customer Satisfaction.

Online-Based Customer Satisfaction

Online customer satisfaction judges whether a product, service, or its features have met or exceeded consumer level of fulfillment (Oliver, 1997, p. 13). Recent studies (Ilham, 2018; Yusra and Agus, 2019) support the importance of examining the satisfaction-loyalty relationship, along with analyzing the mediating impact of customer satisfaction on loyalty. Accordingly, our hypotheses posited that:

H3: Customer satisfaction positively influences customer loyalty.

H4: The relationship between service quality dimensions of third-party OFD apps, and customer loyalty is mediated by customer satisfaction.

Self-Efficacy and Novelty-Seeking

Self-efficacy refers to customers' assessment of their capabilities in using electronic services (Yi and Gong, 2008), while Novelty-Seeking is described as the inclination to explore and engage in new and distinctive experiences (Hirschman, 1980). These personality traits were suggested by Yusra and Agus (2019) to be analyzed as moderators in future studies about service quality, customer loyalty, and satisfaction:

H5: Self-efficacy moderates:

H5a: Service quality dimensions of OFD apps and customer loyalty relationship.

H5b: Customer satisfaction and loyalty relationship.

H6: Novelty-seeking moderates:

H6a: Service quality dimensions of OFD apps and customer loyalty relationship.

H6b: Customer satisfaction and loyalty relationship.

Methodology

This study's conceptual framework is illustrated in Figure 11.1, presenting the mapped associations among service quality dimensions of OFD apps, as independent variables, Customer loyalty (C/LOY), as a dependent variable, customer satisfaction (C/SAT), a mediator, while self-efficacy and novelty-seeking are the moderator.

This study adopts a deductive approach, and the data was analyzed by Partial Least Squares Structural Equation Modeling (PLS-SEM) to test the causal relationships in the conceptual framework. This research is quantitative and we employed a survey questionnaire as the tool of data collection. Regarding the survey design, it was made available in two languages, Arabic and English. It included a screening question, demographics, and variable-related questions. Respondents rated their agreement level on

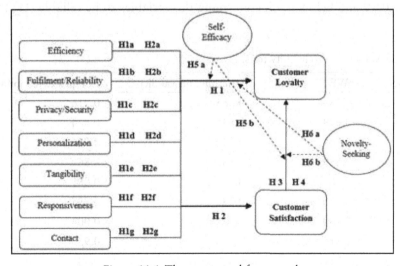

Figure 11.1 The conceptual framework.

Source: Research-based

a five-point Likert scale for the variable questions. Purposive random sampling was used to ensure familiarity with OFD apps among respondents. Users of third-party OFD apps in Kuwait aged 18 and above were the target population. The survey was launched online via Survey Monkey website (www.surveymonkey.com), and was distributed to 480 individuals. Out of the responses, 21 were incomplete, and 27 were disqualified. So, the total sample size is 432 complete responses.

Results and Findings

Demographics Analysis

In this study, users of seven third-party OFD apps in Kuwait were analyzed. The distribution of participants across the apps was as follows: Talabat (37.73%), Carriage (21.3%), Cravez (17.13%), Deliveroo (15.74%), Jeebley (5.32%), Makan (2.3%), and Zitaat (0.46%). Females constituted the majority of the sample size (66.4%), whereas males accounted for 33.6%. The 25–34 year-olds had the highest representation (56.3%), and the following were 18–24 years-olds (23.8%), and 35–44 years old (17.8%). The majority had a bachelor's degree (62%), followed by diploma holders (21.8%), master's degree holders (14.1%), and doctoral degree holders (2.1%).

Validity and Reliability Tests

The measures in Table 11.1 demonstrate that all AVE values are above 0.5, indicating convergence validity (Bagozzi and Yi, 1988). Similarly, the Discriminant Validity values are all above 0.7, suggesting distinctiveness and validity of each measure (Zait and Bertea, 2011). Internal consistency reliability is also satisfactory, with composite reliability values above 0.85. Such values fall within the accepted range of above 0.70 and below 0.95, confirming the variables to be reliable (Hair et al., 2019).

Table 11.1: Validity and reliability tests.

Construct	AVE	Discriminant validity	Composite reliability
EFF	0.783	0.885	0.916
F/R	0.699	0.836	0.874
P/S	0.721	0.849	0.886
PER	0.689	0.830	0.869
TAN	0.667	0.817	0.889
RES	0.720	0.848	0.885
CON	0.760	0.872	0.904
C/SAT	0.815	0.903	0.930
C/LOY	0.744	0.862	0.935

Source: Research-Based

Collinearity Test

Table 11.2 shows no collinearity issues, as the VIF values for all the variables are within the acceptable range of 1.0 to 5.0 (James et al., 2017).

Correlation Analysis

Correlation values below ±0.3 indicate low correlations, whereas coefficients between ±0.3 and ±0.5 are deemed to be moderate levels of correlations, and coefficients greater than ±0.5 affirm high correlations (Cohen, 1992). Table 11.3 shows customer loyalty to be strongly correlated with self-efficacy, fulfilment/reliability, personalization, and tangibility. However, internal correlations among service quality dimensions are generally weak. This contrasts with Yusra and Agus's (2019) findings in Malaysia, indicating cultural differences between Malaysian and Kuwaiti users.

R^2 Results

An R^2 value of 0.795 was noted for customer loyalty (almost 80% of accuracy), and an R^2 value of 0.672 was recorded for customer satisfaction. These results confirm that the mediation model is robust to predict loyalty towards OFD apps in Kuwait.

Path Coefficient Analysis

Table 11.4 presents the first path analysis, as the direct influence of each service quality dimension on customer loyalty was tested to record H1 results. Fulfilment/Reliability significantly influence customer loyalty (beta value = 0.215, t-stat = 6.191, p-value= 0.000), as did personalization (beta value = 0.224, t-stat = 5.649, p-value = 0.000) along with tangibility (beta value = 0.122, t-value = 2.784, p-value = 0.005). Conversely, efficiency (t-stat = 1.674, p-value = 0.076), responsiveness (t-stat = 0.482, p = 0.630), privacy/security (t-stat = 0.563, p-value= 0.574), and contact (t-stat = 1.369, p = 0.171) did not show significant direct impacts on customer loyalty. Therefore, H1a, H1c, H1f, and H1g are not supported, whereas H1b, H1d, and H1e are supported.

The second path analysis examined the association between service quality dimensions and customer satisfaction (H2). The findings noted in Table 11.4 confirm that

Table 11.2: Collinearity test.

Predictor Variables	Predicted Variables		Predictor Variables	Predicted Variables	
	C/LOY	C/SAT		C/LOY	C/SAT
EFF	1.224	1.189	TAN	2.448	2.167
F/R	1.890	1.586	RES	1.551	1.531
P/S	1.344	1.343	CON	1.507	1.502
PER	2.215	2.005	C/SAT	3.050	-

Source: Research-Based

Table 11.3: Internal correlations between variables.

	CON	C/LOY	C/SAT	EFF	F/R	N/S	PER	P/S	RES	S/E	TAN
CON	1										
C/LOY	0.101	1									
C/SAT	0.203	0.841	1								
EFF	0.243	0.255	0.361	1							
F/R	0.187	0.700	0.668	0.228	1						
N/S	0.258	-0.422	-0.329	0.026	-0.333	1					
PER	0.062	0.733	0.674	0.243	0.515	-0.338	1				
P/S	0.411	0.208	0.265	0.259	0.261	0.115	0.170	1			
RES	0.514	0.259	0.347	0.263	0.314	0.169	0.196	0.390	1		
S/E	0.162	0.829	0.802	0.265	0.654	-0.438	0.690	0.213	0.293	1	
TAN	0.084	0.715	0.704	0.302	0.539	-0.293	0.685	0.255	0.241	0.701	1

Source: Research-Based

Table 11.4: Path analysis results.

	Hypothesis	Path coefficient	Sample mean	Standard deviation	T Statistic	P Value
H1a	EFF → C/LOY	−0.046	−0.046	0.024	1.674	0.076
H1b	F/R → C/LOY	0.215	0.216	0.035	6.191	0.000
H1c	P/S → C/LOY	−0.014	−0.014	0.025	0.563	0.574
H1d	PER → C/LOY	0.224	0.223	0.040	5.649	0.000
H1e	TAN → C/LOY	0.122	0.124	0.044	2.784	0.005
H1f	RES → C/LOY	−0.015	−0.017	0.032	0.482	0.630
H1g	CON → C/LOY	−0.038	−0.038	0.028	1.369	0.171
H2a	EFF → C/SAT	0.106	0.107	0.030	3.557	0.000
H2b	F/R → C/SAT	0.316	0.316	0.038	8.231	0.000
H2c	P/S → C/SAT	−0.015	−0.015	0.032	0.462	0.644
H2d	PER → C/SAT	0.262	0.262	0.048	5.473	0.000
H2e	TAN → C/SAT	0.303	0.303	0.045	6.809	0.000
H2f	RES → C/SAT	0.080	0.080	0.038	2.080	0.038
H2g	CON → C/SAT	0.041	0.042	0.032	1.270	0.204
H3	C/SAT → C/LOY	0.494	0.493	0.045	10.859	0.000

Source: Research-Based

Note: Significance Level < 0.05

efficiency (β-value = 0.106, t-stat = 3.557) fulfilment/reliability (β = 0.316, t = 8.231) personalization (β = 0.262, t = 5.473) tangibility (β = 0.303, t = 6.809) and responsiveness (β = 0.080, t = 2.080) have significant positive effects on customer satisfaction with p-values below 0.05 were recorded. However, there were no significant relationships found between privacy/security and contact with customer satisfaction (t-stat < 1.96 and p-value > 0.05). Therefore, H2a, H2b, H2d, H2e, and H2f are supported, while H2c and H2g are not supported. To ensure the validity of satisfaction as a mediator, the direct relationship between customer satisfaction and loyalty was tested, and it was found significant (β-value = 0.494; t-value = 10.859 > 1.96; p-value = 0.000). Hence, H3 is supported.

Mediation Analysis

The influences of efficiency and responsiveness on customer loyalty were found to be insignificant, but when mediated by customer satisfaction, they became significant (t-stat >1.96, p-values <0.05), indicating Full Mediation. Regarding fulfilment/reliability, tangibility, and personalization, the mediating impact of customer satisfaction is partial. On the other hand, customer satisfaction was not noted to mediate the association between privacy/security, contact, and customer loyalty (t-stat < 1.96, p-values > 0.05). Thus, Table 11.5 results partially support H4.

Table 11.5: Mediation analysis.

Indirect relationship	Path coefficient	Standard deviation	T stat	P value
EFF → C/SAT → C/LOY	0.053	0.016	3.383	**0.001**
F/R → C/SAT → C/LOY	0.156	0.023	6.811	**0.000**
P/S → C/SAT → C/LOY	–0.007	0.016	0.462	0.644
PER → C/SAT → C/LOY	0.130	0.027	4.765	**0.000**
TAN → C/SAT → C/LOY	0.150	0.025	5.930	**0.000**
RES → C/SAT → C/LOY	0.040	0.019	2.040	**0.041**
CON → C/SAT → C/LOY	0.020	0.016	1.242	0.214

Source: Research-Based

Note: Significance Level < 0.05

Moderation Analysis

Table 11.6 results show that self-efficacy and novelty-seeking do not have significant moderating effects on the relationships between the service quality factors and customer loyalty, nor between customer satisfaction and loyalty (all p-values > 0.05). This means that H5a, H5b, H6a, and H6b hypotheses are not supported.

Table 11.6: Moderation analysis—self-efficacy (S/L) and novelty-seeking (N/S).

	H	T Stat	P Value		H	T Stat	P Value
	EFF× S/E→ C/LOY	0.247	0.805		EFF × N/S → CL	0.278	0.781
	F/R × S/E → C/LOY	0.905	0.365		F/R × N/S → CL	0.282	0.778
	P/S × S/E → C/LOY	0.581	0.561		P/S × N/S → CL	1.089	0.276
H5a	PER × S/E → C/LOY	0.721	0.471	H6a	PER × N/S → CL	0.279	0.780
	TAN × S/E → C/LOY	0.390	0.697		TAN × N/S → CL	1.450	0.147
	RES × S/E → C/LOY	0.364	0.716		RES × N/S → CL	0.346	0.729
	Contact × S/E → C/LOY	0.480	0.631		Contact × N/S → CL	0.288	0.774
H5b	C/SAT × S/E → C/LOY	0.572	0.567	H6b	C/SAT × N/S → C/LOY	0.304	0.761

Source: Research-Base

Note: Significance Level < 0.05

Discussion

The study identified fulfillment/reliability as the most influential factor affecting both customer loyalty and satisfaction, supported by previous research in various online business fields (Wolfinbarger and Gilly, 2003; Ilham, 2018; Yusra and Agus, 2019). Personalization and tangibility also played significant roles in influencing customer satisfaction and loyalty. Such results align with the findings of Kuo et al. (2016) regarding personalization, while tangibility only showed a significant impact on satisfaction in their study, but not on loyalty. The significant satisfaction-loyalty relationship in this research supports the findings of Yusra and Agus (2019) regarding the importance of this relationship.

While responsiveness and efficiency do not directly affect customer loyalty, they have a significant impact on customer satisfaction, which in turn fully mediates the relationship between these factors and loyalty. These findings partially support the work of Yusra and Agus (2019), who found similar correlations and partial mediation. However, Kuo et al. (2016) reported different results, suggesting no direct or indirect influence of efficiency and responsiveness on loyalty. Such variations could be attributed to cultural differences as the studies were conducted in different countries. Top of FormBottom of Form Contrary to expectations, privacy/security was not found to significantly affect customer loyalty and satisfaction, which differs from the findings of Kuo et al. (2016). This may be due to the trust OFD users in Kuwait place in existing cybercrime laws and the Department of Cybercrimes (Ministry of Interior–State of Kuwait, 2020), which may explain why this dimension did not affect customer loyalty. Similarly, the dimension of contact was also found to be insignificant, possibly because customers prefer resolving order issues within the app rather than through direct communication with a call center agent. This contrasts with the strong correlation between contact, customer loyalty, and satisfaction found by Yusra and Agus (2019).

The moderating effects of novelty-seeking and self-efficacy were found to be insignificant, being partially consistent with Yusra and Agus (2019). They reported mixed results for personal innovativeness, a personality trait, noting a strong negative correlation with the satisfaction-loyalty relationship, but no significant moderation between service quality and customer loyalty. It is likely that personality traits of OFD users in Kuwait may not strengthen nor weaken the relationships examined.

Conclusion

To guarantee the fulfilment/reliability of online food delivery (OFD) apps, leaders should display realistic delivery times, extend the times during peak hours, and maintain updated information of the restaurants in those apps. Personalized services can be provided through advanced algorithms that offer multiple restaurant options based on cuisines, prices, location, and feedback. Tangibility can be improved by regular information updates, clear item displays, and an interesting interface design. Moreover, efficiency requires app updates and easy access, while responsiveness entails instant solutions and prompt response to issues with an innovative app infrastructure, and a qualified team. There are two main customers of OFD firms, restaurants owners and end customers. Accordingly, future studies should explore the association between service quality dimensions, customer loyalty, and satisfaction from restaurant owners' perspectives. Also, this study has a geographical limitation and a limited sample size, focusing on the context of Kuwait. Therefore, conducting research in other GCC countries can provide comparative insights and stimulate interdisciplinary research.

Furthermore, examining predictors of customer loyalty, such as trust and image, used by Singh et al. (2017), and exploring the influence of personality traits like interpersonal interactions and self-consciousness on loyalty towards third-party OFD apps, as suggested by Yusra and Agus (2019), can be valuable areas for future research.

References

Abdul-Ghafour, S. (2019, December 16). Asʿār tawṣīl al-ṭalabāt taʿūd ilā al-dīnār. [Delivery prices go back to one dinar]. *AlQabas Newspaper*, 19. Retrieved from: https://d1wnoevxju5lec. cloudfront.net/storage/pdfs/2019/37385_file2.pdf

Anderson, R. E., and Srinivasan, S. S. (2003). E-satisfaction and e-loyalty: a contingency framework. *Psychology and Marketing*, 20(2), 123–138.

Bagozzi, R. P., and Yi, Y. (1988). On the evaluation of structural equation models. *Journal of the Academy of Marketing Science*, 16(1), 74–94.

Cohen, J. (1992). A power primer. *Psychological Bulletin*, 112(1), 155–159.

Hair, J. F., Risher, J. J., Sarstedt, M., and Ringle, C. M. (2019). When to use and how to report the results of PLS-SEM. *European Business Review*, 31(1), 2–24.

Hirschman, E. C. (1980). Innovativeness, novelty seeking, and consumer creativity. *Journal of Consumer Research*, 7(3), 283–295.

Huang, E. Y., Lin, S., and Fan, Y. (2015). M-S-QUAL: mobile service quality measurement. *Electronic Commerce Research and Applications*, 14(2), 126–142.

Ilham, R. (2018). Improve quality of e-loyalty in online food delivery services: a case of Indonesia. *Journal of Theoretical and Applied Information Technology*, 96(15), 4760–4769.

James, G., Witten, D., Hastie, T., and Tibshirani, R. (2017). An Introduction to Statistical Learning: With Applications in R. New York: Springer.

Kuo, T., Tsai, G. Y., Lu, I.-Y., and Chang, J.-S. (2016). Relationships among service quality, customer satisfaction and customer loyalty: a case study on mobile shopping APPs. In Proceedings of the 17th Asia Pacific Industrial Engineering and Management Systems Conference (APIEMS '16) (pp. 1–8). Taipei, Taiwan.

Ministry of Interior–State of Kuwait (2020). Cyber Crime. Retrieved from: https://www.moi. gov.kw/main/sections/cyber-crime?culture=en.

Oliver, R. L. (1997). Satisfaction: A Behavioral Perspective on the Consumer. New York: McGraw Hill.

Parasuraman, A., Zeithaml, V. A., and Berry, L. L. (1988). SERVQUAL: a multiple-item scale for measuring customer perceptions of quality of service. *Journal of Retailing*, 64(1), 12–40.

Parasuraman, A., Zeithaml, V. A., and Malhotra, A. (2005). E-S-Qual: a multiple-item scale for assessing electronic service quality. *Journal of Service Research*, 7(3), 213–233.

Shafiee, M. M., and Bazargan, N. A. (2018). Behavioral customer loyalty in online shopping: the role of e-service quality and e-recovery. *Journal of Theoretical and Applied Electronic Commerce Research*, 13(1), 26–38.

Sharma, K., and Abdul-Waheed, K. (2018). Consumption of online food app services: an exploratory study among college students in Dubai. *Middle East Journal of Business*, 13(4), 4–11.

Singh, G., Singh, I., and Vij, S. (2017). Antecedents and consequences of customer loyalty: a conceptual model. *International Journal of Applied Business and Economic Research*, 15(23), 237–245.

Wolfinbarger, M., and Gilly, M. C. (2003). eTailQ: dimensionalizing, measuring, and predicting detail quality. *Journal of Retailing*, 79(3), 183–198.

Yi, Y., and Gong, T. (2008). The electronic service quality model: the moderating effect of customer self-efficacy. *Psychology and Marketing*, 25(7), 587–601.

Yusra, Y., and Agus, A. (2019). The influence of online food delivery service quality on customer satisfaction and customer loyalty: the role of personal innovativeness. *Journal of Environmental Treatment Techniques*, 8(1), 6–12.

Zait, A., and Bertea, P. (2011). Methods for testing discriminant validity. *Management and Marketing*, 9(2), 217–224.

Zeithaml, V. A., Bitner, M. J., and Gremler, D. D. (2013). Services Marketing: Integrating Customer Focus Across the Firm (Sixth). New York, NY: McGraw-Hill Education.

Zeithaml, V. A., Parasuraman, A., and Malhotra, A. (2000). A Conceptual Framework for Understanding E-Service Quality: Implications for Future Research and Managerial Practice, report No. 00–115. Cambridge, MA: Marketing Science Institute.

12 Development of a Structural Model for Sustainable Environment Training and Knowledge Transfer for Kuwaiti Private Organizations

Fatma Alkhoder[1,a], Ahmad Alsaber[2,b], and Rania Nafea[3,c]

[1]American University of Kuwait (AUK), Kuwait
[2]Assistant Professor, College of Business and Economics, American University of Kuwait (AUK), Kuwait
[3]Associate Professor, College of Administrative and Financial Services, University of Technology Bahrain, Salmabad, Bahrain

Abstract

The private sector is commonly perceived as a structured and rigid organization. Nevertheless, there is a pressing need for the sector to enhance the quality of its services to address community issues effectively. This study seeks to build a structural model for sustainable environment training and knowledge transfer in the context of private Kuwaiti organizations. The research discovered that the private sector in Kuwait is frequently perceived as a formal and hierarchical organization and, as a result, must improve the quality of its work to successfully solve community issues. Survey questionnaires were distributed to private workers in various departments/divisions of private organizations to investigate this topic. The SmartPLS software was used to evaluate the quality of the study instrument and test the hypotheses. The structural equation modeling test results indicated that sustainable environment training positively impacted knowledge transfer. In addition to that, the study found that the effect of training on knowledge transfer was mediated by how much people wanted to learn. The outcomes of this study have practical significance for practitioners in private Kuwaiti organizations. By understanding the different perspectives on motivation to learn, organizations can design a training program that increases employee motivation to succeed and aligns with organizational strategies and goals in the era of global competition and organizational sustainability. Furthermore, the findings of this study may also have broader implications beyond Kuwait for private-sector organizations seeking to enhance their sustainability practices and improve knowledge transfer among employees. The presented insights can be used to plan and implement effective training programs that raise employee motivation and improve organizational performance. This study examines the significance of sustainable environment training and knowledge transfer in private Kuwaiti organizations. It provides insights into the role of motivation to learn in this context. Hopefully, this research will contribute to developing effective training programs that will strengthen private workers' skills and knowledge, allowing them to address community issues more effectively.

Keywords

knowledge transfer, Kuwait, motivation to learn, sustainable environment training.

Introductions

Private organizations in Kuwait are vital in delivering essential services to the community. Yet, they need help addressing the global marketplace's shifting needs. Private companies must improve their knowledge management processes and training programs in light of the speed at which technology is changing, how quickly the world is becoming more interconnected, and how quickly the environment is deteriorating. The idea of sustainability has become increasingly important to organizational performance in private organizations worldwide in recent years. Programs for teaching about the environment play a crucial role in improving employees' skills and knowledge and encouraging sustainable behaviors in private organizations. Moreover, information transfer is crucial to sustainable environment training since it enables workers to use their expertise and knowledge to solve societal problems. Consequently, this research aims to create a structural model for knowledge transfer and training in sustainable environments in Kuwaiti private organizations.

The sustainable development goals (SDGs) are the core agenda for sustainable development until 2030, as agreed upon by world leaders at a United Nations Conference on September 25, 2015. After the Millennium Development Goals (MDGs) were completed in 2015, the SDGs continued to guide global development efforts. The MDGs consisted of eight goals and twenty-one targets. As a result, the SDGs have grown to include 17 goals and 169 targets. The 2030 Agenda consists of all three aspects of sustainable development: social, economic, and environmental.

The Global Commission on Environment and Development deserves most of the credit for sustainable development. The commission defined sustainable development in its report as "meets the needs of the present without compromising the ability of future generations to meet their own needs." When applied to sustainable development, this word provides crucial input. For present and future prosperity, sustainable development requires protecting natural areas and effectively using available natural resources, especially within institutions.

SDG effectiveness in private organizations can be achieved by developing long-term training programs that foster a positive and comfortable work environment, highly motivated employees, and workplace peace and justice. Furthermore, these programs can sustain positive behavior indefinitely, maintain value qualities in the physical and emotional environment, and maintain the type of development that meets the needs of the present without jeopardizing future generations' capabilities. Sustainability training is frequently interpreted in the development context as an organization's efforts to provide formal or informal employee training to improve task efficiency, increase motivation, drive social change, increase productivity, stimulate innovation, create expertise in ways of thinking and working, and accept sustainability in order to shape and achieve high organizational and social performances.

In private organizations, sustainable environment training is intended to recruit, motivate, and retain competent individuals in order to achieve organizational goals and strategies. Organizations must adopt a more efficient approach to add value and present opportunities for growth in innovation and brand equity. It is possible to achieve this by cultivating highly motivated connections and motivating employees to work sustainably.

According to Paulet et al. (2021), human resource-based sustainability is more critical and emphasizes social and ecological goals in addition to organizational goals and human resources. For example, it is efficient and effective to sustain positive employee behaviors in the future, such as employee development, flexibility, commitment, and well-being. Organizations typically implement sustainable environment training in an organizational context, providing both intrinsic motivation (e.g., social learning, concern/care for others' values, welfare, and beliefs) and extrinsic motivation (e.g., providing principles, justice, ethics, procedures, training, teamwork, leadership, and collaboration) to help employees carry out their day-to-day work responsibilities. As a result, as practiced in successful private organizations, sustainable environment training encourages power delegation, in which superiors empower their subordinates in planning, managing, and monitoring training programs.

The significance of sustainable environment training in any organization must be clearly explained. Recent empirical studies discovered that management's ability to manage intrinsic and extrinsic motivation on a regular basis could positively impact employee motivation to learn and knowledge transfer, resulting in a harmonious environment with long-term responsibilities. Motivation to learn is commonly used in the context of sustainability to refer to the inspiration that can influence changes in cognitive and affective domains and foster positive employee attitudes. Employees' desire and determination to learn and master training content to achieve social sustainability, improve their daily work performance, and achieve organizational objectives is evident. Training management, on the other hand, frequently interprets knowledge transfer as employees' ability to learn and apply knowledge, skills, and positive attitudes gained from training programs attended. When they return to their workplace, they apply their newly acquired knowledge, skills, and attitudes.

This paper will investigate sustainable environment training components and provide measurements, structural models, and hypotheses. This study also uses the research model to examine training for a sustainable environment in private organizations. The findings will then be addressed and analyzed in this paper.

Sustainable Environment Training in Private Organizations

Sustainable environment training is becoming increasingly important in private organizations worldwide as governments and private institutions work to address environmental challenges and promote sustainability. private employees who get this training may be better equipped to apply sustainable practices in their day-to-day operations and support broader sustainability initiatives in their organizations and communities (Bin Mahfodh and Obeidat, 2020).

The design of the training program, the delivery methods, and the employees' incentive to learn and use new information are just a few of the variables that affect how effective sustainable environment training is. According to research, learning motivation is a critical component of training program effectiveness since motivated individuals are likelier to participate in learning and apply what they learn to their jobs (Fischer et al., 2021). The current study sought to determine the connection between learning motivation, knowledge transfer, and training in sustainable environments in Kuwaiti private organizations. The study results indicate that learning motivation moderates this connection and that training in a sustainable setting can favor knowledge transfer. These findings imply that effective training programs should concentrate on teaching knowledge and skills and boosting employee willingness to learn and use new knowledge, which has practical consequences for private organizations in Kuwait and elsewhere. Organizations can improve their sustainability practices and employee knowledge transfer by developing training programs that consider the motivational needs of their workforce.

Literature Review and Hypotheses Development

The literature review presents an overview of the relevant theories and concepts related to sustainable environment training and knowledge transfer. The paper investigates how learning motivation functions as a bridge between knowledge transmission and training in sustainable environments. The evaluation also emphasizes how crucial environmental sustainability training is for improving workers' abilities and knowledge while fostering environmentally friendly behavior in private institutions.

Sustainable Environment Training and Knowledge Transfer

Sustainable environment training refers to programs designed to promote sustainable practices in organizations. Programs for teaching about the environment are essential for improving employees' skills and knowledge and advancing sustainable practices in private organizations, according to research by Setini et al. (2020). These initiatives work to spread knowledge about environmental issues and encourage eco-friendly behaviors that protect the environment and natural resources. Another research conducted by Afsar et al. (2019) further states that sustainable environment training is crucial in private organizations to promote sustainability practices and improve organizational performance. These training programs give staff the knowledge and abilities to handle environmental problems and encourage sustainable practices.

Training in sustainable environments can encompass a variety of subjects, including waste reduction, energy saving, and sustainable mobility. Organizations may help create a cleaner, more sustainable environment by providing employees with the knowledge and skills to address these problems. Azeem et al. (2021) claim that by encouraging sustainable behaviors that lower energy use and waste, sustainable environment training can also benefit enterprises financially. Furthermore, research by Ahmad and Karim (2019) states that highlighting an organization's dedication to environmental sustainability, and training in a sustainable setting can improve the organization's reputation. This can draw in stakeholders and customers who care about the environment and boost the organization's credibility.

Knowledge transfer refers to sharing knowledge between individuals or groups within an organization. According to Milagres and Burcharth (2019), knowledge transfer is crucial for improving organizational performance and ensuring staff members can handle societal concerns. Knowledge transfer, according to Li et al. (2019), also aids in fostering a culture of learning and innovation within a business. In today's context of fast change, knowledge transfer is essential for ensuring that firms remain competitive (Secundo et al., 2019). It enables businesses to utilize staff members' expertise and abilities, enhancing productivity, creativity, and efficiency. Effective information transfer can also result in cost savings, better decision-making, and fewer.

The role of sustainable environment training and knowledge transfer is consistent with the leader-member exchange theory proposed by Dansereau et al. (1975). The theory is a process approach since it emphasizes the necessity of a leader's dynamic relationship with their subordinates. It illustrates two main types of organizational interactions: high-quality and low-quality relationships between leaders and members. In the context of high-quality relationships, it refers to a leader's willingness to encourage more physical and emotional drive in their team members by sharing information and receiving feedback, and being approachable, helpful, empathic, and kind. These traits can boost positive employee behavior. In contrast, in a low-quality relationship, the leaders' incapacity to deliver high levels of physical and emotional drive to employees might have a negative outcome. The core concept of the theory is highly supported by workplace training management research. Hence, the following hypotheses are formulated:

H1: *Intrinsic motivation is associated with knowledge transfer.*

H2: *Extrinsic motivation is associated with knowledge transfer.*

Sustainable Environment Training and Motivation to Learn

Motivation to learn refers to an individual's willingness and desire to acquire new knowledge and skills. Motivation to learn is a key element in evaluating how effective training programs are. Workers driven to learn are more likely to use their knowledge and abilities successfully and contribute to the success of the company as a whole (Fischer et al., 2021). Research conducted by Abdelwhab et al. (2019) states that to encourage someone's involvement and participation in training programs, they must have the motivation to learn. It may inspire a worker to seek out new information and abilities that they may use in their work to further the organization's success.

Adam's equity theory states that sustainable environment training leads to motivation to learn and supports using sustainable environment training as an influential predictor variable for motivation to learn. This theory is widely used when describing workplace behavior. The paradigm focuses on the balance of input and output proliferated in 1963. The input refers to one's contribution to a responsibility, whereas the output refers to the reward or return resulting from the commitment. Management's ability to provide fair resource allocation and exchange treatment can substantially influence individual behavior. The fair distribution of resources is frequently executed in two different ways. The first method involves human psychology (for example, tolerance, support, loyalty, sacrifice, and joy). The second is through physical forms known as equitable norms (e.g., the provision of salary, prizes, facilities, remuneration, recognition, and leave). Thus, according to this hypothesis, managers that can balance input and output can incentivize employees to complete tasks efficiently and effectively. It shows that employees who are satisfied with the services provided will contribute in return. As a result, the following hypotheses are formulated:

H3: *Intrinsic motivation is associated with motivation to learn.*

H4: *Extrinsic motivation is associated with motivation to learn.*

Mediating Effect of Motivation to Learn

According to Knowles (1984), the mediating role of learning motivation in the relationship between sustainable environment training and knowledge transfer is consistent with the adult learning theory. Knowles states that an individual's maturity might alter when an employee accepts the benefits an organization provides to develop their knowledge, skills, positive behavior, and ways of thinking. It explains five critical assumptions of adult learners (andragogy), including (i) self-concept (a self-directed human being), (ii) adult learner experience (accumulation of a growing reservoir of experience acting as a resource for learning), (iii) readiness to learn (learn subjects that have immediate relevance and impact on the learners' job or personal life), (iv) orientation to learning (application of knowledge and problem-centeredness), and (v) motivation to learn. These assumptions are acknowledged as a sign of maturity in adult education. Employers will typically learn and master competencies by carefully monitoring and analyzing a situation, which will significantly drive them to gain valuable competencies. As a result, this drive may result in behaviors that increase the individual drive to develop valuable competencies. Also, it results in activities benefits. Therefore, the following hypotheses are formulated:

H5: *Motivation to learn mediates the relationship between intrinsic motivation and knowledge transfer.*

H6: *Motivation to learn mediates the relationship between extrinsic motivation and knowledge transfer.*

Materials and Methods

Research Model

A conceptual framework was established to explain the relationship between sustainable environment training and knowledge transfer is indirectly affected by the motivation to learn, as shown in Figure 12.1.

Methodology

The research collected data from private employees in different departments/divisions of private organizations in Kuwait using a self-administered survey that required the participant to answer several questions. To assess the effectiveness of the research instrument and test the research hypotheses, the research used Jamovi software. A pilot study was then conducted on a small sample to reevaluate and retest the utility of this research instrument. The survey questionnaire contained three components. The first component was the sustainable environment training, and it contained both intrinsic motivation (IM) and external motivation (EM). Intrinsic and extrinsic motivation had three components that were updated based on organizational training literature according to Burke and Baldwin (1999). The second component, motivation to learn (ML), was measured based on four items developed based on training management

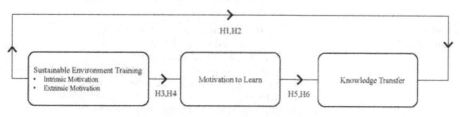

Figure 12.1 Theoretical and conceptual framework.

literature (Burke and Baldwin, 1999). Lastly, knowledge transfer (KT) was measured based on five items modified from organizational behavior literature (Wallace et al., 2011). These items were measured using an answer scale from one (strongly not satisfied) to five (strongly satisfied), and the survey link was distributed to 34 employees for the pilot study who work in private organizations in Kuwait via WhatsApp, email, and LinkedIn then to 151 employees for the research final statistical analysis. Questionnaire items were sorted based on the criteria of having a composite reliability value and Cronbach's alpha coefficient greater than 0.7, as recommended by Henseler et al. (2015), and Sekaran and Bougie (2016), because it generates more neutral feedback and increases dependability according to Lewis (1993). The models were assessed using a simple statistical analysis (e.g., mean, and standard deviation, reliability analysis using Cronbach Alpha tool, and Factor Analysis using PCA to discover the items with higher loading).

Table 12.1 explains the constructs and subconstructs of the study, in addition to the selected items that were used in the survey.

Knowledge transfer served as the dependent variable in the study, with training in sustainable environments and learning motivation as the independent variables. The research also examined how learning motivation affected the relationship between knowledge transfer and training in sustainable environments. The research's findings

Table 12.1: Variables measurement.

Constructs	Sub-Constructs	Items	Sources
Sustainable Environment Training	Intrinsic motivation	1. Encouraging employees to attend the training program 2. Being open to discussing training problems 3. Encouraging employees to renew existing skills	
	Extrinsic Motivation	1. Explaining clearly the objectives of training programs 2. Providing in advance information related to training opportunities offered (e.g., distribution of training calendars) 3. Ensuring that training programs are appropriate for the job requirements	
Motivation to learn		1. Showing interest in attending organized training programs 2. Giving full attention to training content 3. Trying to learn as many new approaches as possible in raining programs 4. Increasing motivation to perform assigned tasks	
Knowledge transfer		1. Improving employees' understanding related to tasks (e.g., knowledge sharing) 2. Applying acquired knowledge systematically 3. Adapting knowledge when the situation changes 4. Utilizing new knowledge in realizing organizational goals 5. Absorbing learned knowledge well	

supported the first hypothesis, which showed that training in a sustainable setting had a favorable and significant impact on knowledge transfer. The findings supported the second hypothesis, which also showed that learning motivation had a favorable and significant impact on information transfer. The research's discovery also supported the third hypothesis that learning motivation mediates the link between sustainable environment training and knowledge transfer. The results show that learning motivation is a key factor in improving the effect of sustainable environment training on knowledge transfer among Kuwaiti private employees. As for the demographic section in the survey, the purpose was to learn more about the employees, such as gender, age, marital status, education level, and work duration.

Table 12.2 shows the respondents' profiles. Most respondents are between less than 27 years old (53%), female (57%), Bachelor's degree holders (54.3%), and single (52.3%). The adequacy of the study sample is measured based on a rule of thumb, that is, the highest number of formative indicators in the survey questionnaire should be more than ten times, and the items for the measurement model must have an outer loading higher than the standard threshold of 0.70 according to Hair et al. (2017). Therefore, the sustainable environment training construct has the highest formative indicators in the survey questionnaires. Based on this guideline, the sample size should be at least 60 respondents. The sample size of this study has fulfilled the above criteria; thus, it can be utilized to assess the research hypotheses.

Table 12.2: Respondents' profiles (Overall N=151).

Respondents' profiles	Sub-profile	Frequency	Percentage
Age	Less than 27 years old	80	53
	28 to 33 years old	23	15.2
	34 to 39 years old	11	7.3
	40 to 45 years old	24	15.9
	46 years old and above	13	8.6
Gender	Female	86	57
	Male	65	43
Highest education	High school	7	4.6
	Diploma	16	10.6
	Bachelor	82	54.3
	Master	27	17.9
	PhD	19	12.6
Work duration	Less than 6 months	40	26.5
	7 months to 3 years	46	30.5
	4 to 8 years	28	18.5
	more than 8 years	37	24.5
Marital status	Single	79	52.3
	Married	52	34.4
	Divorced	8	5.3
	Widowed	12	7.9

Results

Measuring Construct Validity and Discriminant Validity

This research used the SmartPLS software to examine the survey questionnaire data. The data analysis process consisted of the following steps: First, a measurement model analysis was conducted to establish the validity and reliability of the research instruments. Then, a structural model analysis was utilized to investigate the direct effect and mediating models. Hypotheses could be established when the t-value was significant at 1.95. Next, the blindfolding value (Q2) was measured with a value threshold greater than zero, indicating that the construct achieved the level of predictive accuracy specified according to Hair et al. (2017). The SmartPLS program can simultaneously analyze relative and/or formative measurement model data through path analyses.

The instrument validity and reliability investigations for reflective and formative constructs based on the hierarchical component model (HCM) were examined using a two-level analysis combining higher-order and lower-order constructs. Table 12.3 presents the reflective measurement model evaluation performed based on the rate of loading, AVE, and composite reliability values. For the correlation of items with the concept, the loading value was greater than 0.70. Meanwhile, the AVE value was greater than 0.50. According to Hair et al. (2017), the composite reliability value was higher than 0.70, indicating that all the constructs had achieved the convergent validity requirements.

Table 12.4 displays the coefficients of discriminant validity, which are derived from the Heterotrait-Monotrait (HTMT) ratio of correlations among four distinct constructs: Extrinsic motivation (EM), Intrinsic motivation (IM), Knowledge transfer

Table 12.3: Reflective measurement model evaluation for the measurement model.

Constructs/ Items	Outer loading	Cronbach's alpha	Composite reliability (rho_a)	Composite reliability (rho_c)	Average variance extracted (AVE)
IM1	0.861				
IM2	0.879	0.805	0.810	0.885	0.720
IM3	0.803				
EM1	0.841				
EM2	0.847	0.780	0.781	0.872	0.695
EM3	0.813				
ML1	0.742				
ML2	0.803	0.802	0.802	0.871	0.628
ML3	0.815				
ML4	0.807				
KT1	0.755				
KT2	0.831				
KT3	0.784	0.849	0.850	0.892	0.624
KT4	0.792				
KT5	0.784				

Benchmark: Reliability Acceptable Cronbach's Alpha (>0.7)

(KT), and Motivation to learn (ML). Discriminant validity refers to the degree to which a particular notion can be considered separate from other concepts, as indicated by its low correlations with other constructs. Based on the HTMT criteria, it may be inferred that discriminant validity is considered appropriate when the values are below 0.90. According to the data presented in the table, it can be observed that all pairs of constructs exhibit HTMT ratios below the specified threshold.

Table 12.4: Discriminant validity based on HTMT criteria.

Constructs/Items	Extrinsic motivation (EM)	Intrinsic motivation (IM)	Knowledge transfer (KT)
Extrinsic motivation (EM)			
Intrinsic motivation (IM)	0.903		
Knowledge transfer (KT)	0.877	0.765	
Motivation to learn (ML)	0.893	0.859	0.926

Table 12.5 presents the Fornell-Larcker criterion; it was examined to determine whether measurement models had discriminant validity (Hair et al., 2014).

Table 12.5: Fornell-Larcker criterion.

Constructs/Items	Extrinsic motivation (EM)	Intrinsic motivation (IM)	Knowledge transfer (KT)	Motivation to learn (ML)
Extrinsic Motivation (EM)	0.834			
Intrinsic motivation (IM)	0.714	0.848		
Knowledge transfer (KT)	0.714	0.633	0.790	
Motivation to learn (ML)	0.708	0.692	0.765	0.792

Table 12.6 presents the simple statistical analysis test results. It shows the mean value range and the standard deviations for the research variables.

Table 12.6: Basic statistical analysis.

Constructs	Mean	Std. deviation
Intrinsic motivation (IM)	3.557	1.237
Extrinsic motivation (EM)	3.553	1.15
Motivation to learn (ML)	3.593	1.138
Knowledge transfer (KT)	3.514	1.194

Structural Model

The research also discovered that the influence of sustainable environment training on knowledge transfer was moderated by learning motivation. The findings of this research demonstrate that knowledge transfer in Kuwaiti private organizations is significantly impacted favorably by training in sustainable environments. This is consistent with other studies highlighting the value of training initiatives in fostering knowledge transfer inside businesses. The findings are especially pertinent in Kuwait, where there is an increasing focus on sustainability practices and the requirement that private institutions adopt environmentally friendly policies.

The research also discovered that the relationship between knowledge transfer and training in sustainable environments is mediated by learning motivation. This shows that learners are more likely to apply what they learn in training programs to their work than non-learners. Overall, the findings imply that private companies in Kuwait can improve knowledge transfer by offering training programs in sustainable environments that inspire people to learn. These findings have practical ramifications for private institutions in Kuwait and other nations looking to improve staff knowledge transfer and sustainability policies.

According to this research, knowledge transfer in Kuwaiti private organizations is significantly impacted favorably by training in sustainable environments. The correlation matrix reveals that information transfer, training, learning motivation, and a sustainable environment are positively associated. The outcomes of the structural model show that training in a sustainable setting significantly improves knowledge transfer. Moreover, learning motivation moderates the association between sustainable environment training and knowledge transfer. According to the findings, Kuwaiti private firms can enhance knowledge transfer by offering training courses in environmentally friendly settings encouraging students to learn and use new information. Overall, the research emphasizes the value of learning motivation and sustainable environment training in enhancing knowledge transfer in private organizations. The structural model is shown in Figure 12.2.

Outcomes of Hypotheses Testing H1–H4

Table 12.7 provides the results of testing hypotheses 1 to 4, the direct research hypotheses. Hypothesis 1 has ($p = 0.502$; $t = 0.671$), resulting in H1 being accepted. Hypothesis 2 has ($t = 3.663$), resulting in H2 being accepted. Hypothesis 3 ($t = 3.829$), resulting in H3 being accepted. Hypothesis 4 has ($t = 4.502$), resulting in H4 being accepted. The

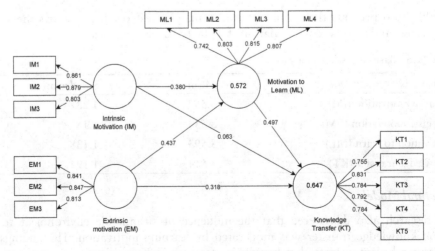

Figure 12.2 Structural model.

Table 12.7: Outcomes of testing hypotheses H1–H4.

Hypotheses	Original sample (O)	Sample mean (M)	Standard deviation (STDEV)	t-values	p-values	Result
H1: Intrinsic motivation (IM) → Knowledge transfer (KT)	0.063	0.064	0.093	0.671	0.502	not Accepted
H2: Extrinsic motivation (EM) → Knowledge transfer (KT)	0.318	0.314	0.087	3.663	0.000	Accepted
H3: Intrinsic motivation (IM) → Motivation to learn (ML)	0.380	0.378	0.099	3.829	0.000	Accepted
H4: Extrinsic motivation (EM) → Motivation to learn (ML)	0.437	0.440	0.097	4.502	0.000	Accepted

Note: Significance level: $t > 3.29$ ($p < 0.001$).

results verify that motivation to learn and knowledge transfer are crucial outcomes of intrinsic and extrinsic motivation.

Outcomes of Hypotheses Testing H5–H6

Table 12.8 Shows the results of the indirect research hypotheses. The relationship between intrinsic motivation and the motivation to learn is significantly correlated with knowledge transfer ($t = 3.172$); therefore, H5 is accepted. The relationship between extrinsic motivation and the motivation to learn is significantly correlated with knowledge transfer ($t = 3.107$); therefore, H6 is accepted. These outcomes are verifying that motivation to learn and knowledge transfer are crucial outcomes of intrinsic and extrinsic motivation. Thus, the relationship between intrinsic and extrinsic motivation to knowledge transfer is mediated by the motivation to learn.

Table 12.8: Outcomes of testing hypotheses H5–H6.

Hypotheses	Original sample (O)	Sample mean (M)	Standard deviation (STDEV)	t-values	p-values	Result
H5: Intrinsic Motivation (IM) → Motivation to Learn (ML) → Knowledge Transfer (KT)	0.189	0.188	0.059	3.172	0.002	Accepted
H6: Extrinsic Motivation (EM) → Motivation to Learn (ML) → Knowledge Transfer (KT)	0.217	0.222	0.070	3.107	0.002	Accepted

Note: Significance level: $t > 3.29$ ($p < 0.001$).

Table 12.9 shows the IPMA's outcomes. The intrinsic motivation has an impact of (0.251) and results in (63.862). The extrinsic motivation has an impact of (0.535) and results in (63.845). Motivation to learn has an impact of (0.497) and results in (64.737) Thus, motivation to learn has to prioritized to enhance training management.

Table 12.9: IPMA analysis.

Constructs	Knowledge Transfer	
	Total Effect	Performances
Intrinsic Motivation	0.251	63.862
Extrinsic Motivation	0.535	63.845
Motivation to Learn	0.497	64.737

Discussions and Implications

The research's findings have practical implications for employees in private organizations in Kuwait. Organizations may create a training program that promotes employee motivation to succeed and aligns with corporate plans and goals in the age of global competitiveness and organizational sustainability by understanding the various viewpoints on motivation to learn. The results of this research may also have wider repercussions outside of Kuwait for public sector firms looking to improve staff knowledge transfer and sustainability practices. The information supplied can be used to create and implement training initiatives to motivate employees and improve organizational performance (Bin Mahfodh and Obeidat, 2020). According to the findings, environmental training, information and awareness workshops, sustainable human intellectual capital, and other similar activities contribute to the accumulation and usage of knowledge. These activities are essential for promoting sustainable development and addressing environmental challenges. By enhancing knowledge and skills, individuals and organizations can make informed decisions and take actions that protect the environment.

Government policies that encourage greater knowledge complementarity and coordination between environmental disciplines will facilitate a greater transfer of knowledge, thereby fostering a more sustainable development. This can lead to the creation of innovative solutions that address environmental challenges while also promoting economic growth. Additionally, it can help build a culture of environmental stewardship and responsibility among individuals and organizations.

Limitation and Recommendation and Future Studies

The research also has implications for policymakers in Kuwait and other countries. Governments must support staff development as they work to raise the standard of services to achieve long-term sustainability and improve knowledge transfer within the business; this study emphasizes creating training programs that suit the private sector employees' unique demands and incentives (Azeem et al., 2021). This research has shed important light on Kuwaiti private sector employees' learning motivational variables. Organizations may create efficient training programs that boost employee motivation and improve organizational performance by understanding the various viewpoints on motivation to learn (Al Bastaki et al., 2021). The research's results can also be applied to other industries, highlighting the significance of employee motivation for long-term organizational performance.

Conclusion

This research highlights the importance of sustainable environment training and knowledge transfer in private organizations in Kuwait. It sheds light on how vital learning motivation is in this situation. This research would aid in creating an efficient training curriculum that improves the abilities and expertise of private employees and equip them to handle issues facing the community. This research emphasizes the value of sustainable environmental education and information transmission in Kuwaiti private organizations. The results emphasize the importance of learning motivation in encouraging sustainable behaviors and enhancing employee knowledge transfer to encourage employee engagement and alignment with company goals; businesses should consider including motivating aspects in their training programs, according to the research's practical implications for employees.

The research adds to the body of knowledge on sustainable private-sector organizations and offers vital information to businesses looking to further their sustainability efforts. Future research could examine the effects of various training program designs on employees' knowledge, skills, and behavior. It is conceivable to create efficient training programs through ongoing research that will empower private organizations to encourage sustainable behavior and support the sustainable development of Kuwait and other nations dealing with similar issues.

The results of this research go beyond the design of training programs. It emphasizes the value of employee motivation and how it can be leveraged to boost organizational effectiveness. Organizations must invest in staff development as the business world becomes more competitive and global (Fischer et al., 2021). This study reveals that employee motivation is a key element in accomplishing this goal. The results of this research can also be used by the public sector and nonprofit groups, in addition to the private sector. Organizations can develop training programs that satisfy these needs by using the insights of this research's findings to pinpoint the elements that inspire their workers (Laallam et al., 2020).

References

Abdelwhab Ali, A., Panneer Selvam, D. D. D., Paris, L., and Gunasekaran, A. (2019). Key factors influencing knowledge sharing practices and its relationship with organizational performance within the oil and gas industry. *Journal of Knowledge Management*, 23(9), 1806–1837.

Afsar, B., Masood, M., and Umrani, W. A. (2019). The role of job crafting and knowledge sharing on the effect of transformational leadership on innovative work behavior. *Personnel Review*, 48(5), 1186–1208.

Ahmad, F., and Muhaimin K. (2019). Impacts of knowledge sharing: a review and directions for future research. *Journal of Workplace Learning*, 31(3), 207–230.

Al Bastaki, S., Haak-Saheem, W., and Darwish, T. K. (2021). Perceived training opportunities and knowledge sharing: the case of the United Arab Emirates. *International Journal of Manpower*, 42(1), 113–130.

Azeem, M., Ahmed, M., Haider, S., and Sajjad, M. (2021). Expanding competitive advantage through organizational culture, knowledge sharing, and organizational innovation. *Technology in Society*, 66, 101635.

Bin Mahfodh, A. B. S., and Obeidat, A. M. (2020). Knowledge sharing tools and their impact on enhancing organizational performance. *Sciences*, 10(9), 91–112.

Burke, L. A., and Baldwin, T. T. (1999). Workforce training transfer: a study of the effect of relapse prevention training and transfer climate. *Human Resource Management*, 38, 227–241.

Dansereau, F., Graen, G., and Haga, W. J. (1975). A vertical dyad linkage approach to leadership within formal organizations: a longitudinal investigation of the role making process. *Organizational Behavior and Human Performance*, 13, 46–78.

Fischer, B., Guerrero, M., Guimón, J., and Schaeffer, P. R. (2021). Knowledge transfer for frugal innovation: where do entrepreneurial universities stand? *Journal of Knowledge Management*, 25(2), 360–379.

Hair, J. F., Gabriel, M., and Patel, V. (2014). AMOS covariance-based structural equation modeling (CB-SEM): guidelines on its application as a marketing research tool. *Brazilian Journal of Marketing*, 13(2)

Hair Jr, J. F., Matthews, L. M., Matthews, R. L., and Sarstedt, M. (2017). PLS-SEM or CB-SEM: updated guidelines on which method to use. *International Journal of Multivariate Data Analysis*, 1(2), 107–123.

Henseler, J., Ringle, C. M., and Sarstedt, M. (2015). A new criterion for assessing discriminant validity in variance-based structural equation modeling. *Journal of the Academy of Marketing Science*, 43, 115–135.

Knowles, M. S. (1984). Andragogy in Action. San Francisco, CA, USA: Jossey-Bass.

Laallam, A., Kassim, S., Adawiah, E. R., and Saiti, B. (2020). Towards knowledge-based waqf organizations. In Challenges and Impacts of Religious Endowments on Global Economics and Finance (pp. 100–120). IGI Global.

Lewis, J. R. (1993). Multipoint scales: mean and median differences and observed significance levels. *International Journal of Human–Computer Interaction*, 5, 383–392.

Li, Y., Song, Y., Wang, J., and Li, C. (2019). Intellectual capital, knowledge sharing, and innovation performance: Evidence from the Chinese construction industry. *Sustainability*, 11(9), 2713.

Milagres, R., and Burcharth, A. (2019). Knowledge transfer in interorganizational partnerships: what do we know? *Business Process Management Journal*, 25(1), 27–68.

Paulet, R., Holland, P., and Morgan, D. (2021). A meta-review of 10 years of green human resource management: is green HRM headed towards a roadblock or a revitalisation? *Asia Pacific Journal of Human Resources*, 59, 159–183.

Secundo, G., Toma, A., Schiuma, G., and Passiante, G. (2019). Knowledge transfer in open innovation: a classification framework for healthcare ecosystems. *Business Process Management Journal*, 25(1), 144–163.

Sekaran, U., and Bougie, R. (2016). Research Methods for Business: A Skill Building Approach. 7th edition. Chichester, UK: John Wiley & Sons, Inc.

Setini, M., Yasa, N. N. K., Supartha, I. W. G., Giantari, I. G. A. K., and Rajiani, I. (2020). The passway of women entrepreneurship: Starting from social capital with open innovation to knowledge sharing and innovative performance. *Journal of Open Innovation: Technology, Market, and Complexity*, 6(2), 25.

13 Exploring Best Practices For Promoting: Entrepreneurship Education in Bahraini University Programs

Saad Darwish

Professor, Kingdom University, Bahrain

Abstract

Our initial idea is to investigate entrepreneurship education in today's educational system. Second, we will look at methods for incorporating entrepreneurship into college curriculum. Finally, as our third supporting argument, we will look at the advantages of real-world experience received via entrepreneurship programs. We will eventually grasp why integrating entrepreneurship into the curriculum is necessary for student success and chances of employability. Entrepreneurship education is becoming more crucial in today's work environment. Entrepreneurship education is needed, and traditional job options may not be as secure as they once were, and people must acquire an entrepreneurial attitude to create their own businesses. Entrepreneurship education may provide students with the skills needed to recognize business possibilities, create a business strategy, and successfully run their own companies. Furthermore, as market demand grows, entrepreneurial education may stimulate creativity and innovation. Entrepreneurship education may assist in fostering an environment of innovation and risk-taking, which will benefit the economy. To summarize, entrepreneurship education is critical for anyone seeking to thrive in today's employment environment. It may provide them with opportunities and contribute to the development and innovation of their sectors.

Keywords

Entrepreneurship education, innovation, talents, ranking, technology.

Introduction

In recent years, there has been a growing interest in incorporating entrepreneurship into college courses. There are several approaches to include entrepreneurship into college curricula. One such technique is to encourage students to participate in real-world initiatives such as formulating company ideas or developing new goods or services. This method enables students to obtain hands-on experience and apply principles learned in class to real-world circumstances. Another approach is to bring in successful entrepreneurs as guest lecturers or mentors for students (Voldsund and Bragelien, 2022). This strategy exposes students to the difficulties and benefits of entrepreneurship while

saad.darwish@ku.edu.bh

also providing them with the opportunity to learn from seasoned professionals. Some studies propose that colleges give tools to foster student entrepreneurship, such as business idea contests and entrepreneurship institutes (Lilischkis and Stalla, 2022). This strategy offers students practical assistance while also fostering an entrepreneurial atmosphere on campus. Incorporating entrepreneurship into college courses requires a diverse strategy that includes hands-on experience and coaching (OECD, 2022). Colleges can equip students to be successful and inventive entrepreneurs by using these tactics (Darwish et al., 2018b).

Research Methodology

This study's purpose is investigative and descriptive, and it takes an informative approach to its methodological strategy. In this methodology, the researcher constructs and validates the authenticity of prior research by drawing on various sources, such as statistical reviews, reports, and other relevant sources relevant to the topic. The approach followed a systematic line of reasoning and used various practices of distinct but interconnected processes. The present investigation used a method that establishes a connection between upcoming research and the problems and worries raised by previous research. Because the fundamental concern is comprehensive gathering, direct analysis, and reflective interpretation, this research method will be the most acceptable of the available options. The researcher adhered to the procedures, which included gathering information, choosing research, and gathering secondary data. Several keywords were used in the search strategy, both independently and in combination. These keywords included, but were not limited to start-ups, entrepreneurs' education, problems, opportunities, and accomplishments.

Research Objectives and Importance

The purpose of the study that is being done on entrepreneurship education is to understand the effects that entrepreneurship education has on people as individuals, organizations, and society. Mainly to identify which approaches to teaching entrepreneurship are the most successful, which abilities and areas of expertise are essential for entrepreneurs to have, and which aspects of a business environment are most conducive to entrepreneurial success.

Research on entrepreneurship education also aims to discover the obstacles that prohibit people from pursuing entrepreneurship and from creating techniques for overcoming these obstacles to remove these obstacles from the equation. This study has the potential to assist in informing policy choices about entrepreneurship education. It has the potential to give direction to educators and trainers who are responsible for teaching entrepreneurship. Research on entrepreneurship education should have as its overarching goals the enhancement of the quality of entrepreneurship education, the rise in the number of successful entrepreneurs, and the promotion of economic growth and development. Researchers can assist in developing an atmosphere that is more encouraging for business owners by gaining a better knowledge of the characteristics that lead to entrepreneurial success.

Research Questions

The answers to these questions could provide valuable insights for educators, policy-makers, and entrepreneurs who are interested in promoting entrepreneurship education and fostering a more vibrant and inclusive entrepreneurial ecosystem.

1. What are the key competencies and skills that students need to develop through entrepreneurship education, and how can these be effectively assessed and measured?
2. How do entrepreneurship education programs impact the creation and growth of new businesses, and what are the key factors that contribute to their success or failure?
3. What are the challenges and opportunities for integrating entrepreneurship education into traditional academic curricula, and how can this be done effectively?
4. What are the key trends and innovations in entrepreneurship education, and how are they shaping the future of entrepreneurship education programs?

Literature Review

Challenges Facing Entrepreneurship Education/Advancement of Technology

Entrepreneurship education has grown in popularity in recent years. With the advancement of technology and the growth of the startup culture, the number of people aspiring to be entrepreneurs has increased (Asian Development Bank, 2022; Cooney, 2012). Nonetheless, despite the increased interest in entrepreneurship education, it faces several obstacles throughout the globe. It may be summed up as a lack of resources and finance, as well as difficulties gauging the performance of entrepreneurship education (UNESCO, 2006).

For decades, the absence of curricular standardization has been a major concern in education. The lack of standardized curriculum leads to considerable variations in educational performance between areas and colleges (Wahl and Münch, 2022). There is no assurance that students in one location or colleges obtain the same education as those in another without a consistent set of criteria. It may generate a feeling of inequity and disadvantage for learners who need access to resources or opportunities that their classmates have. Furthermore, a lack of standardization may lead to confusion and doubt among instructors, who may need clear standards for what to teach or how to teach it. European Commission (2021) advocate putting greater effort into developing and implementing a set of educational standards that can be used by all colleges and districts throughout the nation to solve this problem. Colleges and instructors may guarantee that all students get a high-quality education by doing so.

Many organizations, especially those in underdeveloped countries, need assistance in gaining access to resources and financing. Hill et al. (2022) explains attributes restricted access to resources and finance to a variety of problems, including a lack of political will, poor infrastructure, and a lack of openness in governance. Organizations working in rural and marginalized regions often need assistance with logistical issues, further limiting their access to financing and resources. They may enhance their access to resources and financing through collaborating with other businesses, participating in lobbying and networking, and developing the capability, among other things.

Companies may raise their visibility and reputation by using these techniques, which can help them acquire more financing and resources to support their work (Ernst and Young, 2014; OECD, 2015).

Entrepreneurship education has grown in popularity in recent years as a means of developing people's entrepreneurial skills and capabilities. The effectiveness of such educational programs, however, is difficult to assess. One of the primary obstacles in quantifying the performance of entrepreneurship education is the lack of a clear definition of what defines success. Success in entrepreneurship education may be measured in a variety of ways, such as the number of enterprises launched by participants or their increased entrepreneurial knowledge and abilities (Boldureanu et al., 2020). The results of entrepreneurship education programs may take time to become obvious, making measuring their performance much more difficult. Another issue is the lack of standardization in evaluating the success of entrepreneurship education programs. varied programs may have varied aims and objectives, making it difficult to develop a universal evaluation system. Furthermore, assessing the long-term effect of entrepreneurship education is difficult since people's business experiences are often complicated and multidimensional. Despite these obstacles, measuring the performance of entrepreneurship education is critical to ensuring that these programs achieve their intended aims and objectives.

These problems include a lack of access and resources, insufficient training and assistance, a lack of cooperation between academics and business, and a lack of emphasis on social entrepreneurship. To tackle these issues, governments, educational institutions, and the business sector must collaborate. We can build a more entrepreneurial society that stimulates innovation, produces employment, and contributes to global economic progress.

It is essential to recognize the significance of entrepreneurship education because it equips individuals with the skills and knowledge required to launch and manage successful businesses. Moreover, entrepreneurship, job creation, and innovation have a significant effect on the economy because it creates employment, generates revenue, and contributes to a country's economic development. Various strategies, including financial support, mentorship programs, and access to resources, can be implemented to promote entrepreneurship education. Entrepreneurship education can address a nation's economic needs, the impact of entrepreneurship on the economy, and strategies for fostering entrepreneurship.

Entrepreneurial Education and Economic Development

Entrepreneurship has the potential to help both industrialized and developing countries compete. Introducing entrepreneurship in education and expanding access is critical to developing a creative culture and entrepreneurial individuals and organizations that can promote economic growth, job creation, and worldwide quality of life (Darwish, 2022d). Despite the development of entrepreneurial education, some barriers remain, thus, changing the culture and mentality in countries where business and entrepreneurship are not appreciated or understood is a huge challenge (Khan, 2018). Due to a lack of business and entrepreneurial exposure and role models, many developing countries need help to shift from need to opportunity entrepreneurship. The current financial environment and the education, technology, and innovation restrictions of emerging countries may make funding and compatibility problematic (FATF, 2021; Darwish et al., 2020c).

There is no one-size-fits-all approach to entrepreneurship education. Various areas and educational levels provide various entrepreneurship challenges and opportunities. The local context must be addressed when developing and adjusting programs and activities. Long-term monitoring and evaluation of entrepreneurship education curricula are required. These should be based on broad outcomes rather than just start-ups. For comparable statistics across countries, agreement on entrepreneurial education, the scope of what should be examined, data collection, and coordinating methods is required. Aspiring entrepreneurs should be chosen, motivated, trained, and encouraged through higher education.

Education in Entrepreneurship Meeting Nation's Economic Requirements

Due to the increasing complexity of the business environment, entrepreneurship education is deemed essential in today's world. The current business climate is extremely competitive, and innovation and creativity are essential for business success. Lv et al. (2021) contend that entrepreneurship education equips students with the skills and knowledge necessary to navigate a complex business environment. Education in entrepreneurship enables students to develop their critical thinking and problem-solving abilities, which are crucial for business success. It teaches students to be self-reliant, creative, and risk-takers, which are essential traits of successful entrepreneurs. In addition, entrepreneurship education helps students develop a business perspective, which is essential for identifying business opportunities and transforming them into profitable ventures. In addition to fostering entrepreneurial culture, entrepreneurship education encourages students to create new careers rather than pursue employment. Consequently, entrepreneurship education has a substantial effect on economic growth and development. To empower the next generation of entrepreneurs, innovators, and business leaders, it is essential that entrepreneurship education be incorporated into the curriculum.

Entrepreneurship has a substantial impact on the economy and is a key factor in driving economic progress and development. According to carree and entrepreneurship is a crucial component of any economy because it generates new businesses, employment, and innovations. Job creation is one of the most significant contributions of entrepreneurship to the economy (Szirmai et al., 2011). Entrepreneurs generate employment by launching new businesses and expanding existing ones, which stimulates economic growth and expansion. In addition, entrepreneurship results in the development of new goods and services, which increases competition, expands consumer options, and decreases prices. This results in increased consumer expenditure, which increases demand and stimulates the economy. Entrepreneurship's effect on the economy is not limited to these factors alone; it also fosters economic and social mobility. Entrepreneurs, particularly those from disadvantaged origins, have the chance to generate wealth and enhance their socioeconomic standing. Lastly, entrepreneurship promotes innovation, which results in technological advancements, increases productivity, and enhances people's quality of life. Therefore, entrepreneurship has a positive effect on the economy, and policymakers must foster an environment that encourages and supports entrepreneurship.

Promoting Entrepreneurship Education

It is essential for the formation of new enterprises, the creation of new jobs, and the expansion of the economy. There are several strategies that can be utilized to promote entrepreneurship education.

One strategy is to incorporate entrepreneurship education into the curriculum at all educational levels, including elementary, secondary, and postsecondary. This could involve developing entrepreneurship-specific courses or modules or incorporating entrepreneurial thought into existing courses.

A second strategy is to offer students opportunities for experiential learning, such as internships or apprenticeships with local businesses or entrepreneurs. This provides students with the opportunity to acquire practical experience and learn from real-world examples. Establishing partnerships between educational institutions and local businesses or community organizations is the third strategy. These partnerships can provide entrepreneurship education with funding, mentorship, and networking opportunities, among other resources. In addition, these partnerships can help bridge the divide between academia and industry, fostering collaboration and the exchange of knowledge. By implementing these strategies, educators can assist in preparing students for the challenges and opportunities of entrepreneurship and contribute to the expansion and success of the economy.

In conclusion, entrepreneurship education is crucial to meeting a country's economic requirements. By equipping students with the skills and knowledge necessary to launch and manage successful enterprises, this fosters a culture of innovation and creativity that can stimulate economic growth. Education in entrepreneurship not only creates employment opportunities, but also promotes economic growth, social stability, and wealth creation. Therefore, it is imperative that educational institutions prioritize entrepreneurship education and that policymakers support and encourage its expansion. It is conceivable to create a future in which entrepreneurship drives economic growth and prosperity through these efforts. Besides, Education in entrepreneurship has a significant impact on entrepreneurial intent. To promote economic development, an increasing number of nations have implemented policies and measures to strengthen entrepreneurship education, the importance of which cannot be overstated. Both entrepreneurs and individuals with entrepreneurial ability benefit society. Scholars and practitioners should comprehend entrepreneurship in a broader sense (recognizing and solving problems, identifying opportunities, and creating value for society) than its limited definition (beginning a business). Consequently, entrepreneurial competence is a central concern. In a society that is becoming increasingly complex and uncertain, we can continue to create value for society, foster entrepreneurship, and advance economic growth.

Guidelines for Embedding Entrepreneurship

Here are some guidelines to help educators embed entrepreneurship in the curriculum:

1. Start with the basics: Before diving into entrepreneurship, students need to have a solid foundation in business and economics. This includes understanding basic concepts like supply and demand, profit and loss, and market research.

2. Integrate entrepreneurship into existing courses: Rather than creating a separate entrepreneurship course, educators can integrate entrepreneurship into existing courses like marketing, finance, and management. This helps students see how entrepreneurship fits into the broader business landscape.
3. Provide hands-on experiences: Entrepreneurship is all about acting, so it's important to provide students with hands-on experiences. This can include activities like creating a business plan, pitching a product, or even starting a small business.
4. Encourage creativity and innovation: Entrepreneurship is all about finding new and innovative solutions to problems. Encourage students to think outside the box and come up with creative solutions to real-world problems.
5. Foster a growth mindset: Entrepreneurship is a journey filled with ups and downs. It's important to foster a growth mindset in students and teach them to embrace failure as a learning opportunity. By following these guidelines, educators can effectively embed entrepreneurship in the curriculum and help students develop the skills they need to succeed in the business world.

Actions to Enhance Entrepreneurship Education at University Level

To motivate higher education institutions to enhance their course instruction, they should include entrepreneurial education within professional courses. The teaching of entrepreneurial professional courses is central to the university experience, and the enhancement of students' employability is intrinsically tied to the development of their professional expertise. Conventional talent training courses at colleges and universities must contain entrepreneurial education content to fulfil society's requirement for high-quality and innovative capabilities. Colleges and universities can encourage educators to adopt cutting-edge teaching practices, tailor curriculum to students' interests and needs, strengthen the connection between academic and career success, and foster students' initiative and creativity. By incorporating new pedagogical approaches like case teaching and cooperative learning, which give equal weight to both theoretical and applied learning, we can ensure that today's college students graduate with both strong professional and practical working skills. Cultural influences make many students aspire to graduate and work in government or other non-wealth-generating jobs. Learning entrepreneurship during courses of study requires a combination of theoretical and practical approaches. By taking advantage of these opportunities, students can gain the knowledge and skills they need to become successful entrepreneurs.

The fundamental cause is that students lack innovative thinking and motivation because of unrealistic expectations placed on them in higher education. In many institutions offerings are more theoretical than practical. The design of entrepreneurial education programs does not give enough thought to the development requirements of the overall market or the students' innate need. Problems with colleges include unclear branding, unjustified curricula, and insufficient hands-on experience in talent development. The fundamental reason for the study is the severe absence of teaching resources in the HEI courses put up by college. There is just one approach to teaching, and the curriculum is haphazard at best. Colleges failed to recognize the significance of HEI in the development of inventive, practical talent when it was in operation. Therefore, students are less likely to be motivated to create and launch their own businesses than they would be if entrepreneurship and innovation education were required. So, universities should revamp their models in four ways: idea, model, policy, and social support.

1. Entrepreneurship courses: Many universities and colleges offer entrepreneurship courses that teach students the fundamentals of starting and running a business. These courses cover topics such as business planning, marketing, finance, and management.
2. Business plan competitions: Many universities and colleges organize business plan competitions where students can pitch their business ideas to a panel of judges. This provides students with an opportunity to apply what they have learned in class and receive feedback from experts in the field.
3. Internships: Students can gain practical experience by interning at a startup or small business. This allows them to see firsthand how a business operates and learn from experienced entrepreneurs.
4. Networking: Students can attend networking events and conferences to meet entrepreneurs and learn from their experiences. This can help them build connections and gain insights into the industry.
5. Extracurricular activities: Students can participate in extracurricular activities such as entrepreneurship clubs or student-run businesses. This provides them with hands-on experience and allows them to apply what they have learned in class. See Figure 13.1 below

Overall, entrepreneurship at the university level requires a combination of skills that are essential for starting and running a successful business. These skills can be developed through education, training, and practical experience (Darwish, 2014a).

Creativity: Entrepreneurs need to be creative to come up with innovative ideas that can solve problems and meet the needs of their target market.
Critical thinking: Entrepreneurs need to be able to analyze and evaluate information in order to make informed decisions about their business.
Communication: Entrepreneurs need to be able to communicate effectively with their team, customers, and investors.
Leadership: Entrepreneurs need to be able to lead and motivate their team to achieve their business goals.
Financial management: Entrepreneurs need to be able to manage their finances effectively, including budgeting, forecasting, and managing cash flow.
Marketing: Entrepreneurs need to be able to develop and implement effective marketing strategies to promote their business and attract customers.
Networking: Entrepreneurs need to be able to build and maintain relationships with other entrepreneurs, investors, and industry experts.
Adaptability: Entrepreneurs need to be able to adapt to changing market conditions and adjust their business strategies accordingly.

Figure 13.1 Required skills for entrepreneurship at the university level.

Source: Entrepreneurship Skills for Growth-Orientated Businesses, Prof. Thomas M. Cooney. Dublin Institute of Technology, Report for the Workshop on, 'Skills Development for SMEs and Entrepreneurship', Copenhagen, 28 November 2012

More universities throughout the world are offering courses on entrepreneurship. Market research, financial analysis, and networking are just some of the entrepreneurial skills that students learn. Furthermore, students who participate in entrepreneurship courses can think creatively and produce novel approaches to solve problems, which is an asset in almost any profession. Finally, students in these programs get to work with mentors and professionals in their field, which may lead to invaluable networking and access to resources. Finally, entrepreneurship courses provide students with a chance to explore new paths.

Conclusions

The "Economic Vision 2030" encourages entrepreneurial education to have more students working on real-world projects on their own or with industry partners. Here, I summarize some steps for Bahraini universities to adopt for better standards of entrepreneurship education which could be considered as a road map.

- The limited business-university nexus suggests that concentrating on just one significant economic partner to establish a commercial collaboration framework is a viable strategy.
- The institution employs its website to present a concise booklet or webpage delineating project classifications and corresponding timelines for student engagement.
- Developing content for formal platforms to exhibit the skills and talents of students.
- Adding an entrepreneurship course to all degrees.
- Other courses that explicitly promote entrepreneurial concept, skills and abilities.
- Case studies of successful partners in various media should be considered.
- Support and providing easy access to guest speakers and mentors for colleges.
- The university must think about what activities it can do to inspire students in the sense that universities are hubs for entrepreneurship and play a big part in this.
- Incubate external or student startups within the university campus, plus provide seed funds.
- Students should explore worldwide entrepreneurship and wealth development contests. These are QS-related actions which will help in ranking.
- The academics' capacity to maximize research productivity given their workload, working on topics that maintain the spread of an entrepreneurial culture.
- Academics should help in publishing students' projects quickly.
- industry papers and social media blogs demonstrating the advantages of business partners working with the university.
- Explore high-level, non-resource-intensive cooperation with an enterprise-focused university in a non-competitive location for knowledge exchange, cross-training, and advancement.

References

Asian Development Bank (2022). Park, D., Jinjarak, Y., Petalcorin, C., Estrada, G., Myoda, Y., Quising, P., and Tian, S. (2022). Entrepreneurship in the Digital Age. Asian Development Bank.

https://www.adb.org/sites/default/files/publication/825166/ado2022-update-theme-chapter. pdf,%20Philippines

Boldureanu, G., Lonescu, A., Bercu, A. M., Bedrule-Grigoruta, M. V., Bercu, A. M., and Boldureanu, G. (2020). Entrepreneurship education through successful entrepreneurial models in higher education institutions. *Sustainability*, 12(3), 1267. doi: 10.3390/su12031267, https://www.researchgate.net/publication/339198654_Entrepreneurship_Education_through_Successful_Entrepreneurial_Models_in_Higher_Education_Institutions

Cooney, T. M. (2012). Entrepreneurship skills for growth-orientated businesses, Prof. Thomas M. Cooney. Dublin Institute of Technology, Report for the Workshop. 'Skills Development for SMEs and Entrepreneurship', Copenhagen, 28 November. https://www.oecd.org/cfe/leed/cooney_entrepreneurship_skills_HGF.pdf

Darwish, S. (2014a). The role of universities in developing small and medium enterprises (SMEs): future challenges for Bahrain. *Journal International Business and Management*, 8(2), 70–77.

Darwish, S. (2022d). Socio-economic development via managing entrepreneurship education: critical review. *Journal of Positive School Psychology*, 6(2), 6403–6413. http://journalppw.com

Darwish, S., Aldeeb, H., Al Azzawi, A., and Al Rashid, A. (2018b). New aspects and applications of entrepreneur's. critical success elements. *Applied Mathematics & Information Sciences: An International Journal*, 12(5), 1021–1030.

Darwish, S., Darwish, A., and Bunagan, V. (2020c). New aspects on using artificial intelligence to shape the future of entrepreneurs. *Information Sciences Letters an International Journal*, 9(1), 39–50.

Ernst and Young (2014). Adpating and Evolving. Global Venture Capital Insights and Trends 2014. EYGM Limited, Available at LE/EY_Global_VC_insights_and_trends_report_2014.pdf http://www.ey.com/Publication/vwLUAssets/Global_venture_capital_insights_and_trends_2014/$FI

European Commission (2021). A Guide to Fostering Entrepreneurship Education: Five key actions towards a digital, green, and resilient Europ. https://eismea.ec.europa.eu/system/files/2022-01/A%20guide%20for%20fostering%20entrepreneurship%20education.pdf

FATF (2021). Opportunities and Challenges of New Technologies for AML/CFT. Paris, France: FATF. https://www.fatf-gafi.org/publications/fat recommendations/documents/opportunities-challenges-new technologies-aml-cft.ht

Hill, S., Ionescu-Somers, A., Coduras, A., Guerrero, M., Roomi, M. A., Bosma, N., Sahasranamam, S. J., and Shay, J. (2022). Global entrepreneurship monitor. Global Report Opportunity Amid Disruption; https://www.gemconsortium.org/file/open?fileId=50900

Khan, Y. H. (2018). The effectiveness of entrepreneurial activities for economic development: a route to innovation and job generation. *Socio Economic Challenges*, 2(2), 32–40. https://armgpublishing.com/wp-content/uploads/2016/12/files/sec/volume-2-issue-2/4.pdf

Lilischkis, S., and Stalla, M. (2022). Support for Entrepreneurs through the Centre for Entrepreneurship at the University of Cyprus. He innovate, University of Cyprus, Centre for Entrepreneurship (C4) http://www.c4e.org.cy Ioanna Tsioutsioumi - Manager, T-raining and Outreach, Centre for Entrepreneurship (C4E) University of Cyprus, ioanna@ucy.ac.cy, https://heinnovate.eu/sites/default/files/shared_file/Updated_HEInnovate_C4E_edited_140323_0.pdf

Lv, Y., Chen, Y., Sha, Y., Wang, J., An, L., Chen, T., Huang, X., Huang, Y., and Huang, L. (2021). How entrepreneurship education at universities influences entrepreneurial intention: mediating effect based on entrepreneurial competence. *Frontiers in Psychology*, 12, 655868. doi: 10.3389/fpsyg.2021.655868. PMID: 34295281; PMCID: PMC8289882; https://www.ncbi.nlm.nih.gov/pmc/articles/PMC8289882/

OECD (2015). New Approaches to SME and Entrepreneurship Financing: Broadening the Range of Instruments. https://www.oecd.org/publications/new-approaches-to-sme-and-entrepreneurship-financing-9789264240957-en.htm

OECD (2022). Recent Developments in Entrepreneurship Training, Implications for Inclusive Entrepreneurship, Ireland. BEPT Workshop Report. https://www.oecd.org/cfe/smes/OECD2022_Entrepreneurship_training_for_inclusive_entrepreneurship_IRE.pdf

Szirmai, A., Naudé, W., and Goedhuys, M. (2011). Cusmano, L. (2015). New Approaches to SME and Entrepreneurship Financing: Broadening the Range of Instruments, Economic Development: An Overview. doi:10.1093/acprof:oso/9780199596515.003.0001; https://www.researchgate.net/publication/265064574_Entrepreneurship_Innovation_and_Economic_Development_An_Overview

UNESCO (2006). Towards an Entrepreneurial Culture for the Twenty–First Century. UNESCO and ILO research on and findings from good practice. https://unesdoc.unesco.org/ark:/48223/pf0000147057

Voldsund, K. H., and Bragelien, J. J. (2022). Student peer mentoring in an entrepreneurship course. *Procedia Computer Science*, 196, 856–863. 10.1016/j.procs.2021.12.085

Wahl, D., and Münch, J. (2022). Turning students into Industry 4.0 entrepreneurs: design and evaluation of a tailored study program. *Entrepreneurship Education*, 5, 225–259.

14 Service Quality and Adoption of Artificial Intelligence; Strategies for Improving Student Commitment, Satisfaction, and Retention

Mahmood Ali Akbar[1,a], Haytham Alalawi[1,b], and Fowz Abdulaal[2,c]

[1]Assistant Professor, University of Technology Bahrain, Kingdom of Bahrain, Bahrain
[2]BSBI student, University of Technology Bahrain, Kingdom of Bahrain, Bahrain

Abstract

This research aimed to explore the factors that can enhance the performance of private higher educational institutions. This performance is based on student commitment, satisfaction, and retention. The data were gathered from prior published studies. The results highlighted that student commitment, satisfaction, and retention can be achieved by the adoption of artificial intelligence and improvement in service quality. The proposed conceptual model of this research can be empirically examined by future studies.

Keywords

Artificial intelligence adoption, service quality, student commitment, student retention, student satisfaction.

Introduction

In its quest of academic excellence, Bahrain's government is very concerned about the quality of higher education institutions (HEIs). Higher education is increasingly viewed as a service industry, stressing the satisfaction of its student customers' needs and preferences (Altbach and Knight, 2007). Due to intense rivalries, students' enrollment in most universities is declining, and programs and services that draw students need to be dealt with (Naylor and Mifsud, 2019). Every educational institution and its competitors are ensuring and making efforts that the enrolled student should remain part of the institute until his or her degree completion to earn throughout their tenure. This is possible by attaining the loyalty of students which can lead to retention. Therefore, the universities keenly focus on student retention (Ackerman and Schibrowsky, 2007) and student engagement for quality and sustainable development (Coates, 2005). Similarly, Fam et al. (2021) also highlighted that retention is a process of gaining long-term loyalty. Students' retention is defined as a major consideration in improving academic goals, skills, and self-confidence (Tinto, 2017).

Despite the stronger competition from PHEIs for educational services, the retention rate of students is one of the most important issues for HEIs and PHEIs worldwide

[a]mahmood@utb.edu.bh, [b]shalawi@utb.edu.bh, [c]abdulaalfowz@gmail.com

(Beer and Lawson, 2017). Private universities face a number of obstacles, including a need to make a profit, an inability to recruit talented students who lack adequate financial capital, and a dependence on student income, which forces institutions to regard students as "customers" who pay for services (Yu, 2016). Therefore, this research has also used this context of considering students as customers because the student is also the customer of the institute and his or her retention is equally important as customer retention in any domain. Thus, in today's dynamic academic environment, when students have a variety of options, it is important to carefully consider the variables that enable educational institutions to draw in and keep students.

Prior studies have focused on several factors leading to student retention, but ignored the two important factors (i.e. service quality and Adoption of Artificial Intelligence). Parasuraman et al. (1985) defined service quality as the "ability of an organization to meet or exceed customer expectations." Many researchers investigated the service quality in commercial enterprises, but in comparison to business organizations, the concepts or models of higher educational institutions are different. Similarly, their vision, mission, objectives, processes, strategies, and strategic issues are different from commercial or typical business organizations (Akonkwa, 2013). A considerable amount of literature has been published on student retention, and successful PHEIs know that student retention is a by-product of student commitment and satisfaction (Harrell and Reglin, 2018). Service quality is the biggest factor influencing student retention (Eresia-Eke et al., 2020; Sickler, 2013). Artificial intelligence is established in intelligent behaviors and performance by machines, robots, or computers that are used for the assistance of businesses and human beings. In the context of service quality, artificial intelligence is all about referring digital and robotic services to customers for facilitating their purchases and particularly the consumption journey (Lu et al., 2019). Prentice et al. (2020) quoted that "AI is a component of the services that service providers supply to influence the customer experience in order to promote good attitudes (satisfaction) and behaviors (buying and loyalty) in their clients. In education, the application of artificial intelligence systems and algorithms is becoming very popular (Chen et al., 2020). Chassignol et al. (2018) highlighted that in education, artificial intelligence can be incorporated into administration, teaching, and learning. Therefore, this study has proposed a model for student retention based on service quality and the adoption of artificial intelligence by private higher educational institutions.

Supporting Theory

Student Retention Theory given by Tinto (1993) which is widely cited for student retention. The philosophy of Tinto's theory affected student success most and has contributed to a large number of graduate and observational experiments (Burch, 2018). The idea is that students reach the classroom and pre-school schooling with individual and family characteristics (Dillon and Smith, 2017). The students make other promises, both to graduate and remain at the university. They join an academic system marked by grade and intellectual development, which together contribute to academic integration, and enter into a social system in which connections with peer groups and teachers lead to social integration. According to Tinto's (1993) theory Student

Retention Theory centers on social and academic alignment in relation to a student's contribution to the school and/or external activities.

Service Quality, Student Commitment, Student Satisfaction and Service Quality

Quality in education is defined by Waterman and Peters (1982) as excellence, whereas quality in education is defined by Crosby (1979) as the output of conformance with set goals. Furthermore, Holdford and Patkar (2003) describe service quality as an evaluation of the services provided to students throughout their academic life. It's difficult to define and characterize service quality dimensions, and there's a lot of disagreement over how many should be used. In numerous studies, it is established that diverse cultures, demographic factors, and individual characteristics all contribute to variation in service quality characteristics. In order to understand how users perceived and assessed the quality of services, Parasuraman et al. (1985) listed 97 characteristics found to influence service quality. The first stage of purification had ten dimensions for determining service quality: tangibility, consistency, sensitivity, interaction, reputation, safety, professionalism, courtesy, comprehension, information, customers, and connection. Furthermore, the SERVQUAL model consolidated these ten dimensions into the well-known five dimensions (Parasuraman et al., 1990). There are several patterns for measuring service quality. However, the SERVQUAL model is the most well-known (Moosavi et al., 2017). After extensive field research on service quality, this pattern was introduced in 1998. This pattern is a method for determining user satisfaction with the services based on a model of the gap between user expectation and perception. This is the most widely used paradigm for assessing the quality of services (Tsinidou et al., 2010). Studies have shown that using this model to assess the quality of educational services is also effective (Bayraktaroglu and Atrek, 2010; Moosavi et al., 2017). Although service quality in HEIs cannot be measured objectively, it is a diverse and complex concept that should be investigated (Hameed and Amjad, 2011, p. 151).

In light of this, to continue with the evolution and analysis of the SERVQUAL model, in upcoming sections, there is a brief explanation of the five dimensions and its multidimensional attributes in the context of service quality of PHEIs, particularly in the Kingdom of Bahrain. PHEIs have become increasingly competitive during the last decade. In the higher education market, high-quality service is an important requirement for survival and competitiveness. The most difficult question facing academic institutions is what level of quality they must attain to stay competitive. PHEIs must recognize students' needs and comprehend students perceived service quality to successfully overcome the existing challenges. Students' expectations have a huge impact on how they evaluate service quality and how satisfied they are. In PHEIs, students are seen as primary customers, and their perspectives as the single most important customers can help to improve service quality (Sahney et al., 2006). Students' opinions on all areas of education provided in educational institutions are researched and regarded a significant factor in determining the quality of PHEIs in today's world (Tan and Kek, 2004; Faganel, 2010).

McDougall and Snetsinger (1990) defined tangibility as "the degree to which a product or service can provide a clear concrete image". They investigate the topic and come to the conclusion that tangibility has both a physical and a mental component. The definition of tangibles is given as "the physical evidence of the service" (McDougall and Snetsinger, 1990). While tangibility characteristics emphasize the ability to visualize the service. Asaduzzaman et al. (2014) conducted a study to examine the service quality in private universities by using 550 students. The results highlighted the highest correlation (i.e. 54.6%) between the tangibility of institution and satisfaction. Mwiya et al. (2017) empirically examined the relationship between service quality performance dimensions and overall satisfaction of undergraduate students studying in public university. They gathered the data from 656 students of final year and the results of their study revealed that along with other dimensions, the tangibility of university can play an important in the satisfaction of students. Similarly, Omar et al. (2016) conducted the study to analyse the student satisfaction leaded by service quality. They collected data from 279 students and applied multiple regression. The results of their study also revealed that tangibility can lead to satisfaction of students. Mansori et al. (2014) analyzed the service quality in Malaysian private educational institutions by using SERVQUAL model. They distributed 460 questionnaires for analysis, 29 of them were skipped due to missing data. The findings of their study demonstrated that, among the SERVQUAL aspects, tangibility had the greatest bearing on students' intentions to pursue higher-level education and to disseminate good word of mouth. The tangibility can therefore increase student happiness, which has an impact on fostering loyalty or commitment.

Dependability is also a key characteristic of service reliability, which enable the service provider to handle service problems promptly. Keeping the customer well informed about service availability, provision of correct service from the very first time, and at right time, indicate service reliability, which lead to customer retention (Barusman et al., 2019). Accuracy and reliability exist when educational resources are readily available, and personnel are willing to support students (Parasumaran et al., 1998). The ability to carry out the promised service with dependability and accuracy will promote student satisfaction and commitment, which will result in student retention. If the students are not satisfied with the performance, accuracy, dependability, and consistency of the university, they will give a negative result. Whereas, Mukhtar et al. (2015) found that among all the dimensions of service quality, the reliability has negative effect on student satisfaction.

According to Parasuraman et al. (1988:40), the SERVQUAL assurance dimension refers to the employees' professionalism, civility, and capacity to garner trust and respect. The data of 279 students were used by Omar et al. (2016) to empirically explore the connection between service quality and student happiness. Their study's findings indicated that certainty is the primary variable affecting students' contentment. The qualities of responsiveness include preparedness, readiness, speed, comfort, and eagerness to assist students. Numerous research (Mwiya et al., 2017; Sembiring et al., 2017) underlined the importance of responsiveness in relation to student satisfaction. Comparatively, Sibai et al. (2021) described responsiveness as a deteriorating predictor of student satisfaction. The responsiveness of the instructor can play an important role in developing the commitment of students (Cavanagh et al., 2018). Similarly, Lee and Seong (2020) concluded that along with all other dimensions of service quality, responsiveness can lead to student commitment. Besides student retention, the students' commitment is also an important element to understand in the context of PHEIs.

Empathy in service quality represents the service organization's customer care and personalized attention (Parasuraman et al., 1988). Rioux et al. (2017) also conclude that the personalization of student services is a major indicator of student satisfaction. Service delivery should then in no way annoy consumers to have a strong influence on the degree of customer satisfaction (Parasuraman et al., 1988 as cited in Hwang and Seo, 2016). Lee and Seong (2020) highlighted that in private universities, empathy can lead to student satisfaction and student commitment.

On the basis of the discussion given above, the research has developed the following propositions:

P_1: *Service quality can lead to student satisfaction*
P_2: *Service quality can lead to student commitment*
P_3: *Service quality can lead to student retention*

Adoption of Artificial Intelligence, Student Commitment, Student Satisfaction, and Service Quality

Researchers have argued that there is an urgent need of deploying emergent technologies like artificial intelligence in education (Croxford and Raffe, 2015). Artificial intelligence can customize learning, it can facilitate the needs of all student categories. Every student can enjoy receiving entirely unique and new educational approaches that are developed according to their needs. In higher educational institutes, artificially intelligent libraries can help in facilitating a better learning experience for students (Cox et al., 2019). Moreover, artificial intelligence can help in the customized approach to learning, and different artificial intelligence applications can help in the personalizing learning experience (Kumar, 2019). The adoption of artificial intelligence can help with student retention (Dennis, 2018), commitment, and satisfaction. Therefore, the following propositions are developed:

P_4: *Artificial intelligence can lead to student satisfaction*
P_5: *Artificial intelligence can lead to student commitment*
P_6: *Artificial intelligence can lead to student retention*

The conceptual framework proposed by this research is shown in Figure 14.1.

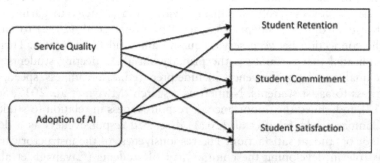

Figure 14.1 Proposed conceptual model.

Source: Self-made by the researcher

Conclusion

The results highlighted that artificial intelligence adoption and service quality of private higher educational institutes can lead to student satisfaction, commitment, and retention. PHEIs should focus on improving service quality and adopting artificial intelligence in their educational institutions for enhancing student satisfaction, commitment, and retention.

Limitations and Recommendations

The research has provided a comprehensive framework for the improvement of private higher educational institutes, but still, it has several limitations that can be considered by future studies. First, the research has proposed the model but it has not investigated it empirically, thus, future studies can empirically investigate the proposed model. Second, the study has focused mainly on the private educational institutes of Bahrain, and studies in the future can focus on public educational institutes.

References

Ackerman, R., and Schibrowsky, J. (2007). A business marketing strategy applied to student retention: a higher education initiative. *Journal of College Student Retention: Research, Theory and Practice,* 9(3), 307–336.

Akonkwa, D. B. M. (2013). Beyond market orientation: an operationalisation of stakeholder orientation in higher education. *African Journal of Marketing Management,* 5(3), 68–81.

Altbach, P. G., and Knight, J. (2007). The internationalization of higher education: Motivations and realities. *Journal of Studies in International Education,* 11(3–4), 290–305.

Asaduzzaman, M., Hossain, M., and Rahman, M. (2014). Service quality and student satisfaction: a case study on private universities in Bangladesh. *International Journal of Economics, Finance and Management Sciences,* 1(3), 128.

Barusman, A. R. P., Rulian, E. P., and Susanto, S. (2019). The antecedent of customer satisfaction and its impact on customer retention in tourism as hospitality industry. *International Journal of Advanced Science and Technology,* 28, 322–330.

Bayraktaroglu, G., and Atrek, B. (2010). Testing the superiority and dimensionality of SERVQLAL vs. SERVPERF in higher education. *Quality Management Journal,* 17(1), 47–59.

Beer, C., and Lawson, C. (2017). The problem of student attrition in higher education: an alternative perspective. *Journal of Further and Higher Education,* 41(6), 773–784.

Burch, J. J. C. (2018). An Application of Tinto's Student Integration Model and Bandura's Social Cognitive Theory to Student Retention in Stem Disciplines. Tarleton State University.

Cavanagh, A. J., Chen, X., Bathgate, M., Frederick, J., Hanauer, D. I., and Graham, M. J. (2018). Trust, growth mindset, and student commitment to active learning in a college science course. *CBE—Life Sciences Education,* 17(1), ar10.

Chassignol, M., Khoroshavin, A., Klimova, A., and Bilyatdinova, A. (2018). Artificial intelligence trends in education: a narrative overview. *Procedia Computer Science,* 136, 16–24.

Chen, L., Chen, P., and Lin, Z. (2020). Artificial intelligence in education: a review. *Ieee Access,* 8, 75264–75278.

Coates, H. (2005). The value of student engagement for higher education quality assurance. *Quality in Higher Education,* 11(1), 25–36.

Cox, A. M., Pinfield, S., and Rutter, S. (2019). The intelligent library: thought leaders' views on the likely impact of artificial intelligence on academic libraries. *Library Hi Tech,* 37(3), 418–435.

Crosby, P. (1979). *Quality is free: The Art of Making Quality.* Certain McGraw-Hill: New York.

Croxford, L., and Raffe, D. (2015). The iron law of hierarchy? Institutional differentiation in UK higher education. *Studies in Higher Education,* 40(9), 1625–1640.

Dennis, M. J. (2018). Artificial intelligence and recruitment, admission, progression, and retention. *Enrollment Management Report,* 22(9), 1–3.

Dillon, E. W., and Smith, J. A. (2017). Determinants of the match between student ability and college quality. *Journal of Labor Economics,* 35(1), 45–66.

Eresia-Eke, C., Ngcongo, N., and Ntsoane, T. (2020). The nexus of service quality, student satisfaction and student retention in small private colleges in South Africa. *Education Sciences,* 10(7), 179.

Faganel, A. (2010). Quality perception gap inside the higher education institution. *International Journal of Academic Research,* 2(1), 213–215.

Fam, K. S., Cheng, B. L., Cham, T. H., Yi, M. T. C., and Ting, H. (2023). The role of cultural differences in customer retention: evidence from the high-contact service industry. *Journal of Hospitality and Tourism Research,* 47(1), 257–288.

Hameed, A., and Amjad, S. (2011). Students' satisfaction in higher learning institutions: a case study of COMSATS Abbottabad, Pakistan. *Iranian Journal of Management Studies,* 4(1), 63–77.

Harrell, J. C., and Reglin, G. (2018). Evaluation of a community college's nursing faculty advising program relative to students' satisfaction and retention. *College Student Journal,* 52(1), 33–48.

Holdford, D., and Patkar, A. (2003). Identification of the service quality dimensions of pharmaceutical education. *American Journal of Pharmaceutical Education,* 67(1/4), 849.

Hwang, J., and Seo, S. (2016). A critical review of research on customer experience management: Theoretical, methodological and cultural perspectives. *International Journal of Contemporary Hospitality Management,* 28(10), 2218–2246.

Kumar, S. (2019). Artificial intelligence divulges effective tactics of top management institutes of India. *Benchmarking: An International Journal,* 26(7), 2188–2204.

Lee, H. J., & Seong, M. H. (2020). A study on the effects of business service quality on satisfaction, commitment, performance, and loyalty at a private university. The Journal of Asian Finance, Economics, and Business, 7(9), 439–453.

Lu, L., Cai, R., and Gursoy, D. (2019). Developing and validating a service robot integration willingness scale. *International Journal of Hospitality Management,* 80, 36–51.

Mansori, S., Vaz, A., and Zarina, M. M. I. (2014). Service quality, satisfaction and student loyalty in Malaysian Private Education. *Asian Social Science,* 10(7), 57–66.

McDougall, G. H. G., and Snetsinger, D. W. (1990). The intangibility of services: measurement and competitive perspectives. *Journal of Services Marketing,* 4(4), 27–40.

Moosavi, A., Mohseni, M., Ziaiifar, H., Azami-Aghdash, S., Manshadi, M. G., and Rezapour, A. (2017). The quality of educational services from students' viewpoint in Iran: a systematic review and meta-analysis. *Iranian Journal of Public Health,* 46(4), 447.

Mukhtar, U., Anwar, S., Ahmed, U., and Baloch, M. A. (2015). Factors effecting the service quality of public and private sector universities comparatively: an empirical investigation. *Researchers World,* 6(3), 132.

Mwiya, B., Bwalya, J., Siachinji, B., Sikombe, S., Chanda, H., and Chawala, M. (2017). Higher education quality and student satisfaction nexus: evidence from Zambia. *Creative Education,* 8(7), 1044–1068.

Naylor, R., and Mifsud, N. (2020). Towards a structural inequality framework for student retention and success. *Higher Education Research and Development,* 39(2), 259–272.

Omar, M. S., Ariffin, H. F., and Ahmad, R. (2016). Service quality, customers' satisfaction and the moderating effects of gender: a study of Arabic restaurants. *Procedia-Social and Behavioral Sciences,* 224, 384–392.

Parasuraman, A., Berry, L. L., and Zeithaml, V. A. (1990). Guidelines for Conducting Service Quality Research. *Marketing Research*, 2(4), 34–44.

Parasuraman, A., Zeithaml, V. A., and Berry, L. L. (1985). A conceptual model of service quality and its implications for future research. *Journal of Marketing,* 49(4), 41–50.

Parasuraman, A. B. L. L., Zeithaml, V. A., and Berry, L. (1988). SERVQUAL: A multiple-item scale for measuring consumer perceptions of service quality. *Journal of Retailing*, 64(1), 12–40.

Prentice, C., Lopes, S. D., and Wang, X. (2020). The impact of artificial intelligence and employee service quality on customer satisfaction and loyalty. *Journal of Hospitality Marketing and Management,* 29(7), 739–756.

Rioux, L., Scrima, F., and Werner, C. M. (2017). Space appropriation and place attachment: University students create places. *Journal of Environmental Psychology,* 50, 60–68.

Sahney, S., Banwet, D. K., and Karunes, S. (2006). An integrated framework for quality in education: application of quality function deployment, interpretive structural modelling and path analysis. *Total Quality Management and Business Excellence,* 17(2), 265–285.

Sembiring, M. G. (2017). Exploratory study of academic excellence associated with persistence in ODL setting. *Asian Association of Open Universities Journal*, 12(2), 125–136.

Sibai, M. T., Bay Jr, B., and Dela Rosa, R. (2021). Service quality and student satisfaction using ServQual Model: A study of a private medical college in Saudi Arabia. *International Education Studies*, 14(6), 51–58.

Sickler, S. L.(2013). Undergraduate Student Perceptions of Service Quality as a Predictor of Student Retention in the First Two Years. Bowling Green State University.

Tan, K. C., and Kek, S. W. (2004). Service quality in higher education using an enhanced SERVQUAL approach. *Quality in Higher Education,* 10(1), 17–24.

Tinto, V. (1993). *Leaving college: Rethinking the causes and cures of student attrition* (2nd edn). Chicago, IL: University of Chicago Press.

Tinto, V. (2017). Through the eyes of students. *Journal of College Student Retention: Research, Theory and Practice*, 19(3), 254–269.

Tsinidou, M., Gerogiannis, V., and Fitsilis, P. (2010). Evaluation of the factors that determine quality in higher education: an empirical study. *Quality Assurance in Education,* 18(3), 227–244.

Waterman, R. H., and Peters, T. J. (1982). *In search of excellence: Lessons from America's best-run companies* (p. 360). New York: Harper & Row.

Yu, S. O. (2016). Reculturing: the key to sustainability of private universities. *International Journal of Teaching and Education,* 4(2), 88–105.

15 Framework on Strategic Succession Management System: A Proposed Reference for Business Organizations

Manolo L. Anto[1,a] and Marluna Lim-Urubio[2,b]

[1]Associate Professor, University of Technology Bahrain, Bahrain
[2]Assistant Professor, University of Technology Bahrain, Bahrain

Abstract

This study aimed to develop a proposed framework on strategic succession management system as reference for business organizations. It compared two benchmark frameworks on succession management system. In conducting the benchmarking process, steps were followed, such as: decide what needs benchmarking, document benchmarking objectives and scope, document the current process, decide on the primary metrics, identify sources and start data gathering, and develop a recommended framework for a system. Resultant commonalities were noted and further analyzed, and the proposed framework on strategic succession management system was developed.

Keywords

Benchmarking, succession, succession management system.

Introduction

Succession management, as defined by Phillips and Gully (2014), is a process to enhance employee performance which will identify, assess, and develop the leadership capabilities of the organization's workforce. The process involves strategic talent planning, retirement and retention planning, and talent development and assessment. It ensures the continuity of the employees' leadership, prevents top ranks from future hiatus, and prevents employees from unlikely promotion.

Succession management thus creates a direct link between the goal of the organization and the employee performance, and thereby makes the employees' contribution to the organization more open and clearer. This study therefore aims to propose a framework for business organizations that would align the succession management system with their organizational goals.

Literature Review

Human resource management as it is has many basic functions, one of which is succession management. Succession management is a vital tool, based on the employer's

---

[a]m.anto@ku.edu.bh, [b]mlurubio66@gmail

perspective, to work at the goals of the organization strategically. The process induces employees to be attracted to the organization because it has an impact on their behaviors and attitudes, and it can be a powerful instrument to make sure that employee's interests are consistent with that of the organization.

Strategic human resource management is associated with business strategy to acknowledge external challenges in order to devise models leading to the reduction or elimination of the effect on business in the external environment. Strategic human resource management supports the human resource management practices to improve employee performance and develop competitive advantage.

"Human resource functions in order to be strategic. By this means to assist the top management fulfil business objectives which are strategic in nature. The performance management system reinforces the individual behavior through linking the organization's goals with individual goals. In doing so, attainment of individual goals contributes to the attainment of the goals of the organization. In addition to this, while in some cases, and for some reason when the goals of individual so not attained, but connecting the goal with that of the organization leads to an opportunity to establish in depth communication in identifying possible initiatives which will satisfy both individual and organizational goals. It is always in the best interest that there is alignment between organizational and individual goals." (Anto, 2019).

Phillips and Gully (2014) stressed on their book that "succession management does not only mean to identify and recognize employees for possible promotion but it should also It should ensure that it integrates the supervision of the company's pool of talent with the strategic plan of the organization. If done far enough in advance, succession management can sometimes affect the choice of which business strategy to pursue. If the firm's succession planning indicates that managerial talent is in short supply, the organization can make hiring employees with the potential to become store managers a key goal of its recruiting and hiring process. Alternatively, the company can plan to hire store managers from outside of the company to staff its new locations. This means that succession management impacts long-term direction of the organization. Diversity of workforce has become significant also that companies nowadays require diverse workforce for the succession management to be successful. Even if the succession management system can identify the replacement of that resigning employee, the company should not limit itself to one candidate only but leave it open for other employees too. It is important therefore that all information about the system should be cascaded to all employees to make them feel that they are more of investors rather than assets".

The key functions needed for an effective succession plan includes understanding development needs of the organization, identifying potential successors, training and development for the identified successors, and promoting employees and providing them with the right compensation. Effectiveness in the implementation of these functions will lead to the achievement of organizational goals and objectives (Ameen, 2014).

In the study of Cardy (2008), he stated that one of the first steps for organizations to self-assessment is to visualize their direction and develop their future plans. Moreover, According to Babu (2010), a successful plan allows organizations to handle progressions in employees' career and thereby achieving the goals for excellent organizational performance and productivity.

The study of Kippist (2013) highlighted the lack of succession planning role of the doctor manager in Australia and implications on individual and the organization. Findings revealed the need for health care administrators to develop a plan for succession in all management levels. On the other hand, in the study of Freiling and Poschl (2020), it was found out by these authors that there is not fully in place a predecessor nor successor in the issue of family corporations involving succession management system pertaining to entrepreneurial tasks range on a top level positions.

The aim of the study of Gliszczynski and Berkowski (2021) is to prove the hypothesis that the lack of effective succession management system is one of the obstacles for SMEs to flourish. While in the study of Liu (2020), it reveals that the succession of the Chief Operating Officer provided a good impression on post-succession

Methodology and Model Specification

For a developmental type of research which purpose is to develop a proposed framework out of the existing plans, benchmarking tool is apt to be used. Benchmarking is a method of comparing one's business processes to industry best practices from other companies (Richey, 2021).

By this benchmarking tool, this study observed the following steps such as: a) decide what needs benchmarking, b) documents benchmarking objectives and scope, c) documents the current process, d) decides on the primary metrics, e) identifies sources and start data gathering, and f) develops a recommended framework for a plan.

The following Tables 15.1 and 15.2 are the research instruments upon which the key components of various succession management frameworks were considered in this study for point of comparison.

The comparison of these two instruments was anchored on the framework in Figure 15.1 by Dessler (2017). In his book, he emphasized that succession planning process is

Table 15.1: Key components of strategic succession management system.

Succession planning and its Effects on Employee Career Attitudes: Study of Iranian Governmental Organizations (Farashah et al., 2011)	Succession Planning and Talent Pool Development Framework in the Federal Government (www.fahr.gov.ae/Portal)
Process and change management	Identify critical positions
Selection of successor	Develop and monitor talent pool
Development of successor	Engage talent pool
	Govern/review succession strategies

Figure 15.1 Steps in succession planning by Dessler (2017).

to enhance employee performance which will identify, assess, and develop the leadership capabilities of the organization's workforce.

Results and Discussion

Two benchmark frameworks were considered in this study: a) Succession Planning and its Effects on Employee Career Attitudes: Study of Iranian Governmental Organizations (Farashah et al., 2011), and b) Succession Planning and Talent Pool Development Framework in the Federal Government (www.fahr.gov.ae/Portal).

Under the framework of Farashah et al., 2011, the process involves three basic steps: a) process and change management, b) selection of successor, and c) development of successor. On the other hand, under the framework of www.fahr.gov.ae/portal, the process involves three basic steps, such as: a) identify critical resources, b), develop and monitor talent pool, c) engage talent pool, and d) govern/review succession strategies.

Table 15.2: Comparison of key elements of strategic succession management system.

Succession Planning and its Effects on Employee Career Attitudes: Study of Iranian Governmental Organizations (Farashah et al., 2011)	Succession Planning and Talent Pool Development Framework in the Federal Government (www.fahr.gov.ae/ Portal)	Comparative Analysis
Process and change management	Identify critical positions	Set objectives for succession management
		Identify critical positions and resources;
Selection of successor	Develop and monitor talent pool	Develop inside talent pool (competency gap analysis, career development, training plan)
Development of successor	Engage talent pool	
	Govern/review succession strategies	Assess and choose those who will fill in the top positions (performance appraisal)
		Evaluate the succession management system

Conclusion and Recommendation

The study concludes by extracting the resultant framework based on the comparison between the two given frameworks which are: a) Succession Planning and its Effects on Employee Career Attitudes: Study of Iranian Governmental Organizations (Farashah et al., 2011), and b) Succession Planning and Talent Pool Development Framework in the Federal Government (www.fahr.gov.ae/Portal).

Figure 15.2 Proposed framework on strategic succession management system.

The two were being compared and the resultant commonalities were noted and further elaborated. Thus, the proposed framework on Figure 15.2 includes processes such as: a) set objectives for succession management; b) identify critical positions and resources; c) develop inside talent pool; d) assess and choose those who will fill in the top positions, and, e) evaluate the succession management system.

For a succession management system to be strategic, it is important that the organization should first set the objectives of the system and align it with the organizational goal. Identify critical positions and critical resources for future roles in the organization. In assessing the potential of the candidates, the managers performs a review of the talent as well as performance of the employee using a variety of data and from different sources. This may include performance review data done on an annual basis, together with a person's development plans. It may also include other types of assessment that can result to uncovering other potentials. Now, using the pre-set objectives for the succession planning which are measurable, then results are evaluated and the system is enhanced or refined as needed.

References

Ameen, F. (2014). Succession Planning Strategy of Bank of Bahrain and Kuwait (BBK) in the Kingdom of Bahrain. MBA Thesis. AMA International University Bahrain. Unpublished.

Anto, M. (2019). Framework on Strategic Performance Management System: A Proposed Reference for Business Organizations. AMA International University Bahrain, Unpublished.

Babu, R. (2010). The Basics of Succession Development. Theoretical Framework.

Cardy, R. L. (2008). Talent management: for the twenty-first century. *Harvard Business Review*, 86(3), 74–81.

Dessler, G. (2017). Human Resource Management. 15th Edition. Pearson.

Farashah, A., Nasehifar, V., Ahmadreza Sanjari Karahrudi (2011). Succession planning and its effects on employee career attitudes: Study of Iranian governmental organizations. *African Journal of Business Management*, 5(9), 3605–3613.

Freiling, J., and Poschl, A. (2020). Family-external business succession: the case of management buy-ins. *Journal of Small Business and Entrepreneurship*, 8, 1–26.

Gliszczynski, G., and Berkowski, F. (2021). The role management succession on the growth of pPolish SMEs scientific papers of silesian university of technology. Organization & management zeszyty naukowe politechniki slaskiej. *Seria Organizacji Zarzadzanie*, 153, 111–131.

Kippist, L. (2013). Bridges or Barriers? Succession planning for Doctor Managers. *International Employment Relations Review*, 19(2), 24–37.

Liu, X. (2020). Impression management against early dismissal? CEO succession and corporate social responsibility. *Corporate Social Responsibility and Environmental Management*, 27(2), 999–1016.

Phillips, J. M., and Gully, S. M. (2014). Strategic Staffing (2nd edn). Prentice Hall: Pearson.

Richey, R. C. (2021). Developmental Research: The Definition and Scope. Detroit: Wayne State University. https://eric.ed.gov/?id=ED373753.

16 Sustainable Packaging: Analysis of the Customer's Attitude Towards Utilization of Paper Based Packaging Material

Marluna Lim Urubio

SFHEA-UK, University of Technology Bahrain

Abstract

The issue of food packaging waste is considered a significant matter due to its adverse environmental effects. Food packaging is an important part of the supply chain whether it is on a local or global level and therefore the kind of packaging material being used is a vital factor. One option is the use of sustainable innovation in product packaging and shifting from non-biodegradable material to biodegradable materials. This study aims to know the consumer's attitude towards the use of both plastic packaging and sustainable packaging materials. The results showed that respondents favored the use of sustainable packaging where the benefits of using these types of materials are made known to them and will lead to their intention to use sustainable packaging materials and eventually promote health and safe environment. Through awareness campaign and activities, consumers can be encouraged to shift to sustainable packaging that result to health benefit as well as environmental benefits. In addition, government support through regulatory policies will have a strong impact coupled with manufacturer's performing life cycle assessment for the packaging materials that they use in their operation.ng.

Keywords

Food packaging, life cycle assessment, sustainable packaging.

Introduction

Manufacturing and Service Operations pertaining to food production and services are one of the biggest contributors of plastic waste. If plastic waste reduction will be on its way, a specific area to explore is on sustainable packaging. While plastic is viewed to be an efficient packaging material considering the perspective form the supply chain, but it results to disastrous environmental effects (Silva and Molina-Besch, 2022). Food packaging is unquestionably indispensable part of food chain. Movement is highly dependent on the reliability of its packaging.

Food packaging's primary concern is ensuring that food reaches the end users in good quality, ensuring safety and health. Another function of food packaging is to ensure cleanliness and sanitation of the products against any bacteria or microorganisms as

mlurubio66@gmail

well as undesirable changes in temperature, presence of moisture. Food packaging ensures protection against product handling during transportation and even storage.

Currently, most of the food packaging is made of plastic which is recognized to have detrimental effects to environment as its disposal results to increase in carbon footprint. Therefore, this study is significant now that Bahrain has declared Zero Carbon Emission or Carbon Neutrality by 2060. The study investigated consumers 'attitudes that will lead to their intention to shift from buying food in plastic packaging to those which use paper based packaging materials.

The objectives of the study include (a) understanding how customers' attitude towards the plastic packaging affect/influence their intention to shift to paper-based packaging, (b) recognizing how customers' attitude towards paper based packaging affect/influence their intention to shift to paper based packaging and (c) understanding how these two (2) attitudes of consumers' can lead to the actual use of paper based packaging.

Literature Review

Packaging is very important as consumers are first attracted to the product through its packaging. While there are many types of materials being used for food packaging, still plastic materials contribute to the biggest percentage. Plastic waste has emerged one of the biggest threat to the environment to be 141 Million tons in 2015 by the industrial sector (Geyer et al., 2017). Putting the overall plastic wastage including consumer, it went to 161 Million tons and out of 161 Million tons, only 2.2 Million tons was recycled or 14.16% (Environmental Protection Agency/ www.billerud.com (??)). Using plastics packaging has some advantages for consumers because of their flexibility and affordability but most plastics are for single use, and with low recycling or reuse ratios which contribute to environmental issues specifically pollution (Weber Macena et al., 2021).

Isak (2021), reiterated the hazardous effect of plastic materials as plastics is made up of both chemical and hazardous substances, one of which is the Bisphenol A (BPA), which are present in all plastic materials and are considered dangerous to human health and environment. The use of plastic leads to voluminous plastic waste which when exposed to ambient radiation contributes to 3.4% of global greenhouse gas emissions throughout their lifecycle (https://www.carbontrust.com/what-we-do/assurance-and-labelling/plastic-packaging-framework). The use of plastic packaging comes with a number of advantages but the disadvantages these plastic materials have caused to environment should be seriously taken into consideration.

Manufacturing companies should have a deeper understanding of their corporate social responsibility through ensuring that their products and operations do not contribute to environmental problems. One way is to avoid the use of plastic based packaging materials (Evans, 2020).

It was said that 40% of plastic garbage is made up of packaging materials, 12% from consumer goods and 11% from clothing and textiles (OECD, 2022). More than clothes, people purchase food items and other consumer goods mores. Measuring sustainability of packaging materials can be a result of the few factors like—level of greenhouse gas emission, proper disposal, amount of energy used to manufacture the packaging material, degree of frequency on reusing, durability, recyclability, time to decompose (Edgington, 2019).

This study used the Theory of Reasoned Action (Fishbein and Ajzen, 1975) which indicates that pre-existing attitudes of consumers are important in the decision making process where there is a relationship of behaviors and attitude to consumers' action. Consumers' beliefs, attitudes, intentions and behavior form a causal chain, that allow these beliefs to lead to consumers' attitudes and finally these attitudes become intentions and leads to actual consumer behavior.

Data and Variables

The study covered respondents who are mixed nationalities which were taken randomly from Dana Mall, Juffair Mall and Bahrain CitiCenter. The survey was done for the whole month of December 2022 until February 2023 where people are into shopping spree due to Christmas season. As of 2021, data from the World Bank indicates that Bahrain has a population of 1,463,265. However, since 2023 data is not available, then the author used 450 samples which is 16% higher than the required sample.

Procedure

Respondents were of different ages but limited to not lower than 20 years old. The questionnaire used was a modified survey questionnaire coming from different researches. Since people were coming in groups during their shopping spree, the researcher asked first whether they are willing to participate in the survey citing the importance of the research. After a short introduction of the research, respondents were given the questionnaire.

Dependent Variable

The dependent variable in this study is the intention of the respondents to use paper-based packaging.

Independent Variable

There are two independent variables which include the attitudes of the respondents toward the use of plastic packaging, a non-renewable packaging, which is considered a negative attitude while the other variable is the attitude towards the use of paper-based packaging, a renewable packaging, which is considered a positive attitude.

Methodology and Model Specification

With the aim of answering the research questions, the researcher used both qualitative and quantitative method for this study. The author used 5 – pt-Likert scale for the questionnaire focused on their attitude towards the existing packaging materials with 13 indicators while 7 indicators were on paper based packaging. The mean and composite mean were taken as well as the standard deviation. Ranking was done to see how respondents given much importance on certain indicators.

The study used Heterotrait-Monotrait (HTMT) ratio to measure the similarity between latent variables. It also measures the discriminant validity of the variables to prove that they are significantly different from each other. It also used SRMR or Standardized Root Mean Square Residual to test how well the data fit the structural model/theory that have been used for the study. The SRMR is defined as the difference between the observed correlation and the model implied correlation matrix. Thus, it allows assessing the average magnitude of the discrepancies between observed and expected correlations as an absolute measure of (model) fit criterion.

Results

The discriminant validity of the two variables have been confirmed through the result shown in Table 16.1. Heterotrait-Monotrait (HTMT) ratio. The researcher used HTMT of the Heteroit-Monotrati ratio to validate the two variables in this study are significantly different from each other. An HTMT value that is close to 1 points out an absence of discriminant validity. However form some authors, a threshold value of 0.85 also proves the lack of similarity of the variables.

Additionally, a path analysis and model fit test were done through Standardized Root Mean Square Residual (SRMR) as presented in Table 16.2. Values for the SRMR range from zero to 1.0 with well-fitting models obtaining values less than .05 (Byrne, 1998; Diamantopoulos and Siguaw, 2000). Hu and Bentler (1999), suggests that values as high as 0.08 are deemed acceptable although an SRMR value of 0 indicates perfect fit. However, but it must be noted that when there is a high number of parameters in the model and in models based on large sample sizes then, the SRMR will be lower.

Table 16.1: Heterotrait-monotrait.

	Intention to adopt	NAT Non-renewable	PAT renewable
Intention to adopt			
NAT non-renewable	0.696		
PAT renewable	0.798	0.803	

Table 16.2: Path analysis and model fit criteria.

Path	Coefficient	P value
Negative attitude → Intention to use	0.164	0.194
Positive attitude → Intention to use	0.441	0.000
Model Fit		
Adjusted R square	0.228	
SRMR	0.070	
NFI	0.032	

Intuitively, since the research goal is to test a model that predicts consumer intention, then SRMS therefore fulfills this job. SRMR measures the overall model fit, ensuring that the model is best fitted and minimizes the residuals of the observed and predicted covariance matrices of the data set (Henseler et al., 2015).

In this case, the positive attitude of using paper based packaging has a p value of 0.000 means that it has significant influence on the dependent variable which is the intention to use paper based packaging. A p value of less than 0.05 is considered significant. The negative attitude pertaining to the use of plastic has a p value of 0.194 and is therefore not significant.

The structural model below in Figure 16.1 shows both the negative and positive attitude of respondents—negative attitude towards non-renewable packaging and positive attitude towards renewable packaging and which between the two leads to the intention to use renewable packaging. The models validates the impact of the 2 latent variables whether they are significant to the intention to use paper based packaging materials.

For Part 1 which focused on the attitude on the existing packaging showed that the indicators pertaining to the plastic packaging materials to be very convenient has a mean score of 4.78 while indicator stating that plastic packaging materials ensures product quality scored 4.67. Respondents also strongly agreed that plastic packaging allows ease of use and recycling (4.61). They also see the plastic packaging as something that can survive extreme environment (4.26) and same time, flexible and adaptable with same mean rating of 4.17. On the other hand, they recognize the risk of BPA which is present in plastic products (4.07) while these materials do not easily degrade in either hot or cold temperature (4.1). Respondents also recognized that inappropriate disposal results to pollution (3.95) and worse is, these materials end in landfills and trash bin (3.76).

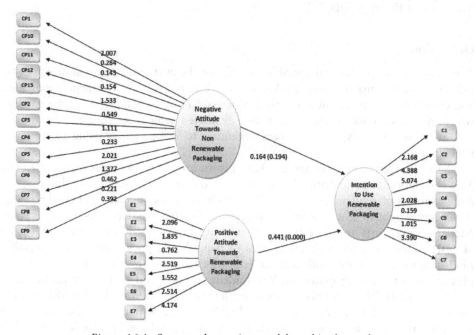

Figure 16.1: Structural equation model used in the study.

On respondents' attitude towards paper based packaging, respondents recognized that using paper based packaging materials is safe to human and environment where the mean rating is 4.5 while respondents also acknowledged that paper based packaging are environmentally friendly with mean rating of 4.45. Both indicators on the ability of the paper based packaging to be disposed easily and its ability to resist bacteria have similar mean rating of 4.34. The ability to keep the food from moisture and humidity is rated at 4.15 while keeping the quality of food is 3.74.

Part 3 tackles the respondents' intention to use paper based packaging materials based on the different indicators. Respondents' 1st consideration is their knowledge that using paper based packaging is better for health (4.37) while the 2nd is that paper packaging keeps the food safe (4.33). The 3rd consideration is the easy disposal of the packaging when its paper based (4.30) and the 4th is being able to help reduce the impact of plastic materials to environment (4.25). Consumers also considered that paper is lightweight material (4.23). Another consideration is that paper based are reusable and easy to use—both with a mean score of 4.07 while the least is its durability (3.98).

Ranking the indicators in terms of how these will influence the respondent' intention to use paper-based packaging shows that the 1st consideration that will make them shift to using food packed in paper based packaging material is their knowledge that using this material is better and beneficial for their health and followed by the ability of the packaging material to keep their food safe (2nd). The 3rd and 4th among the indicators include the disposability of paper packaging materials and that using these will help reduce the impact to environment if plastic materials will be continuously used. On the other hand, the 5th and 6th are the indicators stating that the paper based materials are lightweight and that it is reusable. The last consideration is that the durability of the materials.

Discussion

The study measured the two variables which are the customers' attitude towards the existing products using plastic packaging which is referred to as a negative attitude and customers; attitude towards sustainable packaging or renewable packing which is referred to as positive attitude. It also evaluated which between the 2 variables will affect significantly the customers' intention to use products using paper based packaging.

The respondents strongly agreed that plastics are convenient packaging material. This is supported by the British Plastic Association cited that plastics are durable, safe and shatterproof, hygienic, secured as it comes with tamper-evident and child resistant closures and light weight. However, respondents are also aware that using paper based packaging materials are more beneficial for both human and environment. Vishal et al. (2014), mentioned the characteristics of paper-based packaging to be recyclable, biodegradable, renewable and sustainable product that makes it a lot better than most plastic-based packaging materials. Respondents ranked 2nd that paper packaging is environmentally friendly. This is supported by the discussion in the World Economic Forum (2016) validating that paper is a highly recyclable packaging material which is benign if leaked into the environment. Using paper based packaging instead of plastic packaging is highly efficient and cost-saving alternative for consumers (Sonoco Asia; Oloyede and Lignou, 2021). Paper is far more biodegradable than plastic and very easily recycled (Santos-Moreira, 2020). The heaviest consideration if and when respondents will use paper packaging is the safety it gives to consumers. From a survey conducted in a European consumer, done by Two Sides in 2020, 62% of respondents viewed paper and cardboard packaging to be environmentally friendly while 70% of the respondents expressed that they were actively doing their part to reduce their utilization of plastic packaging (Santos-Moreira, 2020).

The result of the study shows that to make the respondents shift to the use of sustainable packaging material, a positive campaign should be done to make them fully understand the benefits of the paper-based packaging. Living Business Programme (2022) said that consumers from the GCC countries or the so called Middle Eastern consumers, they think that there is a lack of sustainable options available to consumers and that quality of the products is inconsistent. Moreover, product becomes too expensive for using sustainable packaging. This supports the result of the study that a strong awareness campaign is important to expose the consumers on the available options which support sustainability. Moreover, customers' intention to purchase food packed in paper packaging materials is also influenced by the packaging color, the material itself, designs and graphics, shape and size (Yeo et al., 2020). This characteristics for a paper packaging can be another research area.

Murphy (2022) said that between 2019 and 2021, consumers' shopping habits have changed avoiding items presented in plastic packaging. GlobeScan Consultancy concluded that packaging innovations should be explored as consumers' buying behavior is geared towards plastic waste elimination. Consumers are found to associate paper based packaging as unique and possesses high quality aside from its novelty and exclusivity (Chrisant Rystiasih, 2019). In the same research it is noted that consumers are willing to pay more if it means having a food packed in safer packaging material.

Making a campaign showing the negative impact of the use of plastic is not necessarily contributing to their intention to use renewable or sustainable packaging materials as evidenced by a p-value of 0.194. Respondents are already super exposed to all of the media campaign showing climate change, greenhouse effect, pollution among others but while these bother them for quite some time, "that feeling of being bothered" is not at all translated into their intention to use sustainable packaging materials.

Government support is required in terms of formulating regulatory policies that will promote the use of sustainable packaging like tax incentives or tax exemption for manufacturers who opt to use sustainable packaging materials, same with stores who will only carry products packed in paper based packaging.

Manufacturers' cooperation is equally significant making them perform life cycle analysis of all their products or materials to know the impact on the environment.

Conclusion

To summarize, plastic pollution is a global issue that has serious health and environmental impact. Irresponsible and careless disposal leads to release of harmful chemicals to the environment that can go to water sources and air. The findings of the study has proved that consumers are willing to use sustainable packaging materials as environmental advocacy has led consumers today to widely view paper as a more environmentally friendly alternative to plastic (Santos Moreira, 2021). In addition, consumers would be ready to prefer using green packaging if consumers are presented with facts about the benefits of these packaging to environment, the product pricing along with improving their environmental concern and knowledge (Karan Gupta, 2021; Lim-Urubio, 2022).

An Australian research yielded 80% of its respondents indicated their intention to do plastic reduction (Dilkes-Hoffman et al., 2019). The study also said that while many respondents agree to the health and environmental advantage of using paper-based packaging, however this agreement does not translate into action. Reduction on the utilization of plastic rests more in the industry and government while raising awareness on the benefits of saving the environment will be better in making the consumers choose sustainable packaging (Afiza, 2023).

Consumers should be well exposed on the concept of sustainability where their actions and decisions lead to either environmental protection or degradation.

On the part of the Manufacturers, it is important that they conduct a full life cycle assessment to determine a product packaging's environmental impact—not just what it's made of as well as assessment of its ability to decrease food waste, which is essential for a more sustainable food system.

However, government initiatives are one significant support if sustainable packaging will be implemented. There should be stronger and more effective sustainable packaging regulations beyond single use plastic bags but for food packaging which contribute to a bigger percentage when it comes to plastic waste.

Legislation is an essential element of any Recycling Plan. There are currently regulations and legislation that provide the intended purpose, but require modernization to align with technological progression; and provide more authority to ensure the disciplinary and enforcement measures are in place. The Strategy Plan addresses the issue of the need for legislation clearly (Shavanas, 2019).

Caring for the environment means having the right choices and these right choices lead to a better and greener world to live.

References

Afiza, M. N. (2023). Springer Nature Switzerland AG. Publisher, Springer Science and Business Media Deutschland GmbH.

Byrne, B. M. (1998). Structural Equation Modeling with LISREL, PRELIS and SIMPLIS: Basic Concepts, Applications and Programming. Mahwah, New Jersey: Lawrence Erlbaum Associates.

Chrisant Rystiasih, A. (2019). Retail and Consumer Perceptions on Paper Packaging for Flour in Indonesia with Insights on Perceptions of Environmental Sustainability. Published by Division of Packaging Logistics, Department of Design Sciences, Faculty of Engineering, Lund University, P.O. Box 118, SE-221 00 Lund, Sweden, ISBN 978-91-7623-396-2

Diamantopoulos, A., and Siguaw, J. A. (2000). Introducing LISREL. London: Sage Publications.

Dilkes-Hoffman, L., Pratt, S., Laycock, B., Ashworth, P., and Andrew Lant, P. (2019). Public attitudes towards plastics. *Resources, Conservation and Recycling*, 147, 227–235. ISSN 0921-3449.

Edgington, T. (2019). Plastic or paper: which bag is greener?, BBC News.

Environmental Protection Agency/www.billerud.com. The Plastic Packaging Problem, https://www.billerud.com/managed-packaging/knowledge-center/articles/plastic-packaging-problem

Evans, D. (2020). Understanding plastic packaging: the co-evolution of materials and society. *Global Environmental Change*, 65(5), 102166. doi:10.1016/j.gloenvcha.2020.102166

Fishbein, M., and Ajzen, I. (1975). Belief, attitude, intention and behaviour: An introduction to theory and research. Reading, MA: Addison-Wesley.

Geyer, R., Jambeck, J., Lavenderlaw, K., et al. (2017). Production, use, and fate of all plastics ever made. *Science Advances*, 3(7), 1–5. doi:10.1126/sciadv.1700782

Henseler, J., Ringle, C. M., and Sarstedt, M. (2015). A new criterion for assessing discriminant validity in variance-based structural equation modeling. *Journal of the Academy of Marketing Science*, 43(1), 115–135. https://doi.org/10.1007/s11747-014-0403-8

Hu, L. T., and Bentler, P. M. (1999). Cutoff criteria for fit indexes in covariance structure analysis: conventional criteria, versus new alternatives. *Structural Equation Modeling*, 6(1), 1–55.

Isak, A. (2021). Paper survey on the impact of the waste of plastic-made materials, its disposal and their effects on human health and environment: a case study in mogadishu city, the capital of Somalia, horn of Africa quest journals. *Journal of Research in Environmental and Earth Sciences*, 7(2), 17–23. ISSN(Online): 2348-2532www.questjournals.org*

Karan Gupta, R. (2021). Exploring the factors affecting purchase intention towards green packaged products of Indian consumers. *E3S Web of Conferences*, 309, 01084, ICMED 2021.

Lim-Urubio, M. (2022). Relationship of people's knowledge, behavior and government action toward environmental sustainability. (Paper publication on going process).

Living Business Programme (2022). Triple whammy helps green the shopping experience in Bahrain, (2022), https://livingbusiness.com/triple-whammy-helps-green-the-shopping-experience-in-bahrain/

Murphy, C. (2022). The Rise of Single-Use Plastic Packaging Avoiders. Ellen MacArthur Foundation.

OECD (2022). Plastic Pollution is Growing Relentlessly as Waste Management and Recycling Fall Short, says OECD. https://www.oecd.org/environment/plastic-pollution-is-growing-relentlessly-as-waste-management-and-recycling-fall-short.htm

Oloyede, O. O., and Lignou, S. (2021). Sustainable paper-based packaging: A consumer's perspective. foods. 10(5), 1035. doi:10.3390/foods10051035. PMID: 34068639; PMCID: PMC8151435.

Santos-Moreira, M. (2020). Is paper a more sustainable flexible Packaging material than plastic. https://www.forbes.com/sites/woodmackenzie/2020/08/24/is-paper-a-more-sustainableflexible-packaging-material-than-plastic/?sh=4d5a8f9212d4

Silva, N., and Molina-Besch K. (2023). Replacing plastic with corrugated cardboard: A carbon footprint analysis of disposable packaging in a B2B global supply chain—A case study. *Resources, Conservation and Recycling*, 2023, 8–10.

Swaliha Shanabas. (2019). Bahrain: An overview of solid waste management in bahrain. https://www.wasterecyclingmea.com/news/waste-management/bahrain-an-overview-of-solid-waste-management-in-bahrain

(2021). Theory of reasoned action for predicting consumer behavior. https://accounting.binus.ac.id/2021/11/15/theory-of-reasoned-action-for-predicting-consumer-behaviour/.

Vishal, A., Hauptmann, M., Zelm, R., Majschak, J-P., and Retulainen, E. (2014). 3D Forming of paperboard: the influence of paperboard properties on formability. *Packaging Technology and Science*, 27(9), 677–691. 15p.

Weber Macena, Morgana, Rita Carvalho, Luísa Paula Cruz-Lopes, and Raquel P. F. Guiné. (2021). Plastic food packaging: Perceptions and attitudes of portuguese consumers about environmental impact and recycling. *Sustainability*, 13(17), 9953. https://doi.org/10.3390/su13179953.

World Economic Forum Annual Meeting, 20–23 January 2016. https://www.weforum.org/events/world-economic-forum-annual-meeting-2016.

Yeo, S. F., Tan, C. L., Lim, K. B., Khoo, Y.-H. (2020). Product packaging: impact on customers' purchase intention. *International Journal of Business and Society*, 21, 857–864. 10.33736/ijbs.3298.

17 Sustainable Microfinance Principles in Sustainable Development Goals for the Economic Resilience

Jayendira P. Sankar

Assistant Professor, CAFS, University of Technology Bahrain, Kingdom of Bahrain

Abstract

Microfinance gained high popularity in serving poor and vulnerable people. The paper aims to find the importance of microfinance in sustainable development goals (SDGs). Also, the study utilized agency and life-cycle theories to connect sustainable microfinance principles in achieving the SDGs for economic resilience. To assess the connectivity between microfinance and SDGs, SDG 1.4 is linked to "Goal 1 No Poverty", SDG 2.3 is related to "Goal 2 Zero Hunger", SDGs 8.3 and 8.10 is connected to "Goal 8 Decent Work and Economic Growth", and SDG 9.3 is connected to "Goal 9 Industry, Innovation and Infrastructure." Further, the study wants to find the relation and importance of sustainable principles on SDGs. The study strongly proved using SD dimensions, SD sub-dimensions, and domains of 1.4, 2.3, 8.3, 8.10, and 9.3 SGDs connected to the eleven fundamental sustainable microfinance principles. Mainly, microfinance will alleviate poverty along with the financial service available to the poor people in rural areas and some urban areas in all developed, developing and underdeveloped countries.

Keywords

Agency theory, and life-cycle theory, economic resilience, SDGs, Sustainable microfinance.

Introduction

Microfinance is small-amount financing that supports people who do not have access to financial services, are low-income individuals, or are unemployed. Also, microfinance is a quick solution for vulnerable people facing sudden financial requirements. In developed, developing and underdeveloped countries, microfinance plays a vital role in the business generation of poor people (Yoganandham and Sankar, 2022). For over 30 years, small loans through microfinance have successfully reduced poverty in several countries. Moreover, microfinance deals with financial payment facilitation, saving programmes, remittance facilitation, micro insurance, and micro pension. Further, microfinance empowers women and youth in the rural areas of developing countries through microloans by supporting them financially in poverty reduction and gaining economic rewards.

jpsankar@utb.edu.bh

Everyday saving, the basis of microfinance, is a robust financial system in Europe; recently, microfinance has gained massive importance in South Asia (Mustafa et al., 2018). Policymakers view microfinance as the key to income generation, encouraging entrepreneurship, empowering the poor (women and youth), reducing poverty, and increasing social capital, education and health. Further, income generation ensures food safety and self-sufficiency among people experiencing poverty in developing countries, especially people away from conventional banking who will benefit from microfinancing. Hassan and Islam (2019) pointed out that microfinance will alleviate socio-economic problems and increase opportunities to vulnerable groups. Moreover, microfinance will support technology adoption in small businesses, increasing productivity (Pham and Huynh, 2021).

The study utilised two theories to discuss sustainable development goals (SDGs) using the microfinance principles, agency theory and life-cycle theory connected to microfinance institutions (MFIs) and practices. Both approaches deal with microfinancing, the relation between agent and regulation in agency theory, and the maturity of the financial institutions in life-cycle theory. Agency theory (Alchian and Demsetz, 1975; Jensen and Meckling, 1976) deals with the contracts among individuals with self-interest and the behavior of MFI managers on a day-to-day basis. In the agency theory, the agent will act on behalf of the principal with authority and contract; the managers face all the challenges like profit organizations. Life-cycle theory (Hollis and Sweetman, 2001; de Sousa-shields et al., 2004) reflects the "birth, growth, maturity, and death" of the firms. The same concept applies to microfinance and its related institutions, which will help gain experience to enhance the financing to achieve sustainability.

This study connects the microfinance principles to the resilience of SDGs by discussing the agency and life-cycle theories to highlight the importance and need to strategies micro-financial institutions. The study's novelty is through the extensive literature on microfinance to SDGs. Further, an increasing micro-financial contribution will increase micro-entrepreneurs, rural employability and alleviate poverty. Moreover, this study is not limited to any specific country or region; it will give an idea to policymakers across the globe. The study deals with the microfinance components within sustainable goals in section 2, sustainable microfinance principles in section 3, discussion and implications in section 4, and the conclusion in section 5.

Sustainable Microfinance within Sustainable Development Goals

Based on the United Nations General Assembly Resolution A/RES/69/315 (United Nations, 2015), 17 SDGs, the study derived six primary goals connected to micro-financing in economic sustainability as mentioned in the Figure 17.1.

Goal 1.4. The goal is to achieve economic equality by 2030 for all individuals, especially disadvantaged ones, by providing them equal access to economic resources and essential services. This includes financial services, new technology, natural resources, inheritance, and rights to land ownership, including microfinance. Goal 2.3. The goal is to double the agricultural productivity and increase the income of small-scale food producers, fishers, pastoralists, family farmers, indigenous peoples, and women by 2030. This can be achieved by providing security and opportunities for value addition, non-farm employment equal access to land, markets, knowledge, financial services,

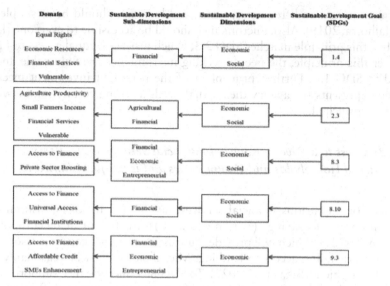

Figure 17.1 SDGs related to access to finance.

Source: Self-made by the researcher

inputs, and productive resources. Goal 8.3. The statement advocates for policies that promote economic development by supporting productive activities and encouraging entrepreneurship, creativity and innovation, growth of micro-, small-, and medium-sized enterprises, facilitating the formalization, and creating decent jobs. These policies should also include access to financial services. Goal 8.10. To increase access to financial services for all individuals. To encourage and expand access to financial services for all individuals, especially those currently underserved or excluded from the financial system. Strengthen domestic financial institutions to improve their ability to provide banking, insurance, and financial services. Goal 9.3. The goal is to increase access to financial services, such as affordable credit, for small-scale industrial and other enterprises, especially in developing countries. This will help integrate these businesses into value chains and markets.

Sustainable Microfinance Principles

Eleven good practices for microfinance services were identified based on fundamental principles of sustainable microfinance (World Education Australia, 2006). These principles were found sustainable and appropriate based on several microfinance institutions globally.

Principle 1: Microfinance Services Should be Tailored to Meet the Needs and Preferences of Clients

The micro-financial services provided to the clients must be more flexible and convenient; usually, the people who avail of microfinance are from low-income groups, so the repayment period and frequency, terms, and loan size should be as simple to the clients (Malhotra, 2019). Also, microfinance should be accessible to everyone (Lensink et al., 2018); this principle matches SDG 2.3, which insists on equal access to financial services. Per this principle, the people seeking microfinance are vulnerable and poor, connected to SDG 1.4. Further, principle 1 of the persistent investment mechanism with clients represents the agency theory that needs a strong connection between the agent and the principal.

Principle 2: Access to a Diverse Range of Financial Services is Necessary for Impoverished Households and Communities and is not just Limited to Loans

Microfinance offers various financial services, not limited to loans, insurance, cash transfers, and access to savings (Karlan et al., 2016). Different financial options are connected to SDG 1.4, which will provide immediate access to economic resources and SDG 8.10 on expanding access to banking. Microfinance must be reasonably priced, flexible and convenient (Bika et al., 2022). To SDG 8.3, microfinance support by giving access to financial services for small and medium enterprises through flexibility. Principle 2 of sustainable microfinance In the life-cycle theory of microfinance institutions, various financial services lie in the second growth stage, which will support entrepreneurial activities (Navin and Sinha, 2021).

Principle 3: Microfinance is a Potent Tool in the Fight Against Poverty

Alleviation of poverty is the primary goal of every country (Haq et al., 2022); microfinance helps reduce poverty by adding assets and income and reducing vulnerability. Microfinance provides people experiencing poverty with various financial services to rural poor dealing with farm and non-farm activities to improve the family's education, health and status. SDG 1.4 deals with financial institutions and microfinance in removing poverty and vulnerability. SDGs 2.3 and 8.3 insist on the need for non-farm employment and small and medium enterprises through various financial services (Gansonre, 2021). Against poverty, principle 3 needs to be associated with solid agency theory and levels 2 (growth) and 3 (maturity) of life-cycle theory because high poverty lies in developing and under-developed countries (Traeger et al., 2020).

Principle 4: Microfinance Involves the Creation of Financial Systems that Cater to the Needs of Impoverished Individuals

Several countries are still building microfinance systems; no perfectly established financial system exists. Those countries view microfinance as unorganized but need socially responsible investors and government interference (Praseeda, 2018). SDG 1.4 insist that micro-financial services should serve people experiencing poverty. Moreover, to prioritize microfinance, governments need to integrate it into the financial sector with industrial bodies, regulators and conventional financial service providers (Sahay et al., 2020). SDGs 8.3, 8.10, and 9.3 insist on the need for economic system access, regulation and market value chain. Generally, principle 4 persists in the need for implementing systematic agency theory, and life cycle theory levels 1 (birth) and 2 (growth).

Principle 5: Financial Sustainability is Vital for Reaching Poor Populations

SDGs 1.4, 8.3, and 9.3 insist on the need for innovative and affordable micro-financial services for poor and rural women for their empowerment. The lack of retail microfinance intermediaries, stable financial institutions, and government intervention will hinder the reach of low-income people (Hannig and Jansen, 2011). Here the need for agency theory plays a vital role in overcoming the hindrance to making the service affordable to low-income people. To reach a significant number of beneficiaries, microfinance should cover all the transaction costs; to achieve this, the cost sustainability agencies need to implement technological innovation to expand the service at a low price (Murshid and Murshid, 2022). Government intervention is the key to financial sustainability; life cycle theory levels 2 (growth) and 3 (maturity) must be instigated to reach the maximum.

Principle 6: Ceilings on Interest Rates Harm the Poor's Financial Access

SDGs 1.4, 8.3, and 8.10 insist on making flexible micro-financial services for people experiencing poverty; agency theory represents a strong connection with the agents in rural areas. Microfinance focuses on vulnerable groups; bank loans with high-interest rates are thorny. It is more challenging to accommodate poor people in remote rural areas than in urban areas. Affordable interest rate less the bank loan interest with flexible microfinance services helps the vulnerable to increase productivity (Borio and Gambacorta, 2017). SDGs 8.3 focus on entrepreneurship and job creation through easy access to financial services.

Principle 7: Credit is not Always a Suitable Option

Level 3 (maturity) in the life cycle theory of microfinance expresses the importance of microfinance to sustainable activities. SDGs 2.3 and 8.3 represent the need for microfinance to concentrate on the opportunities for value addition and encourage people experiencing poverty in small and medium enterprises. Apart from lending, microfinancial institutions should focus on non-financial services like training, employment, education, health, small grants and infrastructure improvements (Kondo, 2007). Also, awareness of people with low incomes on money risk management, credit management, savings and money management (Lusardi, 2019).

Principle 8: Governments Enable, not Provide, Financial Services Directly

Principle 8 represents the need for the solid agency theory to be executed by the government through policy decisions and the business environment. SDGs 1.4 and 8.10 insist on the need for the government to strategize financial services to reach all sets of people in society, especially people experiencing poverty. Microfinance is not possible for the government to provide services directly to vulnerable people (Bangoura, 2012).

SDG 9.3 contends the need for affordable credit by integrating private-public partnerships. Governments should act as facilitators to provide efficient micro-financial assistance through private partnerships in various financial options (Roy and Chowdhury, 2009).

Principle 9: Donor Subsidies Should Complement Private Sector Capital, not Compete

The donor subsidy for the efficient use of microfinance infrastructure development and making financial services available for people experiencing poverty, even in the country's rural areas, with a fixed performance standard (Kondo, 2007). Microfinance aims to serve people experiencing poverty with financial assistance rather than competing with the private (Ghosh, 2013). The life cycle theory of microfinance stresses the importance of level 3 (maturity) to widen the availability of microfinance instead of creating competition among service providers. SDGs 2.3 and 8.10 insist on strengthening the micro financial services by not affecting the private sector capital.

Principle 10: Lack of Capacity Hinders Microfinance Expansion

More micro-financial institutions can reach a more vulnerable set of people in society (Gatto and Sadik-Zada, 2022). As discussed in principle 8, public and private partnerships must widen the availability to people experiencing poverty by including technology (Roy and Chowdhury, 2009). Also, as mentioned in principle, 5 Government intervention is the key to financial sustainability; life cycle theory levels 2 (growth) and 3 (maturity) must be instigated to reach the maximum. SDGs 1.4, 8.3, 8.10, and 9.3 insist on increasing the number of microfinance availability and variety of services that need to be rendered through the microfinance package to exhibit its full potential.

Principle 11: Transparency is Crucial for Financial and Outreach Accountability

SDG 8.3 insists on policies to ensure transparency for effective financial services. Transparent microfinance activities will overcome unfair practices and support economic sustainability (Dörry and Schulz, 2018). Microfinance includes a variety of stakeholders, which need high vigilance and strict monitoring because there is a high chance of exploitation of people experiencing poverty (Hussain et al., 2020). Life cycle theory levels 1 (birth), 2 (growth), and 3 (maturity) represent the need for transparency in financial services. So it is mandatory to have regulations over investors, donors, regulators and bank supervisors (Khan, 2018).

Discussion and Implications

As discussed above, every country aims to achieve SDG 2030. The study revealed some critical SDGs to the micro financial institutions, practitioners, entrepreneurs, policymakers, and scholars in achieving sustainable development. As framed in the study, SDG

Table 17.1: Principles of sustainable microfinance to SDGs.

SDGs	Sustainable Microfinance
1.4	Principles 1, 2, 3, 4, 5, 6, 8, and 10
2.3	Principles 1, 3, 7, and 9
8.3	Principles 2, 3, 4, 5, 6, 7, 10, and 11
8.10	Principles 2, 4, 6, 8, 9, and 10
9.3	Principles 4, 5, 8, and 10

Source: Self-made by the researcher based on the fundamental principles of sustainable microfinance (World Education Australia, 2006) and United Nations General Assembly Resolution A/RES/69/315 (United Nations, 2015)

1.4 is connected to "Goal 1 No Poverty", SDG 2.3 is related to "Goal 2 Zero Hunger", SDGs 8.3 and 8.10 is connected to "Goal 8 Decent Work and Economic Growth", and SDG 9.3 is connected to "Goal 9 Industry, Innovation and Infrastructure."

Table 17.1 revealed that the SDGs 1.4, 2.3, 8.3, 8.10, and 9.3 by United Nations General Assembly Resolution A/RES/69/315 (United Nations, 2015) are connected to the eleven principles of sustainable microfinance (World Education Australia, 2006).

Theories like agency theory and life cycle theory of microfinance were used in the study to embed the importance of theories in the principles of sustainable microfinance to achieve the SDGs. Principles 1, 3, 7, and 9 connected to microfinance services based on the client preference, the key to poverty alleviation, value-added services, and private and public partnerships related to SDG 2.3 (Lensink et al., 2018; Kondo, 2007; Traeger et al., 2020). In connection with SDG 1.4 on principles 1, 2, 3, 4, 5, 6, 8, and 10, equal rights, economic resources, financial services, and vulnerable deals with principles support client preference, poor households, extra services than credit, poverty, financial services for the poor, low-interest rate, and expansion of microfinance (Malhotra, 2019; Haq et al., 2022).

SDG 8.3 on principles 2, 3, 4, 5, 6, 7, 10, and 11 are connected to value-added services, job creation, entrepreneurship, low-interest rates, policies, expansion of microfinance, and transparency (Gansonre, 2021; Khan, 2018; Lusardi, 2019). Principles 2, 4, 6, 8, 9, and 10 are connected to domestic microfinance, banking expansion, government facilitation, public-private partnership and access to financial services related to SDG 8.10 (Gatto and Sadik-Zada, 2022; Roy and Chowdhury, 2009; Ghosh, 2013). SDG 9.3 on principles 4, 5, 8, and 10 are connected to small-scale entrepreneurship, affordable credit, and government interference; the cost sustainability agencies need to implement technological innovation to expand the service at a low price (Praseeda, 2018; Murshid and Murshid, 2022).

Conclusion

Principles of sustainable microfinance, agency theory, life-cycle theory, financial innovation, and access to finance in achieving sustainable development goals (SDGs). Globally, countries are attempting to reach the SDG by infusing lots of effort by policymakers, governments and administrators on socio-economic issues. The study strongly proved using SD dimensions, SD sub-dimensions, and domains of 1.4, 2.3, 8.3, 8.10, and 9.3 SGDs connected to the eleven fundamental sustainable microfinance principles. Mainly, microfinance will alleviate poverty along with the financial service available to the poor people in rural areas and some urban areas in all developed, developing and underdeveloped countries. Also, microfinance will be sustainable with private investors, managers and entrepreneurs—government intervention and regulations like accountability, certificates, reporting, and auditing support microfinance to serve better. Financial innovation and technological advancements like fintech instruments will make microfinance accessible to the vulnerable. Overall, the study strongly suggests a high concentration of principles of sustainable microfinance, theoretical adoption of agency theory, and life-cycle theory to tackle and build the achievement of SDGs practically.

References

Alchian, A. A., and Demsetz, H. (1975). Production, information costs, and economic organization. *IEEE Engineering Management Review*, 3(2), 777–95. https://doi.org/10.1109/EMR.1975.4306431.

Bangoura, L. (2012). Microfinance as an approach to development in low income countries. *Bangladesh Development Studies*, 35(4), 87–111.

Bika, Z., Subalova, M., and Locke, C. (2022). Microfinance and small business development in a transitional economy: insights from borrowers relations with microfinance organisations in Kazakhstan. *Journal of Development Studies*, 58(1), 183–203. https://doi.org/10.1080/00220388.2021.1956472.

Borio, C., and Gambacorta, L. (2017). Monetary policy and bank lending in a low interest rate environment: diminishing effectiveness 612. *Journal of Macroeconomics*, 54, 18–19. https://doi.org/10.1016/j.jmacro.2017.02.005.

de Sousa-shields, M., Miamidian, E., Van der Steeren, J., and King, B. (2004). Financing microfinance institutions: the context for transitions to private capital accelerated microenterprise advancement project. *Histochemistry and Cell Biology*, 122, 52–56. https://www.findevgateway.org/sites/default/files/publications/files/mfg-en-paper-financing-microfinance-institutions-the-context-for-transitions-to-private-capital-2004.pdf.

Dörry, S., and Schulz, C. (2018). Green financing, interrupted. potential directions for sustainable finance in luxembourg. *Local Environment*, 23(7), 713–33. https://doi.org/10.1080/13549839.2018.1428792.

Gansonre, S. (2021). Welfare impacts of non-farm employment in semi-arid areas: evidence from burkina faso. *Heliyon*, 7(10), 1–10. https://doi.org/10.1016/j.heliyon.2021.e08080.

Gatto, A., and Sadik-Zada, E. R. (2022). Access to microfinance as a resilience policy to address sustainable development goals: a content analysis. *Heliyon*, 8(e10860), 1–8. https://doi.org/https://doi.org/10.1016/j.heliyon.2022.e10860.

Ghosh, J. (2013). Microfinance and the challenge of financial inclusion for development. *Cambridge Journal of Economics*, 37(6), 1203–19. https://doi.org/10.1093/cje/bet042.

Hannig, A., and Jansen, S. (2010). Financial inclusion and financial stability: current policy issues. ADBI Working Paper 259. Tokyo: Asian Development Bank Institute. Accessed December 10, 2022. http://www.adbi.org/working-paper/2010/12/21/4272.financial.inclusion.stability.

Haq, M. A. U., Sankar, J. P., Akram, F., and Siddique, M. (2022). The role of farmers attitude towards their resources to alleviate rural household poverty. *Quality and Quantity*, 56, 2133–2155. https://doi.org/10.1007/s11135-021-01205-8.

Hassan, S. M. M., and Islam, M. M. (2019). The socio-economic impact of microfinance on the poor family: a study from bangladesh. *Journal of Asian and African Studies,* 54(1), 3–19. https://doi.org/10.1177/0021909618785399.

Hollis, A., and Sweetman, A. (2001). The life-cycle of a microfinance institution: the irish loan funds. *Journal of Economic Behavior and Organization,* 46(3), 291–311. https://doi.org/10.1016/S0167-2681(01)00179-2.

Hussain, R. I., Bashir, S., and Hussain, S. (2020). Financial sustainability and corporate social responsibility under mediating effect of operational self-sustainability. *Frontiers in Psychology,* 11, 1–13. https://doi.org/10.3389/fpsyg.2020.550029.

Jensen, M. C., and Meckling, W. H. (1976). Theory of the firm: managerial behavior, agency costs and ownership structure. *Journal of Financial Economics,* 3(4), 305–60. https://doi.org/10.1016/0304-405X(76)90026-X.

Karlan, D., Mann, R., Kendall, J., Pande, R., and Suri, T. (2016). *Making Microfinance More Effective.* National Bureau of Economic Research Working Paper Series, No. 22633. Accessed January 14, 2023. http://www.nber.org/papers/w22633

Khan, A. (2018). A behavioral approach to financial supervision, regulation, and central banking. IMF Working Papers. 18. WP/18/178. https://doi.org/10.5089/9781484372289.001.

Kondo, T. (2007). Effect of microfinance operations on poor rural households and the status of women. In *Special Evaluation Study.* SST: REG 2007-19; Operations Evaluation. Accessed February 25, 2023. https://www.oecd.org/countries/bangladesh/39503711.pdf.

Lensink, R., Mersland, R., Vu, N. T. H., and Zamore, S. (2018). Do microfinance institutions benefit from integrating financial and nonfinancial services. *Applied Economics,* 50(21), 2386–2401. https://doi.org/10.1080/00036846.2017.1397852.

Lusardi, A. (2019). Financial literacy and the need for financial education: evidence and implications. *Swiss Journal of Economics and Statistics,* 155(1), 1–8. https://doi.org/10.1186/s41937-019-0027-5.

Malhotra, G. (2019). Microfinance impact on rural household in India. In *SSRN* (No. 3342689). Accessed February 05, 2023. https://ssrn.com/abstract=3342689

Murshid, N. S., and Murshid, N. (2022). Innovations during COVID-19: microfinance in bangladesh. *Affilia—Journal of Women and Social Work,* 37(2), 232–49. https://doi.org/10.1177/08861099211054024.

Mustafa, F., Khursheed, A., and Fatima, M. (2018). Impact of global financial crunch on financially innovative microfinance institutions in south asia. *Financial Innovation,* 4(1), 1–11. https://doi.org/10.1186/s40854-018-0099-8.

Navin, N., and Sinha, P. (2021). Social and financial performance of MFIs: complementary or compromise. *Vilakshan—XIMB Journal of Management,* 18(1), 42–61. https://doi.org/10.1108/xjm-08-2020-0075.

Pham, D. P. T., and Huynh, T. C. H. (2021). The impact of trade credit investment on manufacturing firms profitability: evidence from vietnam. *Acta Universitatis Agriculturae et Silviculturae Mendelianae Brunensis,* 68(4), 775–96. https://doi.org/10.11118/actaun202068040775.

Praseeda, C. (2018). Socially responsible investment, microfinance and banking: creating value by synergy. *Indian Journal of Corporate Governance,* 11(1), 69–87. https://doi.org/10.1177/0974686218769200.

Roy, J., and Chowdhury, P. R. (2009). Public-private partnerships in micro-finance: should NGO involvement be restricted. *Journal of Development Economics,* 90(2), 200–208. https://doi.org/10.1016/j.jdeveco.2008.11.001.

Sahay, R., von Allmen, U. E., Lahreche, A., Khera, P., Ogawa, S., Bazarbash, M., and Beaton, K. (2020). The Promise of Fintech; Financial Inclusion in the Post COVID-19 Era. IMF Departmental Papers/Policy Papers from International Monetary Fund. International Monetary Fund. https://doi.org/https://doi.org/10.5089/9781513512242.087.

Traeger, R., Banda, B. M., Riba, M., Valensisi, G., Joo, K., Lechner, T., Slany, A., et al. (2020). The Least Developed Countries Report 2020: Productive Capacities for the New Decade. United Nations Conference on Trade and Development, Geneva. https://doi.org/978-92-1-005384-6.

United Nations (2015). Transforming our world: the 2030 agenda for sustainable development United Nations. Resolution Adopted by the General Assembly on 1 September 2015.

World Education Australia (2006). Principles of Sustainable Microfinance. Australia: World Education Australia.

Yoganandham, G., and Sankar, J. P. (2022). Organizational credit facilities for microfinance entrepreneurs: an Indian context. *Remittances Review,* 7(1), 117–30. https://doi.org/10.47059/rr.v7i1.2401.

18 Undetectable Message Ciphering Method Based on Cell Engineering

Defaf Shakir Kadum[1,a] *and Sahar Adill Kadum*[2,b]

[1]Research Scholar, department of computer science, Babylon University, Iraq.
[2]Department of computer science, Babylon University, Iraq.

Abstract

With the explosive expansion of internet usage in recent years, concerns about data security have only increased. In response to the rise in unauthorised access, many secure communication mechanisms, such encryption and data hiding, have been implemented. DNA has been increasingly used as a carrier for encryption and data concealment due to its unique biomolecular features. In this research, a DNA ste-ganography system was developed to encrypt data and conceal signals in the genome's naturally occurring variations (single nucleotide polymorphisms). Defects (mutations) inside the encrypted messages might potentially be found by using Alingment Technique. Furthermore, this study will help in the future creation and protection of data concealing strategies based on DNA sequences. Additionally, use SNPs in DNA as hiding locations provide good noise, zero payload, high capacity, low modification rate, high information entropy, low cracking probability, blind algorithm and preserve functionality.

Keywords

Cryptography, DNA, information hiding, SNP.

Introduction

The protection of information against intrusion is known as information security. Current thinking holds that the overarching purpose of security is to protect against unauthorised access to, modification to, or theft of sensitive information (Singh, 2013; Subhedar and Mankar, 2014; Hamed et al., 2016). Cryptography and data concealment, two related concepts, are the most widely used methods in the communication and computer security fields. Both methods are designed to keep information secret and secure, but they are put to different uses. Cryptography is the study of techniques for making information unintelligible via encryption. If cryptography is the process whereby the person in possession of a secret key may influence the meaning of secret writing, data concealment is a hidden form of writing that hides the existence of the message being concealed. After using a method to hide the data, the original medium should retain as few of its original characteristics as is feasible. While encryption is

---

[a]defaf.kadim.gsci10@student.uobabylon.edu.iq, [b]wsci.sahar.adil@uobabylon.edu.iq

the preferred method of protecting sensitive information during transmission over the internet (Amin et al., 2003; Al-Mohammad, 2010; Hamed et al., 2015), data conceal-ment is often chosen due to its higher level of security and more efficiency. DNA-based cryptography is a new discipline that emerged with the discovery of DNA's computa-tional potential, which uses DNA as an informational and computational carrier with the help of molecular technology (Anam et al., 2010).

Related Works

Information security is a growing area that includes information encryption and hid-ing. Some of the previous works is displayed in the Table 18.1.

Table 18.1: The comparisons between previous works.

References	Proposed work	Solved problem
Das et al. (2011)	Insertion, complimentary pair, and substitution are the three options presented.	The "capacity," "payload," and "number of bits buried per character" (bpn).
Peterson (2001)	Binary encoding and complementary-pair concepts are at the heart of the proposed method, both of which have been realised in the cloud.	Maximise privacy and complexity.
Mousa et al. (2011)	Created a technique for hiding DNA sequence data using reversible contrast mapping.	The noise versus the amount of hidden data.
Sahana et al. (??)	Novel algorithms have been used to improve cryptography and steganography. As a result, the proposed technology combines encryption with steganography to produce a very effective system for concealing data from undesirable users.	Modification rate.
Marwan et al. (2016)	DNA hiding was compared to four different cyphers (playfair, vigenere, RSA, and AES).	Hiding capacity and data size.
Lee et al. (2018)	There are other suggested difference expansions for DNA data hiding that would allow for data retrieval in either direction. The string structure of DNA is important to consider when hiding information.	Data watermark bpn and storage capacity
Adithya and Santhi (2021)	DNA computing colour code encryption was proposed as a means to secure information from snooping. The format of the text message is encrypted.	Equilibrium, and energy efficiency.
El-deeb et al. (2021)	It was hypothesised that information may be masked in DNA sequences by making substitutions. Two bits may be encoded by each DNA codon in one of the classes.	Preserves the DNA original biological structure.

(continued)

Table 18.1: Continued

References	Proposed work	Solved problem
Biswas and Hossain (2021)	the proposed method has two fundamental phases. The message is first encoded in DNA using a 10 10 Playfair cypher. Second, they introduce the message into the DNA and conceal it by making changes to the sequence through complimentary base substitution.	Sending a keyword before the encrypted DNA Sequences.
Nabi et al. (2021)	broke down the concept of reversible encryption and data hiding. In the first step, a code is buried in a DNA snippet. Using a "private key to choose a DNA sequence from the database to implant the hidden message," data insertion allows for the covert insertion of data.	Storage capacity, large-scale computation.

Deoxyribose Nucleic Acid Computing (DNA Computing)

Biological methods are now being used to many different industries. DNA is an emerging biological technology with several uses (Al-Wattar et al., 2015). Genetics have a role in this.

DNA has a lot of power in terms of cryptography. The binding properties of nucleotide bases (A-T, G-C) allow for the creation of self-assembling structures, which make excellent platforms for carrying out computations. Another benefit is that DNA has a tremendous capacity for storage, but on the other side, actual DNA cryptography implementation is difficult.

takes a lot of effort and time. There are also various computational restrictions. As a result, it is still challenging to employ DNA cryptography effectively from a practical standpoint (Pramanik and Setua, 2012).

DNA and the immune system are linked (Liu et al., 2021). The DNA computing (Biomolecular computing) experiment was successful. Developed by Leonard Adelman, this method uses molecular instruments. The first one was released in 1994. A section of the typical course of the investigation was solved using biology.

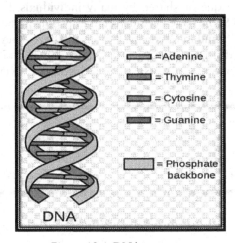

Figure 18.1 DNA structure.

DNA Cryptography

The strength of current cryptographic algorithms is insufficient to offer adequate security because unauthorized users or intruders could access the data for a variety of nefarious purposes. The tremendous information density and massive parallelism inherent in DNA molecules are investigated for cryptographic applications such as encryption (Sadkhan, 2021a). Authentication, signature, and other similar terms are used. DNA cryptography is a combination of encryption and genetics.

DNA cryptography is a bright spot in the cryptography area. Instead of typical digital media like images, text, or video, DNA was used as a carrier, with biological tools serving as implementation tools. Furthermore, the simulation software and the manufactured DNA sequence were digitally and biologically incorporated into custom biotechnical hardware. The main goal is t use DNA as a carrier and contemporary biological techniques as application tools in this project.

The original data was hidden using encryption technology, which was also employed to protect the data. Provides a range of methods for storing and encrypting messages in various formats Sadkhan (2021b) of DNA sequences. Encrypting DNA is part of DNA cryptography. Using DNA computational techniques, the plaintext is generated. It is all about DNA processing. Using DNA for processing presents a whole new computation concept and method. The foundation of the idea of working with DNA is to encode data in a DNA strand structure for reproduction.

Single Nucleotide Polymorphisms

The vast majority of variations in human DNA are SNPs (single nucleotide polymorphisms). Specifically, each SNP represents a variation in a single nucleotide, an element of DNA.

When a single-nucleotide polymorphism (SNP) occurs in a stretch of DNA, cytosine (C) may be switched out for thymine (T) (T). The presence of SNPs is a normal part of the genetic makeup of all humans. They tend to cluster in groups of approximately a thousand nucleotides, suggesting that there are about 4 or 5 million SNPs in a typical genome (https://www.britannica.com/science/single-nucleotide-polymorphism). These differences might be unique or shared by many individuals. Scientists estimate that more than 100 million SNPs have been detected in people all across the globe. Mutations like this are often found in intergenic regions of DNA. They may be used as diagnostic tools to identify disease-causing genes (Gunter, 2023). In Figures 18.2 and 18.3, we see an explanation of SNPs and SNPs. The Detection of SNPs.

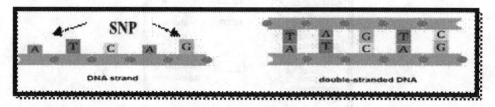

Figure 18.2 SNPs of DNA.

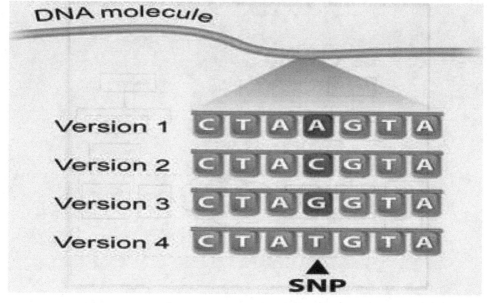

Figure 18.3 SNPs identification.

Proposed System

In this paper, a new direction of ciphering is designed that is extremely secure and efficient using the biological cell engineering concept. The message is encrypted to a DNA form to be introduced as DNA genome barcodes combined with engineered cells as biological assets that play a crucial role in biological synthesis.

These cells were employed as SNPs for ciphering the secret messages in changeable portions of a genome.

Coding the message in a way that reduces the length of the message and at the same time preserves the content of the message. Ciphering message is an extremely Self-coding Method in DNA sequence to achieve confidential transmission using engineering cells. Each message will be ciphered according to cell Engineering synonym using one base called single nucleotide polymers (SNP). Thus, the new method has coded the message in one small region. This leads to the creation of hard, cracking probability and strong security.

Methodology

The proposed methodology is divided into two phases: ciphering and SNP generation. In this method, we will design and implement. An approach for Hiding information that is more secure and efficient using biological cell engineering.

The concept, the main framework of the proposal, is depicted in Figure 18.4.

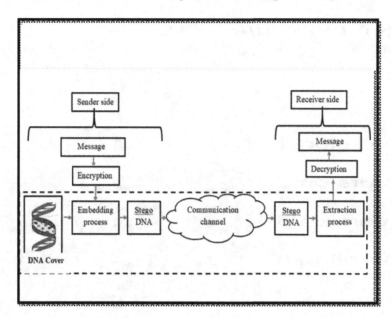

Figure 18.4 Proposed system framework.

Cipher Phase

This phase depicts the ciphering messages to be prepared for the embedding phase. Algorithm (1) explain the message ciphering steps and coding table represented in Table 18.2:

Table 18.2: DNA codons.

A	A	T	G	C
A	AAA(A)	TAA(E)	GAA (I)	CAA (M)
	AAT(B)	TAT(F)	GAT (J)	CAT (N)
	AAG(C)	TAG(G)	GAG (K)	CAG (O)
	AAC(D)	TAC(H)	GAC (L)	CAC (P)
T	ATA(Q)	TTA(U)	GTA (Y)	CTA (c)
	ATT(R)	TTT(V)	GTT (Z)	CTT (d)
	ATG(S)	TTG(W)	GTG (a)	CTG (e)
	ATC(T)	TTC(X)	GTC (b)	CTA (f)
G	AGA(g)	TGA(k)	GGA (o)	CGA (s)
	AGT(h)	TGT(l)	GGT (p)	CGT (t)
	AGG(i)	TGG(m)	GGG (q)	CGG (u)
	AGC(J)	TGC(n)	GGC (r)	CGC (v)
C	ACT(w)	TCA (1)	GCA (5)	CCA (9)
	ACT(x)	TCT (2)	GCT (6)	CCT (0)
	ACG(y)	TCG (3)	GCG (7)	CCG ()
	ACC(z)	TCC(4)	GCC (8)	CCC (.)

Algorithm (1): Message ciphering
Step1: Apply random permute function.
Step2: Messege segmentation.
Step3: Converting The message into DNA sequence according to the able (2).

SNP Generation Phase

This phase includes a DNA coding table in a table 18.3, SNP generation, and distribution.

Table 18.3: DNA coding.

DNA Base	Coding
A	0
T	1
C	2
G	3

Algorithm (2): SNP Generation
Step1: arrange the ciphered message in a 2D array.
Step2: generate SNP for each row and column
Step3: distribute the SNPs for each row and column.
Implementing algorithms (1 and 2) is clarified through a plain message "IRAQ."
According to algorithm (1) steps, the ciphered message will be:
CAA CAT CAGGTG
According to the algorithm (2)
Convert ciphered message into Triple codon {CAA, CAT, CAG, GTG} and arrange as in figure 18.3 below:

CAA CAT	200 201
CAG GTG	203 313

Figure 18.5 DNA coding.

The result of generating SNP as below in Table 18.4:

Table 18.4: SNPs generation.

C	A	A	C	A	T	T
C	A	G	G	T	G	G
A	A	G	T	T	T	A

The new message form is: **CAA CAT T CAG GTGG AAGTTTA.**

Detect Mutation

One of the disadvantages of storing information in DNA sequences is that it is subject to mutation. A nucleotide mutation can affect the meaning of an encrypted message. 'CCA TCA TCA,' for example. The initial nucleotide, C, is replaced with T ('TCA TCA TCA'). The mutation is a significant issue they face while using steganography. Thus, they use this method to identify mutations, modifications, and information manipulation.

Algorithm (3): Detect mutation

    Step1: detect and check for mutation.
    Step2: if it exists, then.
    Step3: correct the mutation
    Step4: else
    Step5: complete the message extraction
    Step6: end {if};

Security Analysis

The suggested algorithm's strength and resilience are based on the following:

- There is a reference DNA sequence S that is used in encryption.
- There are around 163 million publicly available DNA sequences. To prove the strength of the proposed method and security, several measuring tests were used, such as:

Cracking Probability (CP)

There are around 163 million publicly available DNA sequences. AS a result, the possibilities of an attacker making precise estimation of equation (1):

$$CP = 1/(163*)10 (^8)$$

Because the represented coding of A, C, G, and T yields diverse combinations of two Zebari et al. (2021), the likelihood of guessing the represented coding is:

$$1/24$$

Bit Error Rate (BER)

BER computed for encrypted message according to the equation (2) the ideal value of BER = 1 (Zhang et al., 2017).

    BER = number of nucleotides in sender/ number of nucleotides in receiver   (2)

Hiding Capacity

denotes the total amount of data DNA sequence can tolerate. It is the maximum amount of data that can be contained in DNA (Malathi et al., 2017).

    Capacity = Length of DNA Sequences   (3)

Table 18.5: Results of measures.

No. of Message	No. of Segments	Capacity	Cracking probability	Modification rate	BER
Message1	20	2940	11e-1.821	0.04	1
Message2	2	249	11e-1.821	0.003	1

Discussion

Humans have a lot of SNPs and SNP hotspots. The ability to code the information among naturally occurring SNPs is a key feature of our proposed method. On the other hand, this approach cannot be employed with well-established model species with previously recognized DNA sequences and only a small number of SNPs.

The number of SNPs required increases in direct proportion to the message length.

The information will be coded in variable SNP regions to prevent it from being identified by traditional methods such as next-generation sequencing (NGS). As a result, the proposed DNA encryption technology may be a viable method of protecting developed creatures.

Conclusion

This paper developed a DNA coding technology for encrypting secret messages in SNPs to prevent detection. Making it more difficult to hack. The suggested approach increases the level of data security by utilizing encryption at the first level and a new DNA-steganography method called SNP at the second level to embed data into a dedicated DNA data set and Reducing the possibility of the suggested approach being compromised by employing dynamic coding tables that are randomly created at each transition rather than static tables. So, Utilize DNA SNPs as hiding places provide good noise to hide data and Preserve functionality.

References

Adithya, B., and Santhi, G. (2021). Deoxyribonucleic acid (DNA) computing using two-by-six complementary and color code cipher. *Bulletin of Computer Science and Electrical Engineering*, 2(1), 38–45.

Al-Mohammad, A. (2010). Steganography-based secret and reliable communications: Improving steganographic capacity and imperceptibility (Doctoral dissertation, Brunel University, School of Information Systems, Computing and Mathematics Theses).

Al-Wattar, A. H. S., Mahmod, R., Zukarnain, Z. A., and Udzir, N. (2015). Review of DNA and Pseudo DNA cryptography. *International Journal of Computer Science and Engineering (IJCSE)*, 4(4), 65–76.

Amin, M. M., Salleh, M., Ibrahim, S., Katmin, M. R., and Shamsuddin, M. Z. I. (2003). Information hiding using steganography. In 4th National Conference of Telecommunication Technology, 2003. NCTT 2003 Proceedings. (pp. 21–25). IEEE.

Anam, B., Sakib, K., Hossain, M., and Dahal, K. (2010). Review on the advancements of DNA cryptography. arXiv preprint arXiv:1010.0186.

Biswas, S., and Hossain, M. (2021). Fully blind data hiding by embedding within DNA sequences using various ciphering and generic complimentary base substitutions. In Proceedings of International Joint Conference on Advances in Computational Intelligence (pp. 1–13). Springer, Singapore.

Das, S., Das, S., Bandyopadhyay, B., and Sanyal, S. (2011). Steganography and steganalysis: different approaches 1111.3758.

El-deeb, A., Elsisi, A., and Youssef, A. (2021). A Substitution-based method for data hiding in DNA sequences. *IJCI International Journal of Computers and Information*, 8(1), 87–105.

Gunter, C. (2023). Single nucleotide polymorphisms (SNPS), available at: https://www.genome. gov/genetics-glossary/single-nucleotide-polymorphisms

Hamed, G., Marey, M., El-Sayed, S. A., and Tolba, M. F. (2015). Hybrid technique for steganography based on DNA with n-bits binary coding rule. In 2015 7th International Conference of Soft Computing and Pattern Recognition (SoCPaR) (pp. 95–102). IEEE.

Hamed, G., Marey, M., El-Sayed, S., and Tolba, F. (2016). DNA-based steganography: survey and analysis for parameters optimization. In Applications of Intelligent Optimization in Biology and Medicine (pp. 47–89). Cham: Springer.

Hamed, G., Marley, M., El-Sayed, S. A., and Tolba, M. F. (2016). Comparative study of various DNA-based steganography techniques with the essential conclusions about the future research. In 2016 11th International Conference on Computer Engineering & Systems (ICCES) (pp. 220–225). IEEE.

https://www.britannica.com/science/single-nucleotide-polymorphism.

Lee, S. H., Lee, E. J., Hwang, W. J., and Kwon, K. R. (2018). Reversible DNA data hiding using multiple difference expansions for DNA authentication and storage. *Multimedia Tools and Applications*, 77(15), 19499–19526.

Liu, Q., Yang, K., Xie, J., and Sun, Y. (2021). DNA-based molecular computing, storage, and communications. *IEEE Internet of Things Journal*, 9(2), 897–915.

Malathi, P., Manoaj, M., Manoj, R., Raghavan, V., and Vinodhini, R. E. (2017). Highly improved DNA based steganography. *Procedia Computer Science*, 115, 651–659.

Marwan, S., Shawish, A., and Nagaty, K. (2016). DNA-based cryptographic methods for data hiding in DNA media. *Biosystems*, 150, 110–118.

Mousa, H., Moustafa, K., Abdel-Wahed, W., and Hadhoud, M. M. (2011). Data hiding is based on contrast mapping using a DNA medium. *International Arab Journal Information Technology*, 8(2), 147–154.

Nabi, S. H., Sarosh, P., Parah, S. A., and Bhat, G. M. (2021). Information embedding using DNA sequences for covert communication. In Multimedia Security (pp. 111–129). Singapore: Springer.

Peterson, I. (2001). Hiding in DNA. Proceedings of Muse. 2001;22.

Pramanik, S., and Setua, S. K. (2012). DNA cryptography. In 2012 7th International Conference on Electrical and Computer Engineering (pp. 551–554). IEEE.

Sadkhan, S. B. (2021). Information security based on DNA-importance and future trends. In 2021 International Conference on Communication & Information Technology (ICICT) (pp. 310–314). IEEE.

Sadkhan, S. B. (2021). Information security based on DNA-importance and future trends. In 2021 International Conference on Communication & Information Technology (ICICT) (pp. 310–314). IEEE.

Sahana, S., Dey, G., Ganguly, M., Paul, P., and Paul, S. (??) Adaptive steganography based enhanced cipher hiding technique for secure data.

Singh, G. (2013). A study of encryption algorithms (RSA, DES, 3DES, and AES) for information security. *International Journal of Computer Applications*, 67(19).

Subhedar, M. S., and Mankar, V. H. (2014). Current status and key issues in image steganography: a survey. *Computer Science Review*, 13, 95–113.

Zebari, N. A., Zebari, D. A., Zeebaree, D. Q., and Saeed, J. N. (2021). Significant features for steganography techniques using deoxyribonucleic acid: a review. *Indonesian Journal of Electrical Engineering and Computer Science*, 21(1), 338–347.

Zhang, X., Han, F., and Niu, Y. (2017). Chaotic image encryption algorithm based on bit permutation and dynamic DNA encoding.

19 Investigating the Factors That Influence Internationalization of Consumer Service Organizations in Kuwait

Rania Nafea[1,a], Abdulaziz Al-Jassar[2,b], Nidhi Menon[1,c], and Shabana Faizal[1,d]

[1]Assistant Professor College of Administrative and Financial Services, University of Technology, Bahrain
[2]Maastricht School of Management (MsM), Netherlands

Abstract

This study examines the factors that lead to internationalization of consumer service organizations in Kuwait. Kuwait is an economy where oil and gas contribute 40% to the country's GDP and represent about 92% of the nation's export revenues. For the economy to become truly sustainable, a shift needs to take place in the country's strategic direction. A greater focus needs to be given to the internationalization of consumer and manufacturing services to generate export revenue for Kuwait and decrease the reliability on oil and gas income in the long-term. The target is employees of consumer service organizations that have international presence outside of Kuwait. This explanatory study uses a quantitative approach where a questionnaire was developed to collect data electronically. Total 302 valid and complete responses were collected through an online survey using survey monkey, which was then analyzed using Smart PLS v. 3.3. A theoretical framework based on extensive literature review was adapted from Javalgi et al. (2003) and Chelliah et al. (2010) to include four independent variables—firm size, competitive advantage, market characteristics and international knowledge and experience. Findings reveal that three variables—International knowledge and experience, competitive advantage and market characteristics impact the internationalization process.

Keywords

Attitude of the management towards internationalization, competitive advantage, international knowledge and experience, internationalization, market characteristics.

Introduction

Over recent years, many developed nations have been shifting from being largely manufacturing-based economies to being predominantly service economies (Patterson and Cicic, 1995). This might be attributed to the fact that as countries' standard of living increases, citizens start demanding a larger variety of goods and services. This in turn, has turned the globe into a 'dynamic consuming economy', where the demand for services and consumer goods has multiplied rapidly. Moreover, developments in information technology, coupled with less restrictive trade barriers, have facilitated the globalisation and provision of services (Patterson and Cicic, 1995; Yayla et al., 2018).

---

[a]rania.nafea@utb.edu.bh, [b]Aafajq8@gmail.com, [c]nsmenon@utb.edu.bh, [d]s.faizal@utb.edu.bh

This also meant that many businesses now operate in a global market environment (Hassan and Kaynak, 1994; Ekeledo and Sivakumar, 1998).

This expansion of consumer services sector has witnessed increased importance for the global economy and for international commerce and has been the focus of some recent research (Patterson and Cicic, 1995; Lam and White, 1999; Choo, 2012). Nevertheless, there is a scarcity of studies into the role of the consumer services sector within local and global economies (Patterson and Cicic, 1995; O'Farrell et al., 1998). In 2020, a review was conducted, and it was discovered that there remains inadequate research in this area (Paul and Rosenbaum, 2020). This study aims to bridge the gap in literature in terms of factors that impact the internationalization of consumer service organizations in a growing economy like Kuwait.

Literature Review

Internationalization represents a significant stage in the life cycle of many business organizations, which involves a decision to expand its operations to external markets (O'Farrell et al., 1998). Such a decision is fraught with difficulties, especially for companies which manufacture products. However, in the case of companies which provide consumer services, Clark and Rajaratnam (1999) have pointed out that the process of internationalization is often much easier to implement.

Many definitions in the context of consumer services include the notion of the expansion of services beyond local markets to find customers in international markets (Rammal et al., 2014; Hazarbassanova, 2016). This involves business diversification such that it extends its service operations to a new business environment (Javalgi et al., 2003), Prior to deciding whether or not to 'go international', careful consideration needs to be given to the challenges which might confront the organization in deciding to operate in unfamiliar business environments (Etemad, 2004). Dunning's eclectic theory is a development of the cost-based theory that aimed at understanding transfer as well as the internationalization of companies (Dunning, 2015). Resource-based theory focused on the association of the size of the company with the decision to internationalize (Bonaccorsi, 1992; Sousa et al., 2008). Sousa et al. (2008) posited that international expansion necessitated that a company should have sufficient resources to meet the task. The larger the organization, the better its chances of successfully internationalizing.

Factors that affect the success of internationalization

Firm size

Previous studies have shown that internationalization can be successful when a company is of a considerable size (Sousa et al., 2008; Subramaniam and Wasiuzzaman, 2019). Sousa et al. (2008) stressed the importance of certain resources for successful internationalization. Large organizations possess the capabilities, skills and other resources (O'Farrell et al., 1998; Dunning, 2015). Accordingly, the following research hypotheses were formulated:

H1: Consumer service organizations' size has a positive impact on the success of internationalization.

H1.1: Attitude of the management moderates the relationship between firm size and success of internationalization.

Competitive advantage

Wiedersheim-Paul et al. (1978) have shown that having a competitive advantage was a strong motivator for companies to internationalize. This is supported by other authors (e.g. Cooper and Kleinschmidt, 1985; Subramaniam and Wasiuzzaman, 2019. Thus, we hypothesize the following:

H2: Consumer service organizations' competitive advantage has a positive impact on the success of internationalization.

H2.1: Attitude of the management moderates the relationship between a firm's competitive advantage and success of internationalization.

Market characteristics

Dunning (2015) has shown that characteristics of the market like having low trade barriers is a determinant of the decision to internationalize. It is important to note that the effects of trade barriers have been noted by several authors (Yang et al., 2011; Dunning, 2015). It is therefore reasonable to hypothesize that:

H3: Consumer service organizations' market characteristics has a positive impact on the success of internationalization.

H3.1: Attitude of the management moderates the relationship between a firm's market characteristics and success of internationalization.

International knowledge and experience

Vida et al. (2000) have shown the importance of previous experience in operating internationally and how it significantly reduced the risks involved in a new internationalization venture (Chelliah et al., 2010). A competitive advantage is firmly secured by the knowledge that the company possesses which is unique and cannot be imitated by other competitors. It is found that international knowledge and experience has a positive association with attitude of the management towards internationalization (Chelliah et al., 2010). This leads to the below hypothesis

H4: Consumer service organizations' international knowledge and experience has a positive impact on the success of internationalization.

H4.1: Attitude of the management moderates the relationship between a firm's international knowledge and experience and success of internationalization.

Attitude of the management

Ciszewska-Mlinaric and Mlinariè (2010) strongly advised that the relationship between the attitude of the management towards internationalization and the actual expansion should not be taken lightly. The authors argued that having a positive attitude of the management could help in the final approval of the decision to internationalize the operations of the company. Kahiya (2018) found that a positive and significant relationship existed between the attitude of the management towards internationalization and the decision to internationalize. Javalgi and Grossman (2014) actually found the attitude of the management to be the principal factor for the internationalization of consumer service companies.

H5: *The attitude of the management of consumer service organizations in Kuwait has a positive impact on internationalization.*

Conceptual Framework of Research

The conceptual model for the current study has been developed and is shown in Figure 19.1. The model includes the principal factors that are hypothesized as influencing the internationalization of service companies in Kuwait. The model consists of four independent variables—firm size, competitive advantage, market characteristics and international knowledge and experience, which are hypothesized as positively affecting the attitude of the management toward internationalization. These would also help in determining the success of internationalization.

Dependent variable

Success of internationalization is the dependent variable.

Independent variables

Firm size: the size of the organization in terms of the number of employees.

Competitive advantage: a unique strategy that the company has decided to follow.

Market characteristics: the structure and characteristics of the new market such as the laws that govern internationalization and the tax system on external organizations.

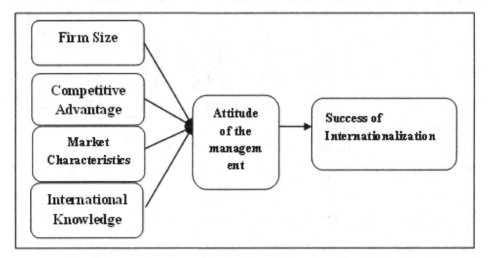

Figure 19.1 Conceptual model of the study adapted from: Javalgi et al. (2003); Chelliah et al. (2010).

International knowledge and experience: the knowledge and information that the organization might hold about internationalization based on its experience from other markets or its observation of similar competitors' experiences.

Mediating/moderating variable

There is one mediating variable in this study which is attitude of the management towards internationalization.

Methodology and Model Specifications

This study is based on quantitative methodology since the researcher aims to discover causal relationships between the variables of the research (Saunders et al., 2016).

Data collection was done using questionnaires that were distributed to employees of organizations in the consumer service industry in Kuwait that have an international presence outside the country. Therefore, the target population is 111 organizations. These organizations vary in size and structure. A total of 302 valid and complete responses were collected. The collected data is used to test the relationships between the four independent variables (measures), the mediator (dimension) and the dependent variable (construct).

Conceptual Model Variables' Analysis

Discriminant validity

A Fornier Locker Criterion tests the discriminant validity. Table 19.1 displays the results below.

Table 19.1: Fornier locker criterion test.

	Competitive Advantage	Size of the firm	International Knowledge and Experience	Attitude of the management	Market Characteristics	Success in Internationalization
Competitive Advantage	0.725					
Firm Size	0.225	1.000				
International Knowledge and Experience	0.522	0.203	0.779			
Attitude of the management	0.522	0.073	0.518	0.772		
Market Characteristics	0.588	0.092	0.445	0.504	0.791	
Success in Internationalization	0.625	−0.096	0.447	0.461	0.686	0.755

Convergent validity

The AVE values obtained for each variable are displayed in Table 19.2. The convergent validity has been established as all AVE values are above the 0.5 threshold.

Composite reliability

Composite reliability was used for this study, as recommended by Hair et al. (2016). The acceptable levels of reliability are values ≥ 0.7 (Hair et al., 2016). Table 19.3 shows the obtained composite reliability values for the research variables. The reliability of the variables is established since all values are above 0.7.

Table 19.2: AVE values.

Constructs	AVE
Competitive Advantage	0.526
Firm Size	1.000
International Knowledge and Experience	0.606
Attitude of the management	0.596
Market Characteristics	0.626
Success in Internationalization	0.570

Table 19.3: Reliability results.

Constructs	Composite reliability
Competitive Advantage	0.885
Firm Size	1.000
International Knowledge and Experience	0.885
Attitude of the management	0.816
Market Characteristics	0.869
Success in Internationalization	0.867

Correlation analysis

The strength of associations between each pair of variables was measured using correlation analysis and the results are tabulated in Table 19.4. All the independent variables have a significant correlation with the attitude of the management towards internationalization except for firm size.

Path Coefficients Analysis

The relative weightage of all the individuals' paths in the model is shown in the SEM, along with the significance of these paths (Hair et al., 2016). Testing of hypothesis is also done. Figure 19.2 represents the SEM model.

Table 19.4: Correlation analysis.

	Competitive Advantage	Firm size	International Knowledge and Experience	Attitude of the management	Market Characteristics	Success in Internationalization
Competitive advantage	1					
Firm size	0.225	1				
International knowledge and experience	0.522	0.203	1			
Attitude of the management	0.522	0.073	0.518	1		
Market characteristics	0.588	0.092	0.445	0.504	1	
Success in internationalization	0.625	−0.096	0.447	0.461	0.686	1

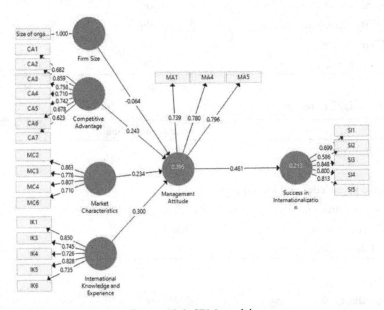

Figure 19.2 SEM model.

Table 19.5 shows the analysis results where the influence of firm size on attitude of the management towards internationalization is examined first. The beta value is −0.064 and is very minimal. The table also shows that the result is not significant (t statistics = 1.452 and p-value = 0.147). So, hypothesis H1 is not supported. In addition, the moderation effect of attitude of the management on the relationship between firm size and the success of internationalization was examined. The results show that the moderation influence is moderate and negative. Moreover, the results show that the moderation is not significant. Hence, hypothesis H1.1 is not supported.

Table 19.5: Research hypotheses testing summary.

Hypothesis	Test statement	Beta	Standard deviation	T-Statistics	P-value of significance	Conclusion
H1	Firm size → Attitude of the management	−0.064	0.044	1.452	0.147	Not supported
H1.1	Firm size → Success in internationalization	−0.03	0.021	1.423	0.155	Not supported
H2	Competitive advantage → Attitude of the management	0.243	0.061	3.995	0.000	Supported
H2.1	Competitive advantage → Success in Internationalization	0.112	0.036	3.142	0.002	Supported
H3	Market characteristics → Attitude of the management	0.234	0.059	3.971	0.000	Supported
H3.1	Market characteristics → Success in internationalization	0.108	0.035	3.056	0.002	Supported
H4	International knowledge and experience → attitude of the management	0.300	0.069	4.370	0.000	Supported
H4.1	International knowledge and experience → Success in internationalization	0.139	0.032	4.372	0.000	Supported
H5	Attitude of the management → Success in internationalization	0.461	0.064	7.205	0.000	Supported

Table 19.5 shows the results of competitive advantage influence. It shows that this variable has a significant influence on attitude of the management towards internationalization. The beta value of the result was 0.243. This indicates that for every one-point change in competitive advantage, there is 0.243 change in success in internationalization. The result is significant (t statistic = 3.995 and p-value < 0.05). Hence, hypothesis H2 is supported. With respect to the moderation effect of the attitude of the management on the relationship between firms' competitive advantage and success of internationalization, results show that the influence is significant (path weight is 0.112). Hence, the attitude of the management acts as a moderator between a firm's competitive advantage and the success of internationalization. Therefore, hypothesis H2.1 is supported.

The impact of market characteristics on the success of internationalization was found to be positive (beta = −0.234). Moreover, the results show that the influence is significant (t statistic = 3.971 and p-value = 0.000). Hence, hypothesis H3 is supported. The moderation effect of the attitude of the management on the relationship between market characteristics and the success of internationalization was found to be significant since the path weight is 0.108 and p-value is less than 0.05. Therefore, it is proven that attitude of the management acts as a moderator in this case. Hence, hypothesis H3.1 is supported.

The influence of international knowledge and experience on attitude of the management towards internationalization was examined next. The table shows that the impact of international knowledge and experience was the highest among all the independent variables (beta = 0.300). This implies that the change in international knowledge and experience leads to a 0.300 change in the attitude of the management towards internationalization. The result is significant (t statistic 4.370 and p-value > 0.05). Therefore, hypothesis H4 is supported. With respect to the moderation effect of the attitude of the management on the relationship between international knowledge and experience and the success of internationalization, it was found that the path weight is 0.139. Moreover, the results show that this influence is significant. Hence, it is proven that the attitude of the management moderates the relationship between international knowledge and experience and the success of internationalization. Therefore, hypothesis H4.1 is supported.

Results in Table 19.5 demonstrate the impact of the attitude of the management towards internationalization on the success of internationalization. It's estimated that the beta value of the influence is 0.461. This influence is high and significant (t statistic = 7.205 and p-value = 0.000). Therefore, hypothesis H5 is supported.

Conclusion

This study was aimed at investigating the factors which impact the success of internationalization for service organizations in Kuwait. The relationship is moderated by attitude of the management towards internationalization. Analysis of the full dataset revealed that international knowledge and experience was the most important internationalization factor that influenced attitude of the management toward internationalization. This implies that having the required knowledge and experience in internationalization allows organizations to take a step forward and expand their operations outside. With this knowledge, the organization would be able to know how to deal with risks and to put together an operation that is most likely to succeed. This conforms with the findings of Chelliah et al. (2010), which state that international knowledge and experience has a positive influence on enhancing attitude of the management toward internationalization.

The second significant factor was competitive advantage. With a stronger competitive advantage, management would be assured that the internationalization decision is a good one and thus would have positive attitude towards it. This conforms with the findings of Javalgi et al. (2003) and Kaleka and Morgan (2019), which confirm the existence of a positive and significant relationship between competitive advantage and attitude of the management toward internationalization.

The third significant factor was market characteristics. This shows that moving into an open market with free trade regulations and well-established policies and procedures in terms of taxes and access to resources, technology and supply chain will reflect positively on the bottom-line of the organization. Hence, management would be inclined to move their operations externally. This confirms the findings of Javalgi et al.

(2003) and Dunning (2015), which showed that market characteristics has a positive influence on the attitude of the management toward internationalization.

However, the study did not find a significant influence of firm size on the attitude of the management toward internationalization. This could be justified by the fact that organization size is mainly related to the structure of the organization and might not indicate capabilities and competencies internally or externally. Hence, we see large organizations in Kuwait that do not have a presence outside. This is in contradiction with the findings of Javalgi et al. (2003), which presented evidence of a significant relationship between firm size and the attitude of the management toward internationalization.

Finally, the attitude of the management toward internationalization has a positive influence on the success of internationalization. This implies that having the right mindset when it comes to internationalization and being invested both financially and cognitively in the decision assists the organization in showing resilience and succeeding in its internationalization efforts. This validates the findings of Javalgi and Grossman (2014) and Javalgi et al. (2003), that had demonstrated the existence of a positive and significant relationship between the attitude of the management toward internationalization and the success of internationalization.

References

Bonaccorsi, A. (1992). On the relationship between firm size and export intensity. *Journal of International Business Studies*, 23(4), 605–635.

Chelliah, S., Sivamurugan, P., Sulaiman, M., and Munusamy, J. (2010). The moderating effect of firm size: internationalization of small and medium enterprises (SMEs) in the manufacturing sector. *African Journal of Business Management*, 4(14), 3096–3109.

Choo, Y. Y. (2012). Efficiency and scale economies in the Japanese non-life insurance industry. *International Journal of Financial Services Management*, 5(3), 239–255.

Ciszewska-Mlinaric, M., and Mlinariè, F. (2010). Small firms in a small country: managerial factors, internationalization and performance of Slovenian SMEs. *Managing Global Transitions*, 8(3), 239–259.

Clark, T., and Rajaratnam, D. (1999). International services: perspectives at century's end. *Journal of Services Marketing*, 13(4–5), 298–310.

Cooper, R. G., and Kleinschmidt, E. J. (1985). The impact of export strategy on export sales performance. *Journal of International Business Studies*, 16(1), 37–55.

Dunning, J. H. (1988). The eclectic paradigm of international production: a restatement and some possible extensions, *Journal of International Business Studies*, 19(1), 1–31.

Dunning, J. H. (2015). The eclectic paradigm of international production: a restatement and some possible extensions. *The Eclectic Paradigm*, 50–84.

Ekeledo, I., and Sivakumar, K. (1998). Foreign market entry mode choice of service firms: a contingency perspective. *Journal of the Academy of Marketing Science*, 26(4), 274–292.

Etemad, H. (2004). Internationalization of small and medium-sized enterprises: a grounded theoretical framework and an overview. *Canadian Journal of Administrative Sciences*, 21(1), 1.

Hair Jr, J. F., Hult, G. T. M., Ringle, C., and Sarstedt, M. (2016). A Primer on Partial Least Squares Structural Equation Modeling (PLS-SEM). Sage Publications.

Hassan, S. S., and Kaynak, E. (1994). Market globalization: an introduction. In Globalization of Consumer Markets: Structures and Strategies (pp. 3–17). Psychology Press.

Hazarbassanova, D. B. (2016). The value creation logic and the internationalisation of internet firms. *Review of International Business and Strategy*, 26(3), 349–370.

Javalgi, R. R. G., and Grossman, D. A. (2014). Firm resources and host-country factors impacting internationalization of knowledge-intensive service firms. *Thunderbird International Business Review*, 56(3), 285–300.

Javalgi, R. R. G., Griffith, D. A., and White, D. S. (2003). An empirical examination of factors influencing the internationalization of service firms. *Journal of Services Marketing*, 17(2), 185–201.

Kahiya, E. T. (2018). Five decades of research on export barriers: Review and future directions. *International Business Review*, 27(6), 1172–1188.

Kaleka, A., and Morgan, N. A. (2019). How marketing capabilities and current performance drive strategic intentions in international markets. *Industrial Marketing Management*, 78, 108–121.

Lam, L. W., and White, L. P. (1999). An adaptive choice model of the internationalization process. *The International Journal of Organizational Analysis*, 7(2), 105–134.

O'Farrell, P. N., Wood, P. A., and Zheng, J. (1998). Internationalisation by business service SMEs: an inter-industry analysis. *International Small Business Journal*, 16(2), 13–33.

Patterson, P. G., and Cicic, M. (1995). A typology of service firms in international markets: an empirical investigation. *Journal of International Marketing*, 3(4), 57–83.

Paul, J., and Rosenbaum, M. (2020). Retailing and consumer services at a tipping point: New conceptual frameworks and theoretical models. *Journal of Retailing and Consumer Services*, 54,

Rammal, H. G., Rose, E. L., Jensen, P. D. Ø., and Petersen, B. (2014). Value creation logics and internationalization of service firms. *International Marketing Review*, 31(6), 557–575.

Saunders, M., Lewis, P., and Thornhill, A. (2016). Research Methods for Business Students (7th edn). Harlow: Pearson.

Sousa, C. M., Martínez-López, F. J., and Coelho, F. (2008). The determinants of export performance: a review of the research in the literature between 1998 and 2005. *International Journal of Management Reviews*, 10(4), 343–374.

Subramaniam, V., and Wasiuzzaman, S. (2019). Geographical diversification, firm size and profitability in Malaysia: a quantile regression approach. *Heliyon*, 5(10), e02664.

Vida, I., Reardon, J., and Fairhurst, A. (2000). Determinants of international retail involvement: the case of large US retail chains. *Journal of International Marketing*, 8(4), 37–60.

Wiedersheim-Paul, F., Olson, H. C., and Welch, L. S. (1978). Pre-export activity: the first step in internationalization. *Journal of International Business Studies*, 9(1), 47–58.

Yang, Q., Zimmerman, M., and Jiang, C. (2011). An empirical study of the impact of CEO characteristics on new firms' time to IPO. *Journal of Small Business Management*, 49(2), 163–184.

Yayla, S., Yeniyurt, S., Uslay, C., and Cavusgil, E. (2018). The role of market orientation, relational capital, and internationalization speed in foreign market exit and re-entry decisions under turbulent conditions. *International Business Review*, 27(6), 1105–1115.

20 Adoption of Methodologies and Popular Tools for Entrepreneurs

Arifusalam Shaikh[1,a], Sandeep Singh[1,b], and Carlos Bazan[2,c]

[1]Department of Marketing, Strategy & Entrepreneurship, University Canada West Vancouver, Canada
[2]Faculty of Business Administration, Memorial University, St. John's, Canada

Abstract

Entrepreneurs have always tried different ways to launch their products to the market in the most viable way since the inception of business and trade. However, there have been some significant contributions to entrepreneurship as the new methodologies evolved to minimize their challenges in recent decades. These methodologies like Lean Startup, Design Thinking, Agile Methodology, Stage-gate-methodology, their variants and other tools like Business Model Canvas, Lean Canvas and Value Proposition Canvas have impacted the entrepreneurial ecosystem, particularly on the institutional side. They have aided entrepreneurs in expediting the process and enhancing the success of a new venture. This paper studies the evolution of successful methodologies and the variants widely accepted by entrepreneurs worldwide. Bibliometric analysis was conducted to analyse the adoption of these methodologies as presented by the researchers. While entrepreneurs adopt a methodology that suits their innovation, they also need to learn about the available tools that can help them efficiently manage the launch of new products. This paper also provides recommendations to aspiring entrepreneurs on the current popular tools that can be utilized for their new ventures along with a brief discussion on sustainability in entrepreneurship.

Keywords

Entrepreneurship, innovation, methodologies, technology.

Introduction

Several methodologies and tools have evolved over a period of time to aid entrepreneurs expedite their process of launching their businesses. While entrepreneurship has always been an important element in the world of business, the growing population and the need for cater emerging problem in the business world in recent decades has been a driving factor for researcher and practitioners to keenly focus on developing effective methodologies and tools that can expedite the process and enhance the success rate. Among the popular ones that were widely accepted include methodologies like Lean Startup, Design Thinking, Agile Methodology, Stage-gate-methodology, their

[a]arifusalam.shaikh@ucanwest.ca, [b]sandeep0578@myucw.ca, [c]cabazan@mun.ca

variants and other tools like Business Model Canvas, Lean Canvas, and Value Proposition Canvas.

Popular methodologies that evolved over a period of time will be discussed in the next section. Popular tools widely used in the initial stages of entrepreneurship will also be presented. In the second part of this article a bibliographic analysis of the literature on AI, entrepreneurship, and innovation will be provided and insights will be discussed in detail.

Popular Methodologies in Entrepreneurship

In the following, key offerings and the benefits of prominent methodologies and tools that evolved over a period of time will be discussed.

Design Thinking

Design thinking is a popular problem-solving approach that involves empathizing with the user, defining the problem, ideating potential solutions, prototyping, and testing. It is a human-centered approach that aims to understand the user's needs and motivations, and then create innovative solutions that meet those needs. The approach was first proposed by Rolf Faste in the 1980s at Stanford University (Brown, 2008). However, it gained popularity in the early 2000s when it was adopted by companies such as Apple, IBM, and Procter & Gamble (Liedtka, 2015).

One of the key reasons for design thinking to be accepted widely was its structured process for innovation that could be applied to a wide range of problems. Additionally, it emphasized the importance of understanding the user's perspective, which helped companies create products that met their customers' needs. It further promoted a collaborative approach to problem-solving, which encouraged teams to work together and share their ideas. However, startups often face challenges in adopting design thinking. One of the challenges is that it requires a significant investment of time and resources to conduct user research and prototype solutions. Additionally, startups may lack the necessary expertise in areas such as user research, design, and prototyping. Finally, startups may struggle to balance the need for innovation with the need for revenue generation, as design thinking can be a lengthy process that may not yield immediate results (Liedtka, 2015).

Agile Methodology

Agile methodology is generally viewed as a software development approach that emphasizes flexibility, collaboration, and customer satisfaction through iterative and incremental development. Agile methodology became popular in the early 2000s as a response to the limitations of traditional waterfall software development methods, which were seen as inflexible, slow, and unable to deliver on customer needs (Cohn, 2009). It was proposed by a group of software engineers in 2001, who authored the Agile Manifesto to define the values and principles of the methodology (Beck et al., 2001). The Agile Manifesto prioritizes individuals and interactions, working software, customer collaboration, and responding to change over following a plan and documentation. It encourages a self-organizing and cross-functional team approach that adapts to changing requirements and customer feedback.

Agile methodologies typically use short development cycles, called sprints, to deliver working software quickly and often, and to allow for frequent feedback and adjustments. One common challenge in adopting this methodology is the need for a highly motivated and skilled team, as well as a strong focus on communication and collaboration. Additionally, Agile can be difficult to implement without proper training, coaching, and support, which may be a challenge for startups with limited resources.

Lean Startup Methodology

The Lean Methodology is a philosophy that focuses on minimizing waste and maximizing value in the production process. It was initially developed by Toyota in the 1940s, and later popularized by Eric Ries in his book, "The Lean Startup" in (Ries, 2011). Ries argued that startups could benefit from applying Lean principles to their development process. The Lean Startup methodology became popular because it offered a more efficient and effective way for startups to develop and launch products. The methodology emphasizes rapid experimentation, continuous feedback, and a focus on customer needs, which are all critical elements for startup success.

Despite its popularity, adopting the lean startup methodology can be challenging for startups. One such challenge is the need for a culture shift towards experimentation and risk-taking. Startups must be willing to take risks and learn from failure to implement the Lean methodology successfully. Another challenge is the need for discipline and rigor in the experimentation process. Startups must have clear goals and metrics for measuring progress and success to ensure they are making progress towards their goals.

Stage-Gate-Methodology

The Stage-Gate methodology is a structured product development process that divides the development cycle into stages or gates, with the aim of reducing risks and ensuring successful product launches. It was proposed by Robert Cooper in the 1980s as a way to improve the product development process and was first introduced in his book, "Winning at New Products" (Cooper, 1986). The methodology is characterized by five stages: idea generation, preliminary assessment, detailed assessment, development, and launch (Cooper, 1986). Each stage has its own set of objectives and criteria that must be met before moving on to the next stage. These criteria are designed to ensure that the product is viable and has a high probability of success before committing significant resources to its development.

The Stage-Gate methodology quickly gained popularity among businesses as it provided a systematic approach to product development, allowing companies to reduce risks and improve their chances of success. It also provided a framework for collaboration between different departments, such as marketing and engineering, improving communication and reducing delays. However, the adoption of the Stage-Gate methodology can be challenging for startups due to the rigid structure and heavy emphasis on planning and documentation. Startups often have limited resources and need to move quickly to bring their product to market, which can be hindered by the detailed assessments and gatekeeping of the methodology (Ollila and Yrjölä, 2017). This methodology suits well for the R&D of complex innovative products that will need a significant duration of time to develop a minimum viable product and involves a huge team to manage with significant amount of budget.

Combining Design Thinking, Lean Startup, and Agile Methodologies

Combining Design Thinking, Lean Startup, and Agile into a single framework involves several distinct phases and was discussed in detail by Galvin and Lee (2022). The framework begins with the discovery phase, where user needs and potential problems or opportunities are explored using Design Thinking and Lean Startup techniques. The define phase follows, refining the problem and solution vision with the help of Design Thinking tools and Lean Startup principles. In the development phase, Agile methodologies guide the creation of a minimum viable product (MVP) through iterative cycles and feedback loops, while incorporating Design Thinking methods for prototyping and user testing. The delivery phase focuses on preparing the validated solution for launch, leveraging Agile principles and Design Thinking techniques to refine the solution further. This process emphasizes the importance of iteration, enabling continuous learning, improvement, and adaptation of the solution based on user feedback and evolving market conditions, using Agile practices and Design Thinking insights.

Six-Sigma

Six Sigma methodology is a business improvement strategy that aims to reduce defects and variation in a process by focusing on data-driven decision-making, statistical analysis, and project management techniques. It was first developed by Motorola in the mid-1980s as a quality control system (Harry and Schroeder, 2011). The main goal of Six Sigma is to achieve a level of quality that meets or exceeds customer expectations, resulting in increased customer satisfaction, reduced costs, and improved profitability (Pande et al., 2000). While Six Sigma has been successful in improving quality and reducing costs in large corporations, it can be challenging for startups to adopt the methodology. The biggest challenge is often the cost of implementation, which can be prohibitive for small businesses with limited resources (Gupta and Kohli, 2006). Additionally, startups may lack the expertise and experience needed to effectively implement and sustain Six Sigma projects.

The above mentioned methodologies evolved with the need of entrepreneurs and complemented well to each other given the stages of launching their businesses. The design thinking concepts are appropriate during the early stages when the new ideas are being explored and to evaluate the product market fit. The lean startup and the Six-Sigma methodology aids the entrepreneurship to speed up the process of building their prototypes that may need several iterations to tweak their products or services to their potential customers.

New Methodologies in Entrepreneurship

Disciplined Entrepreneurship, developed by Aulet (2013), is a comprehensive approach that outlines 24 steps grouped into six major themes for starting and growing successful ventures. The process begins with ideation and generating business ideas, followed by market segmentation to identify target customer segments. The entrepreneur then creates detailed customer archetypes and develops a unique value proposition. A competitive analysis helps identify the venture's competitive advantage, and positioning strategies are devised to differentiate the offering. The value proposition is validated through customer engagement and feedback, leading to the development of a customer acquisition strategy. A robust business model is designed, financial projections are prepared, and a capable team is built to support the venture.

Continuing the process, resources are gathered, intellectual property is assessed and protected, and a go-to-market strategy is formulated. Pilot testing is conducted to refine the product or service, followed by a full-scale launch. The sales channel is established, operations and supply chain are set up, and manufacturing strategies are developed. Strategic partnerships are sought, and the revenue model is optimized based on market feedback. Ongoing financial planning and monitoring are essential, and strategies for scaling the business and diversifying offerings are devised. The Disciplined Entrepreneurship framework provides entrepreneurs with a systematic approach to validate and build their ventures. By following these steps, entrepreneurs can increase their chances of success by ensuring a thorough understanding of their customers, creating a compelling value proposition, designing a robust business model, and effectively launching and scaling their ventures.

Popular Tools in Entrepreneurship

In the following, tools that are commonly used by aspiring entrepreneurs will be discussed.

Business Model Canvas

The Business Model Canvas (BMC) is a strategic management tool proposed by Alexander Osterwalder and Yves Pigneur (Osterwalder and Pigneur, 2010). The BMC is a one-page template that consists of nine building blocks that describe the key elements of a business model. The nine building blocks include customer segments, value proposition, channels, customer relationships, revenue streams, key activities, key resources, key partnerships, and cost structure. The BMC became popular among entrepreneurs and startups due to its simplicity and effectiveness in capturing the key elements of a business model (Teece, 2010). It enables entrepreneurs to identify the key components of their business model and analyse how they create and capture value. By using the BMC, entrepreneurs can also test and refine their business model to ensure its viability and scalability in the market.

However, there are challenges to adopting the BMC, particularly for startups. One such challenge is the temptation to oversimplify the business model or overlook critical components in the rush to fill out the template (Kappel et al., 2015). Another challenge is the risk of failing to accurately identify customer needs and preferences, which can undermine the effectiveness of the value proposition and revenue streams (Kappel et al., 2015). While adopting the BMC, it is apt to mention that entrepreneurs should conduct sufficient research and analysis to accurately represent their business model. To overcome the deficiencies of BMC, another tool called Lean Canvas was introduced by Mourya (2022) which will be discussed next.

Lean Canvas

The Lean Canvas is a significant modification of BMC that included new components that can deal with uncertainty and risk which is an inherent challenge for all entrepreneurs (Mourya, 2022). The BMC was update removing certain components that may be too early for an aspiring entrepreneur and were replaced by those that are more important to deal in the beginning of their journey. The four components that were removed from the BMC are key partners, key activities, key resources and customer relationship. These four components deemed more appropriate to be dealt when the idea has been validated by the market and can help in the scalability stage. The four components that were introduced are problem, solutions, key metrics and unfair advantage. These four components are key for any innovative idea to be accepted in the market and therefore Lean Canvas has to potential for early entrepreneurs to enhance their success in gaining the product-market fit. In terms of comparison, it can be concluded that MBC works better after the idea has been validated while Lean Canvas can be a good too in early stages including customer discovery.

Value Proposition Canvas

The Value Proposition Canvas (VPC) is a strategic tool proposed by Alexander Osterwalder and Yves Pigneur in their book "Value Proposition Design: How to Create Products and Services Customers Want" in 2014 (Osterwalder et al., 2014). The VPC is designed to help entrepreneurs and startups analyse their value proposition, by identifying and addressing customer needs. The VPC is a one-page template that consists of two building blocks, the customer profile and the value map. The customer profile block identifies the customer's jobs, pains, and gains, while the value map block identifies the product and service features that address these elements of the customer profile. By using the VPC, entrepreneurs can identify customer needs and design products or services that effectively address those needs (Osterwalder et al., 2014).

The VPC has become popular among entrepreneurs and startups due to its effectiveness in capturing the key elements of a value proposition. It enables entrepreneurs to understand customer needs and design products or services that effectively address those needs. Additionally, the VPC encourages a customer-centric approach to product or service design, which is essential in today's competitive marketplace (Linder and Cantrell, 2017).

However, there are challenges to adopting the VPC, particularly for startups. One challenge is the temptation to rush through the process and fill out the template without conducting sufficient research or analysis. Another challenge is the risk of oversimplifying the customer profile or value map, which may lead to overlooking critical components or failing to consider the broader market context. Additionally, some startups may struggle to accurately identify and prioritize customer needs, particularly if they are operating in a rapidly evolving industry (Linder and Cantrell, 2017).

Bibliometric Analysis

A bibliometric analysis is now presented on the literature on AI, entrepreneurship, and innovation. The search conducted in this paper covered publications from the inception of AI, that is 1960s to 2023. The search was performed using the string *"(TITLE-ABS-KEY (Methodologies OR Methodology) AND (TITLE-ABS-KEY (entrepreneurship OR entrepreneurs) OR (TITLE-ABS-KEY (management) OR TITLE-ABS-KEY (innovation) OR TITLE-ABS-KEY (startup))"* in the Scopus database.

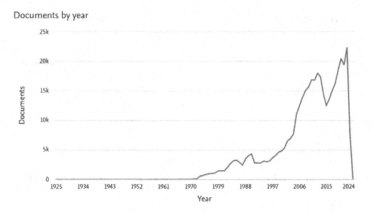

Figure 20.1 Articles published on AI in entrepreneurship and innovation since 1925.

The data was obtained in the form of yearly publications, number of documents by countries, and document by subject area. Each category provided significant insights and will be discussed briefly. Figure 20.1 provides a good overview of the frequency of publications based on the query from 1950s to 2023. The analysis revealed that the number of publications continuously increased, mainly from 1970s until around 2008. There was a drop in the number of publications until 2015 and it started to increase again until the Covid hit and there was a reduction of publications for a short period.

The data obtained was also utilized to learn about which countries contributed most to the field of entrepreneurship in literature. Figure 20.2 (i) provides the top 10 countries since the inception and Figures 20.2 (ii)–(vi) provide details for various period of times. It can be observed that USA and UK have maintained their first and second positions respectively across all periods of time. However, Canada, Australia, Italy, Japan and lately India and China have been among the third to fifth positions after USA and UK. The most recent trend from 2020 to current year revealed that India and China have shown great progress and secured third and fourth position respectively. Not only that India and China have shown progress in contributions, it can also be observed that, India is almost getting close to UK and China is not far away. There has been a significant reduction in the gap between other countries and USA which demonstrates the competitiveness from the developing countries in recent years as shown in Figure 20.3.

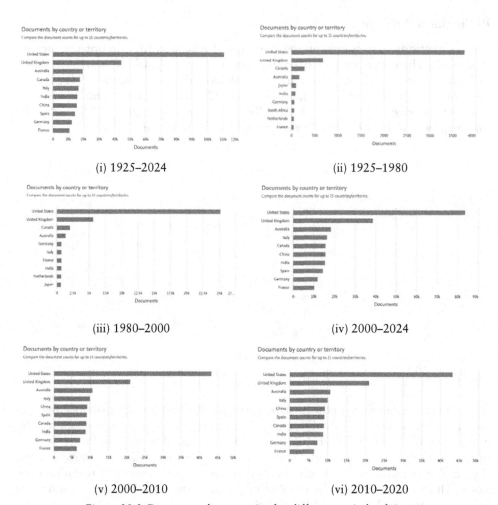

(i) 1925–2024   (ii) 1925–1980

(iii) 1980–2000   (iv) 2000–2024

(v) 2000–2010   (vi) 2010–2020

Figure 20.2 Documents by countries for different periods of time.

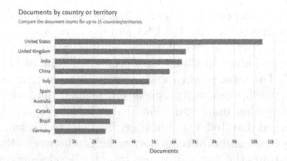

Figure 20.3 Documents by countries from year 2020.

The third category of analysis chosen was the subject area. Since the data collected was from 1965 until the current year, it would be interesting to see which subject areas have been the focus in publication in the field of Entrepreneurship and innovation. The analysis provided great insights that helps understand how the growth of technology has influenced the entrepreneurial ecosystem. It can be seen in Figure 20.4 that major contributions were in the field of medicine for a long period of time. The contributions to other field grew gradually and increased significantly in the recent decades. If the current situation (from 2020) is assessed, it can be seen in Figure 20.5 that most of the contributions are in the field of business and management, followed by engineering, social sciences, computer science, medicine and others. Furthermore, the figure also shows that the contributions are well balanced and the possibility of one subject area taking over the other is quite high and no specific area seem to remain dominant. This is a testimony that innovation has no bar given the technological developments and has led to significant contributions from all subject areas.

Sustainability and Entrepreneurship

Sustainable entrepreneurship has gained significance post-Covid, addressing health care crises and embracing remote work environments area among the priorities while general global orientation on sustainability remains a necessity. A comprehensive discussion on sustainability in entrepreneurship is beyond the scope of this article. However, a brief discussion is presented that can helps aspiring entrepreneurs to align their initiatives with sustainability in their businesses.

Entrepreneurs must prioritize employee and community well-being while reducing carbon emissions and embed sustainability concepts into their business ideas in the early stages of their journey. Equity, diversity, and inclusion (EDI) should be among the key considerations, promoting inclusive work environments and equal opportunities must be an essential component of their strategies.

It is essential to mention that a mindset must be built beyond economical gains towards long term sustainability. Future generations must take precedence over short-term shareholder interests, with a focus on long-term societal health as mentioned by Mulqueen (2022). Mulqueen further suggests that entrepreneurs have a responsibility to integrate sustainability into core practices. By practicing ethical business ethics, sustainable entrepreneurs drive positive change, contributing to a resilient and equitable society.

Building sustainable businesses in the post-Covid era entails several key aspects such as trust, changing minds and openness or transparency (Taffer, 2020). First, trust becomes paramount as businesses prioritize transparency in their operations and build credibility with stakeholders. To stand out from competitors, businesses must find innovative ways to differentiate themselves, offering unique value propositions that address emerging customer needs. Adapting to changing market demands and being open to new ideas is crucial. Embracing openness allows businesses to foster collaboration, respond to feedback, and drive continuous improvement. Lastly, businesses should recognize that it is acceptable to acknowledge and address financial troubles openly, seeking support and implementing necessary measures for long-term sustainability.

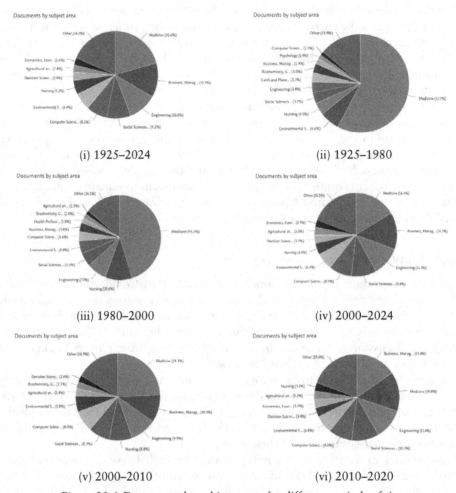

(i) 1925–2024

(ii) 1925–1980

(iii) 1980–2000

(iv) 2000–2024

(v) 2000–2010

(vi) 2010–2020

Figure 20.4 Documents by subject areas for different periods of time.

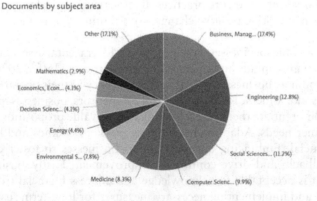

Figure 20.5 Documents by subject areas from year 2020.

Future Trends and Conclusion

The concept of sustainability takes centre stage, with entrepreneurs recognizing the need to balance financial success with social and environmental responsibility. Prioritizing the needs of future generations becomes a guiding principle, ensuring long-term viability and positive impact. Entrepreneurs play a crucial role in driving change and shaping a sustainable future. They become agents of transformation by embracing innovative solutions, practicing ethical business ethics, and fostering inclusive and collaborative environments. By integrating sustainability into their ventures, entrepreneurs create a legacy that extends beyond immediate gains. They contribute to the betterment of society and the planet by addressing pressing challenges and pioneering solutions that align with the principles of sustainable development. As leaders, entrepreneurs have the power to influence and inspire others to follow suit, amplifying the positive impact across industries and communities. By embracing sustainability in entrepreneurship, we can forge a path towards a more resilient, equitable, and sustainable world for current and future generations. In conclusion, as we navigate the post-Covid era, it is imperative to revisit methodologies, effective tools, and embrace contemporary approaches in entrepreneurship. Apart from discussing the popular methodologies and tools, a bibliometric analysis was also presented to provide a good overview of the contributions made by researchers and practitioners to the field of innovation and entrepreneurship along with a brief discussion on sustainability.

References

Aulet, B. (2013). Disciplined Entrepreneurship: 24 Steps to a Successful Startup. John Wiley and Sons.

Beck, K., Beedle, M., Van Bennekum, A., Cockburn, A., Cunningham, W., Fowler, M., Grenning, J., Highsmith, J., Hunt, A., Jeffries, R., and Kern, J. (2001). Manifesto for Agile Software Development. Agile Alliance.

Brown, T. (2008). Design thinking. *Harvard Business Review*, 86(6), 84–92.

Cohn, M. (2009). Succeeding with Agile: Software Development using Scrum. Addison-Wesley Professional.

Cooper, R. G. (1986). Winning at New Products. Addison-Wesley.

Galvin, E., and Lee, N. (2022). Whales Likely Impacted by Great Pacific Garbage Patch. The Ocean Cleanup. https://www.greenbook.org/mr/monthly-dose-of-design/combining-design-thinking-lean-startup-and-agile-into-a-single-framework-part-seven/

Gupta, S., and Kohli, S. (2006). Implementation of six sigma in Indian industry: issues and challenges. *International Journal of Quality and Reliability Management*, 23(3), 290–303.

Harry, M., and Schroeder, R. (2011). Six Sigma: The breakthrough Management Strategy Revolutionizing the World's Top Corporations. Crown Business.

Kappel, T. A., Drobetz, W., and Vallaster, C. (2015). The impact of business model dynamics on startup performance. *Long Range Planning*, 48(6), 362–387.

Liedtka, J. (2015). Perspective: Linking design thinking with innovation outcomes through cognitive bias reduction. *Journal of Product Innovation Management*, 32(6), 925–938.

Linder, J., and Cantrell, S. (2017). Business model generation: A handbook for visionaries, game changers, and challengers. *Journal of Business Models*, 5(1), 54–55.

Mourya, A. (2022). Deconstruct Your Business Model on a Lean Canvas. The Ocean Cleanup. https://leanstack.com/lean-canvas/

Mulqueen, T. (2022). What is Sustainable Entrepreneurship, and Why Does it Matter. https://www.entrepreneur.com/leadership/what-is-sustainable-entrepreneurship-and-why-does-it/354955, Accessed on April 27, 2023.

Ollila, S., and Yrjölä, M. (2017). Applying the stage-gate process in a start-up company. *Journal of Innovation Management, 5*(1), 44–57.

Osterwalder, A., and Pigneur, Y. (2010). Business Model Generation: A Handbook for Visionaries, Game Changers, and Challengers. John Wiley and Sons.

Osterwalder, A., Pigneur, Y., Bernarda, G., and Smith, A. (2014). Value Proposition Design: How to Create Products and Services Customers Want. John Wiley and Sons.

Pande, P. S., Neuman, R. P., and Cavanagh, R. R. (2000). The Six Sigma way: How GE, Motorola, and Other top Companies are Honing their Performance. McGraw-Hill Education.

Ries, E. (2011). The Lean Startup: How Today's Entrepreneurs Use Continuous Innovation to Create Radically Successful Businesses. Crown Business.

Taffer, J. (2020). 3 Ways to Build a Sustainable Business Post-COVID. https://www.entrepreneur.com/growing-a-business/3-ways-to-build-a-sustainable-business-post-covid/352182, Accessed on April 27, 2023.

Teece, D. J. (2010). Business models, business strategy and innovation. *Long Range Planning*, 43(2–3), 172–194.

21 Evaluating the Significance of Indirect Effect of Human Resource Practices and Business Sustainability: An Integrated Mediated Model OLC, Innovation and Change on Banking Sectors

Jeena Ann John[1,a], Saubhagyalaxmi Misra[1,b], Mariam Mirza Al-Salman[2,c], Mona Mansoor Ahmed Hammad[2,d], Esra Abdulaziz Ahmed[2,e], and Mary Benitta Rani

[1]Assistant Professor, University of Technology
[2]Lecturer, University of Technology

Abstract

Sustainability is increasingly important for the banking sector due to several reasons such as social cost and UN (SDGs) 8. Based on the triple point framework, banks aim for social sustainability through higher performance work systems. Strategic objective of the banks are to boost the income by recognizing that social impacts. In this study we have integrated a mediated model to evaluate the total effects of High Performance Work System (HPWS), information technology and Knowledge management towards business sustainability. Based on the several literature reviews, we have decided to consider Organizational learning capabilities, Innovation and change as the mediating variables. The result of 2-tailed indicates that all the independent variables have a stronger correlation with business sustainability at 1% level of significance. Knowledge management has a total effect towards business sustainability through the mediating variable organizational learning but not Innovation and change. The future researcher needs to consider sustainable business value (SBV) and other factors for HPWS, Knowledge management and IT to prove their effectiveness towards the business suitability of bank.

Keywords

Business suitability, high-performance work systems, information technology, innovation and change, knowledge management, organizational learning capabilities.

Introduction

The concept of sustainability in business has become increasingly important in today's economic and social environment. Several studies are done to examine the role of stakeholder partnerships and corporate social responsibility in achieving sustainability in business. Banks contribute significantly to the social and economic advancement of countries by providing creating jobs and financial stability (Canada, 2020). According

[a]annjohn@utb.edu.bh, https://orcid.org/0000-0002-6675-6383, [b]smisra@utb.edu.bh, [c]m.alsalman@utb.edu.bh, [d]mona.hammad@utb.edu.bh, [e]eaahmed@utb.edu.bh

to sustainability performance, a company should examine the influence of its activities on the welfare of all stakeholders, including the community, society, and the environment, in addition to focusing on maximizing short-term shareholder profit (Freeman, 1984). Boon et al. (2019) found that the successful implementation of sustainable business practices involves aligning HR practices with the organization's sustainability goals. This alignment involves both creating HR policies that support the organization's sustainability goals, as well as encouraging employees to actively participate in sustainability initiatives. According to Muhamad et al. (2019) the economic dimension of business organizations has become increasingly important, due to the environmental destruction caused by the present economic activity. As per Umair et al. (2020) study aims to examine a potential mediator in the interaction between information technology (IT) and organizational performance is organizational learning (OL). The employment of technology within the organization, the justification for OL as the primary knowledge process, and the intersection of technology and OL as a knowledge-based method for enhancing organizational performance. The TBL encourages businesses and organizations to consider not only their financial performance but also their social and environmental impacts, and to strive to achieve a balance between the three (Hunt, 2023). This means that businesses must take into consideration the effects of their activities on the environment, the people they employ, and the communities in which they operate. Additionally, companies must also ensure that their operations and decisions are economically sound.

The structure of the paper has 6 sections. Section 1 on the introduction. Section 2 literature review. Section 3 sample of the study. Section 4 methodology. Section 5 discussion Section 6 conclusion.

Literature Review

High Performances Work System and Business Sustainability

Businesses can ensure long-term success by involving their entire employees in projects and training that will support the organization's sustainability (Bhardwaj, 2020). High Performance Work Systems (HPWS) can be very helpful since they have grown in importance for long-term competitive advantage. HPWS can contribute to an organization's sustainability, by allowing them to develop the ability to adapt to external challenges and changes (Suryaningtyas and Irawanto, 2019). In any business, high performance work systems play a crucial role in driving innovation since they have a positive impact on the organization's strategy, structure, workforce, climate, and culture. This led to the development of the hypothesis.

H1a. Organizational Learning mediate between High Performances work system and Business sustainability

H1b. Innovation and change mediate the relationship between High Performances work Practices and Business sustainability

Knowledge Management and Business Sustainability

The study's findings confirmed the predictions that organizational learning influences knowledge acquisition, storage, sharing, application procedures, and long-term organizational performance in a positive way (Kordab et al., 2020). knowledge management is a critical success factor in organizational learning and can mediate the relationship between organizational learning and sustainable business practices (Abdollahi et al., 2023). The results of their study affirm that knowledge management has an important role in helping businesses become more sustainable and innovative (Ochoa et al., 2021). A strong knowledge management system can help businesses develop new and innovative products and services, and in turn, these innovations can lead to greater sustainability, as well as a competitive advantage.

H2a. Organizational Learning mediate the relationship between Knowledge Management and Business sustainability

H2b. Innovation and change mediate the relationship between Knowledge Management and Business sustainability

Information Technology and Business Sustainability

Businesses must design superior technology acquisition and usage strategies to enhance their sustainable performance in dynamic and uncertain contexts (Acosta-Prado and Tafur, 2022). These findings have far-reaching implications for policy makers, as they can be used to increase sustainability in SMEs and help them succeed in competitive and innovative economic environments (Otioma, 2022). It finds that the mediative role of OL in the relationship between IT-c and innovation performance is realized mainly through explorative learning. Research suggests that organizational learning capability can mediate the relationship between Information technology and business sustainability Omar et al. (2019).

H3a. Organizational Learning mediate between Information Technology and Business sustainability

H3b. Innovation and change mediate the relationship between Information Technology and Business sustainability

Based on the above literature review, we propose a conceptual model Figure 21.1 for this study.

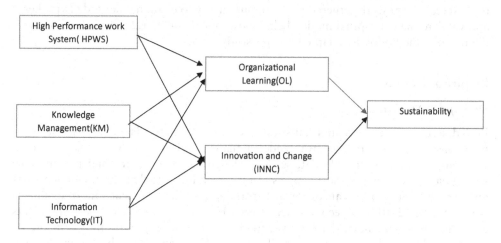

Figure 21.1 Conceptual frame.

The HPWPs are related to organizational learning as they affect organizational performance (Zhu et al., 2018; 2019). Many research have examined the connection between HPWP and organizational results, and they have found a favorable, statistically significant connection between organizational learning and corporate performance (Zgrzywa and Walecka, 2020). Digital technologies can be used to achieve sustainability goals (Guandalini, 2022). The TBL framework takes into account the financial, social, and environmental aspects of performance. A collection of HR procedures known as HPWS aims to raise employee productivity, motivation, and skill levels (Chang et al. 2018). But by combining these ideas, businesses may move toward a more sustainable and regenerative future Tajpour et al. (2022). It can help technology-driven businesses become more sustainable and improve corporate performance. Knowledge management practices can also lead to frugal innovation, which can further enhance corporate sustainability (Kun, 2022).

Therefore, it is possible that HPWS, knowledge management and IT can contribute to the People component of the TBL framework.

Data and Variables

Study Period and Sample

The subject of this research is to get the perception of the managers working in various banks towards the human resources practices and sustainable business of the banks. Total of 369 respondents are considered for the study. As per the central bank there are 100 banks combination of Islamic and non-Islamic banks. The biggest limitation is to collect the data from the managers. An online google survey was distributes and some of the respondents were met face to face to collect the information. It took an approximate of 8 months to collect the necessary data.

Methodology

5-scale Likert scale question is utilized, with the options ranging from strongly agreed to disagreed. Data were gathered via an online survey to examine the study hypotheses and validate the conceptual model. Below flowchart Figure 21.2 gives an overview of the research methodology adapted for this study.

Empirical Results

Descriptive Statistics

Both descriptive and inferential statistics were employed in the data analysis. The arithmetic mean is a measure of central tendency that is used to identify a single numerical value that is representative of a data set. Knowledge management and high performance work system has some of the average strands which indicate that the respondents has an average level of acceptances towards training and development (3.29), employee performance(3.210) and Technological Know How(3.353). 66% of the respondents agree that management conducts survey to identify the employees training demand. By converting knowledge into action, the TNA tool effectively closes the "know-do" gap

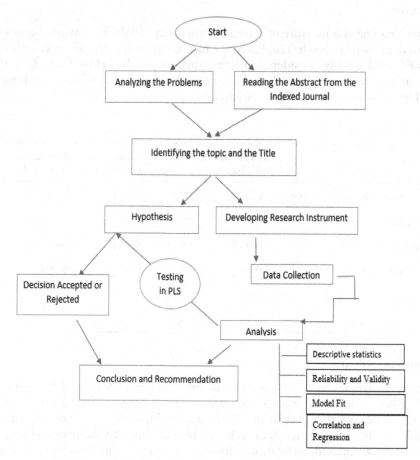

Figure 21.2 Flow chart for the research methodology.

in the world's people resources (Markaki et al., 2021). A healthier organization will have sustainable and higher productive workforce (de Jonge & Peeters, 2019).

Pair Wise Correlation

Correlation indicates the degree of association between two or more variables. When variables move in the same direction it is considered to be positive. (Jaadi, 2019) indicated that more than 0.7 have high positive correlation. Innovation and change have positive correlations with business sustainability value (0.789; p = 000). IT correlation with business sustainability value (0.742; p = 000). Organizational learning correlates with business sustainability value (0.734; p = 000). High performance work systems have moderate correlation with business sustainability value (0.645; p = 000). Knowledge management moderate positive correlation with business sustainability value (0.667; p = 000). Over all the variables are significant at 1%.

Reliability

Cronbach's alpha is a measure of internal consistency reliability that has been widely used for decades to assess the reliability of a measure. It ranges from 0 to 1, with values of less than 0.5 usually considered unacceptable. As per the below Table 21.1 all the latent variable values are more than 0.8 for Cronbach alpha, composite reliability and AVE. The items are highly reliable and accepted.

Table 21.1: Reliability.

	Cronbach Alpha	Rho_A	Composite reliability	Average variance extracted
High performance work system	0.933	0.939	0.944	0.628
Knowledge management	0.937	0.939	0.947	0.641
Information technology	0.947	0.949	0.954	0.656
Innovation and change	0.963	0.964	0.967	0.694
Organizational learning	0.945	0.945	0.953	0.669
Business sustainability	0.951	0.952	0.958	0.673

Discriminant validity

According to Barclay et al. (1995), Fornell and Larcker (1981), and Henseler et al. (2009), all constructs had average variance extracted (AVE) values that were greater than 0.5, indicating that they matched the acceptable criteria for convergent validity. Additionally, all constructs had AVE squareroot values on the diagonal that were higher than the squared correlation with other constructs off the diagonal, demonstrating that all constructs satisfied the required criteria for discriminant validity.

Good fitness model

Table 21.2: Goodness model.

SRMR	0.060

The Standardized Root Mean Square Residual (SRMR) is a measure of model fit used in structural equation modeling (SEM). Table 21.2 shows the result of SRMR value of 0 indicates a perfect fit, whereas values greater than 0.08 indicate a poor fit.

Principal component analysis

According to the principal compound analysis high performance work system which is considered as the compound 1 explains 83.8% of the variance from other components. HPWS accounts for most of the variances in comparison to other variables. Over all it could be assumed that the banks need to give more focus on the high performance work systems which will be the main components towards the Goal 8 of the sustainable development.

Regression Analysis

Business sustainability is a complex issue that involves a number of variables, which can include innovation and change, organizational learning and other factors. The R-squared values for these three variables indicate how well they explain the variation in business sustainability. Specifically, the R-squared value of 0.706 for innovation and change indicates that it explains 70.6% of the variation in business sustainability, while the R-squared value of 0.849 for organizational learning suggests that it explains 84.9% of the variation. Overall the predictive variables HPWS, KM, IT, OL, INNC explain 80% variation in business sustainability.

Result of Path Coefficient

The result shown in the Table 21.3 indicate that the association between knowledge management, innovation and change, and company sustainability does not appear to be statistically significant, according to the t-value of 0.663 and the p-value of 0.507. The association between knowledge management, Organizational Learnings, and company sustainability is statistically significant. Information technology is positively correlated with organizational learning as well as innovation and change and it is proved in several studies (Gomes and Wojahn, 2017; Haile and Tüzüner, 2022). HPWS had a positive significance with both innovation and change and organizational learning capabilities.

Table 21.3: Path coefficient.

Hypothesis		Direct	Indirect	T-Value	P-Value	Decision
H1a	HPWS → OL → BS	0.235	0.568	3.413	0.000	Accepted
H1b	HPWS → INNC → BS	0.191	0.613	3.333	0.000	Accepted
H2a	KM → OL → BS	0.185	0.676	2.106	0.035	Accepted
H2b	KM → INNC → BS	0.049	0.813	0.663	0.507	Rejected
H3a	IT → OL → BS	0.573	0.412	4.848	0.000	Accepted
H3b	IT → INNC → BS	0.596	0.597	3.767	0.000	Accepted

Conclusion and Recommendation

Employees may have an average acceptance towards training and development, employee performance, and technological know-how due to the potential benefits that they can provide to the organization. Training and development can provide employees with the necessary skills and knowledge to perform their job, while employee performance can be improved via training and development. Technological know-how can also help to ensure that the organization is utilizing the latest technology to its fullest potential, enabling it to stay competitive and increase productivity. Stakeholder value is a goal that businesses increasingly strive to achieve for their owners, shareholders, employees, customers, partners, suppliers, the environment, and future generations. To fill these gaps and give businesses the ability to assess their impacts, several researchers has created a brand-new methodology called sustainable business value (SBV). SBV offers a thorough view of a company's effect across six standardized dimensions and can be utilized for decision-making, portfolio management, benchmarking, stakeholder engagement, investor communication, and business development. Future research on high-performance work systems (HPWS) may take into account the following elements: leadership roles, HR practices, work design, and information technology.

Reference

Abdollahi, A., Ghaderi, Z., Béal, L., and Cooper, C. (2023). The intersection between knowledge management and organizational learning in tourism and hospitality: a bibliometric analysis. *Journal of Hospitality and Tourism Management*, 55, 11–28. https://doi.org/10.1016/j.jhtm.2023.02.014

Acosta-Prado, J. C., and Tafur-Mendoza, A. A. (2022). Examining the mediating role of dynamic capabilities in the relationship between information and communication technologies and sustainable performance, *VINE Journal of Information and Knowledge Management Systems*, 11(2), April–June 2021, 1–14. https://doi.org/10.1108/VJIKMS-10-2021-0257.

Bhardwaj, S. (2020). Role of Training in turning the Business Sustainable Role of Trainingin turning the Business Sustainable Snigdha Bhardwaj. *In International Journal of All Research Education and Scientific Methods (IJARESM)*, 8(9), pp. 261–264.

Boon, C., Hartog, D. N. D., and Lepak, D. P. (2019). A systematic review of human resource management systems and their measurement. *Journal of Management*, 45(6), 2498–2537. https://doi.org/10.1177/0149206318818718

Canada, G. A. (2020). Overview of International Financial Institutions (IFIS). GAC. Retrieved from: https://www.tradecommissioner.gc.ca/development-developpement/mdb-overview-bmd-apercu.aspx?lang=eng

Chang, P. C., Wu, T., and Liu, C. L. (2018). Do high-performance work systems really satisfy employees? Evidence from China. *Sustainability (Switzerland)*, 10(10). https://doi.org/10.3390/su10103360

de Jonge, J., and Peeters, M. C. W. (2019). The vital worker: towards sustainable performance at work. *International Journal of Environmental Research and Public Health*, 16(6). MDPI AG. https://doi.org/10.3390/ijerph16060910

Dwivedi, P., Chaturvedi, V., & Vashist, J. K. (2023). Innovation for organizational sustainability: The role of HR practices and theories. *International Journal of Organizational Analysis*, 31(3), 759–776. https://doi.org/10.1108/IJOA-07-2021-2859

Elidemir, S. N., Ozturen, A., & Bayighomog, S. W. (2020). Innovative behaviors, employee creativity, and sustainable competitive advantage: A moderated mediation. *Sustainability (Switzerland)*, 12(8), 1–18. https://doi.org/10.3390/SU12083295

Freeman, R. E. (1984). Strategic Management: A Stakeholder Approach. Pitman, Boston.

Gomes, G., & Wojahn, R. M. (2017). Organizational learning capability, innovation and performance: study in small and medium-sized enterprises (SMES). *Revista de Administração*, 52(2), 163–175. https://doi.org/10.1016/j.rausp.2016.12.003

Guandalini, I. (2022). Sustainability through digital transformation: a systematic literature review for research guidance. *Journal of Business Research*, 148, 456–471. https://doi.org/10.1016/j.jbusres.2022.05.003

Haile, E. A., and Tüzüner, V. L. (2022). Organizational learning capability and its impact on organizational innovation. *Asia Pacific Journal of Innovation and Entrepreneurship*, 16(1), 69–85. https://doi.org/10.1108/apjie-03-2022-0015

Hunt, J. (2023, February 20). Corporate responsibility in 2023: Triple bottom line sustainability. Environment + Energy Leader. Retrieved March 2, 2023, from https://www.environmental-leader.com/2023/02/triple-bottom-line-sustainability/

Jaadi, Z. (2019, October 16). *Eveything you need to know about interpreting correlations.* Medium. https://towardsdatascience.com/eveything-you-need-to-know-about-interpreting-correlations-2c485841c0b8

Kordab, M., Raudeliūnienė, J., and Meidutė-Kavaliauskienė, I. (2020). Mediating role of knowledge management in the relationship between organizational learning and sustainable organizational performance. *Sustainability (Switzerland)*, 12(23), 1–20. https://doi.org/10.3390/su122310061

Markaki, A., Malhotra, S., Billings, R., and Theus, L. (2021). Training needs assessment: tool utilization and global impact. *BMC Medical Education*, 21(1), 310. https://doi.org/10.1186/s12909-021-02748-y

Muhamad, Khalil, Omar., Yusmazida, Mohd, Yusoff., Maliza, Delima, Kamarul, Zaman. (2019). The Effect of Organizational Learning Capability as a Mediating Variable in the Relationship between Green Intellectual Capital and Business Sustainability: Evidence from the Manufacturing Sector. *The International Journal of Academic Research in Business and Social Sciences*, 9(6), 584–599. doi:10.6007/IJARBSS/V9-I6/5974

Ochoa-Jiménez, S., Leyva-Osuna, B. A., Jacobo-Hernández, C. A., and García-García, A. R. (2021). Knowledge management in relation to innovation and its effect on the sustainability of Mexican Tourism Companies. *Sustainability*, 13(24), 13790. https://doi.org/10.3390/su132413790

Omar, M. K., Yusoff, Y. M., and Zaman, M. D. K. (2019). The effect of organizational learning capability as a mediating variable in the relationship between green intellectual capital and business sustainability: Evidence from the manufacturing sector. *International Journal of Academic Research in Business and Social Sciences*, 9(6). https://doi.org/10.6007/ijarbss/v9-i6/5974

Suryaningtyas, D., and Irawanto, D. (2019, August 5). Exploring High-Performance Work Systems for Sustainability in the Hotel Industry. https://doi.org/10.4108/eai.6-12-2018.2286326n

Umair, K., Yongan, Z., and Madiha, S. (2020). The impact of information technology on organizational performance: The mediating effect of organizational learning. *Journal of Asian Finance, Economics and Business*, 7(11), 987–998. doi:10.13106/JAFEB.2020.VOL7.NO11.987

Van der Stappen, E., and Knobbout, J. (2020). A capability model for learning analytics adoption: identifying organizational capabilities from literature on big data analytics, business analytics, and learning analytics. *iJAL*, 2(1), 47–66.

Zhu, C., Liu, A., and Chen, G. (2018). High performance work systems and corporate performance: The influence of entrepreneurial orientation and organizational learning. *Frontiers of Business Research in China*, 12(1). https://doi.org/10.1186/s11782-018-0025-y

Zhu, C., Liu, A., and Wang, Y. (2019, June 10). *Integrating organizational learning with high-performance work system and entrepreneurial orientation: A moderated mediation framework—Frontiers of Business Research in China.* SpringerOpen. https://doi.org/10.1186/s11782-019-0057-y

22 Raising the Cyber Shield: Defending Your Business From the Art of Hacking

Joy Winston James[1,a], Fayzah Jaber[2,b], and Abdul Khadar Jilani[1,c]

[1]University of Technology Bahrain
[2]University of Technology

Abstract

Amidst the fierce competition of modern business, the art of hacking has emerged as a critical skill. With companies vying for market dominance, the quest to gain access to each other's IT resources has become a high-stakes game. From infiltrating databases and networks to stealing sensitive customer information, the stakes are higher than ever. As businesses invest billions of dollars to secure their IT resources and uncover vulnerabilities within their own systems, hackers remain a constant threat. These cybercriminals seek to exploit weaknesses within business networks, using their access to damage reputations or extort money from companies. In this study, we will delve into the world of business hacking, examining the various types of attacks and vulnerabilities that companies face. We will analyze potential solutions for each attack scenario, exploring ways to mitigate the risk of hackers gaining remote access to sensitive information. Ultimately, we aim to provide insight into the ever-evolving landscape of business security, and the importance of staying vigilant in the face of these ongoing threats.

Keywords

DOS, hacking, penetration testing, phishing.

Introduction

In today's fiercely competitive business environment, companies are constantly seeking ways to gain an edge over their rivals. As a result, the art of hacking has emerged as a critical skill, with businesses vying for access to each other's IT resources (Jiang et al., 2021). The stakes are high, and the quest to gain an advantage has led to cybercriminals infiltrating databases, networks, and stealing sensitive customer information. Despite businesses investing billions of dollars to secure their IT resources and uncover vulnerabilities within their own systems, hackers remain a constant threat. These cybercriminals seek to exploit weaknesses within business networks, using their access to damage reputations or extort money from companies (Bansal et al., 2021).

Given the ever-evolving landscape of business security and the increasing sophistication of hacking techniques, it is critical for companies to stay vigilant and proactively

[a]j.winston@utb.edu.bh, [b]fefejaber90@gmail.com, [c]a.jilani@utb.edu.bh

protect their IT resources from these ongoing threats. In this paper, we will delve into the world of business hacking, examining the various types of attacks and vulnerabilities that companies face. We will also analyze potential solutions for each attack scenario, exploring ways to mitigate the risk of hackers gaining remote access to sensitive information. Ultimately, we aim to provide insight into the importance of staying vigilant in the face of these ongoing threats, and the steps companies can take to protect their valuable IT resources (Candallousi et al., 2018).

We will begin by exploring the motivations behind business hacking, discussing the various ways in which cybercriminals target companies and the potential impact of their actions. From there, we will examine some of the most common types of business hacking attacks, including phishing scams, ransomware, and distributed denial-of-service (DDoS) attacks (De Donno et al., 2018). For each attack scenario, we will analyze potential solutions and best practices for prevention and response. We will also explore the role of employee training and education in mitigating the risk of hacking attacks, highlighting the importance of creating a culture of cybersecurity awareness within organizations. Throughout this paper, we will emphasize the importance of taking a multi-layered approach to business cybersecurity. This includes implementing robust security protocols and technologies, regularly testing for vulnerabilities, and establishing a comprehensive incident response plan. As the threat of business hacking continues to evolve and grow, it is critical for companies to stay informed and adapt their security strategies accordingly. By understanding the various types of attacks and vulnerabilities, as well as the best practices for prevention and response, businesses can effectively protect their valuable IT resources and stay one step ahead of cybercriminals.

Literature Review

This article (Wang et al., 2021) details a high-profile case in which European thieves hacked into the First Commercial Bank (FCB) of Taiwan in the summer of 2016, causing its automated teller machines (ATMs) to "spit out" cash and making off with $2.6 million USD. This European criminal network stole over a billion Euros via over 100 similar ATM attacks. Only the FCB case has exposed law enforcement actions and ATM hacking methods. This unique case study examines qualitative data from multiple law enforcement agencies involved in the investigations, highlighting the usefulness of national-local law enforcement collaboration in fighting transnational cybercrime. Police "turf jealousies" are crucial to border security. The European hacker group Carbanak/ Cobalt used a publicly available security tool called Cobalt Strike to get into the FCB's systems and steal money from 41 ATMs spread across 22 locations in three cities.

Encryption technology and protocols make modern ATMs secure. They operate via complex computer networks. Despite these measures, ATM fraud is rising. Hackers may stealthily obtain ATM-processed data and extract cash (Serror et al., 2021).

In this study, they explore the biometric safeguards included in modern ATMs. Additionally, they discuss how conventional ATMs may be replaced with more secure and fool proof biometric technologies (Wang et al., 2021).

Terrorism and other evildoing have caused innumerable devastations, including the loss of human life and the ruin of creative achievements. To avoid such sophisticated attacks and breaches, we need biometric security of comparable complexity. Biometrics has drastically transformed people's perceptions of personal security. Incorporating biometric biometrics into ATM infrastructure and technology might result in a safe and dependable solution. As a result, the buyer is relieved of a major source of concern during the purchase process.

Safety is always a priority. All companies and employees require better security. Enhancing security is difficult and practically impossible due to the IT industry's growing complexity and fast technological advancement.

Banking technology has grown swiftly, providing several trustworthy solutions for tracking funds, data, and processes. ATM innovation has driven account activity. As ATM usage expands, hackers are using technology to steal personal data and conduct fraud. ATM fraud has grown worldwide due to the above shortcomings.

This research (Azmoodeh et al., 2018), examines how hybrid multi-layered security might minimize ATM cubical fraud. They use a PIN, OTP, and pattern lock to prevent fraud in this system. 400 students tested the system. 96% (384 out of 384) entered their PIN on the first attempt, 95% (363 out of 384) passed the second stage, and 99% (363 out of 363) passed the third step, which required them to draw patterns. The evaluation findings show that the suggested security layers are practical, with better performance and sample acceptability.

Today, ATM fraud is quite prevalent, and the following are some of the most prevalent and significant ways (Dovom et al., 2019). Shoulder suffering: It's a way to monitor the ATM and find out whether and when a customer inputs their PIN. Having many ATMs all located in the same office space does not help the situation. Hidden camera: Several image equipment, including a camera and its lens, were used to record the PIN. This is currently one of the most used methods.

Skimmer: Skimming is a method used by hackers to steal sensitive data from the magnetic strip of an ATM card. Indian banks have undergone radical changes in how they operate and provide services to their consumers. Although online shopping is very popular in India, it is not always secure since only the password is secured. All user transaction data is sent through the banking services. "Cloud computing" made scalable computing resources available on-demand at a fee set by usage, changing the computer industry. Cloud computing makes software, processing, and data storage a service. Cloud computing's cheaper initial investment and user ease may boost rural India's economy. Due of rural inhabitants' high-end telephones and expanding Internet usage, cloud computing is straightforward to deploy (Al-Kassassebh et al., 2020).

This study (Abhijith et al., 2022), addresses the security problem by discussing the pros and cons of many different encryption techniques. they arrived at the conclusion that homomorphic algorithm was the best option for securing their sensitive data on the cloud.

ATMs revolutionized financial transactions, but their ubiquity led to more assaults and PIN guessing. This research (Okpe et al., 2018), recommends two-factor authentication to reduce the harm caused by such assaults. Instead of inputting their PIN, customers type their bank card information into the ATM. This method involves a simple mathematical procedure. Encrypting input increased security and reduced the risk of attacks. Hackers are less likely to discover a customer's secret number if they utilize seven-segment digital encryption. Because numerous integers share a code, this encryption method is strong. This method offers good protection without expensive equipment or training (Azmoodeh et al., 2019).

ATMs are used for a variety of financial activities, both personal and commercial, and their security has long been studied. Greater ATMs provide more targets for robbers and fraudsters. Embedded technology protects ATMs against physical attacks at cheap cost. Thanks to the embedded system platform notion, a new system architecture for monitoring operations and putting equipment may be established.

Specifically, this research (Sokolov et al., 2021), makes use of ATM assault sensors. The sensors will immediately lock the ATM's door if they detect any suspicious activity. The system relies on an ESP8266 microcontroller housed on a Node MCU (Micro Controller Unit) board and has RFID (Radio Frequency Identification) tags for shutting off the sensors for servicing and unlocking the door from the outside in case of emergency. The Internet of Things sends all collected data to the appropriate authorities instantly (Internet of Things) (Chen et al., 2018).

The modern technological world permeates almost every aspect of human existence. Data searching and downloading, cloud computing, picture recognition, and video playback are just some of the home and office duties that may be done remotely. The term "Internet of Things" (IoT) is used to describe the global network of physical devices that are networked and monitored remotely through the Internet for use in anything from medical care to city planning (Arzt et al., 2014). Implementing any IoT-based devices in any location offers several issues, the most major of which are security and privacy, due to the nature of the data transmitted between these devices (Chabbouni et al., 2019).

Industry 4.0, often known as the industrial Internet of Things, is a logical progression after the IoT's enormous success in linking devices for consumer use. There are numerous positive outcomes from the increasing interdependence of industrial components, but this connectivity also poses significant security risks.

This paper (Azmoodeh et al., 2018), explores the unique security goals and challenges of IoT installations in the business and manufacturing sectors. The primary motivation for these objectives and concerns is the desire to protect employees and increase productivity. They evaluate the security benefits, explain why it is important to protect the industrial Internet of Things, and list the obstacles that must be solved.

With the use of hacker tools turned against them, the researchers in this study (Falco et al., 2019), have created a lightweight IoT security solution that acts as a vaccination for IoT. Using a "friendly" botnet controlled by a tried-and-true communication infrastructure for distributed systems, the Bitcoin blockchain, their program offers managed security and intelligence to Internet of Things (IoT) devices.

Because of the rising number of Internet of Things-related security problems, the topic of IoT security has received considerable attention. Exploitation of security holes in IoT hardware and software affects many businesses and people. The core reasons of vulnerabilities in the Internet of Things go beyond only technical ones, making it vital to simplify the "security complex" of IoT and give practical solutions for enterprises, consumers, and government agencies.

This paper Robberts and Toft (2019) reports the findings of an initial study into a little-explored corner of the IoT: the potential for integrating crowdsourcing ethical hacking tactics into current vulnerability management frameworks. In particular, they focus on initiatives that incentivize hackers to reveal vulnerabilities by offering financial rewards, such as Bug Bounty Programs (BBPs) and Responsible Disclosure (RDs). A qualitative investigation, supported by a literature research and expert interviews, was carried out to learn how BBP and RD may contribute in the effective detection, classification, prioritization, remediation, and mitigation of IoT vulnerabilities. In addition to providing useful advice for IoT stakeholders, their work sheds light on a methodical integration strategy for merging BBP and RD with existing security processes (such penetration test) to dramatically boost overall IoT security.

The Internet of Things' security is its Achilles' heel (Arp et al., 2014). Unfortunately, most people involved in creating smart devices don't seem to care about something called "Information Security." The reputation of the IoT (Internet of Things) has taken a nosedive in recent years. Keep in mind that almost every organization has at least one person who utilizes a potentially compromised device. It's also possible that attackers might have more sophistication than IoT devices if all potential risks are ignored. This creates a serious vulnerability in terms of cyber safety.

The purpose of this thesis (Anderson et al., 2011), is to investigate a well-known Bluetooth smart lock from the perspective of safety. The system is tested with the use of conventional attack methods to find any vulnerabilities. While it's possible that some of the flaws in the researched lock's design may be considered low-impact vulnerabilities, using the system without taking them into consideration could nonetheless have bad implications for the lock's owner. However, the methods used in this thesis may be valuable in future research into the security of the Internet of Things, even if no critical security vulnerabilities were discovered beyond those presented by bad design.

Common Types of Business Hacking Attacks

In this section, we will explore the most common types of hacking attacks that businesses face, along with the potential impacts and strategies for prevention.

Phishing Attacks

Phishing attacks rank among the prevailing forms of hacking techniques targeting businesses. They exploit fraudulent emails, websites, or messages to deceive users into divulging sensitive information, like login credentials or financial data (Aldoghje et al., 2022). Businesses confronting phishing attacks encounter severe repercussions, including data breaches, financial setbacks, and reputation damage.

SQL Injection Attack

SQL injection (SQLi) refers to a cyber-attack method in which a perpetrator capitalizes on weaknesses in input fields of a web application to insert malevolent SQL code. By leveraging SQLi attacks, the attacker can circumvent authentication, access or manipulate confidential data, and execute arbitrary commands on the underlying database server (Alieyan et al., 2021).

A typical instance of an SQLi attack occurs in a login form where users input their username and password. If the application fails to adequately sanitize user input, an attacker can input SQL commands into the login form, deceiving the application into executing the injected SQL code and bypassing authentication (Bansal et al., 2021).

For example, an attacker could enter the username 'OR 1=1 -- which would cause the application to execute the SQL command SELECT * FROM users WHERE username = ' ' OR 1=1 --' AND password = 'password' where -- is a comment delimiter in SQL and everything after it is ignored (Kariapper et al., 2020). This SQL command would return all the rows in the users table where the username is an empty string or 1 equals 1, which is always true, effectively bypassing the authentication process and granting the attacker access to the application.

Ransomware Attacks

Ransomware attacks encompass a form of malware assault where malicious software is employed to encrypt a target's data, making it inaccessible until a ransom is fulfilled. Such attacks inflict significant ramifications upon businesses, comprising data loss, financial setbacks, and harm to reputation (Ding et al., 2019).

DDoS Attacks

DDoS (Distributed Denial of Service) attacks are a form of hacking assault that involves overwhelming a targeted system with an excessive amount of traffic, rendering it inaccessible to legitimate users. DDoS attacks pose significant threats to businesses, causing downtime, financial losses, and reputational harm.

Insider Threats

Insider threats are a type of hacking attack where an authorized user exploits privileged access to steal or misuse sensitive data. These attacks have severe implications for businesses, resulting in data breaches, financial losses, and damage to reputation (Gaurav et al., 2022).

Social Engineering Attacks

Social engineering attacks involve manipulating individuals into disclosing sensitive information or performing actions that compromise security. They manifest in various forms, including phishing emails, pretexting, baiting, and more (Farris et al., 2018). Phishing emails are particularly prevalent, with attackers impersonating trusted entities to deceive victims into clicking malicious links or providing login credentials on fraudulent websites. Pretexting, on the other hand, entails fabricating scenarios to extract sensitive information, such as an imposter posing as an IT support representative to acquire login credentials.

Man-in-the-Middle (MitM) Attacks

Man-in-the-Middle (MitM) attacks are cyber-attacks where a hacker intercepts communication between two parties, such as a business and its customers or employees, without either party's knowledge (Jothi et al., 2020). Through interception, the hacker can eavesdrop on or modify the communication, potentially gaining access to login credentials, financial data, or other sensitive information. MitM attacks can occur through methods like setting up fake Wi-Fi hotspots or employing malware to redirect internet traffic through the hacker's server (Acharya et al., 2007).

Cross-Site Scripting

Cross-Site Scripting (XSS) is a web-based attack that enables an attacker to inject malicious code into a web page viewed by other users (Gupta et al., 2020). By exploiting vulnerabilities in a website's code, the attacker inserts a script that executes in the victim's browser, allowing for the theft of user data, execution of malicious code, or other illicit activities (Barretto and Varma, 2020).

The Table 22.1 below presents an overview of various types of hacking attacks that businesses may encounter. It includes examples of each attack, the targeted vulnerable resource, and the types of businesses at risk.

Table 22.1: Summary of attacks.

Attack type	Example	Vulnerable resource	Types of businesses at risk
Phishing	An email that appears to be from a bank requesting the victim's login credentials.	Employees, customers	Any business that stores sensitive data, such as banks, e-commerce websites, or healthcare providers (Ceron et al., 2019)
Pretexting	A phone call from someone posing as an IT support representative and asking the victim for their login credentials.	Employees	Any business that has an IT help desk, such as large corporations or government agencies (Alieyan et al., 2021)
Man-in-the-middle (MitM)	A hacker setting up a fake Wi-Fi hotspot and intercepting traffic between a business and its customers.	Network infrastructure	Any business that offers public Wi-Fi, such as coffee shops, airports, or hotels (Dovom et al., 2019)
SQL injection	A hacker inserting a command into a login form that allows them to access the entire database of user login credentials.	Databases	Any business that stores data in databases, such as online retailers or financial institutions (Aldoghje et al., 2022)
Cross-Site Scripting (XSS)	A hacker injecting code into a comment section of a website that steals the victim's session cookie when they view the page.	Websites	Any business with a website, such as news sites, social media platforms, or online forums (De Donno et al., 2018)

Penetration Testing

Penetration testing, also known as pen testing, is a technique used to evaluate the security of an IT infrastructure by simulating an attack. The goal of a pen test is to identify vulnerabilities that attackers could exploit and provide recommendations to mitigate or eliminate them. In the context of business hacking, pen testing can help identify potential entry points for attackers and provide insight into the effectiveness of existing security measures (Aldoghje et al., 2022).

For phishing attacks, pen testing can involve sending simulated phishing emails to employees to test their awareness and susceptibility. The results can help organizations design and implement effective phishing awareness training programs to reduce the risk of successful attacks (Chhbra et al., 2020).

In the case of pretexting attacks (Memos et al., 2020), pen testing can involve simulating a social engineering attack by posing as an IT support representative to obtain login credentials. The test can help identify weaknesses in the organization's security protocols and provide opportunities for employee education and training.

For MitM attacks, pen testing can involve testing the security of public Wi-Fi networks by setting up a fake hotspot and attempting to intercept traffic. This can help identify weaknesses in the network infrastructure and provide recommendations for securing public Wi-Fi networks.

In the case of SQL injection attacks, pen testing can involve attempting to exploit vulnerabilities in the login form or other data entry fields to gain unauthorized access to the database. This can help identify vulnerabilities in the database and provide recommendations for securing it.

For XSS attacks, pen testing can involve injecting code into a comment section of a website to test the effectiveness of input validation and output encoding. The test can help identify vulnerabilities in the website's code and provide recommendations for securing it (Zhou et al., 2021).

Overall, pen testing can help businesses proactively identify and address vulnerabilities in their IT infrastructure before attackers exploit them. It is a critical tool in the fight against business hacking and should be an essential component of any organization's security strategy.

Conclusion

With the continuous advancement of technology, the risks associated with business hacking are also on the rise. Cybercriminals are persistently seeking ways to exploit vulnerabilities in business networks, and the consequences of a successful attack can be catastrophic. However, businesses can significantly reduce their risk of becoming hacking victims by comprehending the various attack types and implementing appropriate mitigation strategies. Some highly effective strategies include regular employee training on cybersecurity best practices, the adoption of strong passwords and multi-factor authentication, regular data backups, and conducting periodic penetration testing to identify and address system vulnerabilities. It is imperative for businesses to maintain a vigilant and proactive stance toward cybersecurity. By taking necessary measures to protect their IT resources, businesses not only safeguard their sensitive data and preserve their reputation but also demonstrate their commitment to customer security and privacy. Undoubtedly, the significance of mitigating business hacking risks cannot be emphasized enough, and the time to take action is now!

References

Abhijith, S., Sreehari, K. N., and Chalil, A. (2022). An IOT based system for securing ATM machine. In 2022 8th International Conference on Advanced Computing and Communication Systems (ICACCS), (vol. 1, pp. 1764–1768). https://doi.org/10.1109/ICACCS54159.2022.9785243

Acharya, T., and Tsai, P. S. (2007). Computational foundations of image interpolation algorithms. *Ubiquity*, 4, 1692–1695.

Aldoghje, F., Jinah, A., and Ilyas, M. (2022). Creating one time virtual encrypted identification number at the ATM. In International Congress on Human-Computer Interaction, Optimization and Robotic Applications (HORA), (pp. 1–7). https://doi.org/10.1109/HORA55278.2022.9799882

Alieyan, K., Almomani, A., Anbar, M., Alauthman, M., Abdullah, R., and Gupta, B. B. (2021). Dns rule-based schema to botnet detection. *Enterprise Information Systems*, 15, 5–45.

Al-Kasassbeh, M., Almseidin, M., Alrfou, K., and Kovacs, S. (2020). Detection of IoT-botnet attacks using fuzzy rule interpolation. *Journal of Intelligent and Fuzzy Systems*, 39(1), 421–431.

Anderson, B., Quist, D., Neil, J., Storlie, C., and Lane, T. (2011). Graph-based malware detection using dynamic analysis. *Journal in Computer Virology*, 7, 2–47.

Arp, D., Spreitzenbarth, M., Hubner, M., Gascon, H., Rieck, K., and Siemens, C. (2014). DREBIN: Effective and Explainable Detection of Android Malware in Your Pocket. In Ndss, (vol. 14, pp. 23).

Arzt, S., Rasthofer, S., Fritz, C., Bodden, E., Bartel, A., Klein, J., Le Traon, Y., Octeau, D., and McDaniel, P. (2014). Flowdroid: precise context, flow, field, object-sensitive and lifecycle-aware taint analysis for android apps. *ACM SIGPLAN Notices*, 49, 2–59.

Azmoodeh, A., Dehghantanha, A., and Choo, K. K. R. (2019). Robust malware detection for internet of (battlefield) things devices using deep eigenspace learning. *IEEE Transactions on Sustainable Computing*, 4, 88.

Azmoodeh, A., Dehghantanha, A., Conti, M., and Choo, K. K. R. (2018). Detecting crypto ransomware in IoT networks based on energy consumption footprint. *Journal of Ambient Intelligence and Humanized Computing*, 9, 11–41.

Bansal, M., Nanda, M., and Husain, M. N. (2021). Security and privacy aspects for internet of things (IoT). In 2021 6th International Conference on Inventive Computation Technologies (ICICT), (pp. 199–204). https://doi.org/10.1109/ICICT50816.2021.9358665

Barretto, G., and Varma, T. (2020). Analysis of ATM security using biometrics. *Journal of Network Security and Data Mining*, 3(3), 1–9.

Ceron, J. M., Steding-Jessen, K., Hoepers, C., Granville, L. Z., and Margi, C. B. (2019). Improving IoT botnet investigation using an adaptive network layer. *Sensors*, 19, 7–27.

Chaabouni, N., Mosbah, M., Zemmari, A., Sauvignac, C., and Faruki, P. (2019). Network intrusion detection for IoT security based on learning techniques. *IEEE Communications Surveys Tutorials*, 21, 26–71.

Chen, H., Su, J., Qiao, L., and Xin, Q. (2018). Malware collusion attack against SVM: issues and countermeasures. *Applied Sciences*, 8, 17–18.

Chhabra, G. S., Singh, V. P., and Singh, M. (2020). Cyber forensics framework for big data analytics in IoT environment using machine learning. *Multimedia Tools and Applications*, 79, 158–81.

Condoluci, M., and Mahmoodi, T. (2018). Softwarization and virtualization in 5G mobile networks: benefits, trends and challenges. *Computer Networks*, 146, 65.

De Donno, M., Dragoni, N., Giaretta, A., and Spognardi, A. (2018). DDoS-capable IoT malwares: comparative analysis and mirai investigation. *Security and Communication Networks*, 1.

Ding, A. Y., De Jesus, G. L., and Janssen, M. (2019). Ethical hacking for boosting IoT vulnerability management: a first look into bug bounty programs and responsible disclosure. In Proceedings of the Eighth International Conference on Telecommunications and Remote Sensing, (pp. 49–55). https://doi.org/10.1145/3357767.3357774

Dovom, E. M., Azmoodeh, A., Dehghantanha, A., Newton, D. E., Parizi, R. M., and Karimipour, H. (2019). Fuzzy pattern tree for edge malware detection and categorization in IoT. *Journal of Systems Architecture, 97,* 1–7.

Falco, G., Li, C., Fedorov, P., Caldera, C., Arora, R., and Jackson, K. (2019). Neuro-Mesh: IoT security enabled by a blockchain powered botnet vaccine. In Proceedings of the International Conference on Omni-Layer Intelligent Systems, (pp. 1–6). https://doi.org/10.1145/3312614.3312615

Farris, I., Taleb, T., Khettab, Y., and Song, J. (2018). A survey on emerging SDN and NFV security mechanisms for IoT systems. *IEEE Communications Surveys and Tutorials, 21,* 8–12.

Gaurav, A., Gupta, B. B., and Panigrahi, P. K. (2022). A comprehensive survey on machine learning approaches for malware detection in IoT-based enterprise information system. *Enterprise Information Systems,* 0(0), 1–25. https://doi.org/10.1080/17517575.2021.2023764

Gupta, B. B., and Quamara, M. (2020). An overview of internet of things (IoT): architectural aspects, challenges, and protocols. *Concurrency and Computation: Practice and Experience, 32,* 49–46.

Jiang, Y., Liu, M., Peng, H., and Bhuiyan, M.Z.A. (2021). A reliable deep learning-based algorithm design for IoT load identification in smart grid. *Ad Hoc Networks, 123,* 102–643.

Jothi, M., Manjupawadharani, A., Meena, S., Meenakshi, J., Student, U. G., Engineering, C. S., and Nadu, T. (2020). Hack prevention over rural banking using cloud computing. *Architecture Diagram, 4,* 1314–1318.

Kariapper, R. K. A. R., Razeeth, M. S., Pirapuraj, P., and Nafrees, A. C. M. (2020). Effectiveness of ATM and bank security: three factor authentications with systemetic review. *Journal of Physics: Conference Series,* 1712(1). https://doi.org/10.1088/1742-6596/1712/1/012007

Memos, V. A., and Psannis, K. E. (2020). AI-powered honeypots for enhanced IoT botnet detection. In 2020 3rd World Symposium on Communication Engineering (WSCE), (pp. 64–68). https://doi.org/10.1109/WSCE51339.2020.9275581

Okpe, O. A., John, O. A., and Emmanuel, S. (2018). Intrusion detection in internet of things (IoT). *International Journal of Advanced Research in Computer Science,* 9(1), 504–509.

Robberts, C., and Toft, J. (2019). Finding vulnerabilities in IoT devices: ethical hacking of electronic locks. In TRITA-EECS-EX NV—2019:311: Independent thesis Basic level. http://kth.diva-portal.org/smash/get/diva2:1334605/FULLTEXT01.pdf

Serror, M., Hack, S., Henze, M., Schuba, M., and Wehrle, K. (2021). Challenges and opportunities in securing the industrial internet of things. *IEEE Transactions on Industrial Informatics,* 17(5), 2985–2996. https://doi.org/10.1109/TII.2020.3023507

Sokolov, S., Gaskarov, V., Knysh, T., and Sagitova, A. (2021). IoT security: threats, risks, attacks. In Mottaeva, A. editors. Proceedings of the XIII International Scientific Conference on Architecture and Construction 2020 (pp. 47–56). Singapore: Springer Nature.

Wang, S. Y. K., Hsieh, M. L., Chang, C. K. M., Jiang, P. S., and Dallier, D. J. (2021). Collaboration between law enforcement agencies in combating cybercrime: implications of a taiwanese case study about ATM hacking. *International Journal of Offender Therapy and Comparative Criminology,* 65(4), 390–408. https://doi.org/10.1177/0306624X20952391

Zhou, Z., Gaurav, A., Gupta, B. B., Hamdi, H., and Nedjah, N. (2021). A statistical approach to secure health care services from DDoS attacks during Covid-19 pandemic. *Neural Computing and Applications, 1,* 1–30.

23 Chronological Impact of Artificial Intelligence on Innovation, Entrepreneurship and Management

Saeedah Zaina Shaik[1,a], Arifusalam Shaikh[2,b], and Carlos Bazan[3,c]

[1]Information and Technology Department, Stanley College of Engineering and Technology for Women, Hyderabad, India
[2]Department of Marketing, Strategy & Entrepreneurship, University Canada West Vancouver, Canada
[3]Faculty of Business Administration, Memorial University, St. John's, Canada

Abstract

This paper explores the impact artificial intelligence (AI) has had on innovation and entrepreneurship since its inception. While understanding the evolution and growth of AI, its initial applications and the popular algorithms that have been developed since the beginning of AI is discussed. It is important to understand how these popular AI algorithms and approaches have created opportunities for innovation. A thorough Bibliometric analysis was conducted to analyse the trends in innovation and entrepreneurship within the scope of AI in terms of research collaboration, citation, and innovation clusters worldwide, among others. The paper also provides emerging trends in the application of AI and how it can impact future innovations.

Keywords

Artificial intelligence, deep learning, entrepreneurship, innovation, machine learning.

Introduction

Artificial intelligence (AI), a rapidly evolving technology, has revolutionized entrepreneurship and innovation, enhanced operational efficiency and effectiveness while enabling the creation of new business models and products. It offers entrepreneurs opportunities for growth and competitiveness in the market. This paper examines AI's evolution, impact, advantages, and limitations on entrepreneurship and innovation, while providing bibliometric analysis on the relevant literature.

To conduct the bibliometric analysis, we used the Scopus database, a leading scientific citation indexing service, to identify relevant publications since inception. We then used VOS Viewer, a network analysis tool, to analyse the data and visualize the relationships between the publications. We used five different queries in the Scopus database to limit our search for publications which we will further be discussing in the paper.

[a]zainashaik99@gmail.com, [b]arifusalam.shaikh@ucanwest.ca, [c]cabazan@mun.ca

Historical Overview of AI

Brief History of AI

Artificial intelligence is the field of computer science that aims to create machines that can perform tasks that typically require human intelligence. The history of AI can be traced back to the mid-twentieth century when researchers began to explore the idea of creating machines that could think and learn like humans (Russell and Norvig, 2010).

One of the first milestones in the history of AI was the creation of the Turing Test in 1950 by computer scientist Alan Turing. The test proposed a way to determine whether a machine can exhibit intelligent behaviour that is indistinguishable from that of a human (Turing, 1950). Turing's work laid the foundation for the development of AI as a scientific discipline (Russell and Norvig, 2010).

During the 1950s and 1960s, researchers made significant progress in developing early AI systems. One of the earliest and most famous AI programs was the Logic Theorist, developed by Allen Newell and J.C. Shaw at the RAND Corporation in 1956. The Logic Theorist was able to prove mathematical theorems using symbolic logic and heuristic search techniques (Russell and Norvig, 2010). In the 1960s, researchers began to explore the idea of machine learning, which involves teaching machines to learn from data rather than being explicitly programmed. One of the pioneers in this field was Arthur Samuel, who created a program that learned to play checkers through trial and error (Samuel, 1959). The years of 1970s and 1980s saw a shift in the focus of AI research from symbolic logic and rule-based systems to connectionism and neural networks. Connectionism involves creating networks of simple processing units that can learn to perform complex tasks through training. Neural networks, which are modelled after the structure of the human brain, can be used to recognize patterns and make predictions (Russell and Norvig, 2010)

In the 1990s, AI research experienced a resurgence with the development of statistical learning algorithms and the availability of large datasets. One of the breakthroughs during this period was the development of the Support Vector Machine (SVM), which was introduced by Cortes and Vapnik (1995) paper. A machine learning algorithm that can be used for classification and regression tasks. The 2000s saw the emergence of a new subfield of AI known as deep learning, which involves creating neural networks with many layers. Deep learning has been used to achieve significant advances in fields such as computer vision, speech recognition, and natural language processing.

In recent years, AI has seen exponential growth, driven by the availability of vast amounts of data, faster computing power, and improved algorithms. AI technologies such as deep learning, reinforcement learning, and generative models have made significant advancements in various domains, including healthcare, finance, transportation, and entertainment. Some notable achievements in AI include the development of AlphaGo, a program that beat a human world champion at the game of Go (Silver et al., 2016), and GPT-3, a language model capable of generating human-like text, the development of autonomous vehicles, the use of AI in drug discovery, and the creation of AI systems that can generate creative content such as music and art.

The Evolution of AI

The evolution of AI can be broadly classified into three stages: the rule-based system stage, the machine learning stage, and the deep learning stage. In the rule-based system stage, AI was based on a set of predefined rules that were programmed into the system. In the machine learning stage, AI systems were designed to learn from data using statistical models. In the deep learning stage, AI systems can learn from vast amounts of data and make complex decisions based on patterns and correlations in the data (Russell and Norvig, 2010). The early days of AI research was focused on creating rule-based systems, where humans programmed the rules that the machine would follow. However, this approach proved to be limited, as it was unable to handle complex tasks that required a high degree of flexibility and adaptation. In the 1980s, the field of machine learning emerged, which allowed machines to learn from data rather than being explicitly programmed (Domingos, 2012).

The first significant breakthrough in machine learning came in the form of neural networks, which are modelled after the human brain. In 1986, a paper titled "Learning Representations by Back-propagating Errors" by Rumelhart et al. (1986) introduced backpropagation, a technique for training neural networks. This paper paved the way for the development of deep learning, which is a subset of machine learning that uses deep neural networks to learn representations of data.

The rise of big data in the early 2000s led to the development of more sophisticated machine learning algorithms that could handle vast amounts of data. SVMs are also widely used for classification and regression tasks and have been applied in fields such as image recognition and natural language processing.

Another significant advancement in AI came in the form of reinforcement learning, which allows machines to learn through trial and error. In 2013, a paper titled "Playing Atari with Deep Reinforcement Learning" by Mnih et al. (2013) introduced a deep reinforcement learning algorithm that was able to learn to play Atari games at a superhuman level. This breakthrough demonstrated the potential for reinforcement learning to solve complex problems in a wide range of applications. In recent years, there have been significant advancements in the field of natural language processing, enabling machines to better understand and produce human language. One notable development is the Generative Pretrained Transformer (GPT) architecture, which was introduced by OpenAI in 2018. This model employs a Transformer network that enables it to effectively handle long-range dependencies and generate coherent text (Devlin et al., 2019).

AI has also made significant progress in computer vision, with deep learning models achieving state-of-the-art performance on tasks such as object detection and image classification. In 2012, a paper titled "ImageNet Classification with Deep Convolutional Neural Networks" by Krizhevsky et al. (2012) introduced the AlexNet model, which achieved a significant improvement in image classification accuracy over previous methods.

The Evolution of AI in Business

One of the key drivers of the evolution of AI in business has been the development of new technologies, including more powerful computing hardware and software. In particular, the development of cloud computing has made it easier for organizations to access the computing power they need to run AI algorithms, without the need to invest in expensive hardware or infrastructure (Armbrust et al., 2010). Another important factor has been the increasing availability of data. As more and more business processes become digitized, organizations have access to vast amounts of data that can be analysed using AI algorithms. This has enabled organizations to make more informed decisions and identify opportunities for improvement that would have been impossible without AI (Provost and Fawcett, 2013).

The application of AI in business has evolved from simple rule-based systems to complex machine learning algorithms that can make predictions and recommendations. The evolution of AI in business has been driven by a combination of technological advancements and a growing understanding of how AI can be applied to solve business problems. The use of AI in business activities has become increasingly prevalent in recent years, with many businesses adopting AI to improve their operations. From expert systems to deep learning algorithms, AI has transformed the way organizations operate and compete, enabling them to make more informed decisions and identify opportunities for improvement (Bughin et al., 2018b).

The Impact of AI on Entrepreneurship and Innovation

AI has had a significant impact on entrepreneurship, revolutionizing the way businesses operate and bringing new opportunities for innovation and growth. The applications of AI in entrepreneurship are diverse and range from customer service to marketing and product development.

According to Autio et al. (2018), the use of AI in entrepreneurship and innovation was initially limited to large corporations due to the high costs of developing and implementing AI technologies. However, the emergence of cloud computing and open-source software has made AI more accessible to entrepreneurs and small businesses.

Entrepreneurs can enhance customer satisfaction and retention by using AI-powered chatbots to deliver quick and personalized support. These chatbots offer 24/7 customer assistance, reducing response times and improving customer satisfaction. H&M and Amazon are examples of companies leveraging AI-powered chatbots for customer queries, recommendations, and analysing feedback to enhance their customer service. AI is also being used to automate and optimize business operations, allowing entrepreneurs to make faster and more informed decisions. For example, supply chain management can be improved with AI-powered predictive analytics. A study by McKinsey Global Institute found that AI can increase supply chain efficiency by up to 20% and reduce procurement costs by up to 25% (Bughin et al., 2018a). AI can enable entrepreneurs to explore new business models and revenue streams. For example, AI-powered platforms such as Airbnb and Uber have disrupted traditional industries by creating new marketplaces that connect buyers and sellers in innovative ways.

Another application of AI in entrepreneurship is in the optimization of business processes. By using AI-powered tools and systems, entrepreneurs can automate many routine tasks, such as data entry, customer service, and inventory management. This can save time and reduce costs, allowing entrepreneurs to focus on more strategic activities such as product development, marketing, and business expansion. Applications of AI in entrepreneurship is in product development has also become prominent in the current era. AI can help entrepreneurs to identify market gaps and customer preferences by analysing large datasets. AI can also be used to optimize product designs and improve the manufacturing process. For instance, fashion retailer Zara uses AI to analyse customer behaviour and market trends to create customized products and reduce the time-to-market of new collections.

In the field of finance and accounting, AI can be used to automate invoice processing, bookkeeping, and financial reporting, which can save time and reduce errors. AI can also be used to analyse financial data and identify patterns and trends, which can help entrepreneurs to make better financial decisions. For instance, MasterCard is using AI to detect fraud in real-time by analysing transaction patterns and customer behaviour.

The main impact of AI in entrepreneurship is its ability to increase productivity and efficiency. By automating routine tasks and providing data-driven insights, AI can help entrepreneurs to make better decisions and focus on high-value activities. Moreover, AI can help entrepreneurs to not only reduce costs, but also to improve customer experiences, and increase revenues, which can lead to higher profits and faster business growth.

Literature Review

The literature on the impact of AI on entrepreneurship and innovation is vast and diverse. The impact of AI on entrepreneurship and innovation has been a topic of interest for many researchers in recent years, with many studies investigating the use of AI in different business processes. AI has also had an impact on innovation. Innovation has been defined as the process of creating and implementing new ideas that add value to society (Schumpeter, 1934).

AI technologies have been used in the development of innovative products and services, as well as in the innovation process itself. For example, AI can be used to analyse customer data to identify new market opportunities or to optimize the design of products (Teece, 2018). One study by Acemoglu and Restrepo (2020) explored the impact of automation on the labour market and found that while automation has the potential to increase productivity and create new job opportunities, it also leads to significant job displacement, particularly in routine and manual tasks. The authors argue that policy interventions, such as investment in education and training, can help to mitigate the negative impacts of automation on the labour market.

This research paper uses bibliographic coupling to analyse the literature on AI, entrepreneurship, and innovation. The articles were obtained from the Scopus database. The articles were analysed using the software VOS viewer, which is a tool for visualizing bibliographic networks.

The literature review conducted in this research paper covered publications from the inception of AI, that is 1950s to 2023. The search was performed through five cases within the Scopus database. The initial search yielded many publications, which were filtered by relevance and date. The final dataset comprised 2000 publications that were analysed using bibliographic coupling. Figure 23.1 provides a good overview of the frequency of publications on AI in entrepreneurship and innovation from 1950s to 2023.

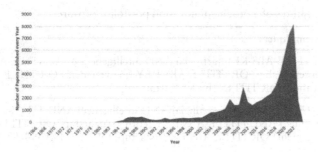

Figure 23.1 Articles published on AI in entrepreneurship and innovation since 1960s.

Limitations

This study has certain limitations. Firstly, it relied solely on the Scopus Database, potentially missing relevant research on AI and entrepreneurship/innovation. Future studies can expand the search to include other databases and sources. Additionally, the study focused solely on bibliographic relationships and did not consider factors like content and document quality. Lastly, the analysis focused on English language documents, which may limit the generalizability of the findings to other languages. Despite these limitations, the following bibliographic analysis aims to understand how researchers and practitioners have perceived the use of AI in the field of innovation and entrepreneurship since its inception.

Bibliographic Analysis

Bibliographic coupling is a technique used in bibliometrics to analyse relationships between scientific articles based on shared references. It helps identify key articles and related research areas, while bibliometric analysis quantitatively examines citation networks, co-authorship networks, and keyword networks to identify patterns and trends in scholarly communication. By applying bibliographic coupling, we can identify co-citation patterns between articles, revealing related content and key themes in the field of AI and entrepreneurship. We utilized this approach to investigate the relationship between AI and entrepreneurship and innovation. Five cases were created for analysis. Case 1 (base case) consisted of keywords AI, Entrepreneurship, Management, Startup, and Innovation. Additional keywords "Algorithm," "Machine Learning," "NLP," and "Deep Learning" were added to create Cases 2, 3, 4, and 5, respectively. The search strings/queries used for each case are provided in Table 23.1. The search period for all cases extended from 1960 to March 2023. The bibliographic data of articles were obtained from Scopus and analysed using VOS viewer for bibliometric analysis.

Keywords Analysis

A base case search in Scopus using five keywords (AI, entrepreneurship, management, startup, and innovation) yielded 59,249 articles. The list was refined to 2000 relevant articles followed for bibliometric analysis using VOS, with a minimum threshold of at least 5 occurrences per document for keyword inclusion in the analysis. Figure 23.2

Table 23.1: Key features of a product innovation portfolio software.

Case	Search string/query
1	**Case 1:** (TITLE-ABS-KEY (artificial AND intelligence) AND (TITLE-ABS KEY (entrepreneurship) OR (TITLE-ABS-KEY (management) OR TITLE-ABS KEY (innovation) OR TITLE-ABS-KEY (startup)))
2	**Case 2:** ((TITLE-ABS-KEY (artificial AND intelligence) AND TITLE-ABS-KEY (algorithms)) AND (TITLE-ABS-KEY (entrepreneurship) OR TITLE-ABS-KEY (management) OR TITLE-ABS-KEY (startup) OR TITLE-ABS-KEY (innovation)))
3	**Case 3:** ((TITLE-ABS-KEY (artificial AND intelligence) OR TITLE-ABS KEY (machine AND learning)) AND (TITLE-ABS KEY (entrepreneurship) OR TITLE-ABS-KEY (management) OR TITLE-ABS-KEY (startup) OR TITLE-ABS-KEY (innovation)))
4	**Case 4:** ((TITLE-ABS-KEY (artificial AND intelligence) AND TITLE-ABS KEY (NLP)) AND (TITLE-ABS-KEY (entrepreneurship) OR TITLE-ABS KEY (management) OR TITLE-ABS-KEY (startup) OR TITLE-ABS-KEY (innovation)))
5	**Case 5:** ((TITLE-ABS-KEY (artificial AND intelligence) AND TITLE-ABS KEY (Deep AND Learning)) AND (TITLE-ABS KEY (entrepreneurship) OR TITLE-ABS-KEY (management) OR TITLE-ABS KEY (startup) OR TITLE-ABS-KEY (innovation)))

Source: Author's compilation

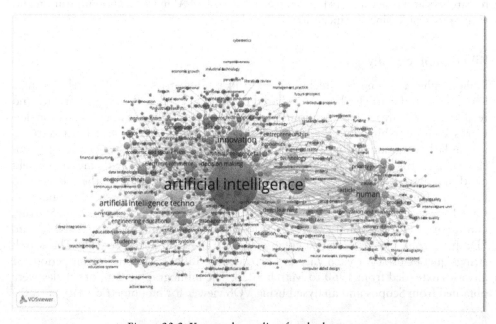

Figure 23.2 Keyword coupling for the base case.

provides major clusters identified and the prominent ones other than the key element of AI and innovation. The clusters also include other keywords which have high occurrence in the papers like artificial intelligence technology, human, machine learning, information management, big data and decision making.

Figure 23.3 presents additional cases generated by adding keywords like algorithms, machine learning, NLP, and deep learning. The results highlight the creation of relevant keywords when specific terms are used in the search string. Deep learning emerged as a prominent and competitive cluster by itself, indicating its popularity among researchers and its adaptability in major business avenues such as innovation and entrepreneurship. Combining relevant keywords from five cases revealed insightful clusters, as shown in Figure 23.4. Notable clusters include innovation, natural language processing, convolutional neural network, cloud computing, resource management, entrepreneurship, and Deep Learning, which emerged as a major cluster after artificial intelligence.

Country Analysis

As the discussion is about entrepreneurship assessing the countries that contribute to the growth of AI in entrepreneurship and innovation is relevant to this discussion. China has surpassed the United States as the largest cluster in AI entrepreneurship and innovation, with other major contributors including India, UK, Canada, Brazil, Malaysia, Germany, Italy, and EU countries, as shown in Figure 23.5. Over the past two decades, technological advancements and innovation have become crucial for economic growth globally. Additionally, countries in the Middle East and South America are emerging as new clusters in AI entrepreneurship and innovation.

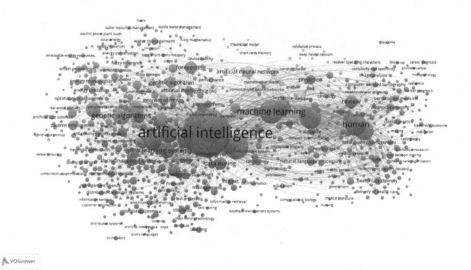

(i) Base case with algorithms

(ii) Base case with machine learning

(iii) Base case with NLP

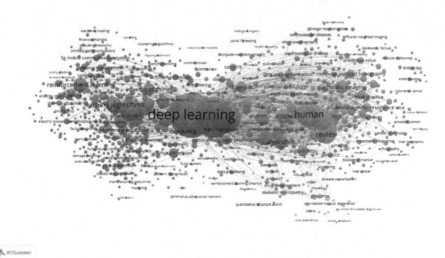

(iv) Base case with deep learning
Figure 23.3 Bibliographic couplings for base case and specific keywords.

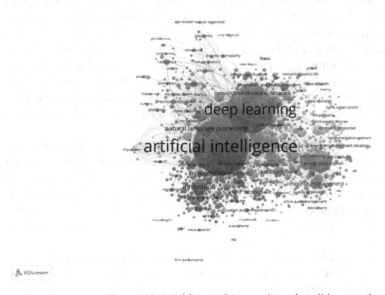

Figure 23.4 Bibliographic couplings for all keywords.

Limitations of AI

While AI continues to make strides in various industries, its potential to revolutionize fields like healthcare, finance, and entertainment is vast. However, AI still faces limitations, particularly in replicating human-level common sense reasoning. Despite advancements in deep learning, natural language processing, and computer vision, AI struggles

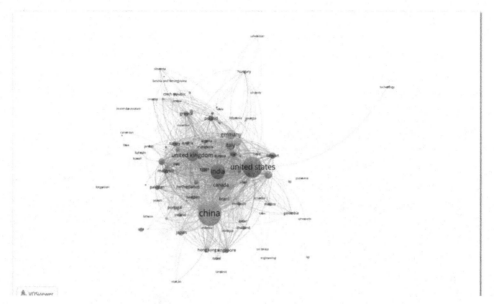

Figure 23.5 Bibliographic couplings for countries.

with contextual reasoning, understanding implicit meaning, and perceiving the world like humans do (Mitchell et al., 2018). Furthermore, deep learning models are susceptible to adversarial attacks, revealing their limited understanding of the world.

Another significant limitation of AI is its inability to handle unpredictable or unfamiliar situations. AI models are limited in their performance when faced with data outside their training set. In the study by Marcus (2018), he argues that current AI systems lack the ability to learn abstract concepts or adapt to novel situations. For example, in autonomous driving, AI models face the challenge of handling unpredictable situations like roadblocks or accidents, highlighting this limitation.

AI's limitation is also in exhibiting true creativity and generating novel ideas stems from its reliance on previous examples, lacking intuition, emotional intelligence, and imagination. This limitation is especially relevant in scientific research, where novel ideas and insights are crucial for advancement. In their study on the limitations of deep learning in biomedical imaging, Litjens et al. (2017) highlight the need for developing AI systems that can generate new hypotheses and ideas, rather than just relying on patterns in existing data.

Therefore, despite significant advances, AI still faces limitations in achieving human-level intelligence, such as common-sense reasoning, handling unfamiliar situations, exhibiting true creativity, and making ethical decisions. Addressing these limitations is crucial for the continued advancement and integration of AI across diverse applications.

Future Research Trends and Conclusion

Future research can explore how artificial intelligence (AI) technologies support entrepreneurship and innovation, including their role in social entrepreneurship and fostering open innovation through collaboration with external stakeholders like customers, suppliers, and partners. Another area of research can explore the practical implications of AI adoption in small businesses and startups, including the influence of government policies, access to financing, and the ways AI can drive business growth and sustainability. Furthermore, ethical and social implications of AI in entrepreneurship and innovation require attention. Research should address topics such as potential biases and discrimination in AI systems, the impact of AI on employment and the future of work, and the ethical considerations involved in AI-driven decision-making.

In conclusion, the integration of AI in entrepreneurship and innovation has been steadily growing globally over the past three decades. This growth is evident from the increasing number of research documents on the topic (Figure 23.1). Bibliographic coupling analysis has identified key research areas in this field. AI has the potential to drive entrepreneurship and innovation, but responsible and ethical use of these technologies is vital for creating a more inclusive and sustainable future for business and society.

References

Acemoglu, D., and Restrepo, P. (2020). Robots and jobs: evidence from US labor markets. *Journal of Political Economy,* 128(6), 2188–2244. https://doi.org/10.1086/705716

Armbrust, M., Fox, A., Griffith, R., Joseph, A. D., Katz, R., Konwinski, A., Lee, G., Patterson, D., Rabkin, A., Stoica, I., and Zaharia, M. (2010). A view of cloud computing. *Communications of the ACM,* 53(4), 50–58. doi: 10.1145/1721654.1721672

Autio, E., Nambisan, S., Thomas, L. D. W., and Wright, M. (2018). Digital affordances, spatial affordances, and the genesis of entrepreneurial ecosystems. *Strategic Entrepreneurship Journal,* 12(1), 72–95. doi:https://doi.org/10.1002/sej.1266

Bughin, J., Chui, M., and Manyika, J. (2018a). Notes from the AI frontier: Modeling the Impact of AI on the World Economy. McKinsey Global Institute. Bughin, J., Hazan, E., Ramaswamy, S., Chui, M., Allas, T., Dahlström, P., and Henke, N. (2018b). Artificial Intelligence: The Next Digital Frontier? McKinsey Global Institute.

Cortes, C., and Vapnik, V. (1995). Support-vector networks. *Machine Learning,* 20(3), 273–297.

Devlin, J., Chang, M. W., Lee, K., and Toutanova, K. (2019). BERT: Pre-training of deep bidirectional transformers for language understanding. In Proceedings of the 2019 Conference of the North American Chapter of the Association for Computational Linguistics: Human Language Technologies, (Vol. 1 (Long and Short Papers) (pp. 4171–4186).

Domingos, P. (2012). A few useful things to know about machine learning. *Communications of the ACM,* 55(10), 78–87.

Krizhevsky, A., Sutskever, I., and Hinton, G. E. (2012). ImageNet classification with deep convolutional neural networks. *Advances in Neural Information Processing Systems,* 25, 1097–1105.

Litjens, G., Kooi, T., Bejnordi, B. E., Setio, A. A. A., Ciompi, F., Ghafoorian, M., . . . and Sánchez, C. I. (2017). The limitations of deep learning in biomedical imaging. *Medical Image Analysis,* 47, 67–78.

Marcus, G. (2018). Deep learning: A critical appraisal. arXiv preprint arXiv:1801.00631. https://doi.org/10.48550/arXiv.1801.00631

Mitchell, M., Wu, S., Zaldivar, A., Barnes, P., Vasserman, L., Hutchinson, B., Spitzer, E., Raji, I. D., and Gebru, T. (2018). Model cards for model reporting. In Proceedings of the Conference on Fairness, Accountability, and Transparency, (pp. 220–229).

Mnih, V., Kavukcuoglu, K., Silver, D., Graves, A., Antonoglou, I., Wierstra, D., and Riedmiller, M. (2013). Playing atari with deep reinforcement learning. arXiv preprint arXiv:1312.5602.

Provost, F., and Fawcett, T. (2013). Data science and its relationship to big data and data-driven decision making. *Big Data*, 1(1), 51–59. doi: 10.1089/big.2013.1508

Rumelhart, D. E., Hinton, G. E., and Williams, R. J. (1986). Learning representations by back-propagating errors. *Nature*, 323(6088), 533–536.

Russell, S. J., and Norvig, P. (2010). Artificial Intelligence: A Modern Approach. (History of Artificial Intelligence). Pearson Education.

Samuel, A. L. (1959). Some studies in machine learning using the game of checkers. *IBM Journal of Research and Development*, 3(3), 210–229.

Schumpeter, J. A. (1934). The Theory of Economic Development: An Inquiry into Profits, Capital, Credit, Interest, and the Business Cycle. Harvard University Press.

Silver, D., Huang, A., Maddison, C. J., Guez, A., Sifre, L., Van Den Driessche, G., Schrittwieser, J., Antonoglou, I., Panneershelvam, V., Lanctot, M., and Dieleman, S. (2016). Mastering the game of Go with deep neural networks and tree search. *Nature*, 529(7587), 484–489.

Teece, D. J. (2018). Business models and dynamic capabilities. Long Range Planning, 51(1), 40–49.

Turing, A. M. (1950). Computing machinery and intelligence. *Mind*, LIX(236), 433–460. https://doi.org/10.1093/mind/LIX.236.433

24 The Contribution of ISO Standards to the Sustainable Development Goals: A Comparative Study Between 2022 SDG Index Scores and ISO Survey

Malak Aoun[a] and Muhammad Rizky Prima Sakti[b]

Assistant Professor, Business Administration Department, University College of Bahrain, Bahrain

Abstract

This study aims to highlight the contribution of ISO standards to the implementation of the sustainable development goals (SDG). This study illustrates the progress of the United Nations in implementing the SDG plan, compares the most recent SDG index scores with the ISO survey results, and recognizes the ISO standards that are directly related to each SDG. The research is based on secondary data from previously published reports, mainly from the United Nations Reports and ISO surveys. The results showed that ISO standards are conceptually related to sustainable development goals; however, there are many challenges that are slowing down the certification and development procedures at both organizational and governmental levels. Future studies are encouraged to empirically evaluate the level of sustainable development and ISO standards implementation as well as businesses, governments and citizens should be aware of the economic, social, and environmental factors and collaborate to attain the SDGs by 2030.

Keywords

ISO survey, SDG scores, sustainability.

Introduction

The widespread definition of sustainability is established on three interrelated pillars including the social, economic, and environmental factors (Purvis et al., 2019). A sustainable future requires the balance between the needs of these pillars and obviously, organizations are ever more expected to show a major role in attaining this. However, the world is facing severe challenges at the social, environmental, and economic levels as shown in Figure 24.1.

Although many certification and international standards bodies provide guidance on how organizations can run ethically and transparently to contributes in the sustainable development, many businesses face challenges while trying to get certified as shown in Figure 24.2.

This study focuses on the most popular certification body, the ISO—International Standards Organization. There are more than 22000 published international standards

---

[a]maoun@ucb.edu.bh, [b]mrizky@ucb.edu.bh

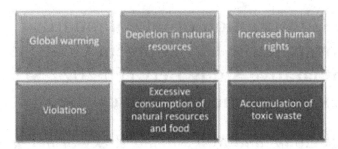

Figure 24.1 Challenges facing the world at the social, environmental, and economic levels.
Source: Jan et al., 2019

Figure 24.2 Challenges facing businesses while trying to get certified.
Source: Mutinda, 2012

which act as a global guidelines and frameworks (ISO, 2018). To highlight the contribution of ISO standards to the SDGs, this research illustrates the progress of the United Nations in implementing the SDG plan, compares the most recent 2022 SDG index scores with the ISO survey results, and recognizes the ISO standards that are directly related to each SDG.

Literature Review

Sustainable Development

Sustainable development is basically defined as the "development that meets the needs of the present without compromising the ability of future generations to meet their own needs". This definition conceptualizes sustainable development based on needs and constraints. Needs refer to the world's poor while constraints refer to obstacles that cease the organizational abilities from meting current and future needs (Keeble, 1988). Many studies (Gasparatos et al., 2017; Kammen and Sunter, 2016; Styles et al., 2015; Chen et al., 2010) have discussed the importance of the most five pioneering models in sustainable development as listed in Figure 24.3.

Solar energy is totally free and accessible in unrestricted quantities. These two factors offer good benefit to consumers and decrease pollution. It is economically and

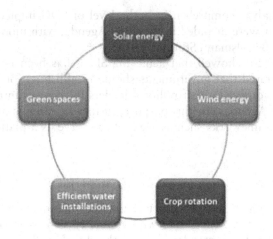

Figure 24.3 The most five pioneering models in sustainable development.

Source: Author

environmentally efficient to replace the non-renewable energy with solar energy. Also, wind energy is an alternative energy source. Employing wind energy entails the usage of windmills and it is projected to serve more than just the individual. It could be a good investment since it can supplement or even substitute the cost of grid energy. Crop rotation occurs when planting different crops successively on the same land. It is chemical-free, and it expands the land's growth potential, while inhibiting soil insects and diseases.

Basically, fresh water represents less than 1% of the Earth's available water supply, thus it important to sustain it for both individual and community usage especially that it takes a lot of energy to produce, transport, and treat wastewater (EPA, 2022). Examples of effective formulations include products from the Environmental Protection Agency's WaterSense program which replace existing building practices and support the efficient installation of water appliances in attempt to conserve this valuable resource. The last category is Green spaces where plants and wildlife are encouraged to thrive. This would provide opportunities for people to enjoy outdoor recreation, especially in crowded cities and protect lakes and streams from polluted runoff (Aldous, 2006).

Sustainable Development Goals

At the end of 2015, the United Nations (UN) approved a plan to implement the 17 SDGs to improve living conditions, preserve the environment, and prospect improvements for both developed and developing countries. These SDGs address the global challenges which are related to "poverty, inequality, climate, environmental degradation, prosperity, peace and justice" (UN, 2021). There are many UN initiatives to follow up and ensure the execution of the SDGs by 2030, including the Sustainable Development Solutions Network, which records information and evaluates the activity of countries in this area. For the same purpose, the Bertelsmann-Stiftung Business Group issues an annual report in collaboration with hundreds of private and public organizations to analyze comprehensively the level of SDG implementation in 80% of the countries that were included in the 2030 Agenda, with more than one million people population (Bertelsmann Stiftung, 2016).

Jabbari et al. (2020) showed that achieving SDGs has been minimal in developing countries and stated that governments should establish national frameworks for achieving the SDGs especially that political leaders in these countries have not fully clarified their 2030 Agenda. For this purpose, further research is needed to highlight how international frameworks such as the ISO can serve as a platform for achieving the SDGs.

The International Organization for Standardization (ISO)

ISO is a non-government, independent international organization that includes 167 members of national standards bodies who voluntary share knowledge and develop market relevant international standards to face the global challenges. Basically, the ISO standards are categorized into 6 areas as follows (ISO, 2018):

- *Quality Management Standards:* reduce product failure and improve efficiency at work.
- *Energy Management Standards:* cut energy consumption.
- *Environmental Management Standards*: reduce wastes and environmental impacts.
- *Food Safety Standards:* avoid contamination of food.
- *Health & Safety Standards:* limits accidents at work.
- *IT Security Standards:* keep confidential information secure.

Figure 24.4 shows the results for recently published annual ISO Survey with data for 2021. It compiles the valid certificates numbers as of 31 December 2020 for the 12 ISO management standards submitted by Certification Bodies accredited by the International Accreditation Forum (IAF).

ISO management standards		Total valid certificates
ISO 9001	Quality management	916,842
ISO 14001	Environmental management	348,473
ISO 45001	Health & safety at work	190,481
ISO/IEC 27001	Information security	44,499
ISO 22000	Food safety management systems	33,741
ISO 13485	Medical devices	25,656
ISO 50001	Energy management systems	19,731
ISO 20000-1	Information technology-service management	7,846
ISO 22301	Societal security	2,205
ISO 37001	Anti-bribery management systems	2,065
ISO 39001	Road traffic safety management systems	972
ISO 28000	Specification for security management systems for the supply chain	520

Figure 24.4 ISO survey results.

Source: ISO, 2021

Methodology

As mentioned earlier, this is a comparative study which is based on secondary data collected from previously published reports and surveys. Table 24.1 shows the most recent SDG Index scores which reflect the overall performance of the top 20 among 193 UN Member countries as published in the Sustainable Development Report 2022 (UN, 2022). The SDG Index and Dashboard determines the global achievement of goals, which is a scale from zero to 100. The worst level of implementation scores zero while 100 means complete compliance with the goals.

Specifically, China was the country with the highest number of ISO certificates worldwide in 2020 as shown in Tables 24.2, 24.3, 24.4 and 24.5 (ISO, 2021) which focus on the top 10 countries based on their valid number of ISO Certificates.

Table 24.1: The 2022 SDG scores.

Rank	Country	SDG score	Rank	Country	SDG score
1.	Finland	86.51	11	United Kingdom	80.55
2.	Denmark	85.63	12	Poland	80.54
3.	Sweden	85.19	13	Czech Republic	80.47
4.	Norway	82.35	14	Latvia	80.28
5.	Austria	82.32	15	Slovenia	79.95
6.	Germany	82.18	16	Spain	79.90
7.	France	81.24	17	Netherlands	79.85
8.	Switzerland	80.79	18	Belgium	79.69
9.	Ireland	80.66	19	Japan	79.58
10.	Estonia	80.62	20	Portugal	79.23

Source: UN, 2022

Table 24.2: Number of ISO 9001 certificates per country.

Rank	Country	ISO 9001 certificates
1.	China	324621
2.	Italy	91493
3.	Germany	49349
4.	Japan	32287
5.	India	32236
6.	Spain	29814
7.	United Kingdom	25995
8.	France	21880
9.	USA	20919
10.	Brazil	17503

Table 24.3: Number of ISO 14001 certificates per country.

Rank	Country	ISO 14001 Certificates
1.	China	168129
2.	Japan	17804
3.	Italy	16858
4.	Spain	12584
5.	United Kingdom	11627
6.	Germany	9955
7.	India	8416
8.	France	6458
9.	Romania	5221
10.	Korea	5091

Table 24.4: Number of ISO 45001 certificates per country.

Rank	Country	ISO 45001 Certificates
1.	China	120134
2.	Italy	10230
3.	United Kingdom	5432
4.	India	5260
5.	Spain	3420
6.	Germany	2310
7.	Romania	2191
8.	Australia	1872
9.	Czech Republic	1823
10.	Taiwan, Province of China	1589

Analysis and Discussion

By comparing the results of ISO Survey Results (2020) and the SDG Scores (2022) as shown in Table 24.6, it was interesting to see some countries such as China missing among the top SDG scores countries. It was ranked 56/163 countries with 72.4 SDG index score although it has the largest total of ISO 9001 certificates worldwide. This is because China has only achieved the "no poverty" and "quality education" SDGs while the other goals are still in significant and major challenges (UN, 2022). The government in China has stated education, science, and technology as the strategic engines of sustainable development. However, China must overcome many obstacles

Table 24.5: Number of ISO/IEC 27001 certificates per country.

Rank	Country	ISO/IEC 27001 Certificates
1.	China	12403
2.	Japan	5645
3.	United Kingdom	3327
4.	India	2226
5.	Italy	1827
6.	Netherlands	1326
7.	Germany	1281
8.	United States of America	1058
9.	Spain	997
10.	Taiwan, Province of China	895

Table 24.6: Comparing the ISO survey results (2020) and the SDG scores (2022).

SDG Score 2022	Top 10 SDGs Scores countries	Top countries with ISO 9001 Certificates	Top countries with ISO 14001 Certificates	Top countries with ISO 45001 Certificates	Top countries with ISO/IEC 27001 Certificates
86.51	Finland	China	China	China	China
85.63	Denmark	Italy	Japan	Italy	Japan
85.19	Sweden	Germany	Italy	UK	UK
82.35	Norway	Japan	Spain	India	India
82.32	Austria	India	UK	Spain	Italy
82.18	Germany	Spain	Germany	Germany	Netherlands
81.24	France	UK	India	Romania	Germany
80.79	Switzerland	France	France	Australia	USA
80.66	Ireland	USA	Romania	Czech	Spain
80.62	Estonia	Brazil	Korea	Taiwan	Taiwan

Source: by Author

to achieve such goals including the lack of social equality, huge population, and the extending urban-rural gap (Xingqian et al., 2007).

The aim of the UN 2030 agenda is to change the world through the 17 SDGs. This requires the involvement of society components including individual, business, industry, and national governments. Therefore, ISO provides a solid background on which improvement can thrive to help governments, business and customers contribute to the attainment of every single SDG. As illustrated in Figure 24.5, the highest number of ISO standards is 13085 including ISO 44001, ISO/TS 37151, ISO 50501 which

SDGs	Number of ISO standards meeting the SDG	Sample of ISO standards
1. No poverty	354	ISO 20400; ISO 37001
2. Zero hunger	544	ISO 22000, ISO 34101
3. Good health and well-being	3042	ISO 11137, ISO 7153, ISO 37101
4. Quality education	534	ISO 21001; ISO /TC 232
5. Gender equality	192	ISO 26000
6. Clean water and sanitation	579	ISO 30500; ISO 24518
7. Affordable and clean energy	885	ISO 50001; ISO 52000
8. Decent work and economic growth	2513	ISO 45001; ISO 37001
9. Industry, innovation, and infrastructure	13085	ISO 44001, ISO/TS 37151
10. Reduced inequalities	551	ISO 26000
11. Sustainable cities and communities	2451	ISO 37120; ISO 37123
12. Responsible consumption and production	2738	ISO 20400, ISO 20245
13. Climate action	1162	ISO 14001, ISO 14080
14. Life below water	298	ISO /TC 234; ISO /TC 8
15. Life on land	1076	ISO 14055; ISO 38200
16. Peace, justice, and strong institutions	174	ISO/TC 309; ISO 19600
17. Partnerships for the goals	2	ISO 44001:2017; ISO/IEC AWI TR 9858

Figure 24.5 ISO standards meeting SDGs.

Source: Summarized by Author

contribute to SDG 9. However, only 2 standards are helping to meet SDG 17 "Partnerships for the Goals" which are ISO 44001:2017 and ISO/IEC AWI TR 9858 (ISO, 2018).

For example, ISO is contributing to SDG 15 through ISO 38200 that promotes traceability in the wood supply chain by promoting better use of wood from sustainable sources which in turn help to combat illegal deforestation. In addition, ISO 22000 standards related to food safety management would help businesses distinguish and control food safety hazards, which contributes to SDG 2. Moreover, ISO 45001 are designed to help organizations globally protect the health and safety of employees, which is directly contributing to SDG 8. Similarly, ISO 29993 covers up different types of lifelong learning such as vocational education and in-company training, which is contributing to SDG 4. Many studies have been recently conducted and identified ISO standards as a driving force for sustainable development (Ikram et al., 2021; Bravi et al., 2020; Fortuński, 2008). Bastas and Liyanage (2018) were pioneers in highlighting empirically the implementation of ISO 9001 methodology. This study suggested significant recommendations for executives who are involved in the ISO 9001 adoption as it can custom their quality management systems. This includes the integrating measurement of financial, environmental, and social key performance indicators for sustainable development. Similarly, Merlin et al. (2012) have developed a basic framework by connecting five popular ISO standards—ISO 14001, ISO 9001, ISO 31000, OHSAS 18001, ISO 26000—with sustainable development. The study categorized the standards into strategic, tactical and operational organizational levels. The findings illustrated that ISO standards would initiate the sustainable development processes in businesses through meeting the minimum criteria related to the strategic alignment.

Conclusion

Conceptually, ISO standards support the three pillars of sustainable development. The standards promote economic sustainability by enabling international trade and strengthening sustainable business practices. The standards also support social sustainability by encouraging countries to advance the health and well-being of their people. In addition, the standards promote environmental sustainability by encouraging responsible consumption. However, the empirical evidence shows that challenges to ISO implementation are similar for both businesses and governments including lack of top management support and commitment, lack of qualified human resources, resistance of employees towards change, lack of regulations, high costs and lack of technical knowledge. Moreover, political, social, environmental, and economic stability has often been a persistent concern for any country. Stability and development are the society's main goals which are the base to establish promising environment and attain balanced economic development.

References

Aldous, D. E. (2006). Social, environmental, economic, and health benefits of green spaces. In XXVII International Horticultural Congress-IHC2006: International Symposium on Horticultural Plants in Urban and Peri-Urban 762 (pp. 171–186).

Bastas, A., and Liyanage, K. (2018). ISO 9001 and supply chain integration principles based sustainable development: a Delphi study. *Sustainability*, 10(12), 4569.

Bertelsmann Stiftung (2016). First SDG Index Delivered to Ban Ki-Moon: Countries need to act Urgently to Achieve the Global Goals. Press release. https://www.bertelsmann-stiftung.de/en/press/press-releases/press-release/pid/first-sdg-index-delivered-to-ban-ki-moon-countries-need-to-act-urgently-to-achieve-the-global-goals.

Bravi, L., Santos, G., Pagano, A., and Murmura, F. (2020). Environmental management system according to ISO 14001: 2015 as a driver to sustainable development. *Corporate Social Responsibility and Environmental Management*, 27(6), 2599–2614.

Chen, F., Lu, S. M., Tseng, K. T., Lee, S. C., and Wang, E. (2010). Assessment of renewable energy reserves in Taiwan. *Renewable and Sustainable Energy Reviews*, 14(9), 2511–2528.

Driver, B. C. (1993). The Environmental Protection Agency's Role in Encouraging Water Use Efficiency in the Western States. Environmental and Energy Study Institute.

EPA. (2022). EPA Programs and Initiatives Addressing Climate Change in the Water Sector. United States Environmental Protection Agency, Office of Water. Available at https://www.epa.gov/climate-change-water-sector/epa-programs-and-initiatives-addressing-climate-change-water-sector#watersense

Fortuński, B. (2008). Does the environmental management standard ISO 14001 stimulate sustainable development? An example from the energy sector in Poland. *Management of Environmental Quality: An International Journal*, 19(2), 204–212.

Gasparatos, A., Doll, C. N., Esteban, M., Ahmed, A., and Olang, T. A. (2017). Renewable energy and biodiversity: Implications for transitioning to a green economy. *Renewable and Sustainable Energy Reviews*, 70, 161–184.

Keeble, B. R. (1988). The Brundtland report: 'Our common future'. *Medicine and War*, 4(1), 17–25.

Ikram, M., Zhang, Q., Sroufe, R., and Ferasso, M. (2021). Contribution of certification bodies and sustainability standards to sustainable development goals: an integrated grey systems approach. *Sustainable Production and Consumption*, 28, 326–345.

ISO (2018). Contributing to the UN Sustainable Development Goals with ISO Standards. Geneva: ISO. ISBN 978-92-67-10790-5

ISO (2021). The ISO Survey of Management System Standard Certifications 2021 Report. International Organization for Standardization Full data available at https://www.iso.org/the-iso-survey.html

Jabbari, M., Shafiepour-Motlagh, M., Ashrafi, K., and Abdoli, G. (2020). Differentiating countries based on the sustainable development proximities using the SDG indicators. *Environment, Development and Sustainability*, 22, 6405–6423.

Jan, A., Marimuthu, M., bin Mohd, M. P., and Isa, M. (2019). The nexus of sustainability practices and financial performance: From the perspective of Islamic banking. *Journal of Cleaner Production*, 228, 703–717.

Kammen, D. M., and Sunter, D. A. (2016). City-integrated renewable energy for urban sustainability. *Science*, 352(6288), 922–928.

Merlin, F. K., do Valle Pereira, V. L., and Júnior, W. P. (2012). Sustainable development induction in organizations: a convergence analysis of ISO standards management tools' parameters. *Work*, 41(Suppl. 1), 2736–2743.

Mutinda, P. B. (2012). Challenges faced by organizations seeking ISO 9001 certification: A case of Kenya Medical Research Institute (Doctoral dissertation, University of Nairobi, Kenya).

Purvis, B., Mao, Y., and Robinson, D. (2019). Three pillars of sustainability: in search of conceptual origins. *Sustainability Science*, 14, 681–695.

Siva, V., Gremyr, I., Bergquist, B., Garvare, R., Zobel, T., and Isaksson, R. (2016). The support of quality management to sustainable development: a literature review. *Journal of Cleaner Production*, 138, 148–157.

Styles, D., Gibbons, J., Williams, A. P., Dauber, J., Stichnothe, H., Urban, B., Chadwick, D. R., and Jones, D. L. (2015). Consequential life cycle assessment of biogas, biofuel and biomass energy options within an arable crop rotation. *Gcb Bioenergy*, 7(6), 1305–1320.

UN (2022). Sustainable Development Report 2022, United Nations. Available on https://dashboards.sdgindex.org/rankings

United States Environmental Protection Agency. Water Planning Division (1982). Results of the Nationwide Urban Runoff Program. Water Planning Division, US Environmental Protection Agency.

Waxin, M. F., Knuteson, S. L., and Bartholomew, A. (2019). Drivers and challenges for implementing ISO 14001 environmental management systems in an emerging Gulf Arab country. *Environmental Management*, 63, 495–506.

Xingqian, S., Wennersten, R., and Mulder, K. F. (2007). Challenges of Sustainable Development in China. Technical Report. URL: https://www.researchgate.net/publication/259267076_Challenges_of_Sustainable_Development_in_China (accessed: 20 May 2023).

Zhao, X., Castka, P., and Searcy, C. (2020). ISO Standards: a platform for achieving sustainable development goal 2. *Sustainability*, 12(22), 9332.

25 The Contribution of Islamic Banking and Finance to the Sustainable Development Goals of 2030

Reem A. Abdalla[a], Hassan Kamal Alaaraj[b], and Gulnar Sadat Mulla[c]

Assistant Professor, University of Technology Bahrain, Bahrain

Abstract

Islamic banking and finance adhere to Islamic principles in order to provide financial services that are adapted to the requirements of Muslim populations while also addressing the needs of all other societies, Islamic microfinance is a crucial component of Islamic finance that will be included as it satisfies one of the Shariah-mandated primary functions of financial intermediary mechanisms, which is to provide financial assistance to individuals who are not eligible for banking services. Microfinance business models can be developed alongside Islamic contracts. This paper will discuss and highlight the various Islamic finance and microfinance Contracts, including Zakat, Waqf, Qard Hassan, Murabaha, Salam, Istisna, Musharaka, and Mudaraba, before examining the effectiveness of each one of them in achieving the 2030 sustainable development goals' dimensions. The methodology will be based on a comprehensive literature evaluation of nineteen published articles of how Islamic banking and finance various contracts uses which advance progress toward the 2030 sustainable development goals (SDGs). The study indicates that there is a strong relationship between sustainable development and the Islamic financial system, which effectively contributes to reducing unemployment and destitution and enhancing the quality of life in developing countries.

Keywords

Islamic contracts, Islamic ethical wealth management, Islamic finance, Islamic microfinance, sharia rules, sustainable development goals.

Introduction

The sustainable development goals (SDGs) outline seventeen specific objectives that aim to eliminate poverty, hunger, inequality, preventable child mortality, and climate change. These goals aim to transform the global community by promoting the long-term health of the economy, society, and ecosystem (Sustainable Development Goals | United Nations Development Programme). Sachs (2015) argues that global problems such as poverty, inequality, and environmental degradation require a collective effort from all nations to address. Priority was given to inclusive, long-term economic

[a]r.abdalla@utb.edu.bh, [b]h.alaaraj@utb.edu.bh, [c]mulla@utb.edu.bh

Table 25.1: Sustainable development goals (Indicators, 2017).

Number of goals	17
Number of targets	169
Number of indicators	232

development in the SDGs in order to solve the urgent social concerns facing nations and promote the SDGs.

This research seeks to investigate the roles of Islamic finance in attaining sustainable development goals and to determine whether Islamic finance institutions contribute to the achievement of these goals. A further objective is to identify the instruments that contribute to the attainment of each SDGs. To show how the SDGs were attained, several articles were studied and linked to the SDGs. On the literature the articles' material was assigned to the relative Islamic contract, and then each contract relative influence was addressed and mapped to the relative goal.

Literature Review

Islamic Sustainable Microfinance Mechanism

Islamic microfinance which is an alternative to the conventional microfinance refers to a financial system that seeks to provide financial support to poor, needy, and low-income small enterprises and individuals. It operates on the concepts of profit and loss sharing, benevolent lending, mutual insurance, and social welfare, with the goal of eradicating poverty and providing economic empowerment to the underprivileged populations, while adhering to the norms of Islamic Shariah law and ethics.

Islamic microfinance offers a variety of approaches based on Islamic religious values. These approaches include the Zakat, Waqf, qard Hassan, Hiba, Murabaha, Salam, Istisna, Musharaka, Mudaraba, Ijarah, and diminishing Musharaka contracts, each of which has its own unique qualities and benefits that are tailored to the needs and conditions. Mudaraba, Ijarah and diminishing musharaka contracts.

Islamic Ethical Wealth Management

Waqf, Sadaqah, and Zakat are social finance instruments that symbolize Islamic ethical wealth and management concepts that highlight the necessity for the affluent to spend part of their assets on the less fortunate members of the society. While Waqf and Sadaqah are voluntary means designed to encourage financially capable individuals contribute back to their community, zakat is obligatory for those who are eligible as a result of their wealth being given to certain beneficiaries stated in the Qur'an (Muneeza and Mustapha, 2021).

Islamic finance is based on the belief that zakat, waqf, and Sadaqah are the most effective means of sharing surplus funds and contributing to the growth of society. Because zakat and Sadaqah come in money that can be spent, they assist those with limited financial resources (Rabbani et al., 2021).

Waqf System (Endowment, Charitable Trust)

A "Waqf" is a charitable endowment in which a parcel, building, or piece of land is gifted. Philanthropy is not obligatory in Islam, yet its payment will lead to societal perfection (Jan et al., 2021). Waqf benefits are enjoyed by a large number of people around the world, and it has the potential to decrease poverty (Wakaf et al., 2020) as mmicrofinance institutions based on Waqf can provide affordable financing to the lower middle class (Rohman et al., 2021). Waqf-based microfinance contributes to the SDGs in several important insights. The flexibility of waqf legislation can enable IMFIs to broaden their services to include social and financial dimensions, besides having a macroeconomic impact on economic growth (Rohman et al., 2021).

Zakat (charity) system

Zakat is an obligatory act of purification in which those who qualify based on their wealth contribute a specific amount to 8 recipient categories, 4 of which are related to sustainability: the poor (those who do not have the cost of his day), the needy (Poor yet better off than the poor), debtors (those who could not pay their debts, and the way-farer (that has been cut off from his country and whose expenses have been expended is given what he can spend to reach his destination or return home, even if he is rich).

According to Anis and Kassim, (2016), zakat is a method for economic empowerment and has a crucial role in the development of small companies owned by the financially disadvantaged. In addition to receiving zakat as start-up capital for small firms, Indirectly, the economic impact of the recipients may have been altered by the fact that zakat was frequently used for medical care, education, and other necessities. Zakat also empowers women economically. If provided the opportunity and resources, women entrepreneurs in underdeveloped countries can achieve the same level of success as men. Women can be encouraged to better their lives and those of their families through hard work and participation in economic activities (Anis and Kassim, 2016).

Hassanain et al. (2016) revealed that the Zakah institution of the Republic of Sudan has the following policy objectives:

i.   To serve as a safety net against natural disasters, infectious diseases, desertification, and drought.
ii. To relieve poverty by providing monetary and in-kind aid.
iii. To create projects that serve the poor and the needy.
iv. To address unemployment by providing money for small enterprises and training.
     Zakat could be an alternate source of funding that is available locally and is not reliant on foreign sources. In this scenario, zakat can have a large positive influence in terms of producing money through modest projects and improving family income and spending (Anis and Kassim, 2016).

Sadaqah (voluntary giving)

"Sadaqah" is defined as "the voluntary offering of something with no expectation of receiving anything in return, with the only intention of pleasing Allah" (Jan et al., 2021).

Islamic Financial Contracts

Qard al-Hasan (Interest-free loans)

Qard al-Hassan is the sole sort of loan permitted by Islamic law in which the borrower repays just the principal and financial institutions are barred from collecting profits. This approach is suitable for people who need financial assistance for personal or emergency purposes. The lender provides the loan without charging any interest, and the borrower is required to repay the loan at a later date. This approach is based on the concept of charity and social responsibility, and it helps to promote social welfare and equity.

Interest-free loans (Qard Hasan) are a form of assistance for the impoverished. In Sudan, for example, the Diwan al-Zakat provides loans to farmers so they can purchase basic supplies and then repay the loans with a part of their crop profits (Hassanain et al., 2016).

The availability of interest-free loans has numerous effects on society, including the facilitation of land acquisition and the assurance of food security (Akanmu Popoola et al., 2021).

Sale Based Contracts

Murabaha (Cost plus mark-up sale)

The Murabaha contract is a type of contract that involves the sale of goods at a profit. The financier purchases the asset or good on behalf of the client and then sells it to them at a profit to be paid in installments over a pre-agreed period. This contract is commonly used in Islamic microfinance to finance the purchase of assets or goods it is suitable for people who need financing for purchasing assets such as equipment or vehicles.

Murabaha provide the members of society the ease of access to textile materials, transportation, and home requirements such as appliances, telephones, and electronic equipment in interest-free installments (Akanmu Popoola et al., 2021).

Salam (forward purchase)

Salam Contracts is a sale in which the seller agrees to deliver certain goods to the buyer at a future date in exchange for full payment of the purchase price in advance.

After the epidemic, (Wakaf et al., 2020) stated that to provide Indonesia with sustainable food security Cash Waqf Linked Sukuk (CWLS) issued under the Salam contract has been used, the Salam contract assist the farmers in cultivating food on productive land (Wakaf et al., 2020), it will also benefit sellers on traditional markets. Given that the majority of Indonesia's provinces are comprised of farmed land, there are significant prospects for Indonesia to achieve sustainable food security (Wakaf et al., 2020).

For relieving financial strain and supporting Nigeria's agriculture economy (Ogunbado and Ahmed, 2015) discussed how Bay' Salam is a practical option. If bankers, financial institutions, brokers, and others invest their money through Bay' Salam, it is envisaged that both contracting parties and Nigerian society will flourish. Agriculture was the primary source of income, food supply, employment, market, and industries in Kano State. The decline in production has been attributed to weak agricultural financing from traditional financial institutions, which has led to a high rate of poverty, unemployment, food shortages, low income of farmers and the government, and the collapse of agribusiness and allied agro-industries, among others; therefore, it is crucial to introduce peace financing to restore Kano State to its former glory (Mohammed et al., 2016).

Rabbani et al. (2021) recommended in his study that governments should use mechanisms like Salam to give cash to farmers and other people who need it.

Istisna'a (Manufacturing contract)

Istisna'a is a construction contract with a step-by-step financing process in which one party agrees to make and sell a specified product at a predetermined price. Better infrastructure is necessary for faster economic growth, and the majority of nations finance these initiatives with interest-bearing public debt. Expansionary monetary policy based on Istisna and Sukuk do not involve public debt and do not require interest payments (Selim et al., 2019). Manzoor et al. (2017) demonstrated that macroeconomic imbalances can be averted by aligning state-owned project financing flows with the real economy, particularly infrastructure. "Istisna-Musharakah-Sukuk" model is most relevant. This design is resilient. The countercyclical "Istisna" Sukuk could finance infrastructure projects. Infrastructure initiatives are compatible with Sukuk, which is based on asset and return, particularly in developing countries(Manzoor et al., 2017).

To finance the new airport, Selim et al. (2019) proposes an expansionary monetary strategy based on Istisna-based Sukuk, with the Central Bank (CB) purchasing and selling these securities on the open market, stated that Istisna'a funding and sukuk will expand monetary policy, increase output and employment, eliminate government debt and interest payments, freeing up funds for public spending, thereby positively influencing the continuation of economic growth, and prevent domestic resources from being used to pay international debts. The most difficult aspect of debt financing is isolating loan repayments from project risk and asset cash flow. The financing of infrastructure is compatible with risk-sharing financial arrangements. These securities are advantageous to the real economy and prevent the issuance and accumulation of debt.

Equity based financing

Musharaka and Mudaraba are equity based Islamic financing that encourage profit-and-loss sharing. Because of their one-of-a-kind qualities, they are appealing to companies and investors looking for financing following Shariah law. Both Musharaka and Mudaraba have the potential to contribute to the achievement of the SDGs.

Equity based financing allow shareholders to earn money through profit sharing from joint ventures, partnership firms, and dividends, so enhancing the social, economic, and financial well-being of cooperators utilizing authorized methods provided by Islamic finance regulations (Akanmu Popoola et al., n.d.). The equity-based IMF has a favorable and large effect on the welfare of rural households, particularly on their income (Fianto et al., 2018). Islam and Ahmad (n.d.) explained how micro-equity instruments, equity-based financing can support small firms and favorably influence the economy. contracts at IMF Stock based financing contracts, such as Musharakah and Mudharabah contracts, have the potential to become a tool for empowering the poor Rohman et al. (2021).

Musharaka

Musharaka is a partnership contract that involves two or more partners in which they share profit and losses. Instead of charging interest as a creditor, the financier will receive a return in the form of a predetermined percentage of the real profits achieved. Unlike conventional creditors, though, the financier will also share in any losses. Musharaka contract is commonly used in Islamic microfinance to finance small businesses. The lender and the borrower become partners in the business venture and share the profits and losses.

Adopting Musharakah and Mudharabah contracts can be a risk management solution since these two types of contracts set the parties on an equal footing, giving them all the same rights and responsibilities to oversee the project's progress until the end of the year (Rohman et al., 2021).

Diminishing Musharaka

Diminishing Musharaka has the potential to have a favorable impact on the income distribution in society and the socioeconomic standing of the poor (Saad and Razak, n.d.). The adoption of diminishing Musharaka into microfinance can be viewed as a sustainable method of alleviating poverty, as this tool gives the poor ownership of tangible assets and can improve the economic performance of customers (Islam and Ahmad, n.d.). A sustainable livelihoods approach can be practiced through the diminishing participation tool. Ownership of tangible assets/fixed property will empower the poor to face economic vulnerabilities and shocks while improving their financial status (Islam and Ahmad, n.d.).

Mudarabah (Profit and loss sharing)

Mudaraba contracts, A partnership in which one partner contributes capital while the other contributes labor or expertise. The capital provider is referred to as Rab-ul-Maal, while the counterpart is referred to as Mudarib. Although this is a credit agreement, the mudarib is not liable for losses except in the case of breach of fiduciary requirements.

One approach in the Islamic microfinance modelis Mudaraba, which is based on the principles of profit and loss sharing. Mudaraba is commonly used in Islamic microfinance to finance entrepreneurial ventures. The capital provider provides the capital, and the entrepreneur provides the expertise. The profits are shared between the two parties based on a pre-agreed ratio.

Small and medium-sized businesses are encouraged to reopen or begin operations by Mudaraba and Murabaha. This encouragement raises one's self-esteem and creates job chances, which increases spending. Investments in various infrastructures, including real estate, equipment, and other assets, can help the economy get back to normal (Rabbani et al., 2021).

Ijarah (Leasing)

Ijarah contracts is a method of medium-term financing that resembles a conventional lease agreement in which the owner rents or leases his property or goods to a lessee for a predetermined period in exchange for a fee. The main difference is that In Ijara contract, the asset is returned to the owner.

This contract is commonly used in Islamic microfinance to finance the purchase of equipment or machinery. The lender purchases the equipment or machinery and leases it to the borrower for a fee. The borrower pays the fee in installments until the full price of the equipment or machinery is paid off.

In (SDGs) ordance with the Islamic concept of ijara, it provides shelter and food to those in need. This notion directly benefits the economy when individuals believe that infrastructure is beneficial for them (Rabbani et al., 2021).

Takaful (Islamic insurance)

Takaful derives from the Islamic principle of social justice, which states that individuals should assist one another in times of need. Takaful is an Islamic insurance system founded on the principles of mutual assistance and community participation. Takaful operates in two directions one as a cooperative system that enables individuals to pool their funds towards protection against unforeseen losses or disasters, and as an investment tool for the Takaful products are based on Islamic principles, such as Mudarabah, Wakala, Wadiah, Waqf, and hybrid. Takaful participants contribute to a Participant Risk Account (PRA) to support other participants with Tabarru contracts. While the participant account will be invested, accumulated, and refunded in conjunction with the PRA coverage amount at maturity or claim, the PRA will utilize funds for claims and reserves (Che Mohd Salleh et al., 2020).

Healthcare is one of the essential industries that contribute to the well-being of individuals and society. Access to decent health care remains a significant obstacle for many people around the world, particularly in low- and middle-income countries. In this regard, Takaful has played a crucial role in providing health insurance to those who cannot afford it.

Che Mohd Salleh et al. (2020) demonstrated that establishing a Takaful model based on the Waqf principle is one of the most effective ways to assist those in need, particularly flood victims.

Sukuk

Sukuk are a form of interest-free bond like financing. They are issued against assets, and their investors are the true asset owners whose return is derived from the asset rather than the voucher or interest rates (Selim et al., 2019).

Green Sukuk

Green Sukuk, is a Sharia-compliant financial instrument that can be used to support environmentally sensitive projects, the association between green sukuk issuances and renewable energy and green real estate is too strong. Green sukuk can be used to finance a wider array of projects, including solid waste management, sustainable land use, and biodiversity protection (World Bank, 2020). The term "green" indicates that the sukuk complies with green bond requirements and that the revenues are utilized to fund climate change mitigation, adaptation, and environmental programs. Green Sukuk have been rated green in accordance with the Green Bond Principles. Waqf Linked Sukuk, also known as CWLS, is a type of sukuk that is environmentally friendly (Wakaf et al., 2020).

Methodology

This is a comparative study based on secondary data obtained from previously published studies and surveys, as mentioned previously. For the purpose of this study, 19 published papers from different databases were analyzed and aligned with the associated Sustainable development objectives.

Conceptual Model to achieve 2030 Sustainable Development Goals

This research focuses on the importance of Islamic financial instruments including as Islamic ethical wealth management, Islamic financial contracts (Qard hassan, Wadia, Sale base contracts, equity base contracts, takaful, and sukuk) in achieving 2030 sustainability development goals.

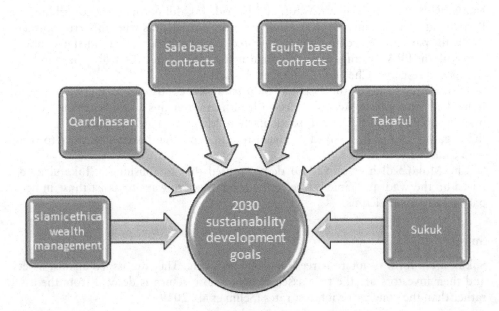

Key findings

IMFI	Effect	Schoolers	Relevant SDG
Waqf	• Charitable endowment in which a parcel, building, or piece of land is gifted. • Decrease poverty. • Financing at affordable prices for the lower middle class. • Having a macroeconomic impact on economic growth. • CWLS is characterized as a green sukuk model.	Jan et al. (2021) Wakaf et al. (2020) Rohman et al. (2021)	Goal 1 Goal 4 Goal 8 Goal 15 Goal 17
Zakat	• An obligatory donation given to certain category. • Mitigation of natural disasters, infectious illnesses, desertification, and drought. • Create projects that support the needy and the disadvantaged. • Economic empowerment of women • Start-up capital for small firms, for education, health, and other emergency purposes	Anis and Kassim (2016) Hassanain et al. (2016)	Goal 1 Goal 2 Goal 8 Goal 3 Goal 5 Goal 4
Sadaqa	• Money that can be spent to assist those with limited financial resources. • Voluntary offering of something with no expectation of receiving anything in return.	Rabbani et al. (2021) Jan et al. (2021)	Gool 1 Goal 4 Goal 8
Qard Hassan	• Assistance for the impoverished. • Provided to farmers for their supplies and then repay after harvesting. • Facilitation of land acquisition and the assurance of food security	Hassanain et al. (2016) Akanmu Popoola et al. (n.d.)	Goal 1 Goal 2 Goal 8
Green Sukuk	• Renewable energy and green real estate	World Bank 2020	Goal 7 Goal 15
Murabaha	• Provides interest-free access to assets.	Akanmu Popoola et al. (n.d.)	Goal 8 Goal 12 Goal17
Musharaka	• Partnership contract, share profit and losses. • Risk management solution. • Equal Rights and responsibilities to oversee the project's progress. • Tool for empowering the poor. • Support small firms and favorably influence the economy.	Rohman et al. (2021) Islam and Ahmad, (n.d.) Rabbani et al. (2021)	Goal 1 Goal 8 Goal 10 Goal 17

(continued)

Key findings Continued

IMFI	Effect	Schoolers	Relevant SDG
Mudaraba	• Tool for empowering the poor. • Enhance the social, economic, and financial well-being. • Large effect on the welfare of rural households, particularly on their income (Fianto et al., 2018). • Support small firms and favorably influence the economy. • Encouraged SMEs startup. • Increase one's self-esteem. • Creates job chances. • Increases spending. • Investments in various infrastructures, including real estate, equipment. • Help the economy get back to normal	Rohman et al. (2021) Akanmu Popoola et al. (n.d.) Islam and Ahmad (n.d.) Rabbani et al., (2021)	Goal 1 Goal 8 Goal 10 Goal 17
Diminishing Musharaka	• Income distribution in society • Socioeconomic standing of the poor. • Sustainable method of alleviating poverty. • Gives the poor ownership of tangible assets. • Improve the economic performance of customers. • Livelihoods approach. • Empower the poor to face economic vulnerabilities and shocks while improving their financial status.	Saad and Razak (n.d.) Islam and Ahmad (n.d.)	Goal 1 Goal 17
Salam	• Provide Indonesia with sustainable food security. • Assist the farmers in cultivating food on productive land. • Solution to maintain the deteriorating agriculture sector. • Relieving financial strain and supporting agriculture economy. • Contracting parties and society will flourish. • Agriculture is primary source of income, food supply, employment, market, and industries.	Wakaf et al. (2020) Ogunbado and Ahmed (2015) Ogunbado and Ahmed (2015) Mohammed et al. (2016) Rabbani et al. (2021)	Goal 2 Goal 8 Goal 9 Goal 12
Istisna	• Advantageous to the real economy • "Istisna" Sukuk could finance infrastructure projects. • Istisna'a is a construction contract. • Two parties, one party make and sell a specified product at a predetermined price paid in advance by the other party. • Do not involve public debt and do not require interest payments.	Manzoor et al. (2017) Selim et al. (2019)	Goal 2 Goal 8 Goal 9 Goal 17

(continued)

Key findings Continued

IMFI	Effect	Schoolers	Relevant SDG
	• Increase monetary policy, raise output and employment, reduce government debt and interest payments, free up cash for public spending, continue economic growth, and prevent domestic resources from being utilized to pay overseas debts.		
Ijara	• Provide shelter. • Benefit the economy. • Enhance the infrastructure.	Rabbani et al. (2021)	Goal 8
Takaful	• Protection against unforeseen losses or disasters. • Investment tool for the participants. • Assist those in need, particularly flood victims.	Che Mohd Salleh et al. (2020)	Goal 3 Goal 8 Goal 17

Discussion

This study focuses on how Islamic banking and finance contribute to achieving sustainable development objectives. According to numerous studies, Islamic banking and finance contribute to the achievement of 12 of the 17 2030 sustainability goals, with seven Islamic finance products contributing to the first goal of poverty alleviation. Four products contributed to the removal of hunger with the aim of promoting health and well-being; zakat and Takaful were the two products directly involved. Then, three products contributed to the achievement of goal 4 of quality education. Only zakat contributes to the goal of gender equality. The only product that contributed to goal 7 of affordable and clean energy was green sukuk. Almost all Islamic products contributed to goal 8 of decent work and economic growth, which is supported by the Islamic moral of eliminating and prohibiting interest, which destroys the economy. Salm and Istisna both contributed to goal 9 of Industry, innovation, and infrastructure, Musharak and Mudarab to goal 10 of Reducing inequality, Musharaka and Salam to goal 12 of Responsible consumption and production, Waqf and Green Sukuk to goal 15 of Life on Land, and Islamic products to goal 17 of Partnerships.

Limitations and Recommendations

The study concentrated on the global contribution of Islamic finance, mapping it to the 17 SDGs. For more research, the scope of the study might be expanded to include Islamic banks' financing methods by country to evaluate their particular contribution to achieving sustainable development goals by mapping it to the targets 169.

In order to establish a connection between Islamic banks and the SDGs, Islamic bank stakeholders must first comprehend the significance of the SDGs and prioritize investments in economic activities that should have an impact on the SDGs. In addition, Islamic institutions can diversify their portfolio investment strategies to incorporate industries that support the Sustainable Development Goals.

Conclusion and Recommendations

Islamic microfinance has been identified as a viable method for alleviating poverty and facilitating sustainable development. This type of microfinance is based on the concept of "profit and risk sharing" and is an ethical alternative to traditional lending practices. By providing access to a range of financial services, Islamic microfinance can support the development of small and medium-sized enterprises, increase employment opportunities, and help individuals and communities become economically self-sufficient and reduce poverty. Moreover, Islamic microfinance has the potential to reduce inequality and promote gender equality by providing access to financial services to those who are traditionally excluded from mainstream banking. Therefore, Islamic microfinance can play a significant role in the sustainable development of Muslim societies around the world, by promoting economic growth, reducing poverty, and improving the economic situation of individuals and societies.

References

Akanmu Popoola, M., Muili, S., Olayekin, A. S., and Olawale, S. M. (2021). Effects of Islamic Finance Principles on Cooperative Societies in OSUN state Nigeria Effect of COVID-19 Outbreak on Socioeconomic Development in Nigeria view project Global Platform to Showcase your Research view Project Effects of Islamic Finance Principles on Cooperative Societies in OSUN State Nigeria, 9(4), 9–24. https://www.researchgate.net/publication/352538683

Anis, F. M., and Kassim, S. H. (2016). Effectiveness of zakat-based programs on poverty alleviation and economic empowerment of poor women: a case study of Bangladesh. *Journal of Islamic Monetary Economics and Finance*, 1(2), 229–258.

Che Mohd Salleh, M., Razali, S. S., Megat Laksana, N. N., Che Embi, N. A., and Abdullah, N. I. (2020). Developing a sustainable model of waqf-based takaful for flood victims in Malaysia. *Journal of Islamic Accounting and Business Research*, 11(9), 1941–1952. https://doi. org/10.1108/JIABR-10-2016-0114

Fianto, B. A., Gan, C., Hu, B., and Roudaki, J. (2018). Equity financing and debt-based financing: Evidence from Islamic microfinance institutions in Indonesia. *Pacific Basin Finance Journal*, 52, 163–172. https://doi.org/10.1016/j.pacfin.2017.09.010

Hassanain, K., Elrahman, A., and Saaid, E. (2016). Zakah for poverty alleviation: evidence from sudan. *International Research Journal of Finance and Economics*, 83–103. http://www.internationalresearchjournaloffinanceandeconomics.com

Indicators, S. D. G. (2017). Revised list of global Sustainable Development Goal indicators. New York: United Nations.

Islam, R., and Rubi A. (2022). Incorporation of Mudarabah, Musharakah and Musharakah Mutanaqisah with Microfinance: A Sustainable Livelihood Approach to Poverty Alleviation. *Journal of Economic Cooperation & Development*, 43(1), 1–29.

Jan, A., Mata, M. N., Albinsson, P. A., Martins, J. M., Hassan, R. B., and Mata, P. N. (2021). Alignment of islamic banking sustainability indicators with sustainable development goals: policy recommendations for addressing the covid-19 pandemic. *Sustainability (Switzerland)*, 13(5), 1–38. https://doi.org/10.3390/su13052607

Manzoor, D., Karimirizi, M., and Mostafavisani, A. (2017). Financing infrastructure projects based on risk sharing model: istisna sukuk. *Islamic Research Journal of Emerging Economies and Islamic Research*, 5(3), 72–84. www.jeeir.com

Mohammed, A. I., Ogunbado, A. F., and Bashir, A. (2016). The viability of salam finance in the growth of agricultural production in Kano State, Nigeria. *Asian Journal of Multidisciplinary Studies*, 4, 2348–7186. www.ajms.co.in

Muneeza, A., and Mustapha, Z. (2021). Islamic ethical wealth and its strategic solutions to 'zero hunger' scheme. In Islamic Wealth and the SDGs (pp. 273–303). Springer International Publishing. https://doi.org/10.1007/978-3-030-65313-2_14

Ogunbado, A. F., and Ahmed, U. (2015). Bay' Salam as an Islamic financial alternative for agricultural sustainability in Nigeria. *Journal of Islamic Economics Banking and Finance*, 11(4), 63–75. https://doi.org/10.12816/0024789

Rabbani, M. R., Asad, M., Ali, M., Rahiman, H. U., Atif, M., Zulfikar, Z., and Naseem, Y. (2021). The response of Islamic financial service to the COVID-19 pandemic: The open social innovation of the financial system. *Journal of Open Innovation: Technology, Market, and Complexity*, 7(1), 85.

Rohman, P. S., Fianto, B. A., Ali Shah, S. A., Kayani, U. N., Suprayogi, N., and Supriani, I. (2021). A review on literature of Islamic microfinance from 2010–2020: lesson for practitioners and future directions. *Heliyon* 7(12), e08549.

Saad, N. M., and Razak, D. A. (2013). Towards an application of Musharakah Mutanaqisah principle in Islamic microfinance. *International Journal of Business and Society*, 14(2), 221–234.

Sachs, J. D. (2015). The age of sustainable development. Columbia University Press, 44(12), 2500–2502. doi:10.1108/IJSE-08-2016-0224

Selim, M., Hasan, K., and Rahman, M. (2019). Financing super-infrastructure using Istisna-Sukuk based monetary policy for faster economic development. *Journal of Economic Cooperation and Development*, 40(4), 139–161.

Sustainable Development Goals | United Nations Development Programme. 2020. Undp. Org. 2020. https://www.undp.org/sustainable-development-goals?utm_source=EN&utm_medium=GSR&utm_content=US_UNDP_PaidSearch_Brand_English&utm_campaign=CENTRAL&c_src=CENTRAL&c_src2=GSR&gclid=Cj0KCQjwwtWgBhDhARIsAEMcxeB1Y2zeYVpV8O3CE-TRpwIDwYtxMH5_egjwV7t45Q8YjNj4tvyjEgUaAo-1HEALw_wcB.

Wakaf, J., Islam, E., and Yunita, P. (2020). Cash waqf linked sukuk (CWLS) model: For Indonesia sustainable food security. *Al-Awqaf: Jurnal Wakaf dan Ekonomi Islam*, 13(1), 59–72.

World Bank, Group. (2020). Pioneering the Green Sukuk: Three Years On. Washington, DC: World Bank

26 Impact of Current and Leverage Ratio Towards the Financial Performance of Iraqi Listed Banks

Hassan Kamal Alaaraj[a], Gulnar Sadat Mulla[b], Jeena Ann John[c], and Reem A. Abdalla[d]

Assistant Professor, University of Technology Bahrain, Bahrain

Abstract

Financial decision–makers in the developing countries face a difficult concern regarding the capital structure due to its relationship with many investment decisions. Thus, the performance, continuity and survival of the companies is closely related to their applied financing structure. However, according to the reports generated from the ILO or the International labor organization perspective, the financial inclusion is low in Iraq. Though the Banks do have higher deposits, the influence of these deposits on financial performance is not very clear. The panel data from 2012 to 2022 were extracted from various portals and tested in the SPSS. Canonical correlations weighted estimated linear regression were utilized to examine the hypothesis. The study's result indicates that current asset has an impact towards ROA and ROE. It could be due to their maintenance of the liquidity. Leverage has only impact towards the ROA but its insignificant to ROE. However, the policy makers must provide incentives for banks to issue debt securities. The suggestions for the researchers is to further investigate more variables related to financial performance and the size of banks in both recession and prosper periods.

Keywords

Banks, current asset, Iraq, leverage, ROA, ROE.

Introduction

Financing decisions play a big part in keeping businesses profitable and competition for a very long period of times. Due to the shortage of funds, especially in emerging countries, the task of providing the necessary funds for companies is considered one of the difficult tasks, and this task becomes more difficult in turbulent countries, both security and political.

Financial leverage is a borrowing instrument that results in an amplification of the effect of profits or losses on the investor. In this context, debt ratios are often used in measurement the profitability as it is one of the most vital and helpful tool in assessing the financing structure of an enterprise at a certain date, in terms of its degree of reliance on financing sources, whether internal or external. The higher the debt ratios, the bigger impact for financial leverage to have on the companies' profits (Anozie et al.,

[a]h.alaaraj@utb.edu.bh, [b]mulla@utb.edu.bh, [c]annjohn@utb.edu.bh, [d]r.abdalla@utb.edu.bh

2023). Overall, the less the dependence relies on loans to finance the assets of the companies, the less it is exposed to risks. Because the interest of the loans may lead to the exhaustion of the liquidity necessary to operate their projects (Cuevas-Vargas et al., 2022).

According to Fitch Ratings (2022), the assets of Iraq's banking sector are anticipated to increase over the medium term. The banking industry in Iraq is poor and undeveloped overall. Shortage of trust in the banking system and deficient public awareness of the Islamic finance sector could impede the sector's rate of expansion. The performance of banks is greatly affected by the borrowed funds, as it represents an important source of financing for growth, expansion and development of the banking services. But at the same time, they can increase the risks of banks if they are used ineffectively. Iraqi banks have a high tangible leverage ratio, which indicates a high level of debt relative to their tangible assets Fitch Ratings (2023).

Thus, the performance, continuity and survival of the banks is closely related to their applied financing structure. It has become necessary to carry out studies related to financing and borrowing decisions for companies, and to search for solutions to many potential problems and risks that threaten companies and impair their performance.

Theories

There are several theories focused on analyzing the leverage and the performance of the companies. One of the first who studied that was Modigliani and Miller in 1958, which concluded that the company's value increases continuously when the percentage of debt increases in the capital structure due to the possible tax savings. However, this theory was criticized by others who argued that Modigliani and Miller ignored the cost of financing by debt which may lead the agency and bankruptcy (En and Malek, 2021) (NazimUddin, 2021).

These criticisms of M&M theory led to the development of what is known as the theory of tradeoff balance, which means that the institution compare between positive consequence of the tax savings and the negative consequence caused by bankruptcy (Qayyum and Noreen, 2019). Although the tradeoff theory has long dominated corporate finance methods, the attention has also begun to shift in Pecking order theory that was firstly founded by Donaldson 1961. The theory was then improved by Stewart Myers, who proposed the Pecking order approach to the capital structure. This theory assumes the first preference is to use the internal financing source represented by retained earnings. Otherwise, it resorts to the external financing source if the internal one is insufficient (Aulia and Gandakusuma, 2020). Finally, NazimUddin (2021) stated that Wurgler and Baker developed the theory of timing for the decision to issue shares. Hence, organizations should borrow or issue shares only if the market conditions are favorable.

Literature Review

The results of this paper show that current ratio (CR) has a considerable favorable influence on return on assets (ROA). Data was gathered by using secondary sources, including the 2008–2017 financial statements of eight companies. Financial statements were produced using panel data and were processed using Eviews 9.0 (Zaman, 2021). The research sample was made up of 12 companies that were chosen from Food and Beverages sector that were collected from website of the Indonesia Stock Exchange (BEI) from 2015–2017. Multiple linear regression analysis is the technique employed for testing the hypothesis. The findings indicated that ROA is impacted by CR (Aminah, 2021) and partly affected by CR based on (Damayanti and Chaerudin, 2021). But conversely to those findings, Qamara et al. (2020) found that ROA is not entirely impacted by current ratio. Moreover Othuon et al. (2021) studied the effect of working capital management on financial performance, they used panel data from 2014 to 2018 and a multivariate regression analytic approach. The results demonstrated that ROA has negatively impacted by CR for the company. These resulted in the development of Hypothesis 1; *Current ratio has an effect on the financial performance in terms of ROA* and it will be evaluated through the linear regression.

According to the findings, the CR has little impact on predicting profitable growth. It can be argued that the current ratio reflects the corporation's capacity to encounter its short-term financial commitments on time, which is useful information for investors (Pernamasari et al., 2020). While the liquidity has significant negative effect on the firms' ROE (Li, et al., 2020). From 2013 to 2019, a sample of 134 listed consumer goods in the MENA area was studied by (EL-Ansary and Al-Gazzar, 2021). They found insignificant evident for the effect of NWC on ROE which is consistent with a result of a study by (Nguyen et al., 2023). They argued the explanation for the insignificance of the ROE model might be understood as MENA area financial managers focusing on how to maximize their profit. These resulted in development of Hypothesis 2; *Current ratio has an impact on the financial performance in terms of Return on Equity* and it will be evaluated through the linear regression.

The result of a study by Zelalem (2020) during a 10-year period (2008–2017) for the 5 commercial banks that were chosen shows that Debt Equity Ratio (DER) has a positive effect towards the ROA and ROE. In another study, the data from 40 listed Jordanian enterprises were collected from 2007 through World Bank's website, Kasasbeh (2021), measured the financial performance through the financial leverage. The study's findings revealed the positive effect of LTD ratio on the financial performance represented by ROA. This effect was along the lines of the findings of a study by (Anozie et al., 2023) on the Naijerian oil and gas firms. Conversely to that and based on "Moody's KMV option pricing model", (Gul and Cho, 2019) the effect on default risk was investigated by Gul and Cho (2019) in the Korean manufacturing companies. The logit model developed by Merton (1974) was utilized to measure the probability of default that is the distance to default as a covariant. From 2005 to 2016, the panel data were collected and analyzed to obtain the regression results. Hence, the results attained recommend that the higher default risk is affected by the dominated amount of short-term debt. However, it showed decrease in term of the long-term. This explains the financing of LTD appreciates the paybacks of tax advantage. This also will prove the theory of trade-off to apply the best structure in the capital using the long-term debt. Hypothesis 3; *Leverage ratio has an impact on the financial performance in terms of ROA* and it will be evaluated through the linear regression.

Bunea et al. (2019) tried to identify the financial factors that have a significant impact on the return on equity (ROE) in their study in the Romanian energy industry.

According to the findings, financial leverage is one of the most important ratios for determining ROE. However, several studies investigated the impact of financial leverage on the financial performance in terms of RoE (Aulia and Gandakusuma, 2020) (Gul and Cho, 2019) (Kasasbeh, 2021) (Abdullah and Tursoy, 2021). For instance, a linear regression model was utilized to determine which factors significantly impacted ROE. Supportively the Leverage can have a negative impact towards ROA but a positive impact towards ROE (Nguyen et al., 2019). Similarly, Rahman et al. (2020) amid to find out whether financial leverage affects company's profitability in Bangladesh's listed textile sector. Using the OLS method, this investigation revealed a significant negative relationship between leverage represented by LTD and STD and financial profitability. However, the partial and simultaneous effect of DER on ROE in the automotive companies in Indonesia was found by (Nasution et al., 2019). These results helps in deriving the hypothesis 4; *Leverage ratio has an impact on the financial performance in terms of Return on Equity* and it will be evaluated through the linear regression.

Data and Methodology

Sample

Four banks that are listed on the Iraqi Stock Exchange provided secondary data, which was obtained. Bank of Baghdad, National Bank, Iraqi Investment Bank, and Mansour Bank panel data were used from 2012 to 2022. The performance of the Iraqi banks' finances was evaluated using variables such as current assets and leverage. Each bank that was used in the study had a stock market listing. The ten-year sample was obtained individually by going to the banks and gathering information.

Descriptive Statistics

70% of their cash on hand was maintained, according to Bank of Baghdad's 2018 financial report. Only by having cash on hand did current assistants increase by 4.2% in comparison to 2017. These increases resulted from cash deposits made by the custodians, while at the same time, investment decreased by 3.0%, credit facilities declined by 4.5%, and property and equipment decreased by 10.6%. Due to the cash payments made to the central banks, these negative indicators exist. Compared to other banks, Bank of Baghdad has low Return on Equity and Return of Assets. These could be due to banks retaining excessive cash liquidity inside the bank (Abbas and Hassan, 2022). The estimated capital structure of National Bank of Iraq maintained a positive returns and margin in the year 2022. The working capital was –0.42 and capital expenditure was 0.14 (Wall Street Journal). Compared to 2019, the investment growth has been declined from 118.75% to 74.16% (2021). But the loan growth rate has been inversely increased to 118.67% (2021) from 45.79% (2019). RETURN ON Assets for the Mansour Bank has a tended growth from the year 2025 to 2021. According to Zawya press release 2022, Mansour Bank had an increase of nearly 4. 2 % in return on average equity. The Iraqi investment bank shows stable growth in current assets 0.5 approx. and Leverage 0.9 approx. ROE

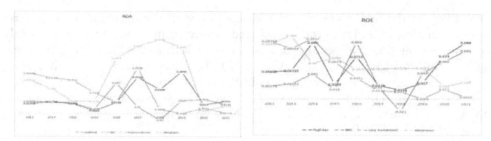

Figure 26.1 ROE and ROA.

has a downward trend compared to ROA. Below shows the Figure 26.1 of ROA and ROE for the period 2012–2021.

Model Fitness

The root mean square error (RMSE), which is stated in the same units as the series itself, is a measurement of how much the actual values of a series deviate from the values predicted by the model. The better the prediction, the lower the RMSE. The result of the RMSE is 0.03 which is closer to zero, indicating it is a good model fit for the study and prediction since a considerable deviance from the residual is explained by the greater RMSE (Padhma, 2021).

Correlation

A statistical measure that illustrates the connection between two variables is correlation. Correlation can be utilized in the context of financial analysis to ascertain the connection between various financial indicators, such as the correlation between current assets and ROA. It is crucial to remember that correlation does not indicate causation. Furthermore, a strong correlation that exists between the two factors does not automatically mean that one factor is the underlying cause of the other. One could compute the correlation coefficient utilizing statistical software or techniques to ascertain the association between current assets and ROA. The study's result indicate that when current asset and leverages are considered to be a controlled variable the correlation between ROA and ROE is very week (0.246). Inversely when the ROA and ROE are controlled variable the correlation between current asset and leverages are very strong at 0.938.

Canonical Correlations

A statistical method called canonical correlation is used to examine the connection between two groups of variables. Thus, to find the linear collection of two groups of variables that have the maximum association with one another is a method of drawing conclusions from cross-covariance matrices. In this study ROA and ROE are grouped in set 1 and CURRENT Asset with leverages in set 2. The scoring value is 2.

Table 26.1: Canonical correlations.

	Correlation	Eigenvalue	Wilks statistic	F	Num D.F	Denom D.F.	Sig.
1	.352	.141	.875	1.243	4.000	72.000	.300
2	.041	.002	.998	.063	1.000	37.000	.804

H0 for Wilks test is that the correlations in the current and following rows are zero

Table 26.1A: Canonical loading.

	Canonical loadings		Cross loadings	
	Set 1	Setn2	Set 1	Set 2
Current asset	0.941	0.34	0.331	0.014
Leverage	0.771	0.637	0.271	0.026
ROA	0.683	0.73	0.24	0.03
ROE	0.902	0.431	0.317	0.018

Wiki lambda test is undertaken to understand the two variance-covariance matrices to the power of 2. As known, the null hypothesis can be rejected when the p-value is below 0.05 or 0.01 we can reject the null hypothesis. From the above Table 26.1 that shows the values are more than 0.01 which indicate there is a correlation existing amongst the variables.

Hair et al. (1998) contend that when given the option, cross loadings are preferable to loadings, which are preferable to weights. Therefore and according to the Table 26.1A, current asset and ROE has the highest loading. Which can be considered that these 2 variables can have the highest effect compared to leverage and ROA.

Weighted Least Square Analysis

Weighted least squares (WLS) is a generalization of ordinary least squares (OLS) and linear regression that incorporates knowledge of the unequal variance of observations (heteroscedasticity) into the regression. The key advantage of WLS versus OLS is that it has the ability to manage regression situations with varied quality data points.

Impact of Current Asset on the ROA

In the Model Summary analysis, the Multiple R of Current Asset to the ROA is 27.1%. R Square indicates that there is only 7 % of the variation in ROA is explained by the

Table 26.2: ANOVA.

	Sum of squares	df	Mean square	F	Sig.
Regression	.006	1	.006	3.004	.091
Residual	.073	38	.002		
Total	.079	39			

Table 26.2A: Coefficients.

	Unstandardized coefficients		Standardized coefficients			
	B	Std. error	Beta	Std. error	t	Sig.
(Constant)	–.006	.020			–.293	.771
CA	.058	.033	.271	.156	1.733	.091

Current Asset. The log – Likelihood functional value is 87.035 which can be considered as a higher value. It could be considered as a best model for the study.

From the above Table 26.2 and 26.2A, the result indicates that there is a significant relation between the Current Asset to ROA at 10% level of significance. In support to the results, the literature review indicated that the current asset have an impact on the ROA (Aminah, 2021). This led to the acceptance of the Hypothesis 1.

Impact of Leverage on the ROA

In the model summary analysis, the multiple R of leverage to the ROA is 26.7%. R square indicates that there is only 7 % of the variation in ROA is explained by the Current Asset. The log – Likelihood functional value is 87.485 which can be considered as a higher value. It could be considered as a best model for the study.

From the above Table 26.3 and 26.3A, the result indicates that there is a significant relation between the Leverage to ROA at 10% level of significance. In support to the results, the literature review indicated that the leverage have an impact on the ROA (Bunea et al., 2019). This led to the acceptance of the Hypothesis 2.

Impact of Leverage on the ROE

In the Model Summary analysis, the Multiple R of Leverage to the ROA is 21.8%. R Square indicates that there is only 4.8% of the variation in ROE is explained by the

Table 26.3: ANOVA.

	Sum of squares	df	Mean square	F	Sig.
Regression	.001	1	.001	2.909	.096
Residual	.016	38	.000		
Total	.017	39			

Table 26.3A: Coefficients.

	Unstandardized coefficients		Standardized coefficients			
	B	Std. Error	Beta	Std. Error	t	Sig.
(Constant)	.019	.006			3.417	.002
LEV	.006	.003	.267	.156	1.706	.096

Table 26.4: ANOVA.

	Sum of Squares	df	Mean Square	F	Sig.
Regression	.003	1	.003	1.903	.176
Residual	.051	38	.001		
Total	.054	39			

Table 26.4A: Coefficients.

	Unstandardized coefficients		Standardized coefficients			
	B	Std. error	Beta	Std. error	t	Sig.
(Constant)	.038	.011			3.553	.001
LEV	.005	.003	.218	.158	1.379	.176

Leverage. The log – Likelihood functional value is 82.306which can be considered as a higher value. It could be considered as a best model for the study.

From the above Table 26.4 and 26.4A, the result indicates that there is no significant relation between the Leverage to ROE at 10%, 5% or 1%. This led to the rejection of the Hypothesis 3. The ROE can be increased only if there is a decrease in Equity. This insignificance may be because highly profitable banks are depending on the internal funds. The ROA will be increased. This finding can be supported by (Jadah et al., 2020). Therefore, LTD is relatively costly resulting in lower bank profitability.

Impact of Current Assets on the ROE

In the Model Summary analysis, the Multiple R of Leverage to the ROE is 26.9%. R Square indicates that there is only 7.2 % of the variation in ROE is explained by the Current Asset. The log – Likelihood functional value is 82.712 which can be considered as a higher value. It could be considered as a best model for the study.

Table 26.5: ANOVA.

	Sum of squares	df	Mean square	F	Sig.
Regression	.002	1	.002	2.954	.094
Residual	.024	38	.001		
Total	.026	39			

Table 26.5A: Coefficients.

	Unstandardized coefficients		Standardized coefficients			
	B	Std. Error	Beta	Std. Error	t	Sig.
(Constant)	.004	.027			.157	.876
CA	.067	.039	.269	.156	1.719	.094

From the above Table 26.5 and 26.5A, the result indicates that there is a significant relation between the Current Assets to ROE at 10%. This led to the acceptance of the Hypothesis 4. In this study, the working capital management techniques used by retail companies in South African are compared to financial performance. The study comes to the conclusion that the financial performance (ROE of the South African retail enterprises was influenced by the methods of working capital management (Mandipa and Sibindi, 2022).

Conclusion and Recommendation

Many studies do not directly examine the current assets of Iraqi banks. The capacity of a bank to cover its short-term obligations with its short-term assets can be determined by looking at its current ratio. Additionally, the liquidity of Iraqi banks can be assessed using the ratio of bank liquid reserves to bank assets. One of the main limitation for the study was the extraction of data from the selected listed banks. The percentages were required to manually convert in order to get the ratio. According to Monetary policy 2020, the values of the Iraqi currency was devalued by 23%. May be this could be the reason that there are weaker correlation between the current assets and financial indicators. In canonical correlations the values are insignificant towards each other. In future the researchers need to identify, the impact of currency devaluation towards the financial performances of the Banking sector.

Reference

Abbas, D. S., and Hassan, A. K. (2022). Indicators analysis of financial soundness, an analytical study on a sample of private banks listed in the Iraq stock. *Al-Qadisiyah Journal for Administrative and Economic Sciences,* 24(3), 207–222.

Abdullah, H., and Tursoy, T. (2021). Capital structure and firm performance: evidence of Germany under IFRS adoption. *Review of Managerial Science,* 15(2), 379–398. DOI: 10.1007/s11846-019-00344-5

Aminah, L. (2021). The effect of current ratio, net profit margin, and return on assets on stock return (Study on food and beverages companies listed on the Indonesia stock exchange 2015–2017 period). *Journal of Management, Accounting, General Finance and International Economic Issues,* 1(1), 1–9. doi: https://ojs.transpublika.com/index.php/Marginal/

Anozie, O. R., Muritala, T. A., Ininm, V. E., and Yisau, N. S. (2023). Impact of capital structure on fnancial performance of oil and gas frms in Nigeria. *Future Business Journal,* 9(1), 1–9. doi:doi.org/10.1186/s43093-023-00186-4

Aulia, H., and Gandakusuma, I. (2020). The effect of capital structure on firm performance of manufacturing companies in ASEAN 5 country. *Advances in Economics, Business and Management Research,* 144, 473–477. doi:10.2991/aebmr.k.200606.080

Bunea, O. L., Corbos, R. A., and Popescu, R. I. (2019). Influence of some financial indicators on return on equity ratio in the Romanian energy sector—a competitive approach using a DuPont-based analysis. *Energy,* 189, 116251. doi:10.1016/j.energy.2019.116251

Cuevas-Vargas, H., Cortés-Palacios, H. A., and Lozano-García, J. J. (2022). Impact of capital structure and innovation on firm performance. direct and indirect effects of capital structure. In The 8th International Conference on Information Technology and Quantitative Management (ITQM 2020 & 2021). (vol. 199, pp. 1082–1089). Elsevier B.V.

Damayanti, E., and Chaerudin, C. (2021). The role of current ratio (CR), debt to equity ratio (DER), and total asset turnover (TATO) on return on asset (ROA) in multi-industrial sector manufacturing companies that registered to the indonesia stock exchange for 2015–2019. *Dinasti International Journal of Management Science,* 2(6), 915–924. doi: https://doi.org/10.31933/dijms.v2i6.921

EL-Ansary, O., and Al-Gazzar, H. (2021). Working capital and financial performance in MENA region. *Journal of Humanities and Applied Social Sciences,* 3(4), 257–280. doi://doi.org/10.1108/JHASS-02-2020-0036

En, J. N., and Malek, A. N. (2021). Capital structure and firm performance of technology of technology sector in Malaysia. *International Journal of Academic Research in Accounting Finance and Management,* 11(3), 601–628. doi:10.6007/IJARAFMS /v11-i3/10660

Gul, S., and Cho, H.-R. (2019). Capital structure and default risk: evidence from Korean stock market. *Journal of Asian Finance, Economics and Business,* 6(2), 15–24. doi:10.13106/jafeb https://www.fitchratings.com/research/non-bank-financial-institutions/iraq-islamic-banks-growth-to-continue-structural-issues-remain-05-07-2022

Hair, J., Anderson, R., Tatham, R. and Black, W. (1998) Multivariate data analysis. 5th Edition, Prentice Hall, New Jersey.

Jadah, H. M., Hassan, A. A., Hameed, T. M., and Al-Husainy, N. H. (2020). The impact of the capital structure on Iraqi banks' performance. *Investment Management and Financial Innovations,* 17(3), 122–132. doi: http://dx.doi.org/10.21511/imfi.17(3).2020.10

Kasasbeh, F. I. (2021). Impact of fnancing decisions ratios on frm accounting-based performance: evidence from Jordan listed companies. *Future Business Journal,* 7(1), 1–10. doi: https://doi.org/10.1186/s43093-021-00061-0

Li, K., Musah, M., Kong, Y., Mensah, I. A., Antwi, S. K., Bawuah, J., and Osei, A. A. (2020). Liquidity and firms' financial performance nexus: panel evidence from non-financial firms listed on the Ghana stock exchange. *Sage Journals,* 10(3), 1–20. doi: https://doi.org/10.1177/2158244020950363

Mandipa, G., and Sibindi, A. B. (2022). Financial performance and working capital management practices in the retail sector: empirical evidence from South Africa. *Risks,* 10(3), 63. doi: https://doi.org/10.3390/risks10030063

Merton, R. C. (1974). On the Pricing of Corporate Debt: The Risk Structure of Interest Rates. *Journal of Finance,* 29(2), 449–470. https://doi.org/10.1111/j.1540-6261.1974.tb03058.x

Nasution, A. E., Putri, L. P., and Dungga, S. (2019). The effect of debt to equity ratio and total asset turnover on return on equity in automotive companies and components in Indonesia. *Advances in Economics, Business and Management Research (AEBMR),* 92, 182–188. (Atlantis Press).

NazimUddin, M. (2021). Leverage structure decisions in Bangladesh: managers and investors' view. *Heliyon,* 7(6), 1–14. doi: https://doi.org/10.1016/j.heliyon.2021.e07341

Nguyen, C. V., Nguyen, T. L., Tran, T. P., and Nghiem, T. T. (2019). The impact of financial leverage on the profitability of real estate companies: A study from Vietnam stock exchange. *Management Science Letters,* 9(13), 2315–2326. doi:10.5267/j.msl.2019.7.023

Nguyen, T. C., Le, A. H., and Nguyen, C. V. (2023). Internal factors affecting the financial performance of an organisation's business processes. *Business Process Management Journal,* 29(5), 1408–1435. doi: https://doi.org/10.1108/BPMJ-10-2022-0486

Othuon, D. O., Gatimbu, K. K., Musafiri, C. M., and Ngetich, F. K. (2021). Working capital management impacts on small-scale coffee wet mills' financial performance in eastern Kenya. *Heliyon,* Sep 1; 7(9). doi: https://doi.org/10.1016/j.heliyon.2021.e07887

Padhma, M. (July 19th, 2023). End-to-end introduction to evaluating regression models. *Data Science Blogathon.* Updated On July 19th, 2023. Merton Retrieved from https://www.analyticsvidhya.com/blog/2021/10/evaluation-metric-for-regression-models/

Pernamasari, R., Budyastuti, T., and Putri, L. (2020). Predicting the profit growth with financial ratio: study at real estate and property companies listed in Indonesia stock exchange. In First

Annual Conference of Economics, Business, and Social Science, ACEBISS. Indonesia. DOI: 10.4108/eai.26-3-2019.2290686

Qamara, T., Wulandari, A., Sukoco, A., and Suyono, J. (2020). The influence of current ratio, debt to equity ratio, and total asset turnover ratio on profitability of transportation companies listed on the Indonesia stock exchange 2014–2018. *International Journal of Integrated Education, Engineering, and Business,* 3(2), 81–93. doi: https://doi.org/10.29138/ijieeb.v3i2.1169

Qayyum, N., and Noreen, U. (2019). Impact of capital structure on profitability: a comparative study of Islamic and conventional banks of Pakistan. *Journal of Asian Finance, Economics and Business,* 6(4), 65–74. doi: 10.13106/jafeb.2019.vol6.no4.65

Rahman, M. M., Saima, F. N., and Jahan, K. (2020). The impact of financial leverage on firm's profitability: an empirical evidence from listed textile firms of Bangladesh. *Asian Journal of Business Environment,* 10(2), 23–31. doi:10.13106/jbees.2020.vol10.no2.23

Zaman, M. B. (2021). Influence of debt to total asset ratio (DAR) current ratio (CR) and total asset turnover (TATO) on return an asset (ROA) and its impact on stock prices on mining companies on the Indonesia stock exchange in 2008–2017. *Journal of Industrial Engineering and Management Research,* 2(1), 114–132. DOI: https://doi.org/10.7777/jiemar

Zelalem, D. (2020). The impact of financial leverage on the performance of commercial banks: evidence from selected commercial banks in Ethiopia. *International Journal of Accounting Finance and Risk Management,* 5(1), 62–68. DOI: 10.11648/j.ijafrm.20200501.16

27 Examine the Impact of Sustainable CSR on Client Satisfaction and Commitment to Islamic Financial Institutions using Carroll's Dimension Model

Gulnar Sadat Mulla[a], Reem Abdalla[b], and Hassan Kamel Al Aaraj[c]

University of Technology, Bahrain

Abstract

The aspiration of this exploration is to assess how clients of Financial Institutions following the Sharia law in the Kingdom of Bahrain perceive the relationship between CSR models. The study examines the impact of different confines of CSR, including economic, ethical, social, and philanthropic values, on client satisfaction and commitment. An aggregate of 204 arbitrary repliers, who are clients of named IFIs, were shared in the study. The data was anatomized using SPSS 20 to test the suppositions. The results indicate that the CSR confines bring a solid and deep influence on client satisfaction and commitment. Specifically, philanthropic and social values were set up to have significant and positive connections, while ethical and economic values showed connections which are a negative affect on CSR. The study highlights the significance of conducting mindfulness and social conditioning to enhance client satisfaction and commitment and alleviate agency problems in IFIs. The findings hold applicability for employers of banks and directors in introducing effective strategies.

Keywords

Commitment, customer satisfaction, economic, ethical, philanthropic, social.

Introduction

Like other conventional entities Islamic financial entities have undergone significant changes as a result of globalization and deregulation, leading to increased risks for investors. The IFI industry has experienced impressive growth due to the incorporation of Islamic principles into its policies. However, there has been a scarcity of research evaluating the effectiveness of CSR within IFIs. Therefore, there is a pressing need for IFIs to identify effective strategies to enhance CSR in the industry. CSR has gained importance as a concept and is now a subject of concern in various research studies. CSR is said to be the integration of social and environmental issues into business operations on a voluntary basis, reflecting stakeholder perspectives by the Election Commission. CSR is also been considered by World Bank as a means to improve the quality of life by encouraging development within communities and the workforce (Al-Ghamdi et al., 2019). Previous research on customer loyalty in Islamic banks has focused on

[a]mulla@utb.edu.bh, [b]r.abdalla@utb.edu.bh, [c]h.alaaraj@utb.edu.bh

economic and ethical indicators, neglecting the environmental aspect, which is equally important (Uhlig et al., 2020). García-Sánchez et al. (2018) suggested that businesses with strong environmental practices are more attractive to stakeholders. The sustainability and functioning of the banking sector are heavily influenced by various aspects of CSR (Fatma and Khan, 2023). Implementing CSR activities can help banks gain a competitive advantage by attracting customers (Shah and Khan, 2019). Research has also shown that incorporating CSR aspects can increase a company's value (Chung et al., 2018). The social exchange theory explains how CSR initiatives, such as charitable donations, environmental protection, adherence to ethical labor practices, and compliance with laws, benefit companies by attracting and retaining consumers through reciprocity and positive word-of-mouth. When communicated effectively, CSR actions foster a strong sense of identification between consumers and companies or brands (Kim et al., 2019).

Bank managers should recognize that CSR is not an additional activity but a core function of the business that requires sufficient attention (Kumar et al., 2022). Integrating CSR initiatives into core operations is crucial for long-term success, benefiting both social and financial performance (Fatma and Khan, 2023).

Literature Review

Economic and CSR Values

In this study, the financial health of Saudi banks was compared to CSR strategies. (Ahmad-Amraji et al., 2021). To examine Zakat, the ratio of net income, and its usage as a stand-in for CSR, they analyzed financial information from 2014 to 2019. According to the report, clients are devoted to banks because of their CSR efforts (Szegedi et al., 2020).

H1: *Economic values negatively affect the CSR activities carried out by IFIs.*

CSR and Ethical

Religious people are significantly more interested in an ethical investment than financial accumulation. By forbidding all varieties of Riba from making ethical investments, this may be accomplished (Szegedi et al., 2020).

H2: *Ethical principles have a detrimental effect on the CSR activities carried out by IFIs.*

The Social Values of CSR

To determine if IFIs are concerned with societal concerns, the perception of managers working for IFIs was put to the test. It became clear from the interviews that CSR was not properly implemented in IFIs. Future difficulties would result from this, and effective collaboration between Islamic and conventional banks was required to improve global welfare to the Pareto optimal level (Ali Aribi and Arun, 2015).

H3: *Social values have a favorable influence on the CSR activities carried out by IFIs.*

CSR and Philanthropic

Provides an in-depth understanding of Islamic banking, its restrictions, and the financial instruments employed. In order to assess the Sharia disclosures made by Sharia in 2017, this study examined the annual reports of Nigeria. They discovered that Banks A and B did not adhere to Sharia in exactly the same way. This article suggested further laws for safeguarding investor and societal behavior using the view of the boards of directors of 159 banks in 9 countries.

Contributions to society can take many various forms, such as funding for institutions, constructing houses for the underprivileged, protecting the environment, etc. Korean businesses understood the value of CSR but were reluctant to invest (Chung et al., 2018).

H4: Philanthropic principles have a beneficial effect on the CSR activities carried out by IFIs.

CSR, Client Commitment and Satisfaction

The brand commitment and loyalty of banks are positively impacted by ethical business practices. Their needs are met, and they will continue to support the brand (Kumar et al., 2022; Fatma and Khan, 2023; Singh and Singh, 2016).

Data and Variables

Study Sample

The responses are taken from the customers of IFIs who are directly involved in the usage of CSR practices in Islamic Finance. According to CBB Report 2018, there are 102 financial institutions in Bahrain. The questionnaire, the most widely used tool was used to collect data, in especially social science research.

Dependent Variable

The satisfaction of customers is the result of cognitive and emotive evaluation based on overall consumption and purchase, where some assessment is generally correlated with genuinely evident performance (Davies, 2006).

According to (Gramer and Brown 2006), loyalty is the degree to which a customer consistently engages in good transactions with and utilizes the services of the same supplier. He consistently transacts with the same seller.

Independent Variable

According to a survey carried out in Lithuania by Ernst & Young, the value of the economy has a long-term impact on CSR. It assessed the level of CSR maturity at which the participating businesses operated. The businesses that practiced CSR produced the highest levels of economic returns. Its reputation and relationship were judged to be favorable. Achieving economic value through moral accountability. The ethical path will assist in achieving high financial performance and CSR in businesses, claims research by EY. The Sharia Board shall authorize the financial services and products provided by IFIs in order to safeguard clients from the IFIs' dishonest business practices.

Social value: Every organization owes a duty to the community. IFI CSR activities ought to further a social cause the results are presented in Table 27.2. Through its Qard Al-Hassan accounts, which are utilized to aid the underprivileged and combat poverty, IFI may provide social value (Muhammad Ayub, 2007).

Corporate philanthropy is a means for organizations to reflect their actions through their corporate social responsibility, according to Carroll (1979) from the Figure 27.1 presents the conceptual framework of dependent and independent variable.

Methodology and Model Specifications

Model Specifications

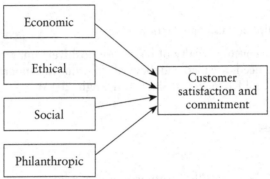

Figure 27.1 Conceptual framework.

Table 27.1: Reliability Statistics.

Reliability Statistics		
Cronbach's Alpha	Cronbach's Alpha Based on Standardized Items	No of Items
.894	.895	5

Table 27.1 after calculating Cronbach's Alpha Coefficient for all possible variables, shows the reliability findings. Because Cronbach's Alpha was 0.894, it is clear that the study scales have very good dependability. If we do an exploratory or pilot investigation, reliability is supposed to be equal to or above 0.60 (Straub & Gefen, 2004).

Table 27.2: Chi-Square.

	Test Statistics				
	EV	SV	ECV	PV	CSL
Chi-Square	183.265a	174.882a	111.000b	127.310c	185.824d
Asymp. Sig.	.000	.000	.000	.000	.000

After calculating Cronbach's Alpha Coefficient for all possible variables, shows the reliability findings. Because Cronbach's Alpha was 0.894, it is clear that the study scales have very good dependability. If we do an exploratory or pilot investigation, reliability is supposed to be equal to or above 0.60 (Straub & Gefen, 2004).

Empirical Results

Correlation

Table 27.3: Correlation.

	Ethical	Social	Economical	Philanthropic
Ethical	1			
Social	.785**	1		
Economical	.763**	.908**	1	
Philanthropic	.409**	.553**	.533**	1
Customer Satisfaction and Loyalty	.353**	.538**	.493**	.948**

**. Correlation is significant at the 0.01 level (2-tailed).

The direction, intensity, and significance of the bivariate correlations between all the variables that were assessed at an interval or ratio level will be shown by a Pearson correlation matrix (Mohamed Ahmed Zaid, 2015). By analyzing how one variable changes when another variable similarly changes, the correlation is determined. According to Table 27.4, charitable giving has a 0.948 association with customer happiness and loyalty.

Regression

Table 27.4: Model summary.

Model	R	R Square	Adjusted R Square	Std. Error of the Estimate
1	.953a	.908	.906	.26684

The predictors in the analysis included Ethical Values, Social Values, Economic Values, and Philanthropic Values, with the constant as the reference point.

The correlation coefficient is a standardized measure that ranges between –1 and +1, indicating the strength and direction of the association between variables (Mohamed Ahmed Zaid, 2015). When the correlation coefficient (r) is significantly different from 0, whether positively or negatively, it indicates a stronger relationship between the variables. Conversely, when r is close to 0, it suggests a weak relationship between the variables. In this case, Table 27.4 regression a correlation coefficient of r = 0.953 indicates a strong association between the two variables (Schober et al., 2018).

Total Variance

Table 27.5: Total variance explained.

Component	Initial Eigenvalues			Extraction Sums of Squared Loadings		
	Total	% of Variance	Cumulative %	Total	% of Variance	Cumulative %
1	3.529	70.574	70.574	3.529	70.574	70.574
2	1.079	21.577	92.150	1.079	21.577	92.150
3	.253	5.063	97.213			
4	.094	1.883	99.096			
5	.045	.904	100.000			

Extraction Method: Principal Component Analysis.

This would be a strong candidate for component analysis because of the relatively significant correlations between the items. Remember that the purpose of the component analysis is to use fewer (latent) variables to model the connections between items. The eigenvalues Table 27.5 total variance revealed that the variation was accounted for by a two-component structure with a total of two eigenvalues greater than one (3.529, and 1.079). Ahmad-Amraji et al. (2021) reports the same outcomes.

Test of Hypothesis

Table 27.6: Coefficients.

Model	Unstandardized Coefficients		Standardized Coefficients Beta	t	Sig.
	B	Std. Error			
1 (Constant)	.375	.093		4.015	.000
Ethical	−.125	.039	−.115	−3.216	.002
Social	.220	.058	.211	3.760	.000
Economic	−.104	.053	−.104	−1.974	.050
Philanthropic	.906	.025	.934	35.831	.000

a. Dependent Variable: Customer Satisfaction and Loyalty

In Table 27.6 coefficients, negative significance for Ethical (−0.125) and Economic Value (−.104) may imply that a rise in one dimension may tend to decrease consumer happiness and loyalty. The B Value displays an estimated slope. When the p-value is significant (.000), the null hypothesis should be rejected in its entirety (Schober et al., 2018).

Conclusion

Except for adhering to Shariah legal requirements regarding product offers, Islamic financial institutions are like conventional commercial banks. They operate according to the same standards as other financial firms in the banking, capital markets, and insurance industries. They must, however, abide by Islamic law, which forbids Riba transactions and necessitates financial expenditures toward legal pursuits. The financial sector which is Islamic has its own set of international prudential guidelines and regulations. The funds dedicated to conventional banking activities and those committed to Islamic banking activities must be kept apart, as guaranteed and made public by conventional banks that intend to offer Islamic products. Similar to other Islamic financial organizations, those in Bahrain are governed by moral standards derived from Shariah law. These principles forbid investing in activities that are not permitted by Shariah and interest-based transactions. It is expected of Islamic financial organizations to explain their ethical principles to their constituents. According to research on CSR and Islamic financial institutions conducted in Bahrain, these organizations fall short of the moral and social standards that Shariah principles imply. (Ali Aribi and Arun, 2015). Agency issues will result from managers who make investments that are not consistent with Shariah. In order to lessen agency issues, it is crucial to develop positive ethical and social interactions (Safieddine, 2009).

References

Ahmad-Amraji, L., Jafarzadeh-Kenarsari, F., Abouzari-Gazafroodi, K., Leyli, E. K., and Soleimani, R. (2021). Translation, Cultural Adaptation, and Psychometric Features of the Persian Version of the Copenhagen Multi-Centre Psychological Infertility-Fertility Problem Stress Scales (COMPI-FPSS). *Journal of Pharmaceutical Research International*, 41–50. https://doi.org/10.9734/jpri/2020/v32i4431079.

Al-Ghamdi, S. A. A., and Badawi, N. S. (2019). Do corporate social responsibility activities enhance customer satisfaction and customer loyalty? Evidence from the Saudi banking sector. *Cogent Business & Management*, 6(1). https://doi.org/10.1080/23311975.2019.1662932.

Ali Aribi, Z., and Arun, T. (2015). Corporate Social Responsibility and Islamic Financial Institutions (IFIs): Management Perceptions from IFIs in Bahrain. *Journal of Business Ethics*, 129(4), 785–794. https://doi.org/10.1007/s10551-014-2132-9

Carroll, A. B. (1979). A Three-Dimensional Conceptual Model of Corporate Performance. *The Academy of Management Review*, 4(4), 497. https://doi.org/10.2307/257850

Chuang, H. (2020). The Impacts of institutional ownership on stock returns. *Empirical Economics*, 58(2), 507–533.

Chung, C. Y., Jung, S., and Young, J. (2018). Do CSR Activities Increase Firm Value? Evidence from the Korean Market. *Sustainability*, 10(9), 3164. https://doi.org/10.3390/su10093164.

Davies, B. (2006). Processes Not Plans Are the Key to Strategic Development. *Management in Education*, 20(2), 11–15. https://doi.org/10.1177/089202060602000204

Fatma, M., and Khan, I. (2023). CSR influence on brand loyalty in banking: the role of brand credibility and brand identification. *Sustainability*, 15(1), 802. https://doi.org/10.3390/su15010802.

García-Sánchez, I., Martínez-Ferrero, J., and García-Meca, E. (2018). Board of Directors and CSR in Banking: The Moderating Role of Bank Regulation and Investor Protection Strength. *Australian Accounting Review*, 28(3), 428–445. https://doi.org/10.1111/auar.12199.

Gramer, and Brown. (2006). Customer loyalty as competitive advantage. Jakarta: Erlangga.

Kim, H., Youn, S., and Lee, D. (2019). The effect of corporate social responsibility reputation on consumer support for cause-related marketing. *Total Quality Management & Business Excellence*, 30(5–6), 682–707. https://doi.org/10.1080/14783363.2017.1332482

Kumar, V., Khan, I., Fatma, M., and Singh, A. (2022). Engaging luxury brand consumers on social media. *Journal of Consumer Marketing*, 39(1), 121–132. https://doi.org/10.1108/JCM-10-2020-4175.

Mohamed Ahmed Zaid. (2015). Correlation and Regression Analysis. Organisation of Islamic Cooperation Statistical Economic and Social Research and Training Centre for Islamic Countries.

Muhammad Ayub. (2007). Understanding Islamic Finance. John Wiley and Sons.

Safieddine, A. (2009). Islamic financial institutions and corporate governance: New insights for agency theory. *An International Review*, 17(2), 142–158.

Schober, Boer C, Schwarte LA. 2018. "Correlation coefficients: Appropriate use and interpretation." Pubmed 1763–1768.

Shah, S. S. A., and Khan, Z. (2019). Corporate social responsibility: A pathway to sustainable competitive advantage? *International Journal of Bank Marketing*, 38(1), 159–174. https://doi.org/10.1108/IJBM-01-2019-0037

Singhal, R., and Rana, R. (2015). Chi-square test and its application in hypothesis testing. *Journal of the Practice of Cardiovascular Sciences*, 1(1), 69. https://doi.org/10.4103/2395-5414.157577

Singh, A., and Singh, M. (2016). Cross country co-movement in equity markets after the US financial crisis. *Journal of Indian Business Research*, 8(2), 98–121. https://doi.org/10.1108/JIBR-08-2015-0089

Straub, D., Boudreau, M.-C. and Gefen, D. (2004). Validation guidelines for IS positivist research. *Communications of the Association for Information Systems*, 380–427.

Szegedi, K., Khan, Y., and Lentner, C. (2020). Corporate Social Responsibility and Financial Performance: Evidence from Pakistani Listed Banks. *Sustainability*, 12(10), 4080. https://doi.org/10.3390/su12104080

Uhlig, M. R. H., Mainardes, E. W., and Nossa, V. (2020). Corporate social responsibility and consumer's relationship intention. *Corporate Social Responsibility and Environmental Management*, 27(1), 313–324. https://doi.org/10.1002/csr.1807.

28 Sustainable Management in Higher Technical Education—Need for Internationalism

Shyamrao V Gumaste[1,a], Ilona Paweloszek[2,b], and Narendra Kumar[3,c]

[1]Department of Information Technology, MET's Institute of Engineering, Bhujbal Knowledge City, Adgaon, Nashik, Maharashtra, India, Savitribai Phule Pune University, Pune, Maharashtra, India
[2]Faculty of Management Science, Czestochowa University of Technology, Czestochowa, Poland
[3]Faculty of Applied Science and Technology, NIET, NIMS University, Delhi–Jaipur Road, Jaipur, Rajasthan, India

Abstract

Higher Technical Education in the need of an hour for developing and development nations to sustain and upgrade itself in this competitive era and to increase GDP. This paper mainly describes the technical education in ancient India relating today's higher education thereby supporting the need of sustainability of education.

Keywords

Curriculum, global village, management, technical education.

Introduction

Higher Education is a backbone of any country for it is development in the era of Information Technology. Only concepts of Information Technology are insufficient to improve the Higher Education. As Higher Education is a vast one, it needs management techniques and skills to manage the scenario as well producing fruitful outcomes. Indian Higher Education undergoes many periods like various cultures: ancient, mediaeval, colonial, post-independence and contemporary. In this expedition, English education structure too gets a position. Institutions of tertiary education are regarded as the most significant body of cultural transformation, social change and above all the whole improvement of the country. Hence, it is the need of an hour to look for sustainable administration of tertiary technical learning for the expedition of tertiary education, from beginning till date is need to be considered while managing the system. In India, ancient educational system in the Vedic era to the post-colonial era is worth enough for a study. The noteworthy transformation in Indian tertiary education was made possible due the initiatives of colonial masters which made an impact both in progressive and destructive ways. Therefore, it is essential to study the cause and pros

[a]svgumaste@gmail.com, [b]ilona.paweloszek@pcz.pl, [c]drnk.cse@gmail.com

especially on the historic progression of tertiary education curriculum in India from ancient times to the present.

Higher Education sector is the most significant aspect of educational system of a nation. Most nations spend more than 5% of GDP to their educational sector. Expanding educational system in terms of size and innovation is thrust area of policy making all over the world.

One major sign of the expansion of the system of Tertiary Education is Gross Enrolment Ratio (GER) which simply means that the total percent of enrolment between ages 18 and 30 in higher education of whole population of a certain nation. Many of the advanced countries hold a inflated GER in higher education of more than thirty percentage (Mukhopadhyay, 1999).

Literature Review

While going with how education system is managed in ancient days.

Education During Buddhist Period

1. Taxila/ Takshshila: It was the most recognised Buddhist centre of wisdom of tertiary education. The Greek travellers, namely, Stravo and Arian had discoursed upon the prosperity of Takshshila. It was popular mainly for the schools of Medicine, Astrology, Law and Military Science and Agriculture that had attained an admiration as a great centre of learning by the mid of the 6th century enticing scholars from various parts of the subcontinent. There was a considerable number of Acharyas and each one of them had a responsibility of educating over a hundred pupils. As the acharyas treated their students equally, there was no question of discrimination the basis of caste, creed etc (Agarwal, 2006).
2. The universities of Nalanda, Vikramshila and Vallabhi: These universities were seen as the ancient significant hubs of Indian universities. Nalanda University situated in Bihar was famous for Buddhist studies. It drew scholars even from China, Nepal, Tibet and Korea as it was considered as a centre of learning for knowledge seekers of higher studies. The University curriculum included a extensive variety of topics. The Vallabhi University of Gujarat, was a competitor of Nalanda for it gave special attention to Hinayana Buddhism as compared to Nalanda which rather a proclivity for Mahayana Buddhism. This learning centre encouraged all faces of higher education from diverse religious systems. To sum up the features of ancient Indian educational system, between 1500 and 1000 B.C, the Rigveda was regarded as the centre of the teaching system which was verbally composed by the religious communities midst the Aryans. Thereafter followed a composition of three more Vedas, namely: Sama Veda, Yajur Veda and Atharva Veda (Basu, 1991).

Higher Education During Mediaeval Period in India

The Mediaeval period in the Indian history is regarded as a key point of socio-cultural amalgamation. The educational history of mediaeval period echoes a wider segment of the study of societal past, social history largely understood through religion, politics and economics (Alam, 1991).

1. The Madrasahs as a System of Education: The 11th century AD witnessed the rise of Madrasahs or colleges as the prominent institutions of tertiary education with a specific intention of promoting religious knowledge.
2. Tertiary Learning in Colonial India: The conventional educational methods were mostly religious and literary in character. The educational system during that period was grounded on early philosophical and religious literature of Sanskrit, Persian and Arabic.

The idea of replicating the model of London Universities on Indian educational system by instituting universities in India can be traced in Sir Charles Wood's Dispatch of 1854 which has been regarded as the Magna Carta of English education in India.

Higher Education Curriculum—International Perspective

It is essential to have sustainable management of higher technical education to share the ideas, to work with mixed culture researchers across the globe. In this direction, it is also essential to view the education curriculum internationally, it is the need of management to involve in the process.

Ralph W Taylor, in his seminal work, 'Basic principles of curriculum and instruction', pointed four major components of curriculum.

i. Setting up of educational objectives.
ii. Identification of relevant subject matter or content.
iii. Selection of suitable instructional strategies appropriate to the content and level of students.
iv. Assessment practices to be followed to check whether or not instructive goals are accomplished (Altbach, 2016).

The Outcomes must also reflect following:

i. Communication
ii. Collaboration
iii. Critical thinking
iv. Problem-solving (Kumar, 2023)
v. Creativity
vi. The management and appreciation of diversity
vii. Learning how to learn.
viii. Teaching learning process.

Challenges

Higher education is confronted with mainly four broad challenges:

i. *The Challenges related to the central pillars of education*
ii. *The degraded quality of teaching and learning process.*
iii. *Limitations on research capacity and innovation.*
iv. *Irregular growth and access to opportunity.*

Five Aspects to Become a Contributing Nation to the Global Village

i.   *Promotion of Research and Innovation*
i.   *University and Community Partnership*
iii. *Emphasis on Skill Development*
iv. *Promoting Open Online Courses*
v.   *Focus on internationalization of higher education*

Curriculum theories: The major agencies and persons for the curriculum formation are learners, teachers, administrators and policy makers. The main stages of curriculum formation are informal discussions and actions of individuals, primary groups and occupational groups.

Objectives of curriculum theory (Young, 2013; Lindén et al., 2017)

i.   *Fixing aims and objectives*
ii. *Specifying the level of learning content*
iii. *Suggesting learning environment*
iv. *Structuring the learning process*
v.   *Specifying different learning experiences to be provided*
vi. *Mentioning evaluation techniques and criteria.*

The nature of curriculum varies corresponding to the nature of various educational systems and level of learning. As per the new educational perspectives in higher education ample curriculum development and effective implementation is highly important. For developing effective curriculum and learning process in tertiary education different theories and a mix of different theories and approaches are useful.

a) *Value-oriented theories.*
b) *Process-oriented theories.*
c) *Structure-Oriented Theories.*

What is Internationalisation of Curriculum?

The aim of internationalisation curriculum should fall beyond increasing the international enrolments inside a classroom. Importance should also be given to raising the self-awareness of an institution's for equipping its students with skills that would enable them to perform efficiently in a globalized world (Schuerholz-Lehr, 2007).

Bearing in mind the diverse backgrounds of the students, a broader notion of internationalisation of the curriculum has been suggested regardless of their national, cultural, ethnic, social class/caste or gender identities to aid them to become competent in an increasingly cooperative culture of communication and hard work (Haigh, 2002).

Internationalisation of the curriculum is, incorporating all understandings, apprising students' affective, attitudinal and cognitive development throughout the period of their tertiary education. It includes a set of principles comprising openness, culturally inclusive behaviour and tolerance. The teachers have greater responsibility of managing and ensuring that cultural variety is meticulously studied and is efficiently employed in the international classroom context (Trahar, 2010).

The concept of intercultural learning is relevant in the internationalization of the curriculum (Knight, 2004; Altbach, 2016; Young, 2013; Lindén et al., 2017;

Accord-on-the-Internationalization-of-Education; Affirming Academic Values in Internationalization of Higher Education; Zhou, 2016; Qiang, 2003).

Need for Internationalism in Higher Education Curriculum

i. *Meeting the demands of a Globalized world*
ii. *Developing a Global citizen*
iii. *For General Goodwill*
iv. *To help people see beyond themselves*
v. *Generate Increased income for universities.*

Why Focus on Internationalization?

The process of internationalizing one's higher education is not a recent development. Early on, a significant number of scholars did extensive travel round Europe; however, during the early modern period, the focus was shifting away from national development to internationalisation. Nevertheless, programs like the Fulbright offer opportunities to Scholars' Programme in the United States and the Erasmus Mundus Programme in Europe. These two programmes have sought to encourage collaboration among institutions of higher education as a means of fostering mutual understanding and promoting the exchange of knowledge. However, in today's world, the quickening pace of globalization has once again brought the topic of student progress, international research alliance, and education as an export business to the forefront of people's minds.

In this day and age, when knowledge and technology are shared all over the world, having a linked network and being aware of the world around you are progressively considered as valuable and sought-after advantages. Institutions are putting a greater emphasis on internationalisation as an outcome of the current state of the labour market, which demands students to possess international, intercultural and foreign language abilities so as to perform effectively in an international situation. The first decade of twentieth century has seen a doubled rate of enrolments of students of higher education outside their home countries (OECD, 2012a); it is speculated that the same pattern would continue in times to come.

On the other hand, student mobility is only the most obvious component of a larger issue, which is known as internationalization and is characterized by its complexity and variety of aspects. One aspect, which is sometimes regarded as "internationalization at home," comprises of inclusion of international and intercultural areas into the programme, teaching methodology, research, and extracurricular activities. This assists learners in honing intercultural and international skills without even exiting their country (OECD, 2004; Wachter, 2003). Other rapidly expanding systems of internationalisation are evolving, such as international education, which is occasionally delivered through overseas campuses, collaborative programs, distance learning etc. These types of internationalisation propose a rather broader approach, particularly in the milieu of tertiary education, which is at present regarded as an essential component of the largescale knowledge economy.

In the field of tertiary education, globalization has significant repercussions, remarkably on the virtual and physical movement of staff and students, information and knowledge, virtual access, as well as the exchange of practices and policies. The countries which are the members of OECD, the shift from higher education being available primarily to an elite population to being available to the general population is nearly complete. Some of these nations are going to face a fall in the number enrolled students from their own nation because the population of the age group ranging from 18 to 25 years old is decreasing. As a result, luring students from other countries is becoming an increasingly popular strategy for making up the difference. Concurrently, there is an ever-expanding need for tertiary education in emerging economies, particularly India, Southeast Asia and China. Internationalisation can also be viewed as a economical substitute to national provision, according to OECD, 2008.

Major Benefits of Internationalization

Students, who, in future would become the world's citizens, scientists and businesspeople, should receive the most applicable education possible, as this is one of the main objectives of internationally oriented tertiary education. Internationalisation should not be regarded as an aim itself; rather, it must be treated as a facilitator for modification and development. It must help produce the abilities that are needed in today's times, encourage novelty, and provide options, and eventually, it should assist stimulate job creation. However, the current state of the economy necessitates a more in-depth investigation of the actual benefits that internationalization brings to economies and society not only within the OECD but also beyond its borders. In contemporary world, internationalisation as a process goes in both directions. It is possible for students to realise their aspirations of pursuing research and obtaining a high-quality education with the help of this resource. It provides students with prospects for pragmatic learning in "real world, real time" in subjects that cannot easily be communicated to them. Besides, institutes may be able to earn a worldwide status in addition to a presence in the international tertiary education community, and they furthermore enhance their aptitude to address the challenges that are connected with globalization. According to Marjolijn, improving student readiness; internationalising the curriculum; increasing the global outline of the institutes; bolstering knowledge production and research and boosting the diversity of both its academics as well as staff are the top five reasons for internationalising an institution.

There is a common understanding that internationalization, when part of a rather comprehensive plan, can provide students, faculty, and institutions considerable advantages. This is the case despite the fact that there are significant differences across countries and institutions in this regard. It can foster strategic thinking that leads to innovation, provide benefits in modernizing pedagogy, increase student and teacher collaboration, and stimulate innovative techniques to assessing students' learning. Students and faculty in tertiary education have the opportunity to broaden their understanding of global concerns and the ways in which educational institutions work in diverse countries, cultural settings, and linguistic backgrounds through the integration of internationalisation into the culture of tertiary education. The majority of technical endeavours can no longer be limited to a single nation because research is already inherently internationalised due to the collaborations and partnerships that occur between different teams. Policymakers face a variety of issues as a result of the numerous facets and the complexity of internationalisation (for example, enhancing mobility flows, ensuring uniform admittance to global learning, safeguarding learners, and ensuring quality assurance. In a similar vein, institutions need to be responsive and continuously orchestrate all of the numerous factors involved so as to obtain the advantages of internationalisation and successfully administer the associated menaces. For instance, internationalization of programs requires refining assistance for learners and providing closer attention to learners who have rather pressing anticipations with respect to the quality of instruction, assessments of students, and the learning atmosphere. Paying special attention to the students having more expectations will certainly help in accomplishment of such goals.

Conclusion

Internationalization is creating a sense of a wider perspective with a view that knowledge is trans boundary in nature for acquiring knowledge from an international perspective. One of the most important aspects of internationalization today is the frame of reference which extends and widens well beyond the local level and even the national level; it is becoming transnational too. Any news about internationalization moves rapidly across the borders. Hence one has to think from all corners to manage the need of an hour for betterment of society as a whole.

References

Accord-on-the-Internationalization-of-Education. https://csse-scee.ca/acde/wp-content/uploads/sites/7/2017/08/Accord-on-the-Internationalization-of-Education.pdf.

Affirming Academic Values in Internationalization of Higher Education. https://iauaiu.net/IMG/pdf/affirming_academic_values_in_internationalization_of_higher education.pdf

Agarwal, P. (2006). Higher education in India: the need for change. Working paper No 180, Indian Council for Research on International Economic Relations.

Alam, M. (1991). Higher education in mediaeval India. In Raza, M. (ed.), Higher Education in India: Retrospect and Prospect. New Delhi: AIU.

Altbach, P. G. (2016). Global Perspectives on Higher Education. Newyork: John Hopkins University Press.

Basu, A. (1991). Higher Education in Colonial India. In Moonis Raza (ed.), Higher Education In India: Retrospect and Prospect New Delhi. Association of Indian Universities, pp. 21–23.

Haigh, M. J. (2002). Internationalisation of the curriculum: Designing inclusive education for a small world. *Journal of Geography in Higher Education*, 26(1), 49–66.

Kumar, N. (2023). Innovative teaching strategies for training of future mathematics in higher education institutions in India. *Futurity Education*, 3(1), 14–31. https://doi.org/10.57125/FED.2023.25.03.02

Lindén, J., Annala, J., and Coate, K. (2017). The role of curriculum theory in contemporary higher education research and practice. In Huisman, J., and Tight, M. (eds), Theory and Method in Higher Education Research. (Vol. 3). https://www.emerald.com/insight/content/doi/10.1108/S2056-375220170000003008/full/html

Mukhopadhyay, M. (1999). Higher education: backbone of national development. In Mukhopadhyay, M. and Parhar, M. (eds), Indian Education Development since Independence. New Delhi: Vikas Publishing House.

OECD. (2004). https://www.oecd.org/corporate/ca/corporategovernanceprinciples/31557724.pdf

OECD. (2008). https://www.oecd.org/greengrowth/42177377.pdf

OECD (2012a). Indicator C4—who studies abroad and where?, education at a glance 2012: OECD indicators. 360–381. doi: 10.1787/eag-2012-en. https://www.oecd-ilibrary.org/education/education-at-a-glance-2012_eag-2012-en

Qiang, Z. (2003). Internationalization of higher education: Towards a conceptual framework. *Policy Futures in Education*, 1(2).

Schuerholz-Lehr, S., Caws, C., Van Gyn, G., and Preece, A. (2007). Internationalizing the Higher Education Curriculum: An Emerging Model for Transforming Faculty Perspectives. *Canadian Journal of Higher Education*, 37(1), 67–94.

Trahar, S. (2010). Developing cultural capability in international higher education: A narrative inquiry. London: Routledge.

Wächter, B. (2003). An introduction: internationalisation at home in context. *Journal of Studies in International Education*, 7(1), 5–11.

Zhou, J. (2016). A dynamic systems approach to internationalization of higher education. *International Journal of Leadership in Education*, 6(1), 1–14.

Young, M. (2013). Overcoming the crisis in curriculum theory: a knowledge-based approach. *Journal of Curriculum Studies*. https://www.tandfonline.com/doi/abs/10.1080/00220272.2013.764505

29 Generation of a New Discipline Key Utilizing the Microfluidic Technique

Hiba Safaa Hashim[a], Sahar Adill, and Ali Yakoob

Computer Science Department, University of Babylon, Iraq

Abstract

The popular modes of communication have been altered by digital networking most. Anyone can readily send and receive data over the network, but this also exposes confidential data to eavesdroppers. Encrypting confidential data, which protects it from eavesdropping users who do not have authorized access, is one of the most effective ways to address this privacy issue. The strength of the encryption algorithm is mostly determined by the strength of the key, and in this research, various scientific disciplines were combined with computer science to develop a comparatively strong and unbreakable random cipher key based on microfluidic technology and DNA sequence. The results of this study revealed that this new approach provides a key with a high randomness ratio that significantly improves the security of the algorithms. These results could be evidence of the potential applications of the proposed approach in both industry and academia.

Keywords

DNA, key generation, microfluidic.

Introduction

Most of us connect in cyberspace barely thinking twice because of today's fast increase in digital communication and electronic data sharing. We share a great deal of our personal data through the internet. Even if we don't like to admit it, we have a digital imprint. To be more specific, the information we send and receive online is frequently unsecured and hence vulnerable to the manipulation of cyber thieves. In order to secure sensitive or secret information, current encryption has an urgent necessity. Data encryption and decryption are the keys of internet security. As a result, information must be encoded in a way that only individuals with certain permissions may access it (Gençoğlu, 2019).

Information security relies on a broad variety of encryption techniques, many of which are easily accessible and frequently utilized. They fall under the following headings:

- As seen in Figure 29.1, symmetric cipher algorithms employ a single key for both encryption and decryption (Gençoğlu, 2019).
- As seen in the Figure 29.2, asymmetric cipher algorithms require two keys: the public key for encryption and the private key for decryption (Zahraa et al., 2020).

[a]hiba.abid.gsci18@student.uobabylon.edu.iq

As long as the encryption key is strong, the key will defy cryptanalysis, even if all system data relating to the encryption key's production or validation is discovered by an attacker (Hasudungan et al., 2019).

Cryptography techniques transfer data with a large amount of space and a low key strength (Vidhya and Rathipriya, 2020). Since the strength of the algorithm depends largely on the strength of the key, the process of generating the key is an important step in the design of any encryption algorithm. So In this paper, a new key generation is adopted based on microfluidic technology using DNA sequencing. the method is an emerging promising direction in generating ciphering keys using DNA sequence and microfluidic technology to provide a high efficiency which is very suitable for cryptographic requirements. The random and unbreakable key is generated.

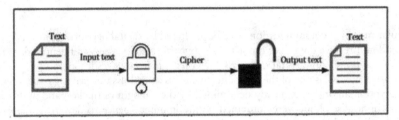

Figure 29.1 Symmetric key cryptography (Zahraa et al., 2020).

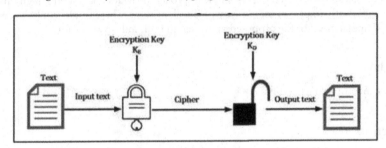

Figure 29.2 Asymmetric key cryptography (Zahraa et al., 2020).

Related Work

Seq	Year	Authors	Description	Result
1	2021	Kolate and Joshi	There has been a proposal for a DNA-based security method. The unique data security strategy might be implemented by utilizing the advantages of DNA-based AES as an information carrier. Using this strategy, multilayer security will be offered. The proposed system protects transactional data throughout communication, which is required while sending or receiving messages or data.	AES-based DNA cryptography can also benefit from compression techniques. This technology can be used to encrypt sensitive data, such as that used in the military, as well as convey and receive business data securely.

(continued)

Continued

Seq	Year	Authors	Description	Result
2	2020	Vidhya and Rathipriya	Describe a selective medical image and use DNA cryptography and the dual hyper chaotic map to encrypt the image and provide a higher level of protection. The strong encryption key is generated by combining the Genetic algorithm and the Diffie-Hellman key exchange technique in DNA cryptography.	Reduce the amount of time it takes to encrypt medical images. The use of entropy values to secure text and image data provides a high level of confidence.
3	2019	Lalit Mohan Gupta Dr. Hitendra Garg and Dr. Abdus Samad	They propose a method that employs a 128-bit DNA-based cryptography key. A new substitution approach follows round key selection, random DNA-based coding, and modified DNA-based coding.	When compared to standard approaches, the proposed methodology reduces the size of cipher text. The technology encrypts and decrypts large files and databases faster thanprior techniques. The proposed method decreases the size of the encrypted text file. When compared to traditional methods, the reduction is around 33%.
4	2017	Yunpeng Zhang, Xin Liu, Manhui Sun	Using a variety of biological processes, present a secure key management mechanism. They use ultrasonic technology to separate DNA fragments from a biological material. Using gel screening, pick cut-DNA pieces of the same length as plaintext DNA fragments and a secure DNA sequence.	The safe keys created straight from the organism are extremely random. Because of the large storage capacity and diversity of DNA chromosomes, there is no link between crucial generations. The transmission of encrypted keys is entirely dependent on biological technologies.

(continued)

Continued

Seq	Year	Authors	Description	Result
5	2017	Shruti Kalsi Harleen Kaur Victor Chang	Proposed are simple, effective algorithms. A technique for key generation based on natural selection theory utilizing the Genetic Algorithm with the Needleman-Wunsch (NW) algorithm, and a method for encryption and decryption based on DNA computing using biological activities. Deep Learning, Transcription, and Translation	This procedure is quick, simple, and adds an additional degree of security. To address computing challenges, DNA computing can function in parallel. Cost and time effectiveness need more effort.
6	2016	Raj and Vijay	This study presents a symmetric DNA cryptography technique. This approach creates an initial cipher and then a final cipher using random DNA sequences to make it harder.	Against specific attacks, this strategy is more effective. This approach provides data transmission confidentiality and integrity.
7	2012	Nafiseh Jafarzadeh, Ali Iranmanesh	offer a new 3D graphical representation based on codon (C-curve) with no information loss.	This model can study DNA codon compositions and distributions. This representation may be used to represent global and local DNA information.
8	2011	Zhao-Hui Qi Ling Li and Xiao-Qin Qi	a novel graphical depiction of DNA sequence is proposed In the transfer of data from a DNA sequence to its graphical representation, the representation can avoid degeneracy and information loss. After that, a multicomponent vector derived from the representation is used to characterize DNA sequences quantitatively.	When a Huffman tree is defined by the frequency of base A, T, G, and C in supplied DNA sequences, the representation is unique.

Microfluidic

Chemical and biological processes can be performed on a smaller scale, at a cheaper cost, and with greater precision using microfluidic devices than by people. The manipulation of small fluid quantities is central to all of these devices, but different techniques offer distinct tradeoffs in terms of size, cost, versatility, and dependability (Stephenson et al., 2020).

We believe that microfluidics will play a bigger role in the future. As a bridge between the fields of computers, chemistry and biology, these devices are a must have. However, computing has historically been used only as a microcontroller or synthesis tool in these systems. 'As a member of a heterogeneous computer system, microfluidic devices can begin to complete loops that would otherwise need the participation of humans (Willsey et al., 2019).

Numerical simulations are needed to help in the design, control, and optimization of analytical processes in this fast growing lab-on-a-chip technology. Often referred to as "microscale total analysis systems (TAS)," microfluidic chips are disposable, single—use devices that imitate the functionality of bigger analytical tools. Sample and reagent consumption is minimized, analysis times are reduced, and TAS is more portable and disposable (Guarnieri et al., 2006). The material used in the microfabrication process is critical to the development of sophisticated and low-cost microfluidic devices. There are times when microfluidic technology fails to achieve its goal of managing fluids (liquid and/or gas) in submillimeter ranges by attempting to miniaturize established laboratory procedures. With devices with critical dimensions smaller than 1 mm, microfluidics is a rapidly expanding field of study that focuses on fluid manipulation at the microscale. In fact, (Ma and Sun, 2019). One of the key components of the microfluidic platform is the micro-selector illustrated in Figure (29.3(a)) (29.3(b)) (Kalsi et al., 2018).

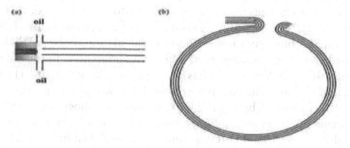

Figure 29.3 Microfluidic platform.

DeoxyriboNucleic Acid

DNA, or deoxyribonucleic acid, is the genetic material found in humans and nearly all other species. Figure 29.4 depicts the four chemical bases (adenine (A), guanine (G), cytosine (C), and thymine (T)) that make up the DNA code that stores information (T). DNA cryptography (DNA cryptography) is an emerging field in bio-inspired cryptography. Cryptography can benefit greatly from DNA's enormous store capacity and huge parallelism in computations (Benyahia et al., 2021).

Organic molecules of the highest complexity are included in this collection. Other cellular components, such as proteins and RNA, rely on DNA instructions (Kolate and Joshi, 2021). Genes are the smallest units of DNA that store genetic data. Genetic information may be used in this way. Zeros and ones are encoded for each of the four

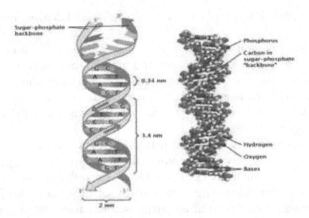

Figure 29.4 DNA molecule.

bases denoted by the letters A (Adenine), T (Thymine), C (Cytosine), G (Guanine). All four nucleotides in DNA have a nitrogenous base, which is the only difference between them. They are commonly referred to as bases. Similarly to A and T, G and C are mutually advantageous (Jafarzadeh and Iranmanesh, 2013). Figure 29.4 depicts the DNA structure (Hasudungan et al., 2019).

Computational processes may be implemented using DNA molecules, which is an inter-disciplinary topic of study Watson and Crick hypothesized that DNA had tremendous parallelism and complementarity (Hasudungan et al., 2019).

Researchers from computer science, biology, mathematics, physics, and chemistry are all interested in DNA computing. This method of computation uses DNA as a data storage medium and bio-operation methods as calculation tools. A DNA molecule is a polymer made up of oligonucleotides, which are monomers. In the meantime, each oligonucleotide in a DNA molecule has three primary components: (1) sugar, phosphate group, and (2) base. The backbone of one DNA strand is made up of nucleotides that are covalently bonded by sugar (deoxyribose) and phosphate residues. A DNA sequence is made up of numerous oligonucleotides, each of which contains one of four bases: adenine (A), cysteine (C), guanine (G), and thymine (T) (T) (Vidhya and Rathipriya, 2020).

The storage capacity of DNA as a computer platform is its primary advantage. A gram of DNA has 1021 DNA bases, or 108 Terabytes of data that may be stored in a very little amount of space. Furthermore, no electricity is required for DNA computing while it is being performed. Without the application of any external energy, the chemical links that make up DNA are produced (Bruce et al., 2018). DNA molecules can also be exploited for non-biological functions, extending their use to the digital world (Kalsi et al., 2018).

Methodology

In this paper, we proposed a new method to generate the encryption key based on the nonlinearity of fluid flow in the microfluidic chip to generate a key in DNA format where the encryption key is in the form of codons (Triple code of DNA bases). In the process of key generation, the behavior of fluid flow is simulated in a microfluidic chip, as the chip consists of inlet channels for fluid flow, the mixer to mix those fluids, and a filter for Choose only the required items. In the proposed method, simulating the chip process for obtaining a ciphered key pad from which the an encryption key can be selected is illustrated in algorithm (1), and Figure 29.5:

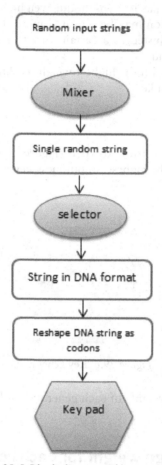

Figure 29.5 Block diagram of key generation.

Algorithm (1): Key pad generation.

Step 1. Generate random strings as input data.

Step 2. Mix these strings randomly to get a new string that will be an entry to the next step (Mixer).

Step 3. From the string obtained from the previous step, only the four bases of DNA are selected (A C G T) (selector).

Step 4. The resulting string from the previous step is reshape into codons (Triple code of DNA bases) representing the key pad from which the key will be selected.

Selecting a strong ciphered key from the obtaining key pad is the next step as illustrated in algorithm (2).

Algorithm (2): Ciphered key selection

Step 1. Each codon is assigned a weight on the key pad based on a specific table.

Step 2. More than one codon may have the same weight, and to solve this problem, the weight of each codon is calculated separately based on a certain equation so that each codon has its own unique weight.

Step 3. Since the same codon may be repeated more than once in the key pad, the weights will be adjusted at a certain rate to reduce the importance of the recurring codon, and

Step 4. Finally, the codon with the highest weight is chosen to be
The best encryption key.

Security Analysis

The process of selection a key from key pad (Figure 29.6) obtained through several processes. Each processing, the highest randomness key is the preferred key.

Figure 29.6 Key generated.

Figure 29.7 explains the weights of each generated codon.

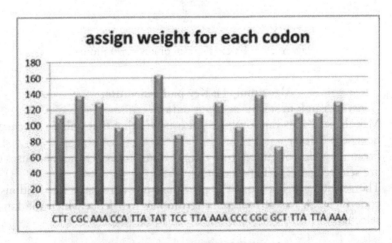

Figure 29.7 The weights of each codon.

Figure 29.8 explains the unified weight for each codon.

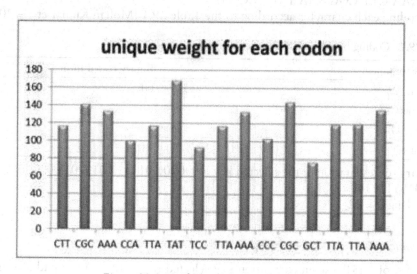

Figure 29.8 Unified weight for each codon.

Figure 29.9 explains the distribution of highest weights codons.

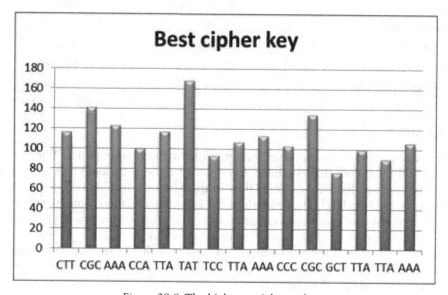

Figure 29.9 The highest weights codons.

Distribution is done according to Figure 29.9, the preferred key is (TAT).

After finding the best codon, the encryption key is the row and column that intersect at that codon, and the length of the key depends on the dimensions of the chosen key pad.

According to the (4*4) key pad
k= AAA CTT CGC AAA TAT CCC TTA
by coding each character according to the Table 29.1 (Mohan Kumar et al., 2020)

Table 29.1: Coding based on DNA nucleotides.

DNA component	Binary coded form
Adenine (A)	00
Cytosine(C)	01
Guanine(G)	10
Thymine(T)	11

Binary representation of the selected key = 000000 011111 011001 000000110011 010101111100
Key length = 42

Randomness Test

The result of NIST test on encryption key selected from (12*12) key pad are shown in Table 29.2.

Table 29.2: Results of NIST tests for the generated key.

NIST test	P_value >0.01	states
Frequency Test	0.609	Success
Block Frequency Test	0.376	Success
Run Test	0.381	Success
Approximate entropy	0.883	Success

Conclusion

In this paper, a new discipline for generating ciphering keys is proposed. Where, relied on a hybrid disciplines that combines Microfluidic technology and DNA techniques. Exploiting the non-linearity of fluids flow in the Microfluidic chip to generate a key with a large random level. The strength of the key in this method came from the high level of randomness in the process of generation and selection process in order to give more strength and security to the encryption process and provides a high level of security because it increases the randomness and confidentiality of the key. This approach is considered relatively new in cryptography field and this method adds a higher level of security to cryptographic algorithms.

References

Benyahia, K., Mustapha, M., and Abdelkrim, L. (2021). A bio-inspired algorithm for symmetric encryption. In: Research Anthology on Artificial Intelligence Applications in Security. IGI Global. (pp. 490–503).

Bruce, K., Gale, I. D., Alexander, R., Jafek, I. D., Christopher, J., Lambert, I. D., et al. (2018). A review of current methods in microfluidic device fabrication and future commercialization prospects. *Inventions*, 3(3), 60.

Gençoğlu, M. T. (2019). Importance of cryptography in information security. *IOSR Journal of Computer Engineering*, 21(1), 65–68.

Guarnieri, F. A., Kler, P. A., and Berli, C. L. A. (2006). Numerical simulation of electrokinetic flow in microfluidic chips.

Guarnieri , Fabio Ariel, kler, Pablo Alejandro; BERLI, Claudio Luis Alberto. (2006): Numerical simulation of electrokinetic flow in microfluidic chips. Repositorio Institucional CONICET Digital.

Hasudungan, R., Pangestuty, D. M., and Latifah, A. J. (2019, November). Solving minimum vertex cover problem using DNA computing. *In Journal of Physics: Conference Series* 1361(1), p. 012038. IOP Publishing.

Jafarzadeh, N., and Iranmanesh, A. (2012). A novel graphical and numerical representation for analyzing DNA sequences based on codons. *Match-Communications in Mathematical and Computer Chemistry*, 68(2), 611.

Kalsi, S., Kaur, H., and Chang, V. (2018). DNA cryptography and deep learning using genetic algorithm with NW algorithm for key generation. *Journal of Medical Systems*, 42(1), 1–12.

Kolate, V., and Joshi, R. B. (2021). An information security using DNA cryptography along with AES algorithm. *Turkish Journal of Computer and Mathematics Education*, 12(1S), 183–192.

Ma, P., & Sun, H. (2019, April). A New Molecular Encryption Model Based on Microfluidic Techniques. *In Journal of Physics: Conference Series* 1187(4), p. 042052. IOP Publishing.

Mohan Kumar, B., Ramya Satya Sri, B., Katamaraju, G. M. S. A., Rani, P., Harinadh, N., Saibabu, Ch. (2020). File encryption and decryption using DNA technology. In: 2020 2nd International Conference on Innovative Mechanisms for Industry Applications (ICIMIA). (pp. 382–385). IEEE.

Qi, Z. H., Li, L., and Qi, X. Q. (2011). Using Huffman coding method to visualize and analyze DNA sequences. *Journal of Computational Chemistry*, 32(15), 3233–3240.

Raj, B. B., and Vijay, J. F. (2016). Secure data transfer through DNA cryptography using symmetric algorithm. *International Journal of Computer Applications*, 133(2), 19–23.

Stephenson, A., Willsey, M., McBride, J., et al. (2020). PurpleDrop.: a digital microfluidics-based platform for hybrid molecular-electronics applications. *IEEE Micro*, 40(5), 76–86.

Vidhya, E., and Rathipriya, R. (2020). Key generation for DNA cryptography using genetic operators and diffie-hellman key exchange algorithm. *Computer Science*, 15(4), 1109–1115.

Willsey, M., Stephenson, A. P., Takahashi, C., et al. (2019). Puddle.: a dynamic, error-correcting, full-stack microfluidics platform. In: Proceedings of the Twenty-Fourth International Conference on Architectural Support for Programming Languages and Operating Systems. (pp. 183–197).

Zahraa, C, et al. (2020). Overview and performance analysis of encryption algorithms. *Journal of Physics*, 12051.

Printed in the United States
by Baker & Taylor Publisher Services